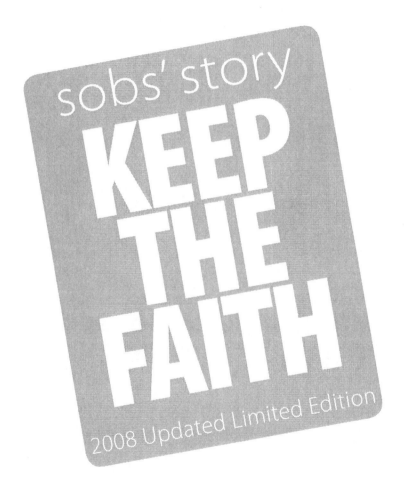

sobs' story

KEEP
THE
FAITH

2008 Updated Limited Edition

Paul Dobson

KEEP THE FAITH
Sobs' Story
By Paul Dobson
One man's life long devotion following Sunderland AFC

First published by ALS Publications in 2005
Limited edition updated version published in 2007

ALS Publications
1 Hodgsons' Buildings
Stadium Way
Sunderland
SR5 1BT

ISBN 978-0-9550364-6-0

Design & Layout: John Longford & Paul Forrest (*www.alsdesign.co.uk*)
Production Editor: Martyn McFadden
Proof Reading: Sheila Seacroft & Andrew Fury

For more ALS Publications literature and information visit
www.a-love-supreme.com

Thanks to Judith for (almost) understanding, to Gary and Ian for following; to everyone else I've shared the Sunderland experience with over the years, and, above all, thanks to Sunderland for being Sunderland.

That was the back end of 2005, and not a lot has changed. Thanks still go to the above people. The intervening two years have seen what Sunderland the football club are all about by producing two seasons which have provided the best and the worst of times. From the lowest points return in our history and the disintegration of the Bob Murray regime to yet another Championship title, the arrival of the Niall Quinn regime and the emergence of Roy Keane as a manager of genuine talent. For the fans like myself, the highs and the lows of this relatively brief period have been just a continuation of what we've lived through all of our lives. Circle of life, that sort of thing. The people around have had to live with us while we've cried tears of joy and tears of despair, they've got up with us for five o'clock starts and been awakened by 5am returns.

They've endured our moods both foul and fair, our stomping around the house and our dancing in the streets. They've also come to know the people who are our acquaintances simply because of the shared passion for all things red and white. For that, they deserve our respect, thanks, and admiration. I did ask Judith if she'd write a few words to explain her side of the story, but she declined on the grounds that she couldn't think of anything. Probably closer to the truth is she'd need something the size of Lord of the Rings to explain half of it... and she's got better things to do with her time, which is fair enough, like. She last saw Sunderland play in a League Cup tie, won by a Niall Quinn goal of sublime quality. She likes Quinny, like every sane person, and she likes to think she knows what Sunderland means to the likes of me. Which means that she's probably accepted me for what I am, and that puts her in there with thousands of other wives, husbands, and partners of whatever denomination or persuasion.

Every time, season after season, it's the same old thing but it's completely different every time. Magic, isn't it? By the way, that's a rhetorical question.

Up, down, turn around, please don't let me hit the ground... and I've never met anyone quite like you before.

This book is dedicated to the memory of
Derek Poskett 1957-2002
Forever Red and White

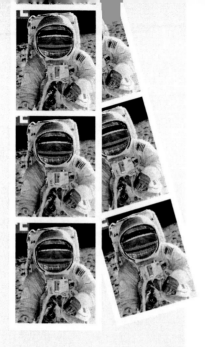

1956-1970

Queen Elizabeth II and I don't have much in common – my ancestors are English for a start, with possibly a bit of Welsh thrown in for good measure, while hers are chiefly German. My parents might have been distantly related by marriage when they met, but the cousins back down my family tree don't have a history of marrying each other – or fratricide, for that matter. What we do share is two birthdays. QE2 has her biological birthday, the date of which I'm uncertain, and an official birthday, which I know is some time in June. I also have a biological birthday, like the rest of mankind, and, slightly more interestingly, a Sunderland birthday. The former is September 5th, while the latter is… well, September 5th as well, but a different September 5th.

The reason for this apparent duplicity is quite simply that my Sunderland birthday celebrates the day that I decided that Sunderland Football Club was something I loved, and wanted to be a big part of my life. That it took fourteen years to realise this might come as a bit of a surprise, as Sunderland had always been my team, even before I knew what football was all about. The Lads were my family team on both my mother's and my father's sides, which is hardly a surprise considering both lots worked underground in the Houghton- le-Spring area. My dad's granddad was in fact born near Roker Avenue eighteen years before the club was formed, and his son used to cleverly divert my schoolboy questions about what it was like in the trenches of World War One by reeling off tales of the antics of SAFC in his pre-army days.

On the bright side, he'd been at St James on the occasion of our 9-1 victory, as part of the Easington Lane Crew, while on the dark side he'd been present when someone decided it would be a good idea to stick a bayonet in a police horse. So the seed was sown, and Sunderland was always part of me from day one – indeed before day one, as my first Roker Park visit was as a three-month-old bump in the Clock Stand (the first home game and I even got in for free) – part of a crowd of 14,824½ against Birmingham in March 1956. One of Bill Holden's nineteen goals for the club was enough to win the game. On the actual day I was born, we lost away to Bolton, despite having beaten Charlton 8-1 four days before. The Suez crisis was in full flow, British forces were "looking after" Cyprus, Russian tanks were rolling into Hungary, and Doris Day topped the charts with Whatever Will Be Will Be – and whatever it was, it was Sunderland for me. The team at that time was full of famous names like Charlie Cannonball Fleming, Shack, Stan Anderson, and George Aitken, but we were sadly in decline. By the time King Charlie arrived a year later, the rot had really set in and we were relegated for the first time at the end of the season.

By the time I was old enough to know anything about football, we'd been promoted, Manager Alan Brown had gone, and I'd moved further away – too far for a ten year old to travel by himself, as Dad didn't go to the matches regularly any more. My standard Sunderland fare was Jim Baxter's Eleven, or Charlie Hurley's Allstars providing the entertainment at charity matches at my local ground, Kingsway in Bishop Auckland. I'd managed a few visits to Roker on the back of family shopping trips, or visits to relatives in the town, but we'd been promoted and relegated again before my big break came. If you're going to support a team properly, then I guess that there's no better time to start than immediately after your team's been relegated, under the leadership of Alan Brown in his second spell – they say "never go back", and in Bomber's case, it would have been the right advice. As relegation has been a regular occurrence on Wearside in the last 50 years, there will be a lot of people who started off in similar circumstances to myself, and that could go some way to explaining the sometimes inexplicable passion with which we stick by the Lads, no matter how bad things are.

So, as season 70-71 got underway, the world was a slightly different place than it had been when I first arrived, but most of the news remained of the bad variety. North Sea Oil was the Next Big Thing, and was definitely of the good news variety, as was England's winning of the World Cup (I'd listened to the final at my grandparents' caravan at Crimdon Dene on the radio, convinced, as I'd never heard of anyone called Nobby, that Mr Stiles was a German). On the other hand, Biafra, the first famine to be covered on a global scale by the mass media, was very much to the fore, as were the USA's increasingly embarrassing attempts to stamp down on communism in Vietnam, and the intensification of the conflict in Ulster. England's attempt at retaining the World Cup, with what looked like a better squad, failed as Germany made a fool of Peter Bonnetti, after Bobby Moore had been the subject of a set-up and jailed for stealing a bracelet. Politically, the Tories had just come back into power with sailor Ted Heath at the helm following Harold Wilson's Labour tenure. I was probably more politically aware than most of my age group, as both Ma and Pa were paid up Labour Party members, who'd both stood for local government. I'd even had tea in my own front room with two MPs. The Tories coming back upset me almost as much as it upset most adults, and developed the slightly left of left political viewpoint that I hold to this day. Musically, we'd been through the heyday of The Beatles, The Stones, and The Who, and, rather depressingly, were back with Elvis and The Wonder of You. Some things simply didn't change that much, apart from the small matter of putting a man on the moon.

1970-1971

Discussions on my birthday present also accompanied the beginning of season 70-71. After much debate, it was decided that my fourteenth birthday present would be a trip to the match. The club thought we'd learnt lessons from the last time we'd been relegated, and believed that promotion would be a mere formality – at least, that's what it looked like from a supporter's viewpoint, as no big signings came in. Experience, in the form of Montgomery, Ashurst, Irwin, and Harvey, was left to bring on the promise of youth, and it was decided that I could become one of these – albeit in a strictly off-the field capacity. We'd lost 3-4 at Bristol City on the opening day, then drawn 3-3 at home to Watford before losing 0-2 at Swindon. Was this football match lark going to be worth it if we didn't win? I had my doubts, but had already decided to give it a go when Charlton visited, a couple of days before my big day. Joe Baker took his tally to five with a hat-trick, and I bowled into the paper shop the next morning, proclaiming that we'd won 3-0, and I was going to the next match.

"Who did they beat?" asked the boss. "Charlton," I replied, and I should have expected his riposte of "Bobby or Jackie?" Sarcasm, and what is now referred to as banter, has always played a big part in following football, but I was a mere apprentice and had a lot to learn. Two days later, and it was off to Roker with Dad and little sister (how come she got to go, when she was several years younger than when I started?) to watch from the family enclosure (well, it had a yellow fence around it and fewer people smoked - but only because they were children and couldn't afford to) as Norwich came to town. Norwich are a team that have broken my heart on a couple of occasions and upset me many times more since then, but on the day Mick McGiven and Billy Hughes scored to make the day a victorious one. More importantly from a personal point of view, we won simply because I was there, they'd done it for me, for my birthday, and I was old enough this time to appreciate the occasion, the passion of the crowd, albeit only 16,682 of them, but I was hooked. It was me, right down to the monkey boots on my feet, right down to the ground. So I celebrated as Sunderland September 5th 1970 became my football birthday.

By the time I got to the paper shop the next morning, I considered myself a fully-fledged Sunderland fan – yeah, they'd been my team since before I was born, and I'd been before, perched on a little swing hanging from a Fulwell End barrier, but this time I'd gone under my own terms (OK, it was in my Dad's car, but I'd gone because I'd wanted it to happen). I talked and talked about the experience with the lads at school, and a small group of us (all right, a gang of youths) of a red and white persuasion decided that now was the time to start going en-masse instead of with parents, big brothers, and other distant and mildly irritated relatives. So began a ritual that would last until I passed my driving test, a ritual that was played out every Saturday morning. Gregg's Butchers in Bondgate for a pork and dip sandwich, then to the OK Travel Office to buy the three shillings bus ticket, then to Doggart's Café for a glass of pop, and to loosen the tops on the salt cellars (showing blatant disregard for the now apparent dangers of excess salt consumption). The OK bus left at one from outside the Sun Inn (now of Beamish Museum), next door to the old police station. The big lads and grown-ups could wait inside, but there was no way we could pass for eighteen, so it was a case of listening to the others getting warmed up inside while we got wet and cold outside.

The next two weeks, leading up to the visit of Sheff Wed, couldn't pass quickly enough, we were high as kites by the time Saturday came, despite having lost at Orient in the league and, typically, to little Cambridge in the League Cup. In the Roker End again, just to show my mates where I'd been a fortnight before, and I can still remember Bobby Kerr's shot curling outside the post before bending back into the net. I was amazed – how did people do that without the help of Match of the Day technology? McGiven scored again, as did substitute Dennis Tueart, on for Joe Baker. Joe might have been the big name at the club, the player that the rest of the nation knew, now that Charlie had gone, but he had been around a while, and ninety minutes wasn't always within his athletic capabilities. 3-1, and definitely down to my presence. This belief in my own importance to the Sunderland cause was further built up when Bolton, captained by one Charlie Hurley, arrived (after we'd drawn at Millwall) and we beat them 4-1.

Porterfield scored a beaut, Gordon "Banger" Harris - so-called because he, like Baker, had been around a bit, and, while once a Rolls Royce of sorts on the field, he was now a bit of a banger - did likewise, and Joe Baker came off the bench to score. Goal of the day, and probably the weekend, came from a young Scotsman by the name of Bobby Park, who ghosted through the visiting defence with a mazy dribble that was the subject of countless inferior copies in playgrounds throughout County Durham over the next few weeks. It was also the first time we all went into the Fulwell together, having decided at the previous game that if we wanted to be taken seriously as Sunderland fans, we'd have to move to where most of the singing came from. This was achieved by waiting outside the Wolsley, where the OK bus stopped, and following the big lads to the ground. We found ourselves halfway back, just behind the big step, and just to the Main Stand side of The Cage – the very centre of the Fulwell, where most of the songs started. We also noticed that most of the people in this part of the ground were from our part of the world – South West Durham, people from Bishop, Spenny, Shildon, Aycliffe, and all of the villages in-between. It became a home from home, somewhere we could always find somebody we knew (not difficult when we usually travelled in bunch of ten or so, but you know what I mean), and somewhere that we knew we'd be safe amongst our own, as there were some pretty scary folks in the Fulwell that we didn't yet know that well.

By late September, I succumbed to a bit of bullying from a mate's elder brother, who said that if I was big enough to go to Sunderland, I was big enough to go with him and his mates to Newcastle. Well, they were all bigger than me and Col, so I agreed to go, but we decided it would only happen if we made our mark somehow, so that we could be absolved of our sin by the lads back in Bishop. We wrote FTM in chalk across the back of one of the older lads, and the rest of the gang watched as he was the subject of a torrent of abuse (funny) and a few random punches (not really funny) between the bus and the ground. The game was horrible, the ground was horrible, and the police took anything resembling boots off people and made them watch the game barefoot. If you're interested, and you shouldn't be, Fatty Foggon missed an open goal and it was 0-0 against Liverpool. I know that you should be able to watch any game anywhere and appreciate it as a spectacle, but all this occasion did was to reinforce my new-found belief that it was the long and winding red and white road for me.

Back with the proper folks, things were going very well for our little band of Fulwell Enders – the scores got better every week, and we believed that our little run (for that's all it was, three games off the belt, and not counting away games) would see us promoted the following May. We'd made big sacrifices to become part of the People's Army of Sunderland. As the wages in the distribution and delivery side of journalism, and, for that matter, the dairy industry, were not particularly high, and attending a match cost six shillings (seven if you wanted a programme, which we usually did), something had to go. Fortunately for my health, it was the visits to the corner shop (no longer a corner shop, so you can't prosecute) for two Number Six and a penny box of matches, for consumption behind the water tower on the way home. Being "on the drag", which sounds like a Danny La Rue show now, was the pre-football pastime of several of my group, and we just couldn't afford both, so there you have it – in 1970, Sunderland was a more attractive proposition to the spotty youth of Auckland than smoking, surely a health awareness programme that could be revitalised to the eternal benefit of the anti-social pre-pubescent youth of the modern era.

Now we'd committed every other Saturday, and occasional Wednesday evenings, to the red and white cause, we felt that we'd collectively become part of something important, something very big and we wanted to stay part of it. It was all part of growing up, of course, and part of us trying to work out our own identity, individually and collectively, as lads (and lasses) in a gang of twelve to fifteen yearolds did, always had done, and always will do. The younger members of the group looked up to the older members for inspiration, and to establish exactly how far rules could be bent or even broken. We all, well almost all, managed part-time jobs to fund our newfound personalities, and we strode forth into the brave new world that was the rest of County Durham, suitably kitted out. Clothes for football were obtained from Jack Sackville's, and consisted, from the ground up, of highly-polished monkey boots (a cheap predecessor to the Doc Martin's that would soon come our way), brightly coloured socks, and ankle-flapping two-tone Sta-Prest held up with braces. Above this was the Ben Sherman shirt (checked, of course, and with short sleeves), and the whole ensemble was topped off with either a football jumper – a woolly effort, available in any two-colour combination of stripes, as replica shirts simply were not part of the fashion scene – and/or a Harrington jacket (tartan lined, naturally). The final flourish was the scarf, tied to the braces, or around the wrist. There we were, all very much the same, but all individuals thanks to the slight variance in scarves, entirely due to the idiosyncratic knitting styles of whichever female relative or friend had been conned into providing the final fashion accessory.

By the Christmas of that first full season, we'd established who our heroes were. Monty Python had moved to BBC1, so that we mere mortals with 405-line TV sets could actually see their programmes, while, on the field, Monty Jimmy was an easy choice, as he'd been there and done that with the club. Joe Baker was the international superstar. Billy Hughes and Dennis Tueart were very much the favourites with the girls, and Bobby Kerr was the one who'd battled back from two broken legs to be a popular figure. Colin Todd was the up and coming superstar, and so on, and we all chose our favourite. I used to try to play right half at school because that was Toddo's position - I remember Monty shouting at him "Up Toddy" in my early games, and up Toddy went, soaring above much taller forwards to head clear.

I might have played in Toddo's position, but my first real hero was one of the old guard, Cec Irwin. After breaking into the team in the same game against Ipswich in 1958, he and Len Ashurst probably (I can't be bothered to count) formed one of the longest-standing full back partnerships in the history of the game. Was it Cec or was it Len, who walloped that winger just then? OK, they played 810 times between them, but Len had drifted out of the first team by the end of the relegation season, replaced usually by Martin Harvey, and eventually became player manager at Hartlepool in March 71, while Cec kept on keeping on. He wasn't a particularly fashionable or stylish player, being bald by then (this was before shaven heads became acceptable in the game), but he was one of the earliest exponents of the overlapping full back, a feature of his game that had been with him since his early days. It was these marauding runs down the right, interchanging with Bobby Kerr, which first caught my eye. Most of his crosses were of the type that could be described as looping, but he could never be accused of over-elaborating. His only goal had come a couple of years earlier, when, with no other options, he simply hoofed it as far upfield as he could. It went in. I loved his style, and after only a couple of games, my screams of "Hawaaaay Cec" became part of the folklore of my little part of the Fulwell. Even the arrival in the October of another future hero, Dick Malone, only kept him out for one game, and when Malone took over at right back, Cec went onto the left.

We had a quite solid defence, with Todd and Pitt flanked by Cec and Harvey, while the midfield was stylish, with Porterfield and Park providing the classy bit, fed by Kerr and McGiven's industry and backed up by Banger's experience when necessary. Hughes and Baker were the hit-men and Dennis Tueart was just beginning to make a name for himself. As Christmas approached, things were just about the right side of moderate with 22 points in the bag, when Mr Brown made a rather wise purchase. In came Dave Watson to replace Joe Baker, and he instantly showed us that, Todd apart, we weren't really that good. In his first game, at Watford, he scored our goal in a draw, and in his next, against Boro on Boxing Day, he curled a lovely ball out to the right, realised no-one had anticipated it, and chased over to collect it himself. He also managed to miss my first experience of football violence since 1966 (Jim Baxter's XI, out the back of the main stand at Kingsway when my scarf had been nicked by a threatening Bishop supporter), when a big-mouthed Boro fan started making threats on his way out of the Fulwell and came into sharp contact with my crake (big wooden rattle), but, even to us inexperienced and spotty youths, big Dave was a piece of class.

The year had just turned when, sitting at my grandparents', news came through to Sports Report of a late goal at Ibrox – a late equaliser for Rangers against Celtic which had prompted those disgruntled home fans leaving early to turn and try to go back up the steps to the terraces. Two masses of people going in opposite directions in a crowded football ground is never a good thing, and on this occasion the sad conclusion was the deaths of sixty six fans as barriers collapsed.

By the time we'd turned up in insufficient numbers to satisfy the chairman's call of "If you want to keep Colin Todd, come and see him play," the lad was off to Derby and it was left to McGiven and Harvey to fill in. Toddo's last FA Cup game for us was my first, a re- arranged tie against Orient at home, playing alongside Banger Harris, who might have been a decent midfielder, but was no centre half. As Orient tore us to bits, the game degenerated into one of the most violent I've seen, in terms of fisticuffs. On at least three occasions, groups of up to ten players stood toe to toe trading punches. Proper punches, mind, with none of the silly slapping, rubbing together of brows, and pushing that is the fashion in the modern game. These lads only fell to the ground if they'd been knocked over, after which they either stayed flat out or jumped back up, John Wayne style, to return to the fray.

Orient won the game 3-0, but I think we won the boxing on points. Two days earlier, what was our strongest side capitulated 0-4 at top team Hull, while Dunny and I watched Where Eagles Dare at the Odeon. When I got home, my dad answered my question of "How did they get on?" with "They didn't play." And it had been true. That walloping signalled a sort of stall in our progress. A couple of days later, Joe Baker moved back to his spiritual home at Easter Road and our league form toddled along in nondescript fashion, for which I personally blame decimalisation, and included an embarrassing 0-4 defeat at home to Cardiff. It was in this game that we took our Roker-touring habit to its extreme.

Normally, we'd run onto the field at the end of the game, just so we could be escorted down the tunnel by the polis, but if we were getting beaten, we'd nip out near the end and try another part of the ground for size. Against Cardiff, we managed all four sides, and were in the Roker End when Cec Irwin put a glancing header past Monty from twenty-five yards to complete the rout. Easter brought three games in four days, and gave us a big chance to move on up the table. On Good Friday at Roker, we warmed up nicely as Tricky Dicky put away one of the hardest shots the game has seen to finish off Orient, and the next morning we set out for our first away game as a "No adults allowed, we can manage nicely enough mam" group.

Knowing from the big lads that Boro station was a very dodgy place, where there would undoubtedly be Bovver with a capital B, we took the number 1 to Darlo, changed at High Row, and rattled into the Smog an hour later. If you think Teesside is an oxygenfree zone now, you should have seen it then – well, you couldn't, actually. Pre-pollution control, the sky was somewhere above a pall of funny-coloured smoke, and the houses in the streets we walked through between the town and the ground were coated in all sorts of strange dusts. OK, you might say, how about the coal dust further up the county, and I say fair enough, but at least we knew what it was. Getting to the ground without mishap wasn't too difficult, as the voices weren't too different, and the scarves the same colour – despite me forgetting that my red and white effort had Kerr, Pitt, Park, etc. stitched onto it, a fact which necessitated rapid removal after the first sideways glance, and tying around my waist inside my jacket. By the time we did get to Ayresome (for any Boro fans reading, it's the place where you used to play before the Riverside, you know, where none of your ancestors ever went), at one o'clock, we'd realised that there was to be no attempt at segregation. That, of course, is utter nonsense, as we'd known fine well that there wouldn't be any – the prospect of having to use our wits to stay in one piece was half the thrill.

Somehow, the Sunderland lads managed to congregate in the same place, in the street on the corner of the Holgate End and the Main Stand, a solid mass of bodies unable to move through the closed turnstiles, and unwilling to move away from the ground. At half one, the ground staff pulled of a masterstroke and opened the turnstiles at the other side of the Holgate and let in the Boro lads. They immediately set about collecting the loose hardcore from the back of the terraces and hoying over the wall at us, along with anything else that could be picked up. It was a frightening experience, but we had a good laugh as a large padlock went through the windscreen of a Morris Minor parked outside the first house – must have belonged to a Boro fan, we thought, so well done, you clever Boro Bootboys.

When our gates did open, my little band was among the first few in, and we had to shelter in the turnstiles as missiles rained down around us. A friendly Policeman urged us to "Take up our positions," so we waited until there were some more of ours inside, and followed their charge across the terrace. By the time the dust had settled, we had "taken" over half of the home end, and took in our surroundings. The source of the missiles quickly became evident, as the entire pie-shop area out the back was made up of loose rocks, and the toilets were no more than a series of railway sleepers laid a foot or so from the wall. No wonder we thought Roker was the absolute pinnacle of arena design – we'd been spoilt. Dave Watson worked his magic up front with our goal in a draw as the warring factions continued hostilities, and then it was dodge the skinhead and back to the bus. We'd survived our first collective foray into the outside world with scarves intact, and the team had secured a point from a 2-2 draw. The only casualty was my voice, which, normally recovering its juvenile squeakiness the morning after a game, after two consecutive afternoons being screamed to its limits, broke to bits and left me a magnificent Basso Profundo from which I only partially recovered.

My voice is what it is because of Easter 1971 and the girls seemed to like it, especially Julie, who was the girl of my dreams around that time –she was nice. Courting at that age and time meant a lot of time sitting on park benches and hiding under coats, inevitably leading to a lot of cracking heads together in the dark. Unfortunately for Julie, she had a friend who was as keen on me as I was on Julie and I spent a lot of time (wasted a lot of time, actually) hiding from one and chasing the other in my C & A matching shirt and tie. That was Easter Sunday taken up and it was ear to the radio the Easter Monday. At Bolton, reserve striker John Lathan scored twice in a 3-1 win to move us up the league, but the top was simply too far to climb, and the final four games brought only four points as the season ended in defeat at home to those nice lads from Millwall - some things never change. We ended up thirteenth with forty-two points, and, while T Rex were replaced at the top of the charts on the last day by Dave and Ansil Collins, Sunderland were my Hot Love – we were faster than most, and we played on the coast, a-ha-ha.

I was born under the Fulwell End
The Fulwell, Fulwell End

1971-1972

Personally, this campaign got off to a poor start, as Julie had found out about her keener friend, courtesy of her keener friend's scary imagination (luckily for my pet rabbit, there was no pan handy), and given me the elbow. Miffed, I took up with her keener friend, but quickly discovered that she was way too much for me at that tender age and gave up on girls for the two weeks I was on holiday. Ah, yes, holidays. I was not yet influential enough in our household to determine the timing, or indeed location of family holidays to dovetail with the wanderings of SAFC. This year's trip had been without parents, but with my Mam's sister, and various older cousins, to a campsite in Brittany. At coming up to fifteen, I was allowed by the liberal French to drink in bars, but only shandy (panache, as they called it) while being fussed over by cute fourteen-year-old French girls who smoked Gitanes (camel shit rolled up in tram tickets), and looked about twenty. So much for a girl-free break.

I attempted to escape for a night by persuading our party to go to the pictures to see Fantasia, reckoning that my schoolboy French could just about cope with a Disney cartoon. It probably could have, but the soundtrack was all but drowned out by our Trevor giggling as it quickly became apparent that translation of the dialogue was unnecessary – as is usual with soft-porn, or cinema erotique as we discovered it to be when we looked more closely at the posters on the way out. All part of growing up, I told Aunty Audrey, but I'm not sure she was convinced. I spent the bulk of my holiday money on a very expensive harmonica, and sat playing by the sea to keep away from temptation. Anyway, Brittany was a good, if Sunderland- free, holiday, and you can still find my name carved into a rock above Douarnenez, courtesy of Uncle Dick, who always carried his stonemason's gear with him, as all good stonemasons do. He drew the line at SAFC.

Arriving at my Aunty Audrey's in Surrey on the evening of the first game of the season, I was informed by my cousins, not only had 7,000 people either side of the religious divide in Ulster had their homes burnt down in just four days, with Prime Minister Heath reacting by leading Great Britain to victory in the Admiral's Cup, but that we'd drawn 1-1 with Birmingham (which I considered not too bad), and some lad called Bobby Park had broken his leg (which I considered very bad). Poor Bobby broke the same leg again before a comeback was possible. We youngsters reckoned him one of the division's most skilful players, and were certain a long career in Scotland's midfield beckoned, so it was ironic that he was filling in at left-back on a rain-soaked Roker pitch when the initial injury occurred, and his career was over before it had begun, at the age of just twenty.

Still the club believed that they had the basis of success in Alan Brown's youth policy, so, again, there was no influx of new blood. After drawing at Watford and beating Orient at home, Carlisle came to town and stuck three past Monty in front of 20,000, a result that, along with a 1-3 exit from the League Cup at Bristol Rovers, knocked 8,000 off the crowd for the win over Swindon. Yet another 0-3 defeat, at Sheff Wed, brought Preston to Roker and Jimmy Hamilton to the subs bench. Goals from Pitt (unusual) and Tueart (two) were Sunderland's share of six when Chico (so-named, imaginatively, after a Villa player of the time – Chico Hamilton) joined the fray. Much like Michael Bridges twenty-odd years later, this frail-looking kid headed a last-minute winner. Unlike Michael Bridges twenty-odd years later, that was about it, as one more goal in another seven starts and eight jumps from the bench in three years saw him off to Plymouth, Bristol Rovers, and a good spell at Carlisle before trying his luck at Morton, Gretna, Australia, and Hartlepool. The win got us in good spirits for Boro's visit, and the spirits worked for us as Kerr, Watson, Tueart, and Hughes (from the bench) gave us a 4-1 win.

It also gave South West Durham's fit young men, as we liked to think of ourselves, the chance to get ourselves on the telly. Highlights of all the local games those days were shown on Sunday afternoon, on Shoot, fronted by the marvellously understated George Taylor, patron saint of the sheepskin coat before Motson had even thought of the idea, on Tyne Tees. Our task at each home game, in those days of enlightened policing (unless you were actually trying to kill each other, anything was OK) was to run onto the pitch after a goal, and whoever got closest to the halfway line (starting from behind the goal, of course) was declared the winner.

It required careful planning, not least because we stood a good way back (but could still make the pitch from a standing start), but most importantly in the choice of where to climb back into the Fulwell. Always choose a young polis, who'd usually chide you with something like "Don't do that again… please", rather than one with stripes or facial hair, as their chiding usually involved what is today referred to as something, good, old-fashioned, and involved the back of their hand and one of your ears. Then we would all congregate at someone's house the next day, and watch our efforts in glorious black and white. The ultimate achievement of your passing legs being recorded by the Clock Stand Paddock camera is something that ITV researchers should scour the archives for, as they put together their next documentary on football culture, but whether or not it really impressed the young girls of Auckland in reality as much as it did in our imaginations we'll never know. Perhaps the girls we're married to today retained a lasting impression of us via those antics… or maybe they didn't recognise us at all.

By the time Christmas arrived, we'd become the favourites of those people who did the pools, racking up another seven score draws, as we kids paid our parents to have a go for us, hoping to spend the winnings on the classic music of the time – Rod Stewart's Maggie May was replaced at the top by Slade's Coz I Luv You, which was in turn replaced by Ernie, The Fastest Milkman in the West. As the year turned, we were thinking of more important things than music and football, as Ted Heath's Conservative government fell out with increasingly more trade unions, and the threat of major industrial action became real and the miners' strike began. While we were wondering where that would take us, a civil rights march in Londonderry went all wrong and thirteen marchers were shot dead – Bloody Sunday entered the history books.

Not a good start to the year for the nation, but a good one for Sunderland, as Kerr and Tueart scored against Sheff Wed on New Year's Day. Unfortunately, we shipped five at Orient the next week, a poor warm-up for Wednesday's visit in the FA Cup. The inconsistency of the side was underlined by a 3-0 victory and we started dreaming of a trip to Wembley – as we did after every cup win. Off we went on the service bus to Boro, and walked around the corner towards the away fans with a group of bigger lads with red and white scarves. No sooner were the aforementioned turnstiles in sight than a similarly sized group, bedecked in red and white, hove into view. Up went a cry of "Come on Sunderland" from the other group, and they charged towards us.

Realising we were in the wrong group, we stepped behind a handy car and allowed the Fulwell End hardcore to pass us, and then bravely tagged on the back. Fifty yards down the road, the Boro gang ran into the rest of their nutters, stopped, turned, and charged back towards us. We stopped, most of us turned, then some idiot at the front shouted "Stay, Sunderland!" A surprising number did, the Boro gang clattered to a halt and a Mexican standoff ensued for a few seconds as the majority, ourselves included, decided whether or not actually trading blows was a good idea. This majority jumped around and did a lot of shouting at the back as the few at the front knocked lumps off each other for half a minute, the Polis appeared and the gangs clattered off in opposite directions. We didn't get as far across the Holgate this time, and neither did the team, losing 2-0. When we got home, our fears about the railway station were confirmed when it was reported that one of the lads using the train had been asked who he supported. Being quick, he replied "Boro," but then answered, "Willie Whigham," when asked who their gaffer was. One broken jaw later, he remembered that Jim Platt had taken over.

We had 3-0 home wins either side of Brian Chambers scoring his second FA Cup goal to earn a replay against Cardiff - which we drew. Two days later, and our first trip out of the region to the building site that was a redeveloping Maine Road for the second replay (on neutral ground). Thankfully, it was the half-term holidays, so we made rail arrangements, only to bump into Neil Duckworth, our games teacher, in the car park – and we'd always thought of him as a cricket man (his uncle actually has a cricket rule named after him), or a Man City supporter. Having braved the bus journey from Piccadilly Station with only an assortment of cutlery borrowed from Woolworth's café as comfort in the face of a bus full of unfriendly Mancunians, the team showed less commitment – they ran out of steam and Cardiff ran out 3-1 winners. Ah well, another cup final on the telly without us in it.

Back to the grind of the league, and a remarkable event – reserve centre forward John Lathan's hat-trick against Portsmouth in a 3-2 win. Well, perhaps the crowd of only 8,000 will give a clue – the miners' strike had meant no coal, which meant no power stations, and therefore no electricity. So no floodlights and the highest occurrence of truants in County Durham, as we took our own version of the three-day week to get to the midweek mid afternoon match. After that, it was win a few, lose a few, and cling onto the heels of the leading few, with the highlight being the 5-0 beating of Watford in a rearranged game – the original being postponed when the floodlights disappeared into the fog as we queued outside. Division One was a real possibility, but perhaps we should have listened to Nillson as he sang Without You, because that's what Division One would be. Home losses to Hull and QPR put a dent in our aspirations, meaning that a draw and a win away from home in the last two games, although promotion form, were just not enough. Still, a brave effort and certain success next season, we thought, as the strains of Amazing Grace rang out from Top Of the Tops and we scoffed at the musical tastes of the nation.

We hate Newcastle but we drink Brown Ale
Puts hair on yer chest like rusty nails
We don't give a widdle and we don't give a w***
We are the Fulwell Boot boys

1972-1973

Appropriately enough, Alice Cooper was singing School's Out as the next campaign got underway, but perhaps it should have been Board's Out. The board of directors of any football club in those days was far lower in profile than now and certainly no director took a wage from a club. We were no different to any other club – we knew precious little about the men who ran the club, apart from the fact some of them were called Ditchburn. As far as we were concerned, the people who mattered off the field were the manager, the trainer (some grizzled old pro who kept the players fit), the coach (some grizzled old pro who understood the offside rule), and Johnny Watters, who glued the players back together when pieces broke off them.

Their biggest decision preceding this season was to enter the Anglo Italian Cup, which matched Dick Malone, he of an infinite number of ways to knock over an opponent and appear innocent (hence the nickname tricky), and Luigi Riva, Italian wonderboy, of Cagliari. A narrow defeat and a draw over there were followed by two draws at home and we were out, but we'd seen Europe and we liked what we saw, despite controversy before the Atalanta game at home, when OK didn't put a bus on. We simply assumed it would be there and when it didn't show, several parents had to be persuaded to visit relatives in Sunderland and Joe went up Durham Road and demanded a bus from the owner of the company. He didn't get one.

Again, the transfer market remained something we didn't bother with and the team that started the season was essentially that which had finished the last campaign. Joe Bolton continued in the side, but Dave Watson wasn't fit for the first game, so John Lathan kept the place he'd earned with four good games against the Italians and scored as we went down at Boro. Our traditional invasion of the Holgate was diluted this time, as the police decided that segregation was a good idea – but they forgot to tell us. The nice adults of Teesside helpfully pointed us out to the local hard men, and with cries of "A-G, A-G-R, A-G-R-O – AGRO!" ringing in our ears, we clambered over the fence into the relative safety of the paddock. Nervous glances were exchanged between those who'd got over and those who hadn't, but there was only Lathan's goal to celebrate. He kept his place for the best run of appearances in his Sunderland career, scoring another five goals, and Billy Hughes struggled with form and fitness.

Seven games unbeaten, but with four draws, was hardly the stuff of which legends are made, so we had little to shout about other than the emergence of Jacky Ashurst as a decent centre-half following an injury to Richie Pitt. Indeed, by the end of November, we'd only won three league games and been dumped out of the League Cup by Stoke and this had been unprecedented (in my time, at least) - the board did something positive. Alan Brown left by mutual consent (i.e. leave now and we'll give you a decent pay-off) and in came Billy Elliott. Ready-made, we thought, being fairly simple young folk – he was one of our own; he'd played for us, he'd coached us - surely he could do the job. He did, for a few weeks, during which we failed to win, but he did have the bright idea of switching Dave Watson to defence. Fair enough, we thought, he's good in the air.

Then the board did what they're there to do and brought in Bob Stokoe, the man who'd been around a bit, but was probably most famous for having been the first manager ever to bring on a substitute. His first game ended in defeat by Burnley at Roker, but, with no new faces, only minor changes to the line-up were made. Whatever Bob did – and he described it as "Allowing the players to express themselves"- he did with a more relaxed attitude to his predecessor and things began to look a little rosier. A win at Portsmouth and a goalless draw at home to Preston preceded an enforced Christmas break as the weather took hold, from which we emerged very obviously refreshed. Joe Bolton's first goal came in the 4-0 thrashing of Brighton in the first game of the New Year, watched by one new signing, Ron Guthrie and playing alongside another, David Young – both arriving from our friends up the road after a combined nineteen years' service to the dark side. It looked like the team, along with us, was growing up. Away from football, at fifteen and sixteen, we were torn between the music that we'd heard our elder siblings (mostly sisters in my group) playing (Led

Zep, Cream, Hendrix, Rory Gallagher, the original incarnation of Fleetwood Mac), the music our parents grudgingly acknowledged as "OK" (Beatles, Stones, Kinks, Lindisfarne – local touch), and the stuff we actually liked (Slade, T Rex). Let's just say we were easily influenced and Slade wore the right clothes in their early days – and made a lot of noise.

Unfortunately, our younger sisters went in for that Osmond/Cassidy nonsense, which at least gave us something to laugh about. I made my way to my first live performance (Butlin's apart), despite being caught out by the inspector on the bus and having to pay full fare (God loves a tryer), at the Top Rank Club, near where the Interchange now stands, around the time Stokoe arrived, to see Slade. They were good, but, as was typical in those pre-arena days, it was the support, Thin Lizzy (who I'd assumed to be a dancer), who left the lasting impression. Even the unbilled Suzie Quatro was a pleasant surprise and within six months she'd joined Slade on Top of the Pops.

So, as we argued about the merits of a whole range of music, we travelled to Notts County for the third round game, taking over the Cattle Market Tavern for the first of several consecutive seasons and being introduced to the delights of a bus full of beer. By the time Monty produced one of his wonder saves and a Dave Watson goal had given us a draw, their ground had frayed seriously at the edges, with several large pieces of wood simply breaking off the away end. Three days later, Watson and Tueart disposed of County and we were back to the league for a while and a few changes were made to the Sunderland squad. Recognising our lack of cover at the back and weight up front (since Watson's permanent move to the back), Stokoe began a series of transfers. After a draw at Swindon, Billy Hughes found his big brother John alongside him against Millwall.

What appeared to be a dream ticket turned sour within half an hour, as Yogi struggled through the remaining fifteen minutes of the first half after a nasty challenge wrecked his knee. Quick to react, Stokoe brought in another big strong forward; although (unlike John Hughes) no-one had heard of Vic Halom. Bob obviously remembered him from their time together at Charlton. Next up were Reading in the cup, and one of the biggest cheers of the night was for their manager Charlie Hurley. The undisputed man of the match, however, was Steve Death in the visitors' goal, as he kept out everything we could throw at them to earn a draw virtually singlehanded. Everything but a goal from Dennis Tueart, that is, and in the replay Reading were well beaten 3-1. The up and down league form continued with a defeat at Wednesday, where Young's injury resulted in Richie Pitt's recall from his loan at Arsenal, followed by a nice 4-0 win over Boro at Roker, Tueart continuing his best scoring run in a Sunderland shirt.

Then the cup began in earnest, with a trip to the Chelsea of the day, Man City, who boasted Cold Hesleden boy and England star Colin Bell alongside Franny Lee, Rodney Marsh, and a host of other footballing pin-ups. The media (known simply as the press in those bygone days) were predicting a cricket score for the Blues, but we thought differently. Maine Road was unusual in that the popular end was at the side, and it was where the away fans were put as well. The Kippax, filled to the rafters with the most vociferous fans of both persuasions, was an awesome sight and the teams responded with a cracking match. A dodgy kick by Joe Corrigan to Willie Donnachie never reached its target and Micky Horswill emerged from behind the girder obstructing my view to score the cheekiest goal of his career. Billy Hughes scored an individual effort in the second half, but a very questionable shove on Monty caused him to knock a corner into his own net and we were justified in being disappointed not to have come away with a win.

Four days later and I was privileged to attend one of the great nights in Roker's history. Almost 52,000 others were there as well and it was one of those magical nights when the home crowd became as one and the Roker Roar was at its passionate, throbbing best. As Slade asked the music world to Cum On Feel The Noise, City felt it all right. It is perhaps fitting that the only footage of this match that survives is a monochrome affair, as it was an event that ranks up there with the best of footballing film archive. Everyone who was there and many others beside, will never forget Vic Halom's thunderbolt, probably one of the old ground's best goals and when Billy Hughes danced through the visiting defence to make it 2-0, the place was bouncing with a ferocious roar. Although City got one back, it was no surprise when Hughes got to Tueart's cross just before Kerr to confirm the win.

As far as the league was concerned, we were in the quarter final of the FA Cup, and we could live with mid-table mediocrity, as promotion was almost certainly beyond our reach. Tickets for the home tie with Luton were in such high demand that the club announced the collection of vouchers at the next league game, against Oxford, would guarantee satisfaction. Good move from a financial point of view, as 39,222, some 13,000 more than the recent Boro game, turned up and there was mayhem at the turnstiles. Dave Watson scored the only goal, Ray Ellison, another ex-Mag reserve, made his debut, and we went home happy with our vouchers clutched to our chests. Our next game was at Luton, and, presumably in an attempt to confuse our opponents for the cup, Stokoe included Ellison again, along with Lathan, Jacky Ashurst, Chambers and Jimmy Hamilton. We lost 0-1, but the big one was at home a week later.

In front of 53,151, Luton frustrated us for long periods, until Ron Guthrie (with an overhead kick) and Dave Watson (with a trademark cannonball header) settled the game in the second half. Semi Final of the cup for the first time in my lifetime? What was all that about? Sunday teatime told us it was Arsenal, the Arsenal of the day, at Hillsborough and the league went firmly to the back of our minds. To the back of the fans' minds, but not the team's, as we went on a run of three wins and a draw to warm up nicely for the next step in our big cup adventure.

Vouchers had been collected, encouraging almost 41,000 to the Carlisle game and only about half of my crowd had been lucky. My ticket came from the detective friend of the boyfriend of someone who worked with my mam and arrived two days before, but turned out to be for the Arsenal end. No matter. I thought I'll swap it when I get there and I'm better off than Dunny, who didn't have a ticket of any description. The back seat of the OK bus was rocking to the sounds of We're On Our Way To Wembley when someone said "Patty, what's your sister doing in the car behind? She's waving something." So she was – a match ticket. All our tickets were located, so it was a shout down to the front "Dad, have you got your ticket?" "Yes," came the reply from Stan, "It's in my pock… aagghh!"

It was Wetherby before they could stop the bus and the ticket was reunited with its rightful owner, who had to endure the Nice One, Stanley song for the remainder of the journey. Strangely enough, Sheffield had held back a handful of tickets, allegedly to beat the touts and we bought one at the ticket office half an hour before the game – again, it was for the Arsenal end. I managed to swap mine with an Arsenal fan who had a ticket for the Kop, but his mate refused to swap with Dunny . "Nah, I'm not bothered about being in the wrong end," was the reply to our plea. No problem, as it turned, with the turnstile man letting him use the ticket to get on the Kop anyway. Not long into the game, we spied the uncooperative Londoner (quite easy, as he was about eighteen stone and wore dungarees) being force to stand on the concrete barrier for the whole of the first half. Served him right.

We managed, by some kind of telepathy, to congregate with the rest of South West Durham's fit young men, and watch, awestruck on the one hand (sensible football fans) and expectant on the other (bitten by cup fever) as we matched, then outplayed, the mighty Arsenal. The breakthrough came when Jeff Blockley trod on a back pass, Vic Halom got there before Bob Wilson and what had been a thunderous noise from the Sunderland fans reached a new level of sound. Imagine 20 odd thousand in a big, open, standing area, all loving each other in the most passionate way. Imagine it happening again, when Tueart's back header was headed on by Hughes and Bob Wilson took off on one of his famous safety first dives (i.e. look like you're trying when, in fact, you've no hope of reaching the ball) and in it looped. Craziness ensued in the Kop, the Paddock and the benches right next to the touchline. You could probably have heard us in Rotherham

Then Monty got half a hand to Charlie George's shot and we all blew at the ball as it bumbled and crept just over the line. Arsenal pressed, but we held firm and all thought of being back on the bus for the prescribed five o'clock departure went up in the air when the whistle went. Back then, managers were just as much characters as they are today, but spent a lot less time in the media spotlight. That day at Hillsborough, though, was the day that Bob Stokoe became as big a star as any of his players, when the fans decided that they wanted to show their appreciation to the man who'd turned their team from a bunch of journeymen to local, soon to become national, heroes. For the first time, the fans chanted the manager's name, and five minutes later, out came Bob, in his Terylene shirt with the arm-bands, planting kisses on his hands and throwing them to the Sunderland fans. I don't know if he was crying – probably not – but I would have been.

Our chests swelled almost to bursting point with pride, we floated back to the bus and bounced our way back, passing a hastily painted banner in hanging from a bridge as we passed through Leeds proclaiming LEEDS UTD FA CUP WINNERS 1973. Bring 'em on, we thought, as we watched the magic all over again on Match of the Day.

Waking the next morning, we found ourselves all over the front pages as well as the back pages – and the fans and manager got almost as much coverage as the team. We were walking on air all week at school – we were going to the FA Cup Final, and we were going to win the cup, no problem.

All hearts and minds on Wearside were on the cup, which is just as well, as we continued our league inconsistency with a vengeance. Win, lose, win, win, lose, win, draw, draw, and the cup final countdown was over. We'd had to endure yet another voucher allocation for the final tickets, but I had the added drama of being in Ibiza when the lucky vouchers were drawn, having left mine in the capable (I hoped) hands of Betty Dunn, not known for her interest in football despite her brother Lawrie Pratt having played for Hunwick in the amateur cup final in 1939.

The poor woman was on the receiving end of my first ever international telephone call, which used up two days spending money, when I discovered that I was indeed going to Wembley, as were all of my mates, as we'd obviously chosen the right turnstile to collect our vouchers from. Nerves were still on edge until we actually had the tickets in our sweaty little hands, after which they were hidden away under mattresses and behind mirrors to outwit the cup ticket thieves who would no doubt be targeting Bishop in a big way. For the first time, my folks paid for the trip to an away game – the result of a foolish statement from dad around the Reading game – "If they get to the final, I'll pay your ticket and the bus." Must have cost him a fiver.

Back to life, back to reality and it was Huddersfield at home. Billy Hughes got all three goals and for the first time, we left early. Only a few minutes before the end, mind you and I can't remember why – we didn't have the money to nip in for a pint and most of us were too young to chance asking for one anyway – but it was early enough to miss Monty's penalty save. The games came thick and fast – four days later we beat Portsmouth 2-0, then two days after that lost by the same score at Burnley, followed by a five day break before three games in four days – two wins and a defeat, with fringe players like Joe Bolton, John Tones, Mick McGiven and Brian Chambers appearing. After a one goal win over Forest on the last Saturday of the league season, even Trevor Swinburne gave Monty a rest at Orient on the Monday, where Dave Young earned a point with his only Sunderland goal.

Four days after that, and arguably the single most memorable day in the club's history and we were just about old enough to appreciate the enormity of it. Few people can remember at the drop of a hat who won the cup in any particular year, but most football folk know instantly when asked the 1973 winners. A six o'clock departure (and I spotted a Sparrowhawk only fifty yards from where I'm now sitting) and the bus, full of the fifty-four people I'd travelled with to home games for the last three seasons, was on its way. Parking up somewhere near King's Cross, it was time for my first visit to Del's Diner, beneath the arches outside St Pancras, then the tube ride to Wembley.

Our first sight of the old stadium on its biggest day of the year was at the end of a huge line of red and white – there hardly seemed to be a Leeds fan in sight. We were offered tickets by touts who we later saw being held upside-down by larger Sunderland fans than us and shaken until their tickets fell to the floor – at least some ticketless lads got lucky. My group was split into two smaller groups by our designated turnstiles, so we arranged to meet up "after we win" at a certain spot, and in we went. Gren, Patty, Johnny, and Tommer in one gate, me, Pos, Dunny and hanger-on (Man Utd fan got his ticket from Bishop Football Club) Natty in another. In those days, the allocation of tickets was 33,000 to each club, and the rest to the FA, to be shared out around the football world – with a fair proportion arriving, as they tend to do on these occasions, in red and white hands, as Sunderland fans have an innate ability to get in where a draught couldn't.

By the time the ground had filled up, we noticed how much space (about a whole paving stone each) we could each command. Then Stan (another hanger-on, who'd got his ticket from Shildon Football Club) stood on my foot, and our little band of five were established, a quarter of the way back, with the West End goal just to our left, in our red and white football jerseys, matching tams, several scarves each and in my case, a doctor's white coat with red trimmings. The fans' travelling treasure, the half-mile-long scarf, made its way around the West End and as the rain came down, the Roker Roar arrived in town. If you're too young to have experienced it, then let me tell you than everything that's been written about it is true.

The passion and throbbing noise that had reached epic proportions for the first time that season at home to Man City swelled up and filled Wembley. Imagine the sound of "Short and fat, he's a tw*t, Billy Bremner" from almost 40,000 Wear-side voices rolling across the turf and out off over the stands. Magic. The game's been written about enough for everyone with even a passing interest in SAFC to know the details, but, as far as I was concerned, memorable moments were Pitt's Welcome to Wembley tackle, kissing the young lass in front when we scored, the rain, the noise, Dick Malone forcing the substitution of Eddie Gray, the goal gaping for what seemed like minutes as Lorimer shaped and shot straight at my face – and the save.

Then the longest last few minutes of any game in the world ever, not hearing the whistle and wondering why Mickey Horswill was his knees – then realising that it must be over because of the roar, Arthur Cox being held back by a steward and Bob Stokoe in his immortal trilby, with his mac over his tracksuit, sprinting towards us and Monty before the most famous group hug in football history. Then came the realisation that we'd actually won the biggest club competition in the world. Sunderland. My team. Dunny's team. My Grandad's team. Then the tears came – the first time in my life I'd cried over something happy. I remember looking around and seeing, as well as my mates, older and uglier people than us doing the same – some who looked as if they could have been standing in the same spot thirty seven years earlier, doing exactly the same thing. The climb up the steps to the Royal Box, get yer medals, drop the cup, stumble down the steps and run around the pitch with captain Bobby and Boss Bob on yer shoulders. "Ee-aye-addio, we won the cup," the best chant of all time.

Out of the ground and our merry band was reunited - and the hugging, jumping, and screaming started all over again. I've smiled since, but that was where I learned just how wide a smile could be. Back to the town, with Pos narrowly surviving being jammed in the tube doors, but we got our own back by rocking it off its rails by the medium of song. We ran down the road from King's Cross, scarves a twirling, dancing singing, shaking hands with bemused strangers, trying to come to terms with what had just happened. Then came our first grown-up, pub-type, trophy winning celebration, as we crowded our under-age bodies into a bouncing pub full of joyful Wearsiders, drank slightly too much, laughed as Natty's sweet sherry was downed in one by a celebrating Big Lad who promptly replaced it with a pint and the advice to "Celebrate like man," then dizzily back onto the bus at midnight for more renditions of the "Ee-aye-addio" song. We slept, but never for long, as Joe awoke every twenty minutes and immediately began singing "We won the cup, we won the cup, ee-aye-addio, we won the cup."

Hell, that was some day. The next morning, we ran to each other's houses just to make sure we had actually been there and seen the same thing. As Tony Orlando was tying a yellow ribbon round the old oak tree, had we been tying red and white ribbons to the FA Cup? We had, so we danced and sang some more. School on Monday was virtually lesson-free and the teaching staff took the time to acknowledge each of us who had been there.

Back to life, back to reality – postponed fixtures still had to be fulfilled and only two days after Wembley, the Lads ran out at Ninian Park to applause from home fans as well as the travelling fans – this appreciation even made the national news – and the 26,000 crowd was well above the average Cardiff gate, as only Guthrie from the winning team didn't play. 1-1, but who cared. Another two days off and League leaders QPR came to Roker and spoiled the home fans' celebrations as Stokoe gave the entire Wembley eleven the chance to perform. QPR had other ideas, and, although we could cite tiredness as an excuse, they kicked seven bells out of us and won 3-0.

While 43,000 were there that night, the same were there when the cup was brought back, plus another 500,000 lining the route from the motorway to the ground. I stood at Carrville in my Wembley attire, slung a gold-painted Adidas Scorpion to a bemused Ian Porterfield on the open top bus, then they were gone, slowly trundling up the A690 to town. We lived that whole blessed summer smiling, talking about that day in May, and firmly believing that Division One was a formality come next season's end.

I'm a Sunderland fan
Amazed at what I am
I saw what I think that the Magpies stink
Yes I'm a Sunderland fan
Oh, you won't get me I'm part of the Fulwell
You won't get me I'm part of the Fulwell
You won't get me I'm part of the Fulwell
'Til the day I die, 'til the day I die

1973-1974

That was the summer of love. We saw our baby jive as presence at the final upped our status amongst the teenage females of Auckland and district. Dunny and I strutted our red and white stuff on holiday with his folks in Cornwall – "Yes, we were there," we answered to trippers from around the nation as they asked the inevitable on hearing our accents. We spent hours decorating our schoolbags with FA Cup related messages and updated the names of our heroes. We bussed it through to Roker to get our photos taken with the cup, as mementoes of the club's achievement and our appalling fashion sense.

The weeks passed quickly to the new season, as well they might and anticipation was high as we started the season as leaders of the promotion gang, the team the subject of young love and old love – fans ancient and modern made up the 28,000 opening day crowd at home to Orient as the course of the season was mapped out for us in its first ninety minutes. With Young and McGiven in for the injured Pitt and Horswill, Orient did what everyone else did that season – regarded us as the team to beat in the division and forced a draw. Newly promoted Notts County gave us a chance to gain momentum, and the same Sunderland eleven ran out 4-1 winners. Here we go – so we thought until Cardiff came to town and battered us for most of the match, a point only being gained by Ron Guthrie's one-man mission to defend, play midfield and score the equaliser in front of a relieved Fulwell.

We managed another draw and win before the real fun began – was the Cup Winners Cup distracting us, or were the opposition really lifting their game every week? September 19th saw most Wearside ears glued to crackling radios and Dunny and I sat with one jammed between our heads as the impossible unfolded through the ether. Out in Hungary, Hughes and Tueart got the goals as we beat Vasas convincingly. We welcomed them home to the Luton game, but that one went all wrong as well. Not only did the Hatters win 1-0, but Ritchie Pitt slid off the pitch after making a typical challenge and the crumpled heap in front of the Fulwell was the last we saw of him as a player. Only twenty-one, he spent the next eight months trying to recover from that knee injury, but retired from the professional game at the end of the season, another local boy made good – but for a desperately short time.

Undeterred, we boarded the coach for West Brom the following week, determined to cheer the lads on to a return to form. The only trouble was they'd given us a driver who didn't know where West Brom was. "Easy," we said. "Straight down the motorway, turn left, and you're there." Fortunately, it's not that far from Walsall to the Hawthorns, so we stopped to ask a young lady the way, she agreed to show us, just as long as we gave her a lift, as that's where she was headed and we completed the journey with five police motorcycle outriders and one extra passenger. Vic Halom did the business, we brought home a point and we made ready for our first visitors in serious European competition. No real competition as it turned out, as Tueart's goal confirmed our progress to the next round. We started to check where the final was to be played, like you do when you get carried away.

While happy with the result, I was less than happy with a 22,000 crowd, as I'd walked through from Bishop and spent the night on a bench (after the expected overnight queues failed to materialise) to secure a ticket. The queues weren't even evident as the ticket office opened and the final straw was when Dougie from school spotted me and Dunny legging it towards the Barnes and got his Dad to give us a lift home – but only after they'd nipped to the ground for their tickets. At least we were through, and three days later we beat Wednesday at home, but had only two days to rest up for the League Cup tie at Derby. On a rare start for reserve striker John Lathan, who scored twice to bring them back to Wearside, as some fans complained that they'd rather forsake the League Cup in the quest for European glory – even then, people were getting picky. Our confidence in the team restored, we headed down to Preston, stopping only to terrorise Kirby Stephen Market, collect some ninespot dominoes in town, then watched in wonder as the daft lads marched across the pitch, returned bearing blue and white scalps and took their places back on the away terracing. That was about as exciting as it got on the pitch, as the cup final team, but for Young and Ashurst in for Pitt and Watson, lost 1-0 and we headed for a night in Black-pool...

Aware of the potential fixture congestion that the pursuit of success on three fronts could bring, Stokoe strengthened our attack by bringing in Rod Belfitt from Everton – having played at Ispwich and Leeds, we'd actually heard of him. So we went to Fulham, Horswill and one of their lads scored for us and we were ready for the big one - Sporting Lisbon came to town four days later. With the surprising choice of keeper Trevor Swinburne as substitute, we produced another bit of a surprise, as we won quite a lot more convincingly than 2-1 suggested and despite the late away goal that would come back to haunt us, looked more than worthy of our place in the competition.

After a goalless draw at home to Palace, along came the Derby replay two days later. Draw and unlike today when at least two weeks is needed for the police to sort out their baby-sitters, we tossed a coin for the location, won and all came back two days after that. Over 38,000 for each game and the second turned out to be Vic Halom's finest hour, as he rattled in all three goals, wrapping Durham-born Derby fullback Robson around a Roker End post in the process, to take us into the next round. Such a victory, naturally enough after the achievements of the preceding season, had us dreaming of Wembley all over again as we chased glory in two knock-out competitions.

Our team at Hull preceding the game in Portugal saw some of our more precious players wrapped in cotton-wool and contained five players from the reserves in Guthrie (played in midfield), McGiven, Lathan, Bobby Mitchell (in his only start) and Belfitt, with Ray Ellison on the bench. Perhaps unsurprisingly, we went down 2-0, but, in reality, all eyes were on the game in Lisbon three days later. Back with our first-choice starting eleven, the radios and the ears were again in close contact, but two goals from the Portuguese meant that their goal at Roker had indeed done the damage and that particular dream was over. Despite this, we received deserved acclaim for our contribution, as, with a side containing exactly no European experience whatsoever, we'd acquitted ourselves well.

Anyway, we still had the League Cup to chase and a chance to claim yet another big scalp, as we'd been drawn at home to Liverpool. Consecutive home games against Swindon and Bolton saw Tueart knock in four goals, Halom two, and Por-terfield the other with only one in reply before Bristol City spoiled our warm-up by winning at Ashton Gate. 36,208 turned up for the visit of the Reds, we simply couldn't match them, though, and in the replay of the Charity Shield that never was, went down 2-0. Well, only the league and the retention of the FA Cup to concentrate on, we told ourselves, but by the time we nipped over the A69 to Carlisle for the third round, the only occurrence of note was the debut of Danny Hegan, over twelve years after originally signing for us.

Two draws, five defeats, and only two wins – one at Blackpool, when the weather and threatened postponement had caused us to cancel and re-book our trip twice – was a pretty miserable run. Hav- used my now legendary connections (my Mam's dentist was related to Monty), I secured a pair of tickets from our keeper, which he said would be at the main entrance. Unfortunately, the gadgie (commissionaire?) wouldn't believe that us scruffy oiks had any tickets awaiting us and it was only when the man himself saw what was going on and had a word with Mr Jobsworth that the envelope bearing my name was found at the front desk. A goal-free encounter and we fully expected to finish them in the replay. By 10pm the following Wednesday, our chances of remaining cup-holder come May had gone, as Carlisle scored the game's only goal.

Just promotion, then.

A draw at Oxford, a defeat at Millwall and a bit of squad-strengthening with the arrival of Dennis Longhorn from Mansfield preceded an upturn in form. By March, we'd won three on the belt before Micky Horswill's last game, a defeat at Boro and Tueart's last game, a two-goal starring role in the defeat of Portsmouth. The pair went to Man City in exchange for Tony Towers and a few quid and while we'd lost two local lads, it has to be said that Tueart had lacked passion for some time and Horswill was more than amply replaced by the classy Towers.

Apart from winning England caps while a Sunderland player, he also made Frosties adverts – surely a sign that we were truly a big club. Denny D's last game was also Denny L's first start – after a couple of games on the bench, Dennis Longhorn won a place in the starting eleven. He certainly looked the part – a tall, elegant midfielder – and scored the only goal in the win over Fulham soon after with a spectacular overhead kick from near the halfway line. We expected great things, but in reality he was a steady, reliable player and no more. After twelve starts that season and another six at the beginning of the next, his best run was four in a row before he eventually left for Sheffield Utd.

Personally, match-day travel (to home games at least) changed for- ever when I passed my test and Grandma dipped into her savings and bought me a mini for £150. LUP 233 D and bright red, it soon acquired the necessary red and black stripes to produce an SAFC colour scheme and I could squeeze Dunny, Johnny,

Patty and Gren into it, charge them a fair price for petrol and make a profit on selling them bottles of beer (profit only realised when I took the empties back). We still parked in the same place, near the end of Given Street, home of the biggest dog-turds in the world, but if I was driving I couldn't drink, so we'd take a ball down to Roker beach and play football for an hour before leaving the ball with Johnny's aunty who lived opposite the Fulwell. If the weather was bad, we played run away from the big waves on the pier, and often got to the match sopping wet. Oh the fun we had, and being in possession of a motor was also a hit with the ladies, even if I could either afford petrol to drive them around, or drinks to ply them with, but not both.

Down at the youth club, we were putting on a show of artiness by listening to Genesis and playing Ouija and describing my car's personalised paint-job. I managed to get a nice girlfriend who was also a regular at Roker, so I could officially take her out by meeting her at the match. The problem was that her family stood in the Roker, so it was a bit of a sacrifice to forego the delights of the Fulwell in the pursuit of romance. I probably let the football get in the way of that relationship a bit too much, but she's been happily married to one of my best mates for twenty-five years, so that all worked out for the best. Having the car also meant that I could ferry the lads to music events and Patty persuaded us to see Rory Gallagher at the Empire – as Patty is of Irish descent and with an older sister, it was hardly surprising – and it turned out to be a turning point for my musical tastes. Everything poppy took a bit of a back seat (although I still maintain that Noddy Holder possesses one of the best rock'n'roll voices of all time) and we progressed to heavier stuff. Most of us could reel off Led Zep's tracks in the order in which they'd been recorded and strange symbols began to appear on our school bags alongside the black cats. All part of growing up. I suppose.

Back to the football. Despite bringing a point back from a Duncan McKenzie-inspired Forest, where we'd been refused pints in Trent Bridge Cricket Club (Joe simply bought twice as many halves), two back from Swindon and gaining revenge over Carlisle at home, our promotion charge stumbled when Longhorn's second goal couldn't prevent Bristol City winning at Roker and fell when we visited Carlisle only four days after they visited us. Being a new driver, I was given the chance to take dad's car, loaded with mates and dad as supervising driver, attending an away game for the first time in ages.

Two in the passenger seat, one in the foot well and four across the back, I duly fell asleep at Stanhope and supervising driver became actual driver. Parked up at Aunty Joan's just round the corner from the ground, we were fed ham sandwiches and trifle and the legend of Sobs having relatives within striking distance of almost every league ground was born. I didn't have the heart to tell them that Joan wasn't biological, merely a friend of my mam's. Anyhow, dad didn't like the swearing on the terraces, or the fact that the terraces bounced, and said that it was back to the Red Lion bus for future away trips. That narrow defeat was put right with a win at Villa, then at home to Blackpool and in spectacular fashion on the last day, at Luton in a 4-3 win. Not enough and we had paid the price of the previous season's success. Everyone wanted to scalp us, some managed to raise their games enough to do just that and like Terry Jacks, we had another season in the sun rather than the First Division.

My old man said follow Sunderland
And don't dilly dally on the way
Off went the bus with the boot boys on it
We took Boro in half a minute
We dillied, we dallied, effed them in the alleys
La la la la la la la la la
If you haven't got a bonnet
With Sunderland written on it
You can't find your way home

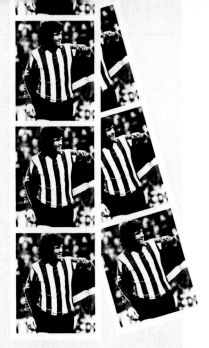

1974-1975

Being the generous sort, I was given to extravagance in the field of family birthday presents. I still offer my mam a trip to the match on her birthday (Boxing Day), but, still she turns me down. For my sister's birthday, in the close season, I took her to see Slade at the City Hall, but, being as daft as I was generous, I thought nothing of wearing a blazer with a club crest on the pocket. My sister's most memorable moment was watching her brother and his pal being threatened with death by a reasonably large and very drunk local who'd wobbled out of the Star on Westgate Road. Anything I admitted to this nutter counted for nothing, as a) he had his fist in my face, and b) I had my fingers crossed. The return journey was a lot safer, as we'd found half of Bishop were at the City Hall as well, discovering the delight of support band the Sensational Alex Harvey Band and we returned en masse, with our colours hidden at the centre of the group.

Pre-season friendlies were generally north of the border in those days, with Berwick being an almost annual fixture. I took my car to its first away match as part of a convoy of South West Durham's finest, we descended on a pub called the Bonarsteads and drank it dry in under an hour. Between eight of us, two paid (half, of course) and six crawled through the legs of the paying customers. We played football on the pitch, got our first sight of new signing Bobby Moncur when he asked us to get off so that they could start the match, then sunbathed our way through the ninety minutes on the grass next to the goal. That's what proper friendlies are all about. Oh, and we won, 4-0 (Finney, Hughes (2) and somebody else) and I almost killed everybody on the way home by failing to spot a Low Fell red light.

Holidays were in deepest Gloucestershire, on the banks of the Severn, where people were still asking us if we'd been at the cup final and West Bromwich was only a short train ride away. Short, but unpleasant, as anyone between the age of twelve and twenty five was considered fair game for a bit of taunting or worse. Dunny and I endured abuse and being pelted with soap by Birmingham fans, as the sure fire way to get battered was to react in any way, and arrived at New Street in one piece (each). New Street is nothing clever now, but in 1974 it looked as if it had been designed to facilitate violence and crime of any description. Just as the Brummies appeared to have given up on trying to get us to bite, we discovered that we had to cross the nastiest bridge in the world – fenced in, roofed in, nowhere to run or hide, its only positive point was that you couldn't be thrown from it. Safely (we thought) on the bus to West Brom, it all started again with the Baggies taunting team poking us with anything they could lay their hands on. We should probably have been awarded the Nobel Peace Prize for not getting involved, but, in truth, getting involved would probably have meant no more than getting one or two good shots in before being pummelled to the floor.

At the Hawthorns, we were greeted by the legendary West Midlands Police, perfectly summed up by the dog-handler at our turnstiles. Despite being – how can I put this? – mentally challenged, he managed to convey a feeling of pure hatred towards us. "Get back, or I'll let the dog off the lead," he screamed, as we threatened the very fabric of society by queuing for admission and – shock, horror – buying programmes. 1-0 to WBA, another wasted journey, and we had it all to do in reverse. Luckily, Man Utd had been playing down the country somewhere and the Brummies saw the massing Mancs as better targets than two miserable Sunderland fans. It was actually quite entertaining, in a totally socially unacceptable way, to watch them trying to fight each other without getting off their respective trains – lots of leaning out of windows and poking rolledup Football Echoes. We told my folks that it had been a poor match but an OK trip, as it was a lot easier than explaining that we were old hands at keeping our heads down and staying intact in the face of extreme provocation – survival skills that I've maintained to the present day, although, thankfully, I don't need them often in today's (mostly) enlightened days of all football fans being brethren in a big sporty family – with the Mags being the half-breed half-cousin kept chained up beneath the stairs.

Anyway, holidays over and back to the business of getting promoted. We thought it a bit of a coup, as well as a gamble on age and fitness, when it was announced that we'd signed Tom Finney. It transpired that it wasn't the Preston Plumber, but an Irish winger from Cambridge who turned out to have a bit of a nasty edge to him. Local boy Pop Robson had eventually arrived at the ground he was born next to and played every competitive game that season, while Stokoe pulled off a bit of a coup by pinching Bobby Moncur from them up the road. Bobby was still captain, still in his prime at twenty- nine and still playing well, so we were probably right in thinking that there was a rabbit off between the management up there and the player. Like Pop, he also played every competitive game that season and after the defeat at West Bromwich, he captained us through two unbeaten months until consecutive defeats at Hull and Cardiff with a largely unchanged team. Joe Bolton had a short run in the side when Guthrie was injured, Porterfield missed the first month and Halom's injury gave Belfitt a month's work. Finney's role was mainly warming the bench, but it was the settled nature of the side that was the real benefit – Kerr, Hughes, and Malone also played every competitive game.

This was also the season when a few of us decided that we could help the club by becoming Roker Bingo agents, with the result that our mates were pestered to part with their pennies every week, (yes, I did sell a £10 winner) and we got free tickets. Free tickets were nice, but they were for the Roker End, and we were Fulwell Enders. This left us with two courses of action (apart from the obvious one of standing in the Roker End), which were to sell the tickets for face value and then pay (half, of course) to get into the Fulwell, or going into the Roker early and, braze-fond, simply walk down the side of the pitch to the Fulwell. Sounds simple, but we didn't look much like we had any business away from the terraces and frequently had to make the last fifty yards with a sprint and a dive for cover. We always beat the stewards for speed, as they were stewards of the old school, not the finely-honed, ex-SAS yellow-jacketed killing machines employed in the football stadia of the 21st century, but middle-aged gadgies with brown coats, flat caps and an armoury of deterrents that consisted of a few well-chosen curses and a swift clip round the lug if they caught you.

A trip to Preston in the League Cup should have given us the chance to progress, but if ever the words lower league and defeat apply to any club, they apply to us and the League Cup. A night game, I had the transport, no problem, it's only a hundred miles straight from school, so in we squeezed and off we went. To say we were poor wouldn't do Preston justice, as they, in general, and a certain Mel Holden, in particular, raised their game and were worth the win. They were so much in control that I was persuaded, for the second and last time, to leave the match early. Big mistake. I'd got into the car and opened the passenger door when all hell broke loose. I was aware of a lot of noise and bodies charging about, then someone got my door open and started kicking my head around the car. As quickly as it had started, it stopped, and I lifted the passenger seat so that the lads could get in the back.

Unfortunately, Gren panicked, and decided to sit in the front, which meant that he put the seat down on top of me. It turned out that they'd run like hell when Patty, curled up in a ball on the floor, started screaming as if they'd done some serious damage to him. Luckily, no serious damage had been done to anyone – which we theorised was down to the fact that our assailants weren't serious hard men, otherwise we'd have been properly minced – and all we took home were a few fat and bruised lips (impressive to the girls for a few days). Passing The Aclet, a mile from home, we were pulled over by the police, who gave us the usual sarcasm (has it been removed from their training these days?), before peering into the car and saying "I know you." Unfortunate. We'd driven two hundred miles, we'd lost the game, and we'd been kicked around a car park, so the reply of "No you f***ing don't" could hardly be classed as a surprise. Having found the car roadworthy, my tax in date, and my breath not smelling of beer, I was left with nothing more than a producer.

No League Cup, but we were looking good in the league despite the two defeats and early October saw us piling into Stubber's Austin 1100 for a rain-soaked trip to Hillsborough. Having used his schoolbag to soak up the water that was coming up from beneath the back seat, we arrived in the nearest pub to be told the game was rained off – just their attempt at humour as it turned out. Billy and Bobby got the goals, two points in the wet schoolbag, and we wrung out the exercise books for a happy but damp homeward journey. Rory Gallagher took us to the Empire for the second time in the same year and we drowned out the Northern Soul Boys at school with awful bootleg tape recordings of his music.

Football-wise, wins at Fulham and at home to Notts County warmed us up for the division's match of the season – later voted match of the decade. Lino and I travelled, for some unknown reason, on the United coach from Darlington and knew the signs were not good when a fellow traveller warned us that it was quite common for the coach not to turn up. Turn up it did, however, away to Old Trafford we went, and into our allocated spot in the Scoreboard End. "Geordies Geordies, give us a song" (everybody called us that in those days, and we generally didn't mind) so we gave them a song. Over the fence they came, and the police swung into action. Well, if you can call keeping well away from the trouble and merely opening a gate in the perimeter fence swinging into action. We spilled onto the pitch like something from a John Wayne film, with bodies tussling in heaps all over the place. Lino and I hopped into the paddock, just behind the dugout, on top of which the police kindly put a portable flashing light, just so that the nutters could see where we were. We ended up holding a tearful five-year-old away from the bother, returning him to a grateful parent a few minutes later, but that wasn't the end of it. Down they came from the back of the paddock, hurling full cans of beer (full – I ask you. What kind of idiots were they?) with a bloke in his thirties eventually confronting us. "You Sunderland?"

"Oh bollocks," I thought, "here we go," as Lino, bless him, stuck his face right into this bloke's nose and said, "Aye, what are you going to do about it like?"

"Er, right, OK then," replied the would be hard-man as he backed away. I think you can call that a close call, situation saved by Lino having more neck than a giraffe. The match itself was one to which the words ding and dong could well be applied. Pearson scored for them, then Billy Hughes scored twice, one of which remains perhaps his finest moment on a football field as he ran fifty yards before applying a Scottish finish (high into the net, when an Englishman would have slotted it along the ground.) 2-1 up at the interval and we were looking good. We all know it ended 3-2 to them and I maintained that their last two goals were both seriously dodgy, but the advent of historical videos has allowed me to see them again and I can't see anything wrong with them. I must have had a much better view from the Paddock than the cameraman did. Being present at such a colossal game is scant reward when you don't win it (fast forward to Wembley 1998) and it was a miserable trip home, made worse when we got back to be told that we'd been on telly, just behind Tommy Docherty – if we'd known how close he was we could have given him some abuse.

We got back on track the following week when Porterfield tore Portsmouth apart as we won 4-1 and I was berated for going to Sunderland when Bishop were playing Bobby Charlton's Preston in the FA Cup. At least I got to see Dick Malone's jinking run and interchange with Bobby Kerr for his second and last Sunderland goal, but then it went horribly wrong. The headlines weren't about whether Porter would be picked for Scotland, but whether he would live or die, after an awful car crash left him with a broken skull amongst other injuries. The feeling around Roker was that we should win promotion for Porterfield, so that we'd be a first division club for his comeback. Dennis Longhorn filled the vacant spot and our form continued to be good, with two wins and two draws taking us to into the New Year and a third round tie with Chesterfield.

They brought fantastic support, raised their game, but couldn't quite match us as Joe Bolton's only FA Cup goal, added to Pop's effort, saw us comfortably through.

Two games in a few days on the south coast returned only one point, then Man Utd came to town for the heavyweight rematch. In probably one of the most entertaining goal-less draws I've seen, Pop contrived to put the ball into the Fulwell rather than the net from a yard or so and Trevor Swinburne deputised well for Monty for the second consecutive game. Still, we looked good and were feeling confident about a trip to the Smog for the fourth round. We shouldn't have been (It took me until Darren Williams headed in Waddle's free-kick to register my first win on Teesside – twenty-six years of trying), as, despite Pop scoring, we never looked like winning and went down, and out, 3-1.

Just the league, then.

The first action after the cup defeat is also something that we're reminded of to this day. We'd had requests played at the Queen's on the Friday night "For all the lads going to Blackpool in the morning," and I managed to get a new girlfriend at the same time, but it wasn't what Sunderland did that we're reminded of. Down at the far end of the pitch, the Blackpool winger cut in from the right and curled a left footer past Monty for the goal of the season, while in front of us the peanut seller performed a crazy war dance behind the goal and distracted Billy Hughes sufficiently to allow Mag-to-be Burridge to save the penalty. 2-3 was not what we wanted, but our first win of the year came at home to Cardiff which, followed by our now customary invasion of Nottingham's Cattle Market Tavern at the pinching of a point, sort of pointed us back in the right direction. We spoiled that by losing at home to Fulham, beating West Brom, then only drawing the next two games before losing at Bristol Rovers and drawing with Oldham at home. Not promotion form, but the first half of the season was keeping us up there, and three wins in a row was promotion form, and we went to Oxford to make it four.

Somewhere in there I'd had to finish with my girlfriend with the excuse of "Sorry, I can't afford football and your Bacardi and lemonade." In reality she lived in West and I couldn't afford the football, Bacardi and petrol, so I took up with a girl who lived in the next street – what a romantic bugger I was. At the Manor Ground, the big away following was more than the local police were expecting, and the segregation was simply non-existent, with the result that we were showered with beer-cans by a lad sitting up in the rafters of the Kop end. He was quickly brought down to earth by a hail of pies – one of those magic moments that can only happen at a football match – and I carried out my first and last act of football violence. As the can-chucker landed on top of his fellow Oxfordians, they took exception to his arrival and charged into the visiting fans. One of them swung a punch at me, I deflected it with my left arm and without thinking, hit him full in the mouth with my right fist. It surprised me almost as much as it surprised him, as is probably the best punch I've ever thrown. Make that definitely, as there aren't many to choose from.

I'm not proud of it, but it was simply a case of self-defence, then hitting him before he hit me. Mind you, the look on his face was precious, unlike the 1-0 defeat. Two games to go and we still had a chance of going up. Up came Bristol City, up stepped Bolton, Robson, and Belfitt with a rare goal and it was all down to the last game, away to Villa. I showed off my Sunderland connections again by getting Monty to kick off a charity match at school (an excuse for people to dress up and roll around in the mud, with two needing medical treatment for injuries caused by over-hard handbags being used as weapons) and he brought along Stan Ternent. Stan said that his knee was coming along fine, which was probably a polite way of telling me that it was knackered and that his two stints on the bench for us were the to be last of his playing career. A bit of a rotten way for a Sunderland fan to end his playing days, but that's football. The Villa game was more important, he said - win that one, the other results go our way and we'd go up.

So we were prepared to cheer the Lads on to Division One. Our party of a dozen or so took enough beer onto the bus to keep a busy pub going for a weekend and we were well up for a promotion party by the time we arrived at Villa Park. If you thought the travelling support at Oxford was impressive, that at Villa would take your breath away. 57,266 in the ground, the huge open end packed with red and white in the blazing sunshine, the atmosphere cranked up to eleven on a scale of ten. We went bare-chested to keep cool (and show off), a decision which backfired when Lucky got bumped and spilled Bovril down my front, leaving an impressive red weal. This was just before the refreshment hut fell over in the crush – another one of those magic moments that can only happen at a football match – and the good old West Midlands Constabulary moved into action.

Someone, somewhere, in the crowd was singing about Harry Roberts being their friend and the police didn't like this, which is understandable, as Mr Roberts was a cop killer. That it was also the name of the Chief Constable in that area at the time of the match is entirely coincidental. In they charged, grabbing Tubby from behind (so they couldn't have seen if he was singing or not) and dragging him up the terraces by his shirt. My question of "What are you doing?" was met with a knee in the danglies and the threat of GBH, so we had to return to watching the football a man down, as it were. Reports from Norwich indicated that results were going our way, but we missed a good chance, Durham lad Brian Little didn't, and we'd blown it. Two points behind Norwich, and finishing in fourth place, was a numbingly disappointing end to the game and the season and it got worse when we went to reclaim Tub from the police station. Once we'd established he was indeed being held there, and that we couldn't have him back, we asked what he was being charged with. When the reply came back "We'll think of something," I snapped, and was halfway across the counter when the others pulled me back by my legs. I don't know what I'd have done if I'd got hold of the desk sergeant, (probably been whacked over the head with a truncheon) but it's as well I didn't.

Bye Bye Baby, sang the Bay City Rollers. Bye Bye Promotion, we sang.

Ee-aye ee-aye ee-aye-oh
Up the football league we go
When we win promotion
This is what we'll sing
We all love you
We all love you
Watson is our king
Oi!

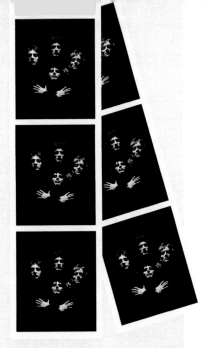

1975-1976

A big summer. We left school, we got jobs, some of us prepared for leaving Bishop and going to College. We had our day in Birmingham court, where the police actually hissed at us and Tubby got done for using the word copper. We'd probably have appealed, but his dad died, no doubt stressed by the court case – nice one, West Midlands Constabulary. My long term (well, five months) girlfriend got sick of sausage in a basket every Friday at the Red Alligator and dumped me at the Queen's (one of a succession of birthday/engagement parties that gave us the chance to wear suits, drink Gold Tankard, Vaux's vilest beer, until the wee small hours and then get belted by the bouncers) to the sound of 10CC's I'm Not In Love. My car having died, as old Minis do, four of us packed my Mam's Mini Traveller (van with windows) full of beer and headed for a week's drinking in Wensleydale. Not a typical holiday for four eighteen- year-olds, you might think, but our second week was to be in the Lake District, which, as any fool knows, is packed with holidaying females. Stubber wound us up with tales of Keswick's pulsating coffee-bar scene and we readied ourselves for a week of romance.

What a load of bull. We spent one night in a B & B in Bowness, where the high point was finding four cans of Special Brew on the pier, and put the lack of girls down to them all being in Keswick for the summer, just waiting for us to turn up. I don't know what part of Keswick they were in, but it wasn't any part we could find and the coffee bars were just that – places to buy coffee. We still work Stubber about that. What do four virile young Sunderland fans do when there are no ladies to impress? A second week drinking, climbing a few hills, playing darts and doms (we knew how to have a good time) and arguing over which of us the landlady of the pub secretly fancied. I treated my sister to her annual birthday present, this time to the sound of Mud at the somewhat safer venue of the Empire, and realised how much my musical tastes had changed the last year or so.

I earned a few bob behind the bar at the Belvedere, got a Danish girlfriend who'd come over on an exchange scheme, went to Denmark on said exchange scheme and got an English girlfriend when the Danish one was late for a date. Survived being attacked by a chair-wielding Danish girl and converted most of that part of Denmark to the Red and White cause, then came back to Bish and got a job driving an ice-cream van. Survived the ice-cream war that raged during the 150 years of the Railway celebration in Shildon and became very popular with my mates because of the size and variety of my iced confections. Got another girlfriend when the last one didn't turn up at a party and caused panic at home when I disappeared for a weekend to visit her at college in Retford.

Amongst all this, Bob Stokoe did a bit of wheeling and dealing and brought in Mel Holden, Tommy Gibb from up the road and Jeff Clarke, a defender with an apparent propensity for own goals, as part of the deal that took Dave Watson, inevitably, to Maine Road. The football started again and we were off on our annual promotion hunt with goals from Longhorn and Robson beating Chelsea, then I decided that I'd take advantage of the folks visiting friends in Newport and got myself a lift to Wales, then the train to Bristol, for our first away game of the season.

I shouldn't have bothered. Trevor Swinburne had no chance behind a shaky defence and we were lucky to keep it to 0-3. An offered holiday in Cornwall with some lads from Trimdon between Bristol and our game at Oxford three days later disappeared in the post-match shenanigans and I took eighteen hours to hitch home. It was an inauspicious start to a reasonably successful career of travelling by thumb and I was off again on the Friday afternoon to ensure timely arrival in the city of the gleaming spires. Bobby Moncur scored, we brought away a point and it took me twenty hours to get home.

Successive home wins over Fulham and Blackpool included Holden's first Sunderland goal and Gibb's only score and we were up and running. For a week. While the team were losing at Plymouth, Stubber and I celebrated our birthday at the Mayfair watching Kraftwerk and even met them in the chip shop afterwards. Apparently, they'd only spoken to us because we were wearing suits as well. The defeat at Home Park, however, was followed by five wins in six and the team had options up front. Robson, Halom and Hughes we all knew about, Holden nobody did – probably not even himself – but he was, in appearance at least, a big target man and, as such, a different option. He was once, in the programme, described as a six-foot enigma and I've heard him called a lot worse, as he was prone to do something fantastic one minute, then fall on his arse the next. Personally, I liked him (check our school photograph that year, and try to spot my home-made Mel Holden is Great badge – you can just make it out on Friends Reunited website), as he always tried to do the right thing.

In the middle of all this, I set out on the adventure of further education. I'd visited Norwich University, but it was a long way from Roker. I'd applied to Durham, but they obviously didn't like the sound of me and I chose the next closest. The fact that it was Newcastle didn't really bother me – I could study what I wanted to study and be even closer to Roker than I'd been in Bishop. So I left home on the OK service bus with Dave, who'd worked the ice-cream with me (and, thirty years on, travels to home games on the same bus as me), wondering what life in bandit country would be like. I was allocated a room with two strangers and met the first as I inspected our big basement room in Jesmond. Canny lad, despite being from Doncaster, and between us we decided that the third roomie was going to ruin our love lives, especially if he had a girlfriend as well. He turned out to be a family Mag (the sort who's family has a history of unfortunate attendance at Gallowgate, but doesn't personally attend often), but a smashing lad despite all that.

Mick from Donny introduced me to Barnsley Rob (who's since turned to the dark side, despite living on Merseyside for the last two decades), who came from the next village to Jeff Clarke and told me that Jeff had a brother or two playing Yorkshire's equivalent to Northern League football (probably called Jud or Wesley, as non-league players in those parts were wont to be called) who considered Jeff a bit of a Jessie for turning pro. Part of our introduction to Newcastle was a free ticket to their game with Spurs and I was disappointed to discover that all of my new pals expected me to a) know the way to the ground from the town itself, and b) actually want to go. I went, and laughed as the Toon hoyed away a 2-0 lead to draw. I persuaded Donny Mick that Sunderland were a better option and both he and the future turncoat Rob accompanied me to Roker many times, enjoying our match day ritual of sleeping until 1, then taking the train to the Central and then to Seaburn before a quick pint or two in the Windmill club or the Bluebell. After the match it was a reverse of that, but with the added excitement of the weekly ambushes carried on by big tough Mags on anyone under seventeen with a red and white scarf sticking out of their coat. New friends, new musical influences, as Mountain and Focus were the sounds that my room-mates preferred.

The season was properly up and running with us in top spot by the beginning of October, and we'd achieved that largely on the back of winning all of our home games – which is always a good idea. We'd got rid of the nonsense of the League Cup by losing at Meadow Lane, leaving only the big two trophies to concentrate on. The small hiccough at Bristol Rovers was matched with both Donny Mick and me receiving matching letters. His began Dear Mick and mine Dear Paul, so you can guess the contents. As his relationship had been on the go for a couple of years compared to mine at a couple of months, his lapse into depression was probably understandable.

The fact that the object of his desires lived in Durham while the object of mine was in Nottinghamshire sent him even further down the tubes, but regular trips to Roker soon brightened him up and we decided to chase every girl on Tyneside for the foreseeable future. Varied female company and five wins in six games soon cheered us both up, before a right thumping at Southampton, then away losses at Chelsea and Bolton. Thank goodness for the home form. Ian Porterfield had remarkably made a comeback at the start of the season, but dropped out of the picture in December, replaced by a variety of vastly different players – Hughes, Finney, Greenwood and Henderson.

At the turn of the year, we were, like Queen and Bohemian Rhapsody, maintaining our position at the top and looking forward to the FA Cup. On came Oldham and out they went thanks to Pop and Mel, then we did what teams in our situation are always told to do – strengthen when you're winning. In came Roy Greenwood, who'd obviously impressed in recent games against us, for a nearrecord £140 grand. He made his debut at West Brom a few days later as we drew after I'd experienced my first driver trying to chat up a young hitch-hiker scenario (I'd carefully got out of his clutches by running away at the motorway services and hiding in the bushes until he'd driven away), but Roy was more remembered for being ginger and refusing to shave off his beard and thus miss the next close-season photo-call than consistent performances on the pitch. Anyway, a win over Plymouth (Mel again and wee Bobby) kept us ahead of the pack. Along came Roy's old club Hull in another home tie and thanks to a rare Finney goal we were on our way. Perhaps the gleaming FA Cup was distracting our focus on the league a little when we travelled to Fulham.

Being experienced in hitchhiking, especially after the West Brom experience, I persuaded Mick that a visit to see his Aunty, who lived in Chelsea Barracks (dead handy for Fulham) would be nice (and two were less likely to be the object of any unwanted desires). Despite being challenged by machinegun-wielding guards who obviously thought we were intent on breaking into the adjacent Buckingham Palace, we survived the night, met up with the Aycliffe lads outside the Cottage and watched Fulham, including Bobby Moore and Rodney Marsh, but not the recently incarcerated George Best, come out on top and Sunderland dropped to third. We spent our last cash on a tube ride to the end of the A1 and arrived back in Jesmond around midnight with a halfpenny between us. Cutting it a bit fine, financially.

Thumb out the next Saturday for the fifth round at mighty-ish (at the time) Stoke, I risked life and limb accepting a ride in a carload of Bolton-bound Mags. Surviving this, I watched the Lads hold on for a deserved draw and took the safer option of a lift to Bishop on the Aclet bus. Three days later and the Roker Roar inspired Mel and Pop to do the business again and the twin towers popped up on the horizon.

Back to the league and we needed to get back to winning ways. I took Keith from London, a Charlton fan, along to Roker for his first visit – one he still reminds me of, as, not only did we win 4-1 to go back to the top, but we were treated to the naughty side of Tom Finney as he put his foot in a little late and broke the keeper's neck. Not a very popular trick with the visiting fans, especially the one standing with me. A night game, a borrowed car and a Carlisle fan was one of my companions as we joined a solid line of traffic across the A69. We reached the back of the terraces just in time to see Tony the Tiger's penalty hit the back of the net, although the 2-2 draw (Mel again) saw us drop to second.

This is where we stayed after the defeat at Luton, but all eyes were on Wembley again as Malcolm Allison's Palace arrived – all big cigars, daft hats, and big talk. Big talk matched by a big performance in front of a big crowd, as blond irritant Alan Whittle scored the only goal. I felt some responsibility, as I'd got a new girlfriend, and, she being from Bristol, I'd taken her to the Rovers home game (draw). She'd also gone across to Carlisle (draw). I should have known that she was destined not to see us win that season, so taking her to a vital cup game was an obvious mistake on my part. Sorry, Lads, my fault.

Just the league then.

Following a busy display against us, Ray Train signed from Carlisle and made his debut three days later in a welcome away win at Orient. Victory came at a cost, with Jeff Clarke's knee injury ending his season and letting Jackie Ashurst in as a capable deputy. The boys are back, we thought, so I biked through to Sunderland and travelled with the Supporters' Club to Forest, my bike sliding all over the luggage compartment at every turn, as Ragworm (sorry, the renowned John Tennick), wouldn't let me leave it in the back of his shop for the duration. Another away defeat, then a late-night bike ride through the Tyne passenger tunnel (highly recommended at that time of night, as there's no one else around, and you can zoom up the walls to your heart's content) and a climb through the window as I'd (as usual) forgotten my key.

Second place was good enough to go up, but there's always more chance of others overtaking you than if you're top, so nerves were starting to fray. Another hitch-hike, this time to Oldham and I met up with Big Harrier from school ("See you in the pub nearest to the ground" – simple times, when all you needed was enough money for a couple of pints, a pie and the junior gate money) and 1-1 was good but not that good, especially when Bristol City were visiting the next week. Yes, I took my Bristolian girlfriend and yes, we only got a draw. There really is something in the superstition business, you know. What we needed was a decent unbeaten run and that's what we got. 3-0 revenge over Southampton, a draw at Notts County and a 3-0 defeat of Blackburn saw us back on top of the pile with only four games left.

Off we went to Hull, where a child-like Mr Rowell opened his account with a soppy shot that trundled under former Darlo keeper Wealands (probably the softest of his century of senior goals for us) and Pop, Mel and the impressive OG (for the second successive game) sent us home more than happy with life, the universe and everything. My family Mag room-mate was finding it hard to take my smug demeanour, although he did excel himself by inviting me and my guitar to a jam session back in his home village, with a mate of his cousin (or a cousin of his mate, I forget which) who turned out to be a Mr McAloon, later of Prefab Sprout – my musical claim to fame. George Maddison, later of the Carpettes (big in Italy around 1980), lived in a nearby room, but he was less willing to share his expertise, and seemed altogether too shy to make a rock star.

Things got happier on the pitch, as 51,000 against Bolton (added to the similar crowd at their place) were expectant at Roker, and they got the win they wanted. We convoyed to Blackpool, all waistcoats and flat caps, on the first day of May, with plans to celebrate victory by staying back after the match for a night on the town, but had nothing to shout about after a narrow defeat, other than the retention of first place. The presence of bit-part players Swinburne and Henderson, in for Monty and Tricky Dicky, couldn't be blamed in any way, but, despite being top, we felt let down. One game to go, and chance for promotion via revenge for another south-coast defeat as Pompey were the visitors. Goals from old favourite Hughes and new cult hero Joe Bolton (his first of the season) meant we were champions. Cue pitch invasion by fans of all ages, but particularly by daft teenagers and TV news images of Pos carrying Pop Robson on his shoulders. North East bragging rights were ours again, and we looked forward to a long summer of celebration, and the next season back at the top.

We are we are Wearside
We are Wearside

1976-1977

Another busy summer, as I got my head down and worked behind the bar to get a bit of cash together for the following academic year. That and my planned holiday, my first big one, of a month riding around Europe's railways. The only problem was that I could only afford to go if I worked right up to the end of August, then missed a month of the season. Well, I was young, daft, and wanted to see the world – or at least the bit across the channel. I managed the first three games, beginning with a tactical (i.e. five defenders) 0-0 draw at Stoke. No new signings graced our starting line-up, with Stokoe trusting the return of Clarke and the experience of the old familiar faces to see us through the season. Further draws, at home to Leicester and Arsenal, seemed to indicate that we could hold our own, so I left them to it as I buggered off around Europe.

It started badly, as the first person we encountered at Calais told us "There's a smashing little café down there does nice cups of tea and scones, not that French muck." We were teenagers, for goodness sake – did we look like we cared about the availability of tea and scones? The day before I celebrated my birthday on the beach at San Tropez, fellow new boys Bristol City thumped us for the second successive season at their place, 4-1, then we went down at the Boro and at home to Man City. All of this went unnoticed by me, as we didn't have a radio, and I hadn't yet persuaded anyone to back my brainwave and open up a string of internet cafes across the civilised world.

By the time I saw my first English paper in almost a month, Europe had been toured, and we were sitting in Amsterdam station. Jim Holton? Alan Foggon? Bob Stokoe hadn't asked me if he could sign these people, but perhaps that was the price I paid for abandoning the Lads for a month. To be fair, Holton was a quick (signing-wise) replacement for the departing Moncur and did reasonably (by comparison) in his 15 games before leaving for Coventry, but Foggon was a big, barrel-shaped let-down, emphasised by the fact that he arrived from Man Utd and left for Southend. Alan Foggon left no real memories of anything positive or dramatic, while Holton did at least score a goal – but his most memorable contribution was the tackle on Graham Paddon of Norwich (in the November defeat) down at the Roker End/Clock Stand corner. Over a hundred yards away, we heard the leg break – eeesh, as they say in the movies.

After the Boro defeat, Mel Holden allegedly fell down the stairs and did his cartilage, so Stokoe went out in a huff and brought in Bob Lee to replace him. At least the News of the World, Dutch edition, brought good news of a Joe Bolton goal at West Ham earning a point, but the events of that Sunday were perhaps more important. We'd bought another goalkeeper – something we hadn't done in over a decade - when Barry Siddall arrived from Bolton and that was the end of an era, as Monty had played the last of his 623 games for us. Off he went Southampton on loan, then Birmingham on loan before a permanent transfer, but, for lads like me who'd never known a Sunderland team without Monty in it, this was a big, big loss – something like when King Charlie left. At about the same time, Pop was enticed back to West Ham (must have had his brain addled by playing for the Mags at the start of his career) with promises of a lifetime's supply of whelks and jellied eels. Still, life goes on, but Barry's first two games, at home to Villa and at QPR, ended in defeat. The Villa game also turned out to be the straw that broke the camel's back as far as Bob Stokoe was concerned and he decided that, after three years of working to get them up, he wasn't the man to keep them there. Perhaps if we'd had a little more luck in the League Cup, he'd have thought otherwise, but, after barging Luton out at home, we managed two 2-2 draws with Man Utd, with, spookily, Towers and Train scoring in each game, before running out of ideas in the second replay at their place.

With no manager appointed, Bob Lee's first goal turned out to be the winner at Coventry and we thought the corner had been turned. If it had, we kept turning and lost at home to Liverpool, then spent ninety minutes running up and down the paddock at Old Trafford, trying to keep sight of the ball in the fog as we were well worth a 3-3 draw - Bob Lee's size made him easy to pick out, by both fans and his team-mates alike, and he scored twice, then again as we beat Spurs. Corner turned? Nah. 1-3 at home to Ipswich, then 0-1 at Derby after a night out in Nottingham and night's sleep on the floor of a friend of a friend, just before Jimmy Adamson's arrival, was only the start of it. A gloomy Christmas saw the New Year arrive without a win, then we managed a draw at mighty Wrexham, with Holton's solitary Sunderland goal, in the FA Cup before going out at their place.

Just the league, then.

Adamson brought three players with him from Burnley - Mick Docherty going in fairly quickly at right-back, as Malone was gradually falling out of favour and the new manager obviously didn't fancy local lad Micky more than a bit mad Henderson as first choice, Colin Waldron being decent cover at centre-half, and Doug Collins – ah, Doug Collins. It said footballer on his passport but, sorry pal, you never convinced me while at Roker – but, to be fair, nothing seemed to go right for any of the players. The goal-less draw at home to Stoke was our ninth league game without a goal, and we were attending matches out of blind faith rather than blind optimism, which was evaporating as fast as Bovril on New Year's Day.

Gradually, however, since the turn of the year, some new faces had been appearing. As the music world was trying to come to terms with the bright young things of punk rock, so Sunderland were introduced to our own band of young upstarts. It was hardly Anarchy in the UK, but it was certainly a small revolution. Rowell we'd seen glimpses of over the last couple of seasons, Alan Brown won a couple of starts after knocking a few defenders over for the reserves, Arnott showed a touch of class, and Elliott got his chance. The game at Highbury may have been another scoring blank, but we didn't concede either and we looked half decent. Perhaps the biggest factor was that, in that game, we played with freedom and a smile on our faces, with Pat Rice's would-be retaliation being met with a peck on the cheek from Bobby Kerr and ending in a nice cuddle between the two of them.

The next week, the unthinkable happened, as Mel's goal beat Bristol City (girl-friend safely kept away from the match, obviously). Could this mean anything, especially as a crazy fixture list meant that Boro were second in a string of four successive home games? Oh yes it did. 4-0, you fume-breathing small Yorkshire club, despite Jeff Clarke's knee going off again. Then West Brom, 6-1, with Micky Henderson at centre half and West Ham lucky to get nil against our six as Waldron took over at the back. Sixteen goals in three games was actually a record, but we were still neck-deep in the brown stuff. When Mel's perfectly good goal was adjudged offside the football world agreed with us for once, as we lost at

Maine Road, but Colin Waldron headed in a corner to beat Ipswich and in the Wearside version of The Great Escape, the tunnels were being dug again. In the middle of this, Ray Train decided that he couldn't take the excitement and after exactly a year in the stripes, nicked off to Bolton.

Just when I was getting into the feel of helping us towards a successful (by our low standards of the time) campaign, my folks announced that they'd booked a holiday on the Norfolk Broads and that me, my sister and our other halves, were invited. At Easter, I ask you. It was bloody freezing, it snowed, we hung the boat at Great Yarmouth when the tide went out further than we'd thought possible and I missed three games in a row, including the 2-2 draw with the Mags at our place. At least we managed to stop off at Elland Road on the way home to watch another local boy, Micky Coady, look solid at the back in his debut, but not solid enough to keep out the equaliser. Mighty Man Utd were then beaten and by way of celebration, we went off to see Focus at the Mayfair, as Donny Mick's favourite band. Unfortunately, they'd recently parted company with Jan Akkerman (the guitarist, that's who) and replaced him with a French bloke who only played acoustic guitar – bad news when 99% of your output is in the form of instrumentals based on the electric guitar. Imagine Cream without Eric Clapton, or Led Zep without Jimmy Page. Mick spent the night getting my girlfriend to supply French insults to convey his displeasure, which was nice, but I was already planning next weekend's trip to Spurs.

We were visiting her folks in Bristol, so, naturally, I got her dad to drop me off near the motorway for a hitch to the smoke. If you know the motorway out of Bristol, you'll know it has a roundabout where it joins the M4. Well, this is where I got done for being a pedestrian on a motorway, £10 fine and they didn't even offer me a lift off the road. I just hid in the bushes (again) until they'd gone, then got to London as quick as you like. London, not Tottenham. It might say London on the address, but White Hart Lane is as far from the end of the M4 as Bishop is from Sunderland. I got there OK, witnessed another fighting performance on and off the pitch as the Lads drew 1-1 and I got a boot up the arse for straying out of the away section. Outside, it was worse. I put on my best cockney accent as they sang It's a long way to Seven Sisters, and I duly walked to Seven Sisters, past all of the nonsense going on around the Sunderland coaches.

I got lost on the tube – you know the green line that goes to Wimbledon and Fulham – and ended up at Earls Court in the aftermath of the Chelsea v Forest game. Wrong place, wrong time, but I managed to keep my head down and make the Brentford flyover and a lift back to Bristol. All that hassle for a point, but it was worth it.

A disappointing draw at home to was followed by a trip to West Brom, so I got my thumb out and nipped down to spend the Friday night in Toxteth (what a delight) as a guest of Big Harrier, then off again to the Hawthorns the next morning. The travelling fans were in the form of their life, as the Roker Roar had a weekend in the West Midlands. We sang Haway the Lads for thirty minutes without a break and you could see their players glancing at the away end and wondering when we'd run out of breath. We didn't, neither did the team and 3-2 was just fine, thank you very much. Next up was Birmingham, which isn't normally a match with much of an edge, but we needed the points, and they had a new goalie. "I can't win," said a certain Mr Montgomery – he was a professional, but a Sunderland boy at heart. Mel Holden's header both spoiled and made Jimmy's day, we had the points and we had two games left to make the survival dream a reality.

Pos booked us a full-size bus for the trip to Norwich, so we gambled, drank and peed in bottles all the way to Norfolk, where the police stopped us a few miles short of town and we scared the life out of a tiny roadside pub – but paid for their holidays for the next few years as we feasted on Watney's Red Barrel. Another fighting performance, another point in the bag and only the Forest fans celebrating their promotion in Newark to survive on the way home. Our appearance on Match of the Day meant an impromptu stoppy-back, as the landlord couldn't shift us until the programme had ended (no remote controls in those day and we surrounded the telly and the plughole).

One game to go, we could do it, we were up for it – it was only at Goodison, after all. Lectures abandoned, out came the thumb and Liverpool was awash with the proper red and white as we packed the bouncy end. On a Thursday? Who thinks these fixtures up? Outside the ground, Jeff Clarke signed my programme and said his knee was coming along fine. I thought back to Stan Ternent and prayed he was being honest. Enough has been written about what went on at Highfield Road for you all to know that although we were deservedly beaten at Everton, we were cheated by Coventry, Bristol City and the FA. The fact that Coventry were censured proves that they cheated and I've no doubt that, had we been the offenders, we'd have been docked points, fined and probably had all our first-born sons thrown off Roker Pier rather than be told "Don't be so naughty – can we buy that nice Mr Hill a drink?"

No-one expected me to show up at lectures the next day, but I did – life goes on, as they say and I had to get meeting the rest of the world over as soon as possible. Rod Stewart's latest single was obviously selling well on Wearside, and was number one by the weekend. The First Cut is the Deepest doubled up with I Don't Want to Talk About it. Bloody right, mate.

Number one is Gary Rowell
And number two is Gary Rowell
Number three is Gary Rowell
And number four is Gary Rowell (Repeat and improvise...)

1977-1978

Close seasons have always been a big disappointment to me. OK, you get to see some (less than) interesting friendlies, you get to work at weekends without missing the football and you get to go to exotic places on your jollidays. I snuck behind the bar again, saved up my money and bought a top of the range Mini van. I had a week in a tent over in the Lakes – no Keswick coffee bar nonsense this time, as I took my own female company with me. My night off was Tuesday and this was Chilton Club disco – taking punk rock on board very slowly. Transfer activity had been fairly low-key – who'd want to come to a newly-relegated club anyway? Wilf did. "It's the Willuf!" we cried (you had to know the popular cartoon series of the time to understand) as local boy Wilf Rostron signed from Arsenal. Somebody told me that I'd once played against him for the school team, but I don't remember (I was that fast as a winger that he probably never saw me either) and in came our midfield utility man.

Out went another piece of history, as Tricky Dicky joined Hartlepool and links with the spirit of 73 were getting fewer by the minute. Tommy Gibb also jumped ship, sailing off with his 1900s moustache - also to the Pools. I blagged a week on a cabin cruiser out of Poole Harbour (owned by a friend, loaned for zero pence), then stuck a mattress in the back of the mini van and hit Reading Rock Festival with Stubber and Tommer. Despite almost killing the pair of them when I started the engine with the tent doors open behind the van and filling the tent with exhaust fumes, we had a hell of a time. Alex Harvey, Thin Lizzy, Doobie Brothers, Hawkwind, Uriah Heep, Aerosmith (who stunk) a pile of wannabe punksters, loads of beer and a whole sea of mud. You had to do these things, they were part of growing up and at least they showed some ambition, which Sunderland hardly had.

One summer signing was hardly going to turn us from (unfairly) relegated failures into promotion favourites. On the positive side, you could say we had a settled goalkeeper, as Barry Siddall missed only one game in his first three years at the club, while on the negative side, Adamson could never decide on his first choice in midfield or attack. Rostron, Elliott, Kerr, Arnott, Rowell, Henderson, Ashurst and (just the once) Stronach – the lad touted as the new Colin Todd – had a go in the middle, while Holden, Lee, Greenwood, Brown and Rowell were tried up front in the first couple of months. Billy Hughes, only a bit-part player the previous season, left for Derby.

Well, we'd give it a try anyway. Hull to start with? Easy peasy, 0- 3 defeat. Then we turned the scoreline around at home to Burnley and followed that with three draws – hardly the stuff that promotion dreams are made of – especially when we followed the draws with a winless run that stretched into mid-October. We'd also done the usual with the League Cup, drawing at home to Boro (who makes these draws?) before losing at their place –c'est la chose, c'est la meme chose. A win over Millwall was at least a start. Another three points from the visit to Mansfield was just what we needed. Punk had taken to the terraces as well, with chants of "Sit down!" being obeyed by the travelling masses (all standing then, remember), before someone shouted "boogie!" and everyone leapt into the air and pogoed for five minutes.

The Wonder Wilf bagged two –one direct from a corner as I remember - and the homeward journey was only spoiled when my gearbox fell to bits in Jesmond, outside Stubber's place. Replacement engine came as a 21st birthday present, and was installed in the street. Shame I forgot to check the sump plug, as the bloody thing seized up on my next trip to Bishop – a curse on Mini vans and their silly little engines, as I couldn't afford the petrol to travel far in it, and it spent most of its life parked up gathering dust. I preferred hitching to the away games, to be honest, as, along with being cheaper and having the added element of unpredictability, I had gained a bit of a reputation as part of an elite band of thrifty travellers. I'd meet up with the same faces on the way down the country, and we'd swap tales of easy lifts, bad places to try from, and sleeping under hedges. My fast deteriorating jacket, matching jeans (with self-inserted flares) and flat cap meant that I was variously referred to as "patches" or "Andy Capp" among my travelling companions. Little things, but they do give you a certain amount of kudos.

That Millwall win was the start of a seven game unbeaten run, as Elliott took over from Waldron at the back, and included a 5-1 demolition of Bristol Rovers, when any sort of success against a Bristol Club was good for me in that I'd win a fish supper from my girlfriend's cousin. On the other hand, her kid brother was a Rovers fan – from Bedminster, which is a bit like me being a Sunderland fan and living in Jesmond – and it didn't go down too well with him. Still, I didn't support Sunderland to keep him happy. As usual, just when we had picked ourselves up, square one was waiting, and we lost the next three, despite a debut goal for Wayne Entwistle, our very own punk-up-front, at Charlton. He'd arrived from home-town club Bury at the same time as Roly Gregoire arrived from Halifax. Blackpool were then beaten at home in a game remembered less for Rowell's brace as Joe Bolton's sending-off (Joe clatters opponent, opponent retaliates, opponent hits the deck – and stays there for several minutes – Joe gets the rubber duck out) on Boxing Day.

Dowse nicely volunteered to drive to Blackburn the next day, and we bumped into both Sunderland and Blackpool players in the pub on the way down. Two Blackpool players caught the eye – the one with the black eye, and Bob Hatton, who, not for the last time, came over and spoke to us. Who he thought we were I'll never know – perhaps we looked like we had some status in the game – or perhaps he was just a nice bloke. Stan Ternent also had a chat, as he knew that we did have some status in the game, and he was just a nice bloke. Maybe he remembered the charity football match. Strangest of all, though still welcome, was Jimmy Adamson buying a round of beers for the Bishop lads. Well, they did tell him he had to.

Up front we had the strange combination of Greenwood and Entwistle, backed up by Rowell, and Tim Gilbert filling in for Joe Bolton in his full debut, a year after his substitute appearance at Sid James Park. Joe, not allowed to travel with the team (who presumably knew they'd be sharing a dinner table with the Blackpool lads) had travelled down with his mates from the Barley Mow, and stood next to us on the terraces as his deputy scored our only goal and earned us a point. A couple of days later, and Tubby volunteered his driving services to get us to Burnley, and even stopped off in Accrington for a pint. If ever a town has mirrored the demise of its football club, this was it. Only the tumbleweed was missing as we watched a car burst into flames at the traffic lights, and all the locals, including the token scrap-metal dealer in his Rolls Royce (which all carry a fire extinguisher as standard) leave the scene as fast as possible. On the pitch, Adamson dropped a forward and brought Mick Docherty into the midfield role that would earn him the respect of the fans. No goals, another point, and home to see in the New Year to the sound of Freebird across the A66.

Said New Year began in good fashion with Mr Rowell getting both goals as we beat Hull, then took a dip as we lost at Bristol Rovers – another debit in the fish supper account – and were out of the FA Cup.

Just the league, then.

Rowell took on the guise of an assassin in front of goal, notching six in four league games, including a 5-1 win over Sheffield Utd followed by a 2-5 defeat at Cardiff, and it all started to fall apart again. Four games without a win, despite an impressive debut (and only appearance) by Peter Weir at Bolton were hardly good for the nerves, and a sneaky win over Mansfield was followed by another winless four. Having achieved some degree of success, performance-wise if not in the ultimate goal, the previous season, Adamson brought in local youngster Keith Armstrong for seven successive games, but with limited effect, eventually winning against Stoke and Fulham (where Roly Gregoire got his only Sunderland goal). We camped out on the steps of the City Hall for Alex Harvey tickets, armed only with a crate of beer each and a bemused policewoman for company.

We bought fifteen front row tickets, and he cancelled (sore throat) a week before the concert. Bugger. I only ever queued overnight for concert tickets once again (Rod Stewart) and the City Hall box office sold me four that turned out to be bad fakes. Like I've always maintained, never trust a Mag. (I did get in, and in better seats, thanks for asking). We still had our regular Sunday night entertainment at the Poly Disco, which had livened up into something of a new musical occasion over the past year. Since I'd arrived in '75, student discos had changed from a mix of "disco" music, which I've never been fond of, and "classic rock" (old stuff, with a bit of Quo and Thin Lizzy mixed in) to sweaty evenings of pogoing part-time punks (we wore old school ties, and safety pins in our lapels, and I had a converted Slade T-shirt with "never mind the Geography" across the front). The sweatiest Sunday of all was when Eddie and the Hot Rods played, and we were right at the front. Lively stuff.

The Lads were also getting lively, and making a bit of an effort on the field. I watched another win, over Notts County, put us in a good mood, then headed for a week in the Dordogne (educational visit, that sort of thing) as, in reality, we were never going to catch the top three. Having visited vineyards and chateaux, developed an unhealthy taste for Pastis (the aniseed based drink, not Tyneside's food of choice), and eaten oysters in Bordeaux market at four in the morning, I screwed up my hitch-hiking on the way back and missed us winning at already promoted Spurs - a game that is well up the Match of the Day league of dramatic comebacks. That left only Charlton at home in a pretty pointless fixture, but Joe went and made it a day to remember by scoring twice as Rowell got the other to go three up. Then we got a penalty. What would you do in that situation? Correct – give the ball to the bloke who'd scored twice. Having scored two snorters, Joe calmly placed the ball on the spot, took aim…. to hoof it over the back of the Roker End – and this was before they took the back few rows off it.

Never mind, even if we were sixth and twelve points off the important third place, we'd showed a few signs that things could get better.

Bob Lee
Bob Lee
Bob Lee, Bob Lee, Bob Lee
Bob Lee, Bob Lee, Bob Lee, Bob Lee
Bob Lee, Bob Lee

1978-1979

Another big summer – graduation, wedding, proper work. I'd done my final preparations for my final exams by watching the finals of the World Cup, and finding a personal hero in gangly Swedish striker Ralf Edstrom, the man no-one could handle. I found this an enjoyable, if ineffective, method of study, as no-one could find me, and my only interruption was Generation X playing down the corridor and drowning out the commentary. Which of these intercontinental superstars would be cutting a swathe through the Roker Park grass come August? Dream on. Having declined the opportunity to study for a PhD in the restorative effects of Irn Bru and its effects of the development of the punk culture, (actually, either working – unpaid – for the Meteorological Office on a roof at the end of Jesmond Road, or hitting the ice with the British Antarctic Survey) I decided on working for a living.

Welcome to the real world of getting up early five days a week, at a time when there weren't that many jobs to be had. I grabbed the first two that came along, doing four evenings behind a hotel bar in Whitley Bay ('cos I liked bar work, even if it was selling watereddown whisky to expense account travelling salesmen, or watching the Round Tablers compete with each other to see who could drink the most before driving home) and five days labouring ('cos it paid better). See that Seaton Sluice harbour? I built that, I did - a minor miracle, as we were under the supervision of a particularly unpleasant local who knew sod-all about how to build things.

After a few weeks I'd had enough of him, so I swung a shovel at his head and walked off. That was Thursday, and I managed to fix up a job interview the next day. I'd only just got into the car when the interviewer tapped on the window. "We forgot to ask – do you play football?"

"Yes"
"Can you play 5 a side next Tuesday?"
"Yes"
"You've got the job. Start Monday"

Jammy beggar, as they say in these parts, and off to HM Factory Inspectorate, Kenton Bar, it was, a little concerned at signing the official secrets act – what if the Tories got in? I'd be working for them, which I didn't fancy much, but work was work. The Tuesday football was a disaster, not because I or any of my team-mates were particularly bad, but because the opposition were Newcastle CID, and they had an ex-Carlisle player up front. Players may lose their pace, their appetite, and their energy, but they never lose their touch. This bloke never touched the ball more than twice at a time, and every time it ended up a goal. We didn't play again, but I was "in" at the office – one of the lads. That cosy situation nearly went pear-shaped when they made me my first cup of coffee, and I said that I couldn't drink it. "Too much milk?" they enquired. "Black and white cup," I replied. Stony silence, as the fact that I rode on a different bus sank in, but they fairly quickly accepted that I was still just another human being. A far more intelligent and cultured one than they were, but that was something beyond the grasp of these poor, simple creatures.

So, grown-up life began in earnest. Bijou flat on Whitley Bay seafront, job with the Civil Service, easy drive to the match. Actually, I was still a bit tight with the money (old habits die hard) and often chose to cycle there, leaving said bike in someone's yard - just knock and ask, I never got refused. Having messed about in the Anglo-Scottish Cup (i.e. played three, won one, and lost two in the all- English qualifiers, thus cunningly avoiding having to play anyone from Scotland), we set off on yet another promotion campaign. Mel Holden became another ex-Lad at Blackpool, and Rowell carried on from last season with the goal that beat Charlton on the opening day, but we followed that with successive away defeats. By the end of August, we'd rid ourselves of the bothersome League Cup, 0-2 at home to Stoke. Gordon Chisholm was a new starter in a half-back line that allowed Elliott or Ashurst, depending on exactly who else was playing, to try midfield a bit.

The next five games brought three wins and two draws, and things were looking up when I nipped down to Sheffield United via Bishop (I needed a lift). We'd signed only Mick Buckley, part of the Everton side that put us down a year earlier, while the Blades had Alex Sabella, fresh from Argentina's world cup squad. While the English media were raving about the arrival of Ardiles and Villa at Spurs and, to a lesser extent, the flop Tarantini at Brum, I think that Sabella was the pick of the South Americans who flew in that summer. He tore us apart that day, and I was one in a rapidly dwindling Sunderland section that remained when substitute Bob Lee brought it back to 2-3. Having remembered my early-leaving present at Preston a few years earlier, I stayed to the (very) bitter end, and reaped the benefits when I was first shoulder-charged, then punched in the face, by a group of Sunderland fans who thought I was a local because I "had a red, white, and black scarf." Cheers lads, you made my day complete, and I had to explain away a fat lip to the wife. Magic, and a bad warm-up for the next game – the Mags at Roker. Only Roy Greenwood, from the bench, saved us a point that day, before Alan Brown's first goal helped beat Millwall – along with Rowell's third double of the season. Mick Buckley might have been Adamson's summer signing, but he only made his debut in the goal-less draw at Oldham, and stayed there for the next two months. Which is more than Adamson did, buggering off to Leeds.

To be honest, few mourned his departure, as, on top of failing to keep us up, he'd come across as a bit of a big-timer. I'd encountered him several times around Whitley Bay, me in my Mini van and him in his flashy silver Granada. With Dave Merrington in as caretaker, Stoke came to Roker and won for the second time that season, then we picked things up with by completing the double over Charlton and gaining revenge over Brighton before losing at Preston. Eight goals in the games against Luton and Bristol Rovers not only won me a fish supper, but saw old tennis-ball head Wayne Entwistle, our very own punk-rocker, notch a hat-trick. A draw at Cardiff, then we lost at home to Cambridge (Cambridge!), a defeat I missed because of my sister's wedding – a blessing in disguise, but it wouldn't happen these days, as her children have so far (two down, one to go) picked international weekends for their weddings, thus ensuring the full attention of Uncle Paul. I was charged with picking the cakes up on the way back to Bishop, so the decision of my top of the range Mini van to suffer electrical failure was not a wise one. Perhaps Basil Fawlty had been in my dreams the previous night, or perhaps Merrington's decision to resign the previous week, as my neighbours were witnesses to me, in my finest late 70s blue velvet pinstripe and high heels, swearing and kicking seven bells out of said vehicle, then burning my hand on the makeshift earth-strap (wire coat hanger) that saved the day and got me, and the cakes, to the church on time.

In came Billy Elliott, after four years coaching in Norway, and with one of those slicked-back haircuts that said "I played in the fifties, you soft bugger", he set about imposing himself on the team. I played the responsible adult, rented a house in Ambleside for Christmas, and invited disparate in-laws and out-laws over for the festivities. Spectacular Lakeland scenery and weather, along with spectacular Lakeland beer and hospitality in the Golden Rule just down the road made for a nice break, but didn't make up for missing the games. Four score draws made us the darlings of those who did the football Pools, then Wilf Rostron started scoring goals, which went no small way to keeping the club on a good points-gathering run. 3-1 over Burnley, then 3-3 at West Ham, and the small matter of a trip to Gallowgate came along. Using the skill and local knowledge gleaned from three years of Toon living, I parked up early, forewent the pre-match pint for the first time in three or four yonks, and got into the Leazes early. About twenty of us were in the Leazes when the world's daftest man entered. Well, either daft or suicidal. Decked out from head to foot in black and white "favours", he took up his position in the middle of the terraces, and stood, arms folded, staring at everybody and nodding his head in that "aye, want to make something of it?" way that nutters do. We shook our heads, and watched as the police picked him up bodily and carried him away, as he refused their pleas to move.

As it turned out, it would have completed a beautiful day had he been allowed to remain. Rowell's hat-trick, taking him to nineteen for the season, and Entwistle's coup de grace to a wonderful move, are part of Sunderland folklore, and we were cocks of the north, make no mistake. I could scarcely disguise my smile (sorry, make that big daft grin) as I tried to get back to the car. "All Sunderland fans to the Central Station" was the police instruction, and that's the way we were ushered. I managed to scurry under a police horse and get into Leazes Park, where I managed to look depressed enough to avoid the attention of the ambush parties that lurked amongst the bushes. Safely back behind the wheel, I let my smile (sorry, make that big daft grin) back out and sang all the way to the seaside.

That momentous win filled the sails of our promotion warship, but not the FA Cup dinghy. After a nice scalping of Everton, and a draw at Burnley, Ian Watson marked his first competitive game between the sticks (sorry, I don't count the all-English Anglo-Scottish tournament) by letting in three goals. Not his fault, but it was down to just the league again, then.

About this time we had some bad weather at Whitley Bay, the sea come in through my aptly named bay window, so we took advantage of being up to date with the rent and did a bunk up the road to Seaton Delaval. Watson actually kept his place for the following game, showed his worth, and helped us to a 1-0 win at Millwall. Joe Bolton then went mental and scored in consecutive games as we beat Oldham but lost to Palace, both at home, before Rowell did what he did best and beat Orient – again at home. That game was the end of Mick Henderson's season, as Steve Whitworth came in from Leicester. An England international? Coming to Sunderland? Would he be up for a challenge? Well, he played sixty-odd games off the belt, looked every inch the experienced pro, defended generally well, and looked as likely to score as, well, a long line of Sunderland right backs. A bit of solidity could be just enough to galvanise our promotion push, and things started to look a bit classy. Just as punk music realised there were two ways to go – either shout more and get louder on the subject of political dissatisfaction ("Oi!" as Gary Bushell imaginatively called them, the UK Subs, the Lurkers, our very own Angelic Upstarts, whose Mensi used to sup in the Blue Bell before home games) or think a bit more about what you were doing and go a bit arty or melodic about love – both unrequited and the other sort – and general angst (Magazine, Buzzcocks) – Sunderland began to use craft and guile to supplement their work ethic, and became one of the favourites to go up.

Whitworth's first four games were defensive shut-outs, as we steadily accrued points, but the board refused to give Elliott the manager's job on a permanent basis. As fans, we saw someone who'd played over two hundred games for the Lads, before managing Libya, coaching the US forces in Germany, and numerous other jobs on the touchline. Hell, he'd even been on the bench at Wembley in '73, the coaching guile to Arthur Cox's scary sergeant-major trainer. He was one of our own – give him the job, we thought, and just when they might have been thinking of doing just that, Billy showed why they shouldn't. At home to Blackburn, and a win would have sent us top, but injuries left us a bit restricted for choice up front. Rather than use experienced players and arrange the formation to suit those available, Billy picked Roly Gregoire for his first game, and the poor lad just wasn't ready for the likes of Blackburn. Roly wasn't the type of player Alan Brown (hardly a seasoned pro himself, and not yet twenty) was used to partnering, and Roly watched the game go by as Blackburn became the fourth side to take two points away from Roker that season.

A revenge win at Cambridge left us with three games to go and the first division firmly in our sights. When Sheffield Utd came up to Wearside, we needed to beat them by three goals to go top. On one of those special Roker Park nights, the Roar came out of its box, and we witnessed one of those games that any sane person would pay money to watch. Gilbert, Brown, and Lee scored, but it was the Wonder Wilf who was on a one-man mission to top the league, as he scored a hat-trick in a thrilling 6-2 win. Thirteen goals in the two games between us and the Blades that season - we should have played each other more often.

I celebrated by getting promoted (oooh) at work, moving to the Ministry at Longbenton, taking on more responsibility, and taking home more money from sorting out pensions. The place was like a prison camp, in that we worked in what looked like Nissen huts, and there were thousands of us. My uncle Tommy worked there, and I never once saw him in the whole four months of my stay. Career picking up, just like the team. After the Sheffield game, we thought that was it – promotion only required the "i" to be dotted and the "t" to be crossed.

Yeah, right. Cardiff might have been at the bottom end of the table, but they made a mockery of our midweek drama and became Roker guest winning team number five. Billy Elliott? Still, if we won at Wrexham the next week, we'd be OK – where's the fun in making it easy? So, the Racecourse Ground became a home from home, bursting at the seams with Sunderland's finest, determined to get the best from their precious Lads – and they did. Rostron and Brown won the game, but, as we celebrated, we forgot to take into account the fact that Palace still had a game left to play. None of that last day drama that we have now, with synchronised kick-offs (unless, of course, you're Coventry, but that's another story). Palace duly won, and we finished – only a point adrift of second place – fourth, after a season of three managers and numerous chances to collect at least that point.

Bright Eyes sang Art Garfunkel. "Red eyes" we thought, as we cried into our beer. If only Bobby Kerr, only three games that season before joining Bob Stokoe at Blackpool, had been there to extract a bit of that spirit of '73, it might have been so different.

Wherever I wander
I follow our team
The famous Sunderland
A love supreme
Wherever I go
You're sure to know
We'll keep the red flag
Flying high...

1979-1980

Some summer this was. Billy Elliott went the way of all flesh, and the board started looking for a big name replacement – or so the press would have us believe. Clough (why would he leave Forest when they'd just won the League Cup and the European Cup?), McMenemy, and Revie were among the names bandied about, but it was from within that the next boss came. Ken Knighton had worked for the previous two managers, and knew how the club and chairman Collins worked. Ex-Mag Frank Clark left Cloughie and became our first assistant manager. My first college reunion was held in Whitley Bay (which was nice), where we showed up the youngsters by taking over the big(ish) wheel and dodgems, drank beer and ate chips for the weekend before going back to our new adult lives. I'd had enough of the Ministry after being reprimanded for going to the front gate to discuss a pension problem with a bloke who lived just across the road. I was, temporarily at least, Delaval's best home-improvement salesman (look, if it's fallen off, I sold it to you twenty five years ago – how long do you expect brick dust and glue to last?).

Then my better (or worse) half decided she'd be better off with a short, older, unemployed Mag, the home improvement market on North Tyneside dried up, and I ended up cleaning Corning's glass factory in Sunderland. I moved in with a mate (another surprised singleton) and, after being down to one Citroen Dyane and £13 in halfpennies at one stage the pair of us hit Camp Africa. This might sound romantic (it might have been if the intended partner had accompanied me), but it was basically some straw-roofed hut on a beach. Everyone got the Tangier trots at some stage – the most violent case of the squirts I've ever come across, with someone literally crawling to the lavs at any time of day or night, and we just stepped over them. Back in sunny West Denton, the pair of us set out on a mission that involved beer, darts, and most of the barmaids in Newcastle.

We set about the league with a solid defence of Siddall, Whitworth, Bolton, Clarke, and Elliott, with Chis or Rob Hindmarch (known as flapper because of the way he moved his arms when he ran) covering while Elliott moved forward a bit. Up front, Alan Brown started the campaign alongside new-old boy Pop Robson, who, having had his fill of jellied eels, re-signed just before Knighton took charge, and the pair both scored early on. Entwistle joined them after a couple of games, but was soon on his way to Leeds, in a partial swap for big John Hawley. Results hadn't been that good – a decent draw at Chelsea was followed by home wins over Brum and Fulham then bad losses to Oldham and West Ham either side of a win over Cambridge wasn't really promotion stuff, but we settled down with a couple of draws and John Hawley's debut hat-trick against Charlton – a nice way to start. Our other autumn signing made his way from the bench to the wing for a decent run in the side – local boy Barry Dunn arrived via Tow Law, Bishop, and non-league big-boys of the time, Blue Star.

The flying gasman was already twenty-seven when he joined us, and he provided some good moments that season. As we picked up the points we wanted, the forward line changed on a weekly basis. Brown, Robson, Rowell, Hawley and Lee (optimistically touted as a Ray Kennedy style forward-turned-midfielder England prospect) all had a go, and kit-man Cooke made his debut. Another local boy, Stan Cummins, arrived from Boro for a massive £300,000 (not quite Jack Charlton's £2 million estimate, but a few years' wages to you and me), and scored on his debut against Notts County. This came a week after a reshuffled team, including Gilbert, Chisholm, and debutant Ian Hughes lost 1-3 at Swansea. That was Ian's only game for us, as, despite being re-signed from Barnsley a few years later, he "did his knee" before restarting his hometown career, and had to make do with a long stint as a coach.

As the team was moving on up, my attendance was interrupted on several Saturdays because of working weekends. I'd cleaned the factories of the North East, and became Tyneside's most qualified car park attendant. I did get to meet several Mag players as they paid up at the Central Station (Peter With: "Hello, thank you." Me: "Hello Peter, I thought you only got Saturdays off."), but it was hard to

Sobs' Story
KEEP THE FAITH

keep a straight face when they'd lost at home, and were trooping gloomily past. I'd shouted joyous congratulations from my little kiosk to passing, victorious Watford fans (yes, they were once a good side), only to be attacked by a lunatic Mag in full storm trooper gear – jackboots, coalscuttle helmet, trenchcoat – and it took six of my friends, the transport police, to carry him away. They warned me to keep my views to myself in future, but, hell, you can't keep schtum forever, or you'd burst. Taking the proverbial is one of the joys of being a football fan.

By the time Christmas arrived, Pop was into double figures, little Stan had settled in nicely, and, while not setting the league alight, we'd started to look a bit on the canny side, but this wasn't the biggest news at the club. Following the trail blazed by Spurs, Leeds, and Birmingham the previous season, Ken Knighton went out and broke the club record by signing our first ever Claudio. Señor Marangoni was also our first Argentine, arriving from San Lorenzo for a whopping £320,000, and showed some unbelievable tricks before it became apparent that he was not, in fact, from South America, but somewhere in a galaxy far, far away. It was plainly obvious that the man had more skill than most league teams, but it was equally obvious that his style and Sunderland's style were totally incompatible. A typically disconnected performance, as Knighton sought to get the best from his man, came on the first day of the New Year in the worst place possible – Gallowgate.

Having spent the night – or rather, the last part of it – asleep on some friends' stairs in Benwell, and rudely awakened by being repeatedly sat upon as said friends took turns to answer seasonal telephone calls of goodwill, the last thing I needed was a freezing cold day at Sid James Park. A couple of pints in the Benwell Tavern, and it was onto the Gallowgate terraces (yes, I know it was the wrong end, but I didn't have a ticket – if, indeed, you needed a ticket. I don't remember. I'd been out late). I survived my inability to keep quiet by restricting my support to shouts of "Haway the Lads" (when it's spoken, you can't see the subtle difference in the spelling) and punching Robbo in the back when little Stan scored what turned out to be our consolation.

Señor Marangoni was obviously the inspiration for Ardiles and Villa a couple of years later, as he showed them what not to do in the FA Cup, when his only appearance in the competition ended in home defeat to Bolton.

Just the league, then.

Just the league indeed. Alan Brown got out the new boots he'd been bought for Christmas, and smacked in his second hat-trick of the season in his second-finest game in a Sunderland shirt as we beat Oldham 4-2, then he scored again (as did Marangoni, for the last time) in a 3-3 draw at Cambridge. Along came Burnley, along came another finest hour – this time for little Stan, as he joined an elite band by scoring four of our five. He'll doubtless still treasure the match ball, but whether or not he still cherishes the grainy images of two of his goals, taken by Stubber's less than steady hand from the middle of the Fulwell and sent to the wee man as a memento of a famous day's work, is less clear. Back down to earth we came in the next game as we lost at Preston. Not only that, but an injury to rock-steady (and rock-hard) Joe Bolton precipitated Joe Hinnigan's arrival from Wigan, then in Division Four. Could Joe 2 make the grade, we asked? Yes, as it happened, because Sunderland's number three shirt was obviously made for Joes, and he fitted in comfortably and remained there for the rest of the season.

That Deepdale defeat was the real turning-point of the season. Kitman Cooke scored his first goal for us in the win over Luton, and we followed up with a couple of goal-less draws before sticking another four past Charlton – they must have hated the sight of us that season. In fact, we let in only six goals in the last fourteen games as we chased the top spot. Our Lads were becoming celebrities again (in the world in general as well as the world in red and white), and Whitworth, Clarke, and the injured Hawley caught a few eyes at the Pretenders gig at the City Hall. When I questioned big John about his wearing of a black and white hooped shirt in a public place, despite being a Sunderland player, he simply replied "Hull" – I believe it's something to do with rugby, so I let him off with a warning. I took a five-day holiday in that London to escape from football for a while, and spent the time divided about equally between Doncaster Mick's couch and my latest discovery, the best thing I ever found in the capital – the Lamb. My interest in music began to change slightly, in that I began to listen to the words more than in the past. Hence a lot more Elvis Costello in my collection, as well as Ian Dury, and some miserable lads from Manchester who had started to get themselves noticed, in the music press if not in the charts. Joy Division suited my mood at the time – probably because of the amount of Saturday football I was missing. The Lads were doing well, and I couldn't be as much a part of it as I wanted, with home games following a 2:30 finish and away games largely out of the question.

I got a bit tired of missing the occasional Saturday game, and took the chance to be part of the "team opening the company's new Darlington facility", with promises of more flexible (and less Saturday) working and promotion opportunity. So, it was back to the spare room at Ma and Pa's in sunny Bishop, where I got a warm welcome, and my old seat back at the Cumberland. What I got at work was a gaffer who was more concerned with ensuring that the building contracts went his brother's way, and said brother duly obliged by laying the rooftop car-park upside down, thus causing a flood downstairs every time it rained. Negative comments about our less than storm-proof building resulted in the removal of what few Saturday afternoon privileges there had been, and things got really strained when I was forced to miss our Stan Cummins-inspired win over the Mags as Rowell made his return to the side in place of the baffled Marangoni, and my workplace demeanour of a Saturday afternoon should have been enough to allow me to pick my own shift rather than scare off the customers. I listened instead of watching, and I didn't like it one bit. From a personal point of view, it's much better to listen to a defeat than a victory, but from a team point of view, of course, aural victories are still bloody good, especially when Shaun Elliott scores twice and we get five without reply (Watford, in case you'd forgotten).

By the time I saw Dowse and the rest of the carload heading for Cardiff as I headed home from work on a Friday night, I was ready to jack it all in and live under the Roker End, earning a crust selling peanuts, or programmes, or as a turnstile operator – anything to get back to the match. By the time the last game came around, I could barely remember my way to Roker, but, thanks to West Ham doing even better in the FA Cup than they had in the League Cup (probably why they didn't get promoted) and winning against Arsenal the previous Saturday – yes, and I didn't have to work that day – it was a re-arranged night game. I was met by Hanrad (WBA, Everton, and Sunderland whenever he could get a lift) and Shacks (Mag, but of the variety that I drank with, and who'd been handy to have around on a couple of occasions during my sojourn in the shadows of the Castle of Darkness) at work, and revved up for a bang-on-the-dotsix pm finish. "You should have asked," said my gaffer. "You could have got off early."

"Cheers, George," was my public reply. My muttered reply was less audible and even less printable – the two-faced bugger.

By the time we got near the ground, it was apparent that something was amiss. Night games always concentrate the times of arrival of the crowd, as most of them had to work and didn't have the luxury of a whole morning to get there, but this one was something else. I was two people from my usual turnstile when it shut, prompting a mad scramble around the ground to find an entrance. No luck – despite the official attendance being over six hundred less that the Mags game, there was no room for us (or a few thousand others). We tried climbing the walls, and Hanrad got as far as the chimney stack on one of the cottages out the back of the Fulwell, but, it being a cottage, and the Fulwell being rather taller, he could see nothing but corrugated iron and a floodlit sky. With mixed emotions (both sad and disappointed, but glad that we only needed the one point), we set off home and did the radio listening thing again in the car. Arnott's tenth of the season as we passed Ramside Hall added to little Stan's, and an apparently hung-over West Ham were beaten.

Trevor Brooking had spent most of the game celebrating his Wembley winner by cuddling Pop, and we had the point we needed to clinch promotion. By leaving Sunderland before half-time, at least we were back in the Cumberland in time for a few celebratory pints, but I'd have swapped them for just a few minutes of live action and a chance to watch the lap of honour. If I felt a bit cheated, how about the supporters who'd booked the holiday with the team? Sunderland had arranged an end of season jaunt to Florida for the team, and invited supporters to join them. For many, the chance to spend their jollies in the company of their sporting heroes was too tempting to turn down. They were faced with the prospect of either losing their money and seeing the match, or flying to Florida and waiting for the team to arrive a few days later. I don't know how many chose which option. I didn't see the match, I didn't go to Florida– but I've got the "Roker Roar on Tour" T-shirt. Whoopee, that makes up for everything.

From the banks of the River Wear
To the shores of Sicily
We're gonna fight, fight, fight for Sunderland
'Til we win the football league
To Hell with Man United
To Hell with Liverpool
We're gonna fight, fight, fight for Sunderland
'Til we win the football league

1980-1981

Another summer of wonders got off to a stinker of a start when my new-found musical hero Ian Curtis did what troubled souls tend to do and topped himself, which raised my mood no end. College reunion 1980 was held in Isleworth, West London, purely because two of the lads lived there. Highlight of the weekend was Murph refusing to believe that a jumbo jet could fly despite watching one do just that on a trip to Heathrow. He is, of course, a Mag. Passing up a holiday with the lads in Cornwall (and the prospect of another season of Saturday working), I left work, and Johnny and I became builders for the summer. The result of our labours still remains as the extension on the back of my Mam's house, so we can't have done that bad a job. While building the house extension was one thing, living there was another, as I'd been left home for four years and was used to a certain degree of mess-making incongruous with living with one's parents. I didn't even realise it at the time, but when Shacks (Mag) and Davy (family Mag) and I rented a rather big and posh house between Darlo and Stockton, I was becoming part of a house that was 66% black and white.

The village itself was my first experience of a place that had more than two Boro fans in it, and was therefore a new and strange experience. It was officially in that mythical land of Cleveland, the product of an over-imaginative local government official (the same fool that gave us Tyne and Wear, no doubt), but for once I was with my Mag housemates when they refused to accept this, and established an outlying province of County Durham for our own personal satisfaction. How I survived the excess of Boro boys, the proximity to a near lunar atmosphere, and the regular sound of explosions at ICI ("Hear that big one late today? My Dad did that." was a regular conversation opener in the pub of an evening) is down to my native wit, hunting skills, and, above all, a skin thicker than a rhino's.

A new journey to the match for me – up the A19 with all the Teesside Sunderland Boys, and it was business as usual. With Jeff Clarke's knee having gone again, in came Sam Allardyce at about the same time as Tom Cowie realised his dream and became chairman, but they were our only two summer signings – perhaps Ken Knighton thought that Marangoni would adapt better to the game in the top division.

Chris Turner started off as first-choice keeper, and Joe Bolton had his place back ahead of Hinnigan. We had a winning start as little Stan, fit-again John Hawley, and one of the best own-goals ever seen at Roker (a twenty-five yard lob) saw us hit the ground running against Everton. Things got even better a few days later when we met up in the Kippax, shaking hands and hugging each other as if we'd been separated for years rather than the three months it had been since the end of the season (as you do every August), and Mr Hawley rewarded our attendance with another hat-trick – is two hat-tricks out of a total of eleven goals something of a record? Little Stan scored again to complete a 4-0 away win – which is a damned good start for a newly promoted team. The fact that Shacks (parttime Mag that he is) held the map upside down as we left resulted in our trip to Bury for a quick pint starting off with a southward section, which wasn't quite as bad as Pos finding his opportunistically parked car towed away to the police pound (and him having to pay a small fortune to get it back), but you put up with these things for a performance like that. Oh, and my exhaust fell off in Moss Side, so there was no sneaking quietly away.

Kevin Arnott had been replaced after the Everton game by Gordon Chisholm, so with a team that included Chis, Big Sam, Elliott, and Rob Hindmarch, (corner kicks were fun with that lot charging into the box) we were never going to let in many goals. On paper, at least, as we let in one too many against Southampton as the Bolton Butcher scored his first Sunderland goal at Roker the following Saturday, and then a draw at mighty Stockport in the League Cup showed us that we weren't established Big Boys just yet. A draw at Old Trafford thanks to Alan Brown's goal and a reasonable performance from Marangoni – perhaps the big stage did suit him better – was a good recovery, but then Stockport came to Roker. Cummins did score, but they scored twice. The winner came from Tommy

Sword, who was a bit like a bigger, harder-looking (and tackling, by a mile) Brian Kilcline, and formerly of Bishop Auckland FC. To say that he was pleased is a bit like saying we were disappointed. Still, it was only the League Cup, and we could concentrate on the league for four months.

On September 6th, the day after our shared birthday, Stubber got married, and the ears pressed to radios at the George, Piercebridge, were rewarded with a win at Leicester courtesy of Mr Hawley. The following Friday, Consett Steelworks closed for good, leaving a big, red hole in the north west of County Durham. Perhaps this makes the technical drawing of one of the furnaces that have some-how come into my possession worth a few quid – maybe I'll find out some day, but I hope I don't need to. There had been the almost compulsory, but ultimately futile, march to London, in the manner of the Jarrow Crusade, but there was an-other chunk of heavy industry gone. This preceded a home defeat by the Boro, and Marangoni's last run in the side was over, as Arnott took his place. A draw at Spurs was followed by a 4-1 thumping of Leeds – which is always nice – and we could be forgiven for thinking that we were back on track. Villa, on the other hand, were a big team then, and comfortably stuck four past Turner, so a home draw against Forest, who were European Cup and Super Cup holders, was prob-ably not a bad result. Not as good as a win over Palace, though.

On September 24th, John Bonham died a rock'n'roll death – in his sleep, on his own vomit, at his mate's house. That was the end of one of the most influential bands of all time – Led Zeppelin had sold more albums than the Beatles at that stage, and they're still influencing kids as I write. Well, my kids at least. Along with being older than some of the players, the fact that my musical heroes, the ones who weren't that much older than myself, had started to pop their clogs with alarming regularity was a worrying sign of the inevitable ageing process.

Being between remunerative engagements and relying for beer and football money on ducking and diving of various sorts, I accepted my folks' offer of a week in the Isle of Wight, knowing that we'd be stopping at Aunty Audrey's in Surrey on the way down, so that I could nip across to Highbury for the match. Nipping across to Highbury wasn't nearly as much fun in those days, as anyone without Gunners tattooed on their forehead was considered fair game. The open end had no segregation, and the police/steward combination provided no se-curity whatsoever. When the local hard men challenged a lad next to me about which team he supported, his girlfriend told them to get stuffed. His groan of resigned acceptance preceded his grabbing her hand and legging it to the Pad-dock, where, allegedly, folks are more tolerant. I sucked my teeth, watched Brian McDermott star for the gunners, and little Stan and a back-on song Rowell get us a 2-2 draw. Not a bad result to take across the Solent for a spot of rest and recuperation, and certainly better than the defeat at Coventry that followed. Barry Siddall went for a month's loan to Darlo just to keep his hands in, so to speak. Pop had lost his place to kit-man Cooke, who eventually scored in the win over Man City, but then we lost at Everton and Norwich, which wasn't really the preparation we wanted for the visit of Liverpool.

In a hugely entertaining game (if you can forget the fact that we lost), we looked briefly as if we might sneak something. 2-4 down, and Shaun Elliott burst through their defence at the Fulwell to leave only Jellylegs Grobelaar to beat. Had it been Brown, Cooke, Robson, or Cummins, the outcome might have been different, but Shaun was a player whose game was based on defence, any goal he did score was usually one that didn't have to be thought about too much, and the chance was duly fluffed. This might sound a touch cruel on a fine player, but that sort of chance has to be taken by any member of the team before you have a really good side. Never mind. Judith, after this, her second visit to the match, said "That was good!" So at least she'd enjoyed herself. What can I say? Some ladies just never completely grasp the concept of really supporting a football team. My housemate Davy might have been a Mag, but a week before the City game, his girlfriend Pauline had introduced me to her friend, Judith, which was nice for me.

I think I originally got the sympathy vote, as Pauline always said she was worried about me sitting up all night, listening to "miserable music" and drinking Davy's gin. Either that or skanking around the house to the Clash's Bankrobber all night. Quite socially perceptive for someone whose other half was a Mag – in fact her brother was as well, and he always came up with the same question whenever we met. "Been to see the dopes lately?" Oh, how I laughed as I swiftly drew the samurai sword from the scabbard on my back and, in one movement, neatly cleft him from crown to crotch. In my head. I think I still owe Davy for a bottle of gin, but Mag 2 still owes me for the bottle of my finest homemade apple wine that he drank, despite the label bearing the words "Mathew Stace, to be drunk on your 21st birthday on May 25th 2000". We re-labelled another one, and my nephew was none the wiser when he eventually reached his landmark birthday. Mind you, he was certainly none the wiser when he'd drunk the stuff.

So, personal life having taken a decided turn for the better, it was the turn of the fortunes of the Lads to do likewise. Hmm.

Another defeat, at Brighton, continued the miserable run, and I took solace in the Rock Garden, Middlesbrough, where boyhood idols Slade, following their storming performance at Reading the preceding summer, were continuing their "Scare The Youth Of Today" tour – magic stuff that took me back seven or eight years. At least they were all still alive. A couple of days after that some nutter decided it would be a good idea to shoot John Lennon – to see what it was like - and there was another icon shuffling of the mortal coil. I've never classed myself as a big Beatles fan, despite the first 45rpm single we ever bought being She Loves You (6 shillings and 6 pence at the House of Andrews in Durham, it was the only one we had and we played it that much the needle wore through to the B side), but his massive contribution to and influence on music is undeniable. Mark David Chapman's act of madness just went to emphasise the lengths people go to in order to investigate the possibilities of the human mind. Three out of the next four number ones were Lennon songs, the fifth (Shaduppa Your Face) best forgotten about.

After the music world in particular and the world in general had wept and moaned for a few days, we were back to life, back to football. Surprising how, no matter what goes on in the world at large, football always seems to pop back up and give us something else to think about. Along came Arsenal, and John Hawley made his comeback after three months injured. He cited his inability to run more than a few yards at a time as the reason why he'd tried a shot from nigh on forty yards rather than carry the ball forward. As it was, his screamer was one of Roker's most memorable goals, and, along with Arnott's effort, gave us our last win of the year. On Boxing Day, West Brom gave us a point and one of the best laughs of the festive season as they turned out in their away kits of green and yellow striped shirts (bad enough) blue shorts (sorry, they just don't match) and, having forgotten their own, borrowed red socks (definite no-no). 28,000 people gave a collective "euch" as they took to the pitch, and our Lads were so distracted by this sartorial disaster that they couldn't score and only our tenth point since September left us in a pretty unhealthy position. On the other hand, my Christmas came a few days early with a decent job offer and a January start. So, personal life having taken a decided turn for the better, it was the turn of the fortunes of the Lads to do likewise.

Sorry, I've heard that one before, and it's Sunderland we're talking about. Still, the FA Cup could perhaps provide us with some light relief and a bit of impetus to carry into the league. A rare Chis goal earned a decent enough draw at St Andrews, but we flopped at home and lost the replay.

Just the league, then.

Whatever Ken Knighton said after the Brum game seemed to work, as Rowell and Cummins got back to scoring work in a 3-0 win over Norwich, then the manager brought in some experience in the form of Ian Bowyer – a fairly recent league champion and European Cup winner with Forest – and he helped us to a 2-0 win over Man Utd. Knighton responded to this by bringing in more experience – this time Tom Ritchie from Bristol City, making the rather strange claim that skinny Tom was a proven First Division goalscorer, when in fact he'd had one season there when City had been promoted alongside ourselves a few years earlier, and he'd been relegated. It's nice how a couple of home games can apparently change your fortunes, but it only lasted seven days until defeat at the Dell, where Siddall began his half season in the green jersey. Bigger news that day was that Mel Holden had died – someone who had played for the lads and was barely any older than I was. To me, anyone who clocks up more than fifty games for us automatically becomes "one of the Lads" (although some, by dint of a particular skill, or attitude, or circumstance, can attain that honour with less – like being a local lad, or rattling in a particularly spectacular or important goal – providing they don't spoil it by moving to the Mags). Mel had scored 28 goals in 83 games, so he was well in as far as I was concerned. It certainly makes you begin to put things into perspective.

All of this preceded another defeat at Judith's first away game, at the Boro. Joe Bolton had been injured in that game on Teesside when Terry Cochrane's cheek caught him a nasty blow on the forehead, and Joe Hinnigan took his place for the three game rest that was compulsory following blows to the head. A win at Leicester was nice, so I persuaded Judith that Leeds would make a nice weekend away, as I'd taken advantage of regular decent income to swap the 1964 MG Midget for a 1974 version - with a roof that fitted. So we stayed over in Harrogate to mull over the inevitable defeat. "Why are they keeping us locked in?" was her question ten minutes after the whistle, and, when the hail of bricks and other Yorkshire debris came over the wall, she understood. Bowyer, the Richard Harris look-alike whose every kick produced a boom that could be heard a mile away, scored his only Sunderland goal to earn a draw with Spurs, during which the steady-away Whitworth was injured. Joe Bolton, having recovered from suspension, got back his number three shirt, and Hinnigan moved across to number two, and went a bit mad. Obviously feeling that someone needed to take on the mantle of goal-poacher supreme following that week's departure of Pop Robson (no, not to West Ham, but to Carlisle as some sort of player/coach.)

Although Villa won, Joe scored, then repeated the trick a week later with the winner at Palace. If that wasn't wild enough for a Sunderland full back, he scored two of our three in the win over Coventry a week after that. Would Joe 2 be the goal scoring saviour of the season? The man whose goals we could normally rely on came off the bench to get a consolation as we were sunk 1-4 at Ipswich, then we lost to Wolves and Stoke, where local boy Rob Vincent made his league debut as a substitute. Somehow I persuaded Judith that Stoke in April would be a nice trip, but she unhappily completed a hat-trick of away defeats. Some amusement was found when she spotted the Pink Panther and Andy Pandy, complete with Sunderland scarves, hitching up the M6, but the laughter stopped when the clutch went near Burnley, and we had to complete the homeward journey in third gear, which made us slightly less miserable than Knighton and Clarke, who'd been handed their P45s that day. Mick Docherty, forced in to retirement two years earlier, took over as caretaker manager, and, along with the fans, patiently waited for Mr Ritchie, the "proven First Division goalscorer", to actually score a goal and set us on the road to recovery and First Division safety. As he'd scarcely looked like doing the necessary with eleven consecutive blanks, his hat-trick against Birmingham was more than a mild shock, and we thought he'd finally cracked it when he scored in the next game at WBA, but we lost, and then let Brighton beat us at home to drop us right in it.

One game left, right in the smelly stuff, and that one game needed to yield no less than two points. Against Liverpool. At Anfield. Where we hadn't won for twenty years. Or forty-five years in the league. No problem, one – nil, Stan Cummins, get in. (OK, so Norwich lost anyway and got relegated, so it didn't matter, but it's a much better way to stay up). Rumour has it that Bob Paisley sent a case of champagne into our dressing room after the match, which was nice, but perhaps not surprising as he was a Hetton lad and had Sunderland in his heart despite all his years at Anfield. Safe, but why had we made such an arse of a season that had started with such promise? Who knows, but if Mr Ritchie had scored more than four goals in fifteen games it might have been different (I know it doesn't sound that bad a ratio, but one against Birmingham would have been enough, and they'd have been better shared out more evenly). Some players never quite hit it off at a club, and Tom was one at Sunderland. It's not that I have anything personal against him (well, he did once try the "Do you know who I am?" trick on me in a pub near Bristol, so I did have a bit of a grudge, but I'll give anyone a chance so long as he's wearing a Sunderland shirt), but he didn't do it for Sunderland when needed. What if Jeff Clarke's knee hadn't gone at the end of the previous season? Still, we were safe, we'd lived to fight another day, and we'd give the top flight another crack come August.

The ground filled up
The Fulwell first
Then the Roker, then the Paddocks
And finally the seats
Zigga zagga
Zigga zagga
Oi oi oi

1981-1982

I celebrated Sunderland's survival with a spectacular college reunion in Droitwich, ten of us sharing the living room floor and scaring the neighbours. Two weeks back at work, then a camping holiday with Robbo, ex-flatmate from Tyneside. Bolton-le-Sands is less than a hundred miles away, so we could stop off for a beer in Barnard Castle, then Kirkby Stephen, on the way, and it's also a nice place. Lancaster was the closest town and it was OK (has lots of pubs), Morecambe was next, was crap, and is still crap. The most memorable thing about the town was a huge pile of horse muck on the promenade, waiting for the council gardeners to do their stuff. So, for a week we forgot football and work, drank beer, and ran away from the tide on Morecambe Bay as we tried to play one-aside football. Then it was back to work for a few weeks before the proper holidays (it was an easy life) of factory fortnight in Dorset. The tent was a work of art, held up as it was with a broom shank - the result of Robbo falling on it at Bolton le Sands and my refusal to spend money on a new pole when the company I worked for manufactured sticky tape.

While Judith and I were gadding about Wessex, Mr Cowie persuaded Alan Durban to become our new manager. I decided that I should move closer to work, and chased the personnel department to help me out, so they chased the council, and found me a delightful first-floor flat with Redifussion radio (free

– a leftover from the first cable experiment) and a strange tendency to fill up with steam if the water heating was left on. Despite a south facing balcony and a one-mile journey to work, I couldn't settle in sunny Aycliffe, and I took up an offer from my folks to move back in with them while I looked for a house to buy. A real grown-up, settle-down decision.

Barry Siddall earned a few quid extra by playing the summer months for Vancouver Whitecaps, and in came Iain Munro to replace Joe Bolton, who'd only lasted a month after the arrival of the new boss. Selling a legend like Joe was bad enough, but selling him to the Boro was awful, and I think Durban made a big mistake in doing so. Imagine his reception at Ayresome Park – "Didn't you nut our star winger a couple of years ago?" It's not that Munro was a bad player, far from it - and he was as hard as nails and as mad as a bicycle - but Joe had years left on the clock and should have stayed. The other signing was the talk of Scottish football – Alistair Murdoch McCoist from St Johnstone. Durban painted a better picture of Sunderland than the managers of Boro and Wolves did of their clubs, and Rangers also missed out (yes, I know – only for a while). £400,000 was our record fee, and we justifiably expected great things of the lad.

Perhaps the biggest change of the summer, however, was that to the strips. Red socks – fine. Red shorts - fair enough, but not as good as black. Andy Pandy Candy-stripe pyjama shirts – no, I'm sorry, not for me. Supposedly created to emphasise that Cowie and Durban meant business and were about to take us in a new direction, but they were horrible. Yes, my eldest lad admitted in the match programme a few years later that he never went to the game without his "Ally McCoist pyjama top", but it was bought at a jumble sale by his gran, and the bairn wouldn't part with it. It's still in the bottom drawer to this day, awaiting a call from Antiques Roadshow or some such source of surprise wealth.

Not many new signings, but a few new faces in the squad. Local boy Pickering had turned professional on his eighteenth birthday just before the season started, and was straight in from nowhere on the left of midfield. Barry Venison, likewise local, appeared in the squad but didn't make it onto the field of play until a couple of months in. Away to Ipswich for starters and only Munro was an unfamiliar face at the back, with Turner getting first go at the green shirt. Jeff Clarke was back in place of big Sam, alongside his mate Chis Hindmarch, with Elliott temporarily unfit. In midfield, Buckley was there to do the work, Chisholm to win the ball for him, and Pickering and Rowell to link up with the attack, where all eyes were looking for McCoist to partner Brown. It was not to be, as Ritchie started, and scored, with young Ally coming off the bench. The goal scoring hero of the day was not Scottish, however, but English, in the unlikely shape of Mick

Buckley, who decided to score 25% of all his Sunderland goals that day. (Two, in case you were wondering). 3-3 away from home wasn't a bad start, and I began to question my opinion of Tom Ritchie when he scored again against League Champions Villa the next week as we won 2-1.

A sound start was continuing. My birthday wish of a win over West Ham was not granted, and we slumped into a league run of four draws and seven defeats that lasted until late November. Ritchie had regained his form of last season and stopped scoring, big Sam had gone to Millwall once Elliott's return to fitness filled up the defensive side of things, and Cooke, McCoist, Cummins, and Brown were all given a try up front. None could force Ritchie to score, but at least we got to see another new face, as amateur Venison got his first start at Notts County. Needless to say, it was one of five 0-2 defeats that Autumn, and even Judith, despite her apparent ability to be entertained whatever the team's ineptitude, conceded that, at the County Ground, we were poor – but Venison had nice hair and looked too young to be playing. I had to explain that we were at an age where several of the players were actually younger than us, and that it was part of growing up that this was the case. Durban must also have liked what he saw in Venison, as he sold Whitworth, after his only three games that season, to Bolton in October. The Spurs defeat saw Colin West come into the defence, but despite scaring the life out of the opposing defence, he couldn't save us.

Personally, I blamed our poor form on the fact that we didn't join the League Cup until October, when Tom Ritchie finally scored in the first leg win over Rotherham, then scored twice in the second leg. See what happens when we get a lower league team to practise our shooting on? A cup run of sorts? Nah. Up came Palace at the beginning of November and took advantage of our sterile attack to dump us out. One-time midfield genius and fans' idol Kevin Arnott went to Blackburn on loan, and never came back, signing for Sheff Utd at the season's end before playing all over Europe, and Jarrow. We didn't hold out much hope when Everton came calling, but Ritchie hopped off the bench to score the winner. Buoyed by victory, Durban brought back Ian Bowyer, about whom most of us had forgotten, to play against his old club Forest the next week. Despite a rare goal from Hindmarch and McCoist's first, we lost 3-2, and despite another (slightly less rare, obviously) goal from Hindmarch, we made it two home defeats on the trot the next week against West Brom, then lost at Brighton, who were actually a quite successful team at that time. They even had a home of their own, just like me. I'd spotted, bought, and moved into a little two-up, two-down job in Bishop town centre, and life got even more settled.

Every Friday up the Blue Bells at Etherley (three miles away, but a nice walk home that I'd been practising on visits to Bish over the last few years), most Saturday nights in the same place, and heading for the match with the lads from the pub. One Saturday night, discussing our five-a-side antics, we decided that we should try eleven a side (on the basis that we had a man for most positions, and Harry's mate was wicket-keeper for Shildon and therefore could catch a ball = goalie), and so the Bittermen came into being. Yeah, we were only a Sunday morning side, but we survived for eighteen seasons, never went into debt, and never fell out with anybody. (Apart from some sweary lads from Tindale, but that was just the once). Typically, I missed the first ever game, a poor show for the joint manager, but I'd just invested in a twin-tub washing machine, and Dad said he was coming round on the Sunday afternoon (we couldn't get eleven men out of bed on a morning for something that new and untried), and I couldn't risk the other potential home-improvements that might occur if I wasn't there to say "Fatha, no!" By the end of October, I was domestically established, socially established (in the Bells twice most weeks), sportingly fulfilled, and, unfortunately, supportingly worried.

Things were beginning (beginning?) to look decidedly dodgy by the time we travelled to Maine Road, but the football world was about to experience the Barry Venison Show, as that day's edition of Match of the Day was to become known. Trailing 2-1 to the career 150th and 151st goals scored by Trevor Francis after taking a cheeky lead through Cummins, Venison came off the bench, provided the pass that Cummins crossed for Rowell's equaliser, and celebrated like a lunatic. A few minutes later, his volley over a stranded Joe Corrigan left the home crowd stunned, the visiting fans celebrating in the snow, like you only can when you've come from behind to win away, and young Baz to celebrate as only a seventeen-year-old can when he's a bit of an extrovert and had just provided the moments of high drama. At least it took us into Christmas with something to smile about, but the weather put paid to our chances of continuing our (one-match) winning run on Boxing Day, and it was kit-man Cooke who popped up with the winner at Wolves at the end of January, after the FA Cup had been sorted for another year. Curiously, as in the League Cup, we drew Rotherham, in the FA Cup. Draw away, win at home - same as the League Cup – and we drew Liverpool at home. We simply weren't at the races, and 3-0 probably flattered us a bit, to be honest.

Just the League, then.

We'd given up on Ian Bowyer, who followed his heart back to Forest at the start of the year, and Jimmy Nicholl had arrived in December to add experience to our defence, but didn't get a League start, after playing in our last two FA Cup games, until Arsenal at the beginning of February. A creditable 0-0 draw was followed by a home defeat to Stoke, which marked the debut of John McGinley. Signed from Gateshead, we should have seen the warning signs. The new Barry Dunn was a winger, but built like a centre-half at six foot two, and only managed three games before he was back at Gateshead. Still, if you don't try them, you'll never find a gem from the amateur game. Nicholl's loan spell was up, so he opted for sunnier climes with Toronto Blizzard, and we lost to Birmingham and Swansea before drawing with Notts County – McGinley's last game. Ally McCoist showed us what he was capable of with a beaut past Peter Shilton in the win over Southampton, but we didn't score in the next four games, and collected only one point – although it was at Old Trafford. At this time, Durban brought in our first Dutchman, attacking midfielder Loek Ursem from Stoke on loan, but his four appearances out of six substitute chances provided little reward, and we reckoned he didn't Loek very good anyway. Sorry, but that's the way the mind of the football fan works when the team isn't doing very well – you attempt to cheer yourselves up by any means available, however pathetic.

As we attempted to cheer ourselves up with that sort of rubbish, real life decided to wake us up. Following the trend of my personal icons, on the eve of his 47th birthday, Alex Harvey died of a heart attack in Belgium, and joined his brother Les, electrocuted on stage with Stone The Crows in 1972, on the rock'n'roll highway out of this world, after a working life as a musical itinerant. If you watch archive footage of the 6-5 special from the late 50s, you'll see Alex hovering about over Pete Murray's shoulder in the background, in his guise of warm-up man for the programme. There's another one gone, I thought. In the bigger world, the Argentinians invaded some sheep-strewn outpost of the British Empire, and the Falklands war (or "conflict", as Mrs Thatcher would have us call it) was underway. While forces commanders claimed that "Nobody really wants a war," one lady certainly did, as it's long been a Tory belief that there's nothing like a war to breed patriotism, and get a few more people off the dole queue.

Is it worth it
A new winter coat and shoes for the wife
And a bicycle on the boy's birthday
It's just a rumour that was spread around town
By the women and children
Soon we'll be shipbuilding
Well I ask you
The boy said "Dad they're going to take me to task, but I'll be back by Christmas"
It's just a rumour that was spread around town
Somebody said that

Someone got filled in
For saying that
People get killed in
The result of this Shipbuilding
With all the will in the world
Diving for dear life
When we could be diving for pearls
It's just a rumour that was spread around town
A telegram or a picture postcard
Within weeks they'll be re-opening the shipyards
And notifying the next of kin
Once again it's
All we're skilled in
We will be shipbuilding

Colin West had been given his chance at the expense of the misfiring McCoist, and his first goal for the club saved us a point against Ipswich. Goal-machine Mick Buckley (8 in 135 appearances) won the game at Stoke, then Westy got both as we beat Birmingham. After eight barren games, Gary Rowell remembered his purpose in life as he and Nick Pickering nicked a point at Spurs, then he grabbed another two as Everton were beaten. He and Pickering again scored away, this time at West Brom, and little Stan weighed in to give us a 3-2 win. Just when everything in the garden was looking distinctly red and white, along came the rearranged game at Coventry, and out of the window went our recent good performances. 6-1 was a real kick in the teeth, but we took it as a kick up the arse, as Rowell (2) and Westy beat Brighton 3-0. Games to make our position safe were fast running out, and a point at West Ham was very welcome, but a narrow defeat at Southampton and a 1-0 over Man City (Buckley again) left us in eighteenth and safely in the top flight for another year. 42 games and only 38 goals sum up the season pretty well, and if Westy and Rowell hadn't got six apiece in the last eleven games, we'd have been right in the mire. It'd all be better next season, we told ourselves.

Number one is Gary Rowell
And number two is Gary Rowell
We all live in a Gary Rowell world
A Gary Rowell world A Gary Rowell world

1982-1983

Summers were getting busier. The thing is, we're pretty good at fighting wars, especially against countries which think that mass conscription and propaganda is a substitute for training and tactics, and who complain that it's not fair when you start shooting their troops. In June, the Argentinians surrendered, and we could let the Falklands get back to their Falks. Oh, and the Israelis invaded Lebanon, objecting to their use of the cedar tree as their national symbol – or something like that. I'd long given up why the Middle East can't pass up the chance to have a go at each other for being Jewish, or Arab, or left-handed, or having a VW camper van.

In the space of a month, Davy and Pauline got married, I was best man to the other Mag from our Cleveland sojourn, and Judith and I got married. Parties all over the place in County Durham for July, not least to celebrate the sale of Tom Ritchie after his loan spell at Carlisle. I say sale, I mean we gave him back to Bristol City after ten goals in eighteen months and wrote off the £180,000, presumably because we'd lost the receipt, but there you go, that's the way these things sometimes work out. We did the South West again for our honeymoon – by tent, of course. I know how to show a girl a good time.

News at SAFC wasn't that good, as they'd made the mistake of having a structural survey, and, surprise, surprise, it was discovered that the Roker End was falling to bits. As we weren't that well off, repairs or replacement weren't an option, so the end was closed, then had the back third knocked off, and the face of Roker changed forever. While previous changes at the old place had given cause for optimism (the roof on the Fulwell, for example, created one of English football's most renowned Kop ends), this one was seen by many as ominous. For a start, we could see from the Fulwell over the Roker for the first time, and those roof-tops were not a welcoming sight, marking as they did the beginning of the end for Roker Park. Over the next few seasons, the capacity shrank with monotonous regularity as safety measure after safety measure made it more comfortable (so they tell us) and easier to evacuate. Apparently, the ground could be emptied in two and a half minutes, which is slightly slower than it would fill up when the Dagenham Girl Pipers were the pre-match entertainment.

Slightly less welcome than the departure of Tom Ritchie was that of Alan Brown to Shrewsbury, perhaps precipitated by his highly unusual loan spell at Gal-lowgate over Christmas, but, by throwing in an extra £20,000, we brought their midfield star of the previous campaign to Roker. Ian Atkins had been at Gay Meadow for nine years before attracting a great deal of attention, but we got to the front of the queue with Browny plus cash, and the deal was done. Barry Siddall also decided that the bright lights of Port Vale were preferable to Sunder-land reserves, and off he went on his own personal tour of another sixteen or so clubs that took him well into his forties. Three men out, one man in and we stuck with those awful candy-stripe shirts in the hope that Ally McCoist would find his shooting boots and propel us to glory.

Or something like that. We could hardly have asked for a tougher start, as first up were team of the day Villa, at their place. Pos and the Aycliffe boys took advan-tage of an invitation from Wink's cousin Gordon Cowans to a tour of the ground and some posh seats, and spent the pre-match wandering about the pitch in suits, waving at those of us on the terraces - we thought that they looked a bit fa-miliar. Hopes for the season took an upward turn when West, McCoist, and Nicky Pick gave us an odds-busting 3-1 win. Possibly the least likely away win of the campaign was followed by Notts County at home, when only a goal from Rowell, the sub, saved us a point. That goal got him a start in place of Westy against West Ham at home the next week, and he responded with the only goal. So Durban sensibly kept the same team, and we lost at Coventry, with three more defeats ending in a horrible record-equalling 0-8 at Watford. Never mind that Watford were in the middle of the best period in their history, that kind of scoreline is just the sort of thing to have us lining up on the parapet of Newton Cap viaduct with our pockets full of bricks.

It certainly didn't provide inspiration for my Sunday morning antics, where the fortunes of the Lads reflected in how confident I'd be for the Bittermen, taking my lead from anything spectacular that had happened the previous afternoon. The importance of team spirit has been talked about many times over the years with regard to Sunderland, but just how important it really is you never fully appreciate unless you've been part of a team yourself. No, I'm not talking about workplace teams, the lifeblood of the performance coaches of modern industry, but a proper sports team where you rely on your mates to help you out. I know that Sunday morning football is typified by ten blokes with hangovers standing, in the rain, in a pub car park, waiting for the goalkeeper to arrive, but even at that level you soon find out who you can trust when you get onto the field of play. That's probably why reunions of teams that last achieved anything half a century ago are still well attended – the Bittermen only ever entered one real competition (i.e. sanctioned by the local FA), but, twenty-odd years on, we still get together to reminisce, drink beer, and laugh at old photographs. Good teams aren't just those that win loads of trophies (they're called successful teams), but ones whose spirit endures even beyond the team's demise as a sporting entity.

Team spirit was probably the last thing on Jimmy Nicholl's mind after his second Sunderland debut. Having eventually got his papers in order and returned from Canada in time to play at Watford, he must have been considering the viaduct and the pockets full of bricks as a suitable career move after that one. No wonder the crowd was down to 13,000 for the visit of Norwich, but we reacted correctly and won 4-1, which led us nicely into a League Cup draw at Wolves (Rowell again). Jimmy chose life, and kept his place for the Norwich game, and played in the two league draws that followed, as well as the home leg against Wolves. While McCoist and Rowell might have been expected to score, two from Chis and one from Hindmarch were a bit of a pleasant surprise as we knocked in five without reply. Wembley here we come? Well, we lost badly in the league at mighty Swansea, aka Liverpool old boys, before a home draw with Norwich in the next round, and then saw Atkins get his first red and white goal in a home draw against Luton. That bloke could hit the ball almost as hard as Dick Malone, but he didn't manage it as we lost to Forest and Birmingham, or at Carrow Road as we went down 3-1 and out of the League Cup.

Having brought experience to the defence in the form of Nicholl, Durban decided to do likewise up front, and signed the footballing nomad that was Frank Worthington, who'd already had five English and two American clubs. On the field, there was no doubting Frank's ability and willingness to encourage younger players, take them under his wing, and give them the benefit of his experience. Off the field, this was also the case, but not always to do with football. Perhaps strangely, he was put in the same hotel as McCoist, and famously claimed that the pair were always back early – but declined to confirm whether this was early evening or early morning. Had we been in a slightly more comfortable league position, we would probably have appreciated his contribution more, but, even where we were, there was no denying his entertainment value. Taking Westy's place, he scored on his debut against Ipswich, but, despite Atkins adding a second, we let in three, and things took a definite downward direction when Mark Prudhoe, in for the injured Turner, could do little about the three that West Brom put past him.

That didn't really put us in the best spirits for the visit of Arsenal, but Nicky Pick tore them apart, Frank took the mickey, and Rowell applied three killing blows. OK, if a blow's killing, then only the one is needed, but three sounds so much better. Another hat-trick for the Earl of Seaham, and that raised our standards a bit, as we kept clean sheets against three of the top sides of the day – Man Utd, Liverpool, and Forest – although it would have been nice if we'd managed just one ourselves. Forest's neighbours County made it a Nottingham double-header over the New Year, so Judith and I set off, waited twenty minutes for Rossy from work, gave up, headed to Meadow Lane, and parked up in the jolly old cattle market. Walking into town for a swift libation, we bumped into Dougy from school, so we treated him to a scandalously cheap New Year pint in the Pheasant. Once in the ground, we fell in with Shaun the Hartlepool Bitterman, and watched as County let little Stan score our first goal in four games. We kept yet another clean sheet, all of the available points, and landed back in Bish in plenty of time to hit the Bells and clean up at darts (me) and doms (Judith. I believe that I still owe her £100,000 in unpaid domino-related debts). Even more defensive effectiveness, against Man City at home in the FA cup, coupled with another blank from our front men took us down to Maine Road for the replay, but despite a goal from Chis, and the return of Worthington after a three-game New Year absence (for the festivities – it was probably in his contract), we let in two and it was yet another case of…

Just the league, then.

Frankie was back on the scoresheet as he and a bloke called OG scored in the win over Villa – a notable league double – which marked the first appearance of Durban's experience-bringer in midfield, Leighton James. Like Worthington, he was one we'd loved to hate when he played against us (Billy Hughes and Joe Bolton at Derby in '77 comes to mind), but like Worthington again, he relished the opportunity to work with the youngsters and nurture them in the big time. He was also a bit of a lad off the field – still is, according to a workmate of mine and long-time friend of the Jamesy from Swansea, but that sort of class is always welcome in a typical Sunderland situation. Around this time I made my only appearance on stage at Whitley Bay ice rink – with The Jam. A trip to the toilets led to me getting lost under the seats, and, thanks to lax security, wandering onto the back of the stage before I noticed the man with the spotty shirt and the guitar. Oops, time for a quick exit. We managed an awful lot of music during that season – Simple Minds (twice), OMD, and Madness spring to mind – and it was generally more inspiring than the football. Never mind, you can't have music as a way of life if you're not professionally involved, unlike football. Which is why dedicated fans of a particular football club are thought of as loyal and worthy folks, while people who apply the same dedication to a particular music act are often thought of as stalkers. Just my theory.

A draw at Spurs, a win over Coventry and our now usual capitulation at Southampton preceded three wins off the belt, inspired by five goals from Gary the Great. Another earned a draw against Swansea, then Jamesy got his first as Pickering again ran the show and got the other two at Luton. Not a bad start to the year, but a narrow defeat at Liverpool set us back a bit. I'd taken Judith to the home draw with Man U in the hope that the vibes would get through to the baby we were expecting, much as they had to me all those years ago, but it nearly went all wrong when I was threatened with ejection from the Posh Stand (I know how to treat a lady) for hurling abuse at Remi Moses – never did like him. The next week, we decided to take advantage of the fact that my mate Pop (Robson, what else did you expect) is a West Ham fan (what else did you expect, Etherley is full of them) and forced him into arranging a Bittermen trip to the East End, and so began a series of trips to the capital that started at the Lamb, and, hopefully, will last for the rest of my life. Brothers Reg and John accompanied Pop and I, and Reg won a free programme for daring to ask for one in a Durham accent – not realising that he'd strayed into enemy territory out the back of the stand, where segregation went only as far as two stewards holding up a piece of plywood between the would-be warring factions in the gents' netty.

Mark Proctor had come from Forest on loan as we set about what seemed like one of the most drawn-out permanent transfers in history, and showed his usual ability to cross the ball from behind himself, but could do little to add to Nicky Pick's goal as we went down 2-1. Trust the damned cock-a-nees to spoil what was developing nicely into a good run. Jimmy Nicholl had returned to Toronto (what kind of stupid contract had we given him?), so local boy Mick Whitfield became our new right back at Norwich, where we gave McCoist a try, but lost again as Turner was injured. A clash with future Sunderland man Keith Bertschin reportedly ended with Chris suffering a broken jaw, but my mate Phil was the dental surgeon on duty at Sunderland General when he was admitted, and he said it was a lot worse than a few loose teeth.

Sure enough, a fractured skull was eventually diagnosed. Not good for a keeper (actually, pretty bad for anybody), and very bad for Sunderland. Nicky Pick saved us a point at home to Brighton with Mark Prudhoe in goal in the next game as we steeled ourselves for the remaining games without our inspirational number one. While the record books show his goal as the moment of the match, most of those present will remember the game for Worthington pulling visiting centre-half Steve Foster's trademark headband down over his eyes as we attacked a corner at the Fulwell. A bad loss at Ipswich, 4-1, was followed by defeat at home to Birmingham, then, with Shaun Elliott having a go at right back, we drew at home to Watford, keeping us just above the drop-zone.

Two games to go, and Westy had been banging on the manager's door, telling him that he was the best centre-forward at the club, and demanding a game. He got one at Arsenal, and made it a league double with the only goal of the game. The last game, a draw at home to West Brom, left us sixteenth, our highest position for fifteen years, but it was hardly worthy of celebration. We'd need to make some changes if we were going to finish in the top half of the top division, but at least we were still in it. As Spandau Ballet sang at the time, True.

We'll take more care of you
Ally McCoist
Ally McCoist

1983-1984

Big changes indeed. Son Gary arrived in June, and, from being a pair of DINKYs (dual income, no kids yet) with a trendy VW Beetle and an equally trendy MG Midget, to an expectant couple with just the Beetle, to parents with an Austin Maxi. Austin Maxi with two of the biggest speakers you'd find in a family hatchback at the time – I'd fitted them myself, as I'd bought the car off my Dad, and his factory-fitted radio cassette just wasn't special enough. Holiday was a couple of days in Alnmouth - Judith's folks, us and the bairn – as we had other priorities for our cash, like furniture and nappies. At Roker, some changes were also underway, with Stan Cummins turning down a new contract because it was not better than his existing one, and going to Palace for nothing. Then McCoist was sold to Rangers for half of what we'd paid for him, after scoring only nine goals in sixty-odd attempts had proved that he was never going to make it as a forward. Fifteen years and 250 goals later, I think he's made it, and it doesn't bear thinking about what he'd have done for us if the club could have afforded Paul Bracewell without selling first.

Frank Worthington went to Southampton, the first of another fifteen clubs before I lost count. He must have lived in a caravan. Behind the scenes there were changes as well, with Johnny Watters, the white-coated, horn-rimmed spectacle-wearing, Brylcreme-plastered physio, and Charlie Ferguson, the brown-coated scout who'd had schoolboy goalkeepers all over the North East diving in extraspectacular fashion just by turning up at a school game, both retired. From the coaching staff Monty, Peter Eustace, Jimmy Greenhalgh, and Mick Docherty all left, and there were also rumblings about possible changes in the boardroom. As well as Bracewell, we finally finished signing Mark Proctor, and brought back Pop Robson – at the age of 37 - as player-coach. Perhaps the most significant change was to the shirts, as, on top of them reverting to proper red and white stripes, they carried our first sponsor's name – Cowies, as you'd expect.

Against Norwich at home, local lad Paul Atkinson made his debut, and Westy got us off to a winning start with the only goal, but we followed that with two away defeats. At home to Wolves, Atky got his first goal, added to by Rowell and that nice man OG for a 3-2 win. Shamefully, I'd gone to work - well, I was on shifts and couldn't get a swap, but when I did get there the following Saturday, we lost to Southampton. A shocking 0-3 at QPR was followed by a narrow win over Coventry, then Rowell did the business in another equally narrow, but far more satisfying, win at Anfield. Were we at last settled into the season? Why no. You'd have been mad to try and predict any of our results, and they obviously disturbed the board, as Collings and Heywood resigned in September, and Barry Batey joined. He'd prove to be real fun, but he probably didn't bet on any of our results either, as we won at Arsenal, lost at home to West Ham, beat Watford 3-0, and let in six at Notts County.

In the League Cup, we'd enjoyed an entertaining, if ridiculously close 7-5 aggregate win over Cambridge, with Rowell getting two in each leg. In the next round, we thought we'd done the hard bit with a draw at Carrow Road, but Norwich (again) won the replay. Back in the league, Pop made his third debut, against West Brom, and scored after only a few minutes. Big news, but not as big as Bracewell scoring twice. (Two goalscorers who had, between them, nine spells at the club if you count le Brace's loan preceding his spell, and Pop's non-playing jobs with the club. Remember that one for the pub quiz). While Pop's goal was nice, you can't rely on a bloke that age to do all of the scoring for you, and in came Lee Chapman from Arsenal, where he'd had a miserable time since moving from Stoke as the Next Big Thing. Unlike Pop, he didn't score on his debut, but Pick and Chis did as we beat Luton, then his partner West did as we lost at Coventry. West and Chapman – twelve feet three inches and twenty-seven stones of forward power – was an interesting combination, later reunited at Sheff Wed, that should have got more goals than it did, as it was one which was, in theory at least, more than a bit daunting for central defenders.

New Year, new direction? Well, after the Coventry game, at least. John and I picked up Stubber from his new abode in Bradford as we set out on the road to Wembley, and off to Bolton we went for the third round. Using my tried and tested Good Beer Guide, I managed to get us to a pub that was the only part of the original street still standing in some God-forsaken suburb of Bolton. It was like a scene from A Bridge Too Far, with piles of burning timbers and abandoned furniture scattered amongst the rubble. At least it was a nice pint. Lee Chapman did manage to score in the clarts, but his celebrations (sliding along the ground in the mud, hardly worthy of mention these days) didn't go down too well with Durban. Westy and Rowell made it convincing, and it was probably the big smiles on our faces that attracted the group of local youth out to make a name for themselves.

Before John or I had realised what was happening, one of them had thrown a punch at Stubber, who'd responded in true Bish fashion by decking the biggest one, with the unarguable logic that if he's out of the way, those remaining will be neither keen nor able to do you as much damage. It did the trick, as they disappeared as quickly as they'd appeared, and we locked ourselves in the car and got back to what we should have been doing all along – celebrating. Birmingham at home in round four was a decent enough tie, and one that we expected to win, as we'd already won at their place. Sadly, there was a big, ugly centre-forward from Plains Farm, called Mick Harford, in their side, and he did for us despite Westy's goal from the bench.

Just the league, then.

The league and Sunderland in early 1984 were not a good pairing. Barry Batey climbed the career ladder in the boardroom to become financial director, and so began a good deal of disagreement behind the scenes over what money went where. Having held off the challenge of Neil Kinnock's Labour Party, Thatcher set about implementing her plans for the destruction of British industry, and the mines in particular. Fired on by Arthur Scargill the miners went on strike, and all manner of conflicts took place over the following weeks. On the pitch, the goals from Rowell and West dried up, and we didn't win a game until sneaking past QPR in March, and that didn't signal a change in fortunes. In fact it came two games after a defeat at Old Trafford, when Stubber had me pick the Great North Run sticker off my car window "In case the Manchester boys recognise it and ambush us after the game." Safety first, I guess. Anyhow, that defeat resulted in Durban being sacked, and that news being conveyed to the players by Pop Robson during a Roker Park training session.

It was more than just the bad results that got Durban the sack, as it had been obvious for some time that the board didn't have the patience that would have allowed the man to bring his plans to fruition. Feeling among the players was that he was still the man for the job, but players don't decide who the manager is. Bad ones might get a manager the sack, but the board does the hiring and firing. Pop became caretaker manager, presided in a 2-2 draw with Arsenal, then ended the shortest managerial reign on Wearside (three days, from the 2nd to the 5th of March) when Len Ashurst took over. Wise move, we thought, the lad has played more games for us than any other outfield player, and you couldn't get much more red and white. We fans are great judges of that sort of thing.

After his initial win, which had turned things around (we thought), the team quickly slipped back into its old ways, and didn't win again until mid April at West Ham. On FA Cup semi-final day, I thought it would be funny to shout "Come on you Reds" down the escalator at the Everton fans who'd just passed us on their way down as we came up. I didn't expect them to turn around and head back up (thankfully the down escalator). Our annual trip to the capital with our own Pop saw Chis score with his chest, much to the delight of the travelling fans. It's always good to win away, a bit special to win in London, made better when a defender of the cult hero type scores the goal, and absolutely hilarious when he does it in a slightly unorthodox manner. Cue much poking of our Pop on the train – once we'd got away from the vicinity of the Boleyn and we no longer needed his claret and blue scarf for cover. When West and Pop scored against Everton the next week, we were in seventh heaven – Len was the boy for the job. Even a blip against West Brom was followed by a win over Birmingham, when Jamesy scored both. Safe? You must be kidding, as we lost at Ipswich and could only draw at home to County, meaning our only chance of avoiding the drop was winning at Leicester. As with every last away game of the season, the travelling support was extra large, but this time we outnumbered the home fans in the 12,000 crowd. Guess what? Pop entered the record books as our oldest ever scorer, and Lee Chapman got the second as we got the points we needed. End of season drama? Nobody does it as well, or as often, as Sunderland.

Aye, aye, aye, aye
Monty is better than Yashin
And Toddo is better than Eusebio
And somebody's in for a thrashing

1984-1985

A bit of a miserable summer for the whole arts spectrum, as Richard Burton, James Mason, John Betjeman, J.B. Priestley, and Eric Morcambe died. We'd seen the industrial unrest reach a peak at the battle of Orgreave, and the miners' dispute looked further away than ever from a resolution. Our first foreign holiday as a family – actually our first trip abroad together as a couple – came courtesy of the fabulous offers available for fans to follow the team's defence of the Gore Trophy. Paul Atkinson had been the star of the tournament last summer, so we'd no doubt unearth another gem this time around. There was a fair chance of that, as Len had been a bit busy in the transfer market. Lee Chapman was obviously too much of a pretty face for Len, and off he went for a good four years at Sheff Wed. Pop Robson left (as he kept doing) for Carlisle (again), Jamesy went to Bury, Flapper Hindmarch to Derby, and Everton took Atkins and Bracewell off our hands. These moves were as nothing to me, however, when the first signs of something not being quite right with Len's managerial head appeared, as he sold Gary Rowell to Norwich. Gary Rowell? You can't get rid of Gary Rowell – he'd scored nigh on a hundred goals for the Lads and he wasn't even a striker.

OK, so he'd had couple of nasty knee injuries, but he'd just scored thirteen in a decidedly dodgy season for the team. He was a local boy, he'd been a Fulwell Ender, he was as red and white as any man on the terraces. I'll never understand that decision as long as I live, but gone he was, and it was a host of new faces on the ferry to the Isle of Man. We travelled with the team, and fellow competitors Carlisle, by ferry, and mingled with the new stars of Len's red and white army. Roger Wylde came from Sporting Lisbon (oooh), and sat alone reading The Times. Steve Berry came from Portsmouth, was never, as far as I can remember, referred to as Chuck, and I can't remember him doing anything on the boat. Gary Bennett came from Man City via Cardiff, Len's previous managerial post, and wandered about looking ridiculously cool and tall, and smiling at the female fans, who seemed to melt into their seats. Clive Walker came from Chelsea, and spent the entire journey in the casino. Hell, this was a player we'd actually heard of, signing for us. What was the world coming to?

Our hotel for the week was a B & B in Douglas, sharing our breakfast table with two young lads living on a shoestring because of their positions as striking miners from Wearmouth Colliery. We fed young Gary his Weetabix every morning, then set off to for the daily 48-a-side game against Carlisle or Blackburn fans. We retained the Trophy thanks to Westy's trick header in the final against Blackburn, and young Gary thought it a brilliant experience – not for the football in particular, but for Gary's newly formed female fan-club shouting "Benno" every few minutes. That and our Gary repeatedly running onto the field, which activity finally ended when Mark Prudhoe grabbed him and sat him on the bench for the rest of the game. Sunderland's youngest ever bench-warmer at eleven months? Quite possibly.

Back home to prepare for the new season, and two more players we'd heard of arrived – David Hodgson, once of Boro, came from Liverpool, and Howard Gayle from Birmingham. Also one we hadn't heard of – Peter Daniel from Wolves via Minnesota Kicks with a League Cup Winners' medal. Well, the more football-soaked of us had heard of him, but either way, it added up to a vastly different squad to the previous season. We began with a bit of a test at home to Southampton, but Benno set the scene for the achievement of legendary status by knocking the ball past Peter Shilton after only a few minutes.

The bright start was short, as Walker's old mates, then Forest, beat us with David Corner suffering a difficult debut as Peter Davenport scored a hat-trick, before Westy won the home game against Spurs, then a rare Berry strike earned a point against West Brom. Pop, (my Pop) decided that it would be a good idea to get married, and being a West Ham fan, picked a Sunderland home game for the happy day, which meant a few empty spaces on the Fulwell, and an afternoon spent with the radio pressed to my ear (only real non-league saddoes possessed headphones in those simple days). As we listened to the speeches, best man Reg shouted out "What's the score, Sobs?" so I replied "1-1, Berry's scored, but I can't hear because the reception's rubbish".

Three people got the joke. I don't know why I bother.

Wylde Roger, as we liked to call him in the Fulwell as we made pirate noises, came off the bench to sneak us a point at Anfield,which made us think that the wily old campaigner might just win us a few games. This was part of a five-draws-in-a-row league run, before we fell into the pattern that marked that season – win, lose, win, lose, lose, win. No consistency. Even two 3-0s on the trot couldn't settle the side and we lost the next, before Stan Cummins decided that whatever he'd fancied about Palace wasn't that good after all, and came back to Roker in time to face Man Utd. Clive Walker scored a two-penalty hat-trick in the dramatic win that saw Hodgson and Mark Hughes sent off for sort of waving their arms at each other in front of the Clock Stand. Not even that victory could drive us on, as we lost at Villa then 0-4 at home to Leicester with a performance that looked devoid of any hope or enthusiasm. Obviously sick and tired of our constant piracy references, Wylde Roger left for the sunnier climes of his home county, Yorkshire, and joined Barnsley. A home win over Ipswich brought us our only other points before the end of the year to leave us closer to the top of Division Two than Division One, but, despite this lack of league form, there was still an air of optimism on the terraces. Why? Well, for the first time since the competition was just a bairn, we were doing well in the League Cup. Back in September, we'd watched Wylde Roger (aarrrr) knock in both goals past Palace, Cummins and all, who thought that they'd done the business with an away goal and a second leg at their place. Turner and the defence did their job, won a goalless draw – maybe this was what Stan saw that brought back the memories - and it was Forest away at the end of October, where Hodgy scored to bring Cloughy's lot back to Roker. I celebrated by doing something stressful, and moved house, a mile or so away from the town centre, for the extra bedroom – like you do. I'd barely got settled in when the replay came around, and it was into the Fulwell with the Bittermen, and one of those special Roker nights unfolded. It's a shame that whenever people talk about great nights at the old ground this one is often forgotten, but it was one of the best.

Cold, damp, and, as it tends to be in November, dark, there might have been 10,000 empty spaces, but the 23,000 who were there took a collective deep breath, smiled at one another, and unleashed the Roker Roar into the night. OK, so the chant of the day might have been the bloody irritating "earwig-oh", but it was relatively new at the time, TallPaul loved it, and the Fulwell rocked as one as we belted it out. No goals at full time, then Howard Hamstring Gayle set away down the right wing towards the Roker, wearing, as he did, the shortest shorts in the history of the game. Would he end his run in the Alan Brown position – at the back of the terraces? Not this time, as, rather than cross, he cut inside and, from fully 25 yards, hit a screamer off the outside of his left foot, and the split second it took to swerve and dip into the net seemed to stretch to ten. As the net twitched and the keeper landed, the ground erupted – that was a goal worthy of winning any game – as we celebrated one of Roker's finest moments. A home tie with Spurs ended 0-0, and the Londoners could have been forgiven for thinking that they'd done the hard bit. They'd obviously not been watching Turner, who kept out almost everything they could throw at us, including a Graham Roberts penalty, and Chis popped up to deflect a goal in off his shoulder (Sunderland's record scorer of goals with the most different body parts?). Walker also scored, and 2-1 was good enough to keep us in the competition – through to the quarter-finals, no less – in to the New Year.

As our winter grew more miserable, in the world at large the crisis of African starvation prompted Bob Geldof and Midge Ure to come up with the Band Aid single as a fund-raising effort. Straight in to number one, but the down side was that ever-charitable Prime Minister Thatcher wouldn't promise to forego the half-million pound VAT bill. Nice lady.

Spurs had their small revenge in 1984's last game, beating us 2-0, then we began the year at Gallowgate, which is never a good idea. The game became immortalised in song not because of Westy running away from goal then half turning and whacking it virtually over his shoulder and into the net, but because of the fact that we'll be ever ready to avenge the 1-3 defeat. The form carried over into the FA Cup, when we went to The Dell and laid down meekly in the face of four goals from the Saints.

Just the league and the League Cup, then.

Makes a nice change – or it would have done if the league hadn't been such a rotten place for Sunderland. Liverpool at home took place on a frozen pitch, was memorable for two things. Firstly that it should never have been started, as players tappy-lappied about for the entire time they were on the field, and secondly for Len's bizarre notion that we should take all goal-kicks short and try and play the ball out of defence. Against Liverpool, on a frozen pitch, both of which facts pointed to the option of hoofing it over the opposition defence and seeing what happened. So the ref took pity on the fans and called it off.

Len went shopping again and brought in Ian Wallace, once a million pound buy for Forest, from Brest (stop it) for £50,000, in the hope that he'd score the goals that would push us up the league. He also brought in our first Nigerian (well, London of a Nigerian parent) when Reuben Agboola (also our first Reuben) arrived from Southampton to keep it tight at the back. After a couple of substitute appearances, Paul Lemon got his full debut, but nothing seemed to work for the Lads. By the end of March, we'd only won one and drawn two before the game at Norwich, which we won 3-1. Significant for the win, it was also significant for the fact that it was a warm-up for the following week's game.

What game could that be? The League Cup quarter-final had been at Vicarage road, on a pitch with more ash than grass, and Turner was up to his old tricks again. 1-0 thank to Clive Walker at the other end, we had a semi-final to worry about – against Chelsea, over two legs. At Roker, the hapless Jason Gavin made our job easier by giving away a penalty in each half. Westy put the first away nicely, then had to rely on netting the rebound for the second in front of a joyous Fulwell, to give us a two-goal cushion for the trip to the Bridge. Talk was not so much of the football that would be played, but how the travelling supporters would get home in one piece. If hooliganism was a general football malaise in the seventies, then it was a Chelsea speciality in the eighties.

They'd already had our seats out of the Posh Stand at Roker, and seemed to exercise their perceived God-given right to violence every week. The word was that they'd stop Sunderland winning if their team couldn't, and they almost managed. Clive Walker ignored his history and scored twice against his old mates, but the defining moment, not for its importance to the result, which was virtually decided in our favour anyway, but for its bizarre image it provided. With Chelsea's delightful fans charging across the pitch towards the visitors, the mounted police trotted onto the field of play. Westy collected the ball, rounded one of the horses, and calmly scored our third goal.

Sunderland 3, Chelsea 2, Shed End nil, and the small matter of a trip to Wembley. I duly arranged floor space at Big Harrier's place in West Ealing – he lived alone and had only one spare bed. John got that, I got the mattress on the floor in the front room, but not until we'd travelled down on the day before the match (Saturday, and there were people there who'd wrongly assumed the match was to be played that day, including two Norwich fans playing chess on the platform at Kings Cross), and met up with Harrier at Richmond Rugby club, where he turned out for London Scottish fourth team, or something like that. Several jugs of beer later, it was a fitful night's sleep then into town to meet the TallPaul and Reg, who'd done the sensible thing and taken the wives down for the weekend, with a West End show thrown in.

We feasted on Jelly Babies and peanuts (all we had to eat that day, come to think of it), and hit Wembley. If they'd done anything by way of decoration or maintenance since our visit in '73, it didn't show. The place was a mess, with the urine from the overflowing toilets streaming down the stairs and dripping off the landings only adding to the general air of decay. Our view from the back of the terraces was so bad that we had to duck to see the crossbar at the far end. As for the game, we started in lively fashion with Hodgson and Walker firing over early on, but it was all downhill from there.

Another crack appeared in the selection-making part of Len's brain, as Westy, semi-final hero and the man in goal scoring form in the cup at least, didn't even make the bench as Ian Wallace was preferred. If Wallace had reproduced the form of his Forest days, then fair enough – the man was a good finisher – but the truth was that he spectacularly hadn't, having managed just the one in the win at Norwich the week before. Maybe that's what Len was impressed by, but he barely had a kick, and Westy was a forlorn, unwanted figure beside the bench.

Without the suspended captain Elliott, Venison, at nineteen, became a Wembley final's youngest ever captain, and we failed to click into gear. The first penalty missed at Wembley, and Corner, Elliott's inexperienced replacement, at eighteen and with only four games under his belt, slipped up, and the ball went in off Chisholm's chest (again, but in the wrong end). The sight of Gary Rowell, injured, carrying the cup around the ground, was too much to bear for most Sunderland fans, and perhaps the only positive thing to come out of the day was the fact that the opposing fans chose to be nice to each other instead of following Chelsea's example.

There's supposedly a special bond between the two sets of supporters still, but this perception is probably down to the fact that we don't actually hate each other, and Tom Cowie had business interests in the vicinity of both clubs. Sunderland cars, Norwich tractors, naturally. So, we contrived to contribute to one of the worst finals Wembley had seen (and yes, there have been several worse since then), and I was surprised to learn, on the homeward train, that Steve Berry had actually played. I couldn't remember him being there. What if Elliott hadn't been suspended? What if, what if... what if the miners' strike had ended sooner, instead of running for a year, give or take? It might have ended, but, unlike the League Cup, there were no winners.

The miners certainly didn't come out on top, as the Tories had ensured that, during the dispute, the foundations of the mining industry in Britain were well and truly, well, undermined, paving the way for the collapse of that and the majority of heavy industry. Things change, things move on, but they should not be forced to simply because a particular government, or worse still, a particular politician doesn't feel like taking responsibility for them. Government by abdication of responsibility, in other words. The government certainly didn't come out on top, however much they might have thought that they did. Their actions, and perhaps more importantly, their attitude of almost mediaeval snobbery, ensured that they'd never have the trust of large parts of the electorate again. Not that large parts of the electorate had ever trusted them in the first place, but attitude counts for an awful lot.

Back in the escapist world of football, away from some of the nastiness of politics and industrial strife, Westy showed his displeasure by demanding a transfer, and Watford, obviously remembering his efforts in the quarter-final, nipped in. The fact that big Colin scored more goals in the rest of that season than the whole of the Sunderland side speaks volumes. Back into league action, and John Moore from Consett was chosen as Westy's replacement on the bench, but Chelsea were in no mood to let another Durham boy cut them down to size and beat us 2-0 at Roker. He started the next game, as Liverpool came back to finish what they'd threatened to do on the ice-rink a couple of months earlier, and we repeated our ploy of playing the ball to feet from goal-kicks. Result? 3-0 to The Reds. Ian Wallace had the temerity to score after a few minutes against team of the moment Everton, but they replied in frightening fashion with four goals of their own that were forever replayed on Match of the Day.

At least we managed a draw against the Mags, then won at Coventry, where Moore marked his last start with the winner. That was it as far as wins went that season, as we managed only three more goals and one more point. Gordon Armstrong, later to make a name for himself as a midfielder, made his debut as a centre-half in the defeat by West Brom. John Cornforth, later to make a name for himself as a sort of classy midfielder, made his debut in the last game, at home to Ipswich, at right back, but despite Wallace netting his third of the season via a shot that went into the turf a-foot from his boot and looped over the visiting keeper and into the Roker End net, we were a team of dead men from the kick off. As we watched our side eke out the last few minutes of their First Division stay, the fans eighty miles away at Bradford were celebrating their side's promotion to the division we were heading for.

As we made our way out of the Fulwell, we began to hear assorted radio reports about something going horribly wrong at Valley Parade. No-one knows why the fire started, but if you looked under any wooden stand in the country, you'd find a pile of assorted flammable material. You'd also find the chiefly wooden stands populated with folks happily puffing away on their tabs before hoying the still-smouldering ends anywhere convenient. Forty-odd people burnt, or were trampled to death in the panic that ensued that afternoon. You can't fail to be affected when this sort of thing happens, especially when it's not that far away, and at a club which is of a size that means that everybody knows everybody, and at a ground where you've stood with your mates watching a game. It was a bad enough tragedy in its own right, borne out of lack of attention to safety and the "It'll never happen to us" attitude towards smoking, cleanliness, and general safety, but still not a lot happened to make football a more user-friendly experience – it was still very much a this is it, take it or leave it situation.

For us, it was no consolation that it was the first time that both finalists in a major domestic cup competition were relegated, more of a resigned acceptance. In truth, Len was lucky to last until the end of the season. Great player, no argument. Manager of any sorts with us, I don't think so.

Hark now hear the Sunderland sing
The Magpies ran away
And we will fight for evermore
Because of New Year's Day

1985-1986

Only two weeks after the Bradford tragedy and the end of the season, I'd accepted an invitation from Stubber to do some paid work as a photographer – pay coming in the form of free travel and accommodation – on holiday sites on the French Riviera. On our first night there, we headed to a bar with a TV to watch the European Cup Final, Liverpool against Juventus. The TV was a small black and white job, and the picture quality was awful, meaning that it was a long time before we could work out that what we were watching was not a game of football, but a lot of fans dying on the crumbling terraces of the Heysel Stadium in Brussels.

By the end of the evening, we'd decided that English football was kaput, and by the end of the week, spent pretending to be German and watching the Italians kicking seven bells out of any English coaches they spotted across the border, we were unsure whether we could carry on watching the so-called beautiful game. The reaction of the governing bodies was not to make grounds safer, or to handle fans in a cleverer way, but to ban all English clubs from European competition for several years. This probably affected the quality of European football as much as it did English football, as no-one could question the achievements that league winners Everton might have produced, but it never once took into consideration the weekly goings-on in Holland and other parts of the continent.

Even today, the Italians get away with behaviour inside football stadia that would see the average Briton locked up for several years. We're no angels, but we've all been tarred with the same brush as the minority of right-wing bigots that people notice and that roam free to attend matches on mainland Europe. An awful time for football, but it would get worse.

After the Band Aid/Live Aid concert had pricked our collective conscience into contributing vast sums of money to charities, many of us looked on the world as a whole as a much more accessible thing. Celebrities began to refer to themselves as citizens of the world and championing various global charities. Judith, Gaz, and I chose to express our concern by taking our holiday in the gloomiest flat Whitby had the misfortune to contain. Rumours that Dracula had refused to stay there because it was too dingy have not been proven, but at least it was time away from the euphoria that was surrounding Sunderland.

The close season got off to a fairly predictable start, when, after only a couple of weeks, Len was on his bike, and the usual round of speculation over the managerial replacement was in full swing. Tom Cowie had made it clear who he wanted, and at the beginning of July Lawrie McMenemy became the new boss. Possibly the biggest managerial name we'd had to date, his arrival sparked scenes of joy amongst the fans, with many turning up to welcome him to Roker. One fan's greeting of "Gan on, Lawrie, the world's ya lobsta," may have sounded amusing at the time, but turned out to be eerily prophetic. From Whitby we awaited news of any new signings. Predictably, Chris Turner's heroics of the ill-fated League Cup (sorry, Milk Cup) campaign ensured a move to Old Trafford, where their keeper, Gary Bailey, was prone to extracting descriptions such as "headless chicken" from Stuart Hall, and the fact that Turner was so sparsely used by the Manchester club showed that Ron Atkinson could be a poor judge of talent. Little Stan had obviously had enough of his native climate, and buggered off back the USA, where he spent the next decade, applying for the managerial post at Sunderland every time it went on offer. Just the two players out, but in came Frank Gray, Dave Swindlehurst, and Eric Gates, who had two things in common – firstly, we'd heard of them, and secondly, they were all thirty, or almost thirty.

We all remembered how Big Lawrie had managed Southampton to FA Cup victory from Division Two (whoever gave them that idea?), and some of us even remembered that he was the last manager to take Bishop to the Northern League title. How could he fail to bring success? Well, watching the first five league games might have given us a clue. By the end of that month, we'd failed to score, and failed to pick up a point. Turner's replacement, the first of several that season, had been described as "Six feet tall and with hands like shovels". Personally,

I'd describe Seamus McDonagh as six hands tall and with hands like feet, but, thankfully, he was only here on loan, and after seven games and fourteen goals (against) he was replaced by another loaner, Bob Bolder. As the second string at Liverpool, he too should have performed a bit better than he did, but, with only Shrinking Seamus to improve on, he looked relatively good, and we turned the loan into a permanent move after a month in which we managed to win a game – just the one, mind. McMenemy's plan soon became apparent as in came Alan Kennedy, the Sunderland boy who'd scored two winning goals in European Cup finals for Liverpool, and then George Burley, who had won the Cup Winners' Cup with Ipswich. The roles of Alan Ball, Dave Watson, and a whole host of senior professionals at Southampton became clear - Lawrie might have picked the team, but they did the team-talks. As one of these experienced signings said to me years later about the manager – "Nice bloke, knew eff-all about football."

As a belated birthday present for me, Gates and Swindlehurst shared three goals against Coventry, but we also let in three, then Frankie Gray scored at his old home to earn a draw against Leeds. The next week we went one better, and Nicky Pick scored both as we won at Shrewsbury. Sorted, we're away at last, and we can gain momentum against Swindon in the League Cup. (Look, you'll have to forgive me if I constantly refer to this competition by its original name, but I just can't keep up with its many and varied manifestations, so you'll have to bear with me). Again, we scored three, but actually won. However, the two we let in sunk us as we lost 3-1 at the County Ground in the second leg.

There had also been the small matter (and I do mean small) of the Full Members' Cup, the purpose of which I admit to forgetting – if indeed there ever was one. It started with a 3-2 defeat at Grimsby (yes, Grimsby), wobbled through a 2-1 home leg win, and ended in a penalty shoot-out of such poor quality that only Durham boys Kennedy, Gates, and Paul Atkinson were called on to take a shot. The same three hit the target after a 0-0 at Maine Road, but this shoot-out went the wrong way, and that was the end of that glamour competition as far as we were concerned.

Wins over Huddersfield, Boro, and Carlisle, then consecutive victories over Fulham and Wimbledon (our ever first encounter with the Dons) gained us points, but the defeats that dominated the first half of the season were killing us. I stayed at home for the visit of Norwich, which predictably ended in defeat, as Judith was expecting our second child at any moment. Had we been winning games, I'd probably have been the bloke in the Fulwell who was the subject of the weekly tannoy announcement "Could Jonty Smith please go home, as his wife is about to give birth." As it turned out, Ian arrived a day late, just as I had got myself comfortable in front of the snooker on the hospital telly, but it was an excuse a lot of lads would have paid good money for. Another child-seat into the back of the Volvo (Volvo, eh? Real family car), and further advertisement of my skills as South Church's Numero Uno exponent of that particular skill. I fitted about six in our street alone, at very reasonable rates.

By the time we got to Christmas, Peter Daniel had gone to Lincoln, Chis to Hibs, and Clive Walker, who'd never really got over his Wembley penalty miss, to QPR. It's a shame MacMenemy couldn't have worked some man-management magic there, as Clive went on to become one of the few people to score one hundred goals in both the professional and amateur games, and his undoubted ability would have been very useful.

The chance for progress in the FA Cup was there with a home tie against Newport County, and a crisp shot from Burley and a tap-in from Corner saw us up against Man Utd – just what we needed. With ourselves resigned to a heavy defeat (yes, things were that bad), the Lads produced one of the performances of that sorry season, and held out for a replay with a goalless draw in front of 35,000. Alas, we'd used up all of our cup charm in the first game, and let in three without reply at Old Trafford.

Just the miserable old league, then.

If ever there was a season in which we needed to concentrate on the league, this was it. Even in January, you could see Division Three waving hello over the horizon, and offering bargain trips to Brentford and Doncaster as incentives. We steeled ourselves for the inevitable relegation dogfight, as we usually did around this time of year, but we would have been arming ourselves with metaphorical knuckledusters had we realised just how bad things would get. The loss of Gary Bennett to injury didn't help, but, despite this, we had experienced international defenders Gray, Kennedy, and Burley to fill the void. Allegedly. On paper, we should have had no trouble, but the problem was obviously that the idiot in charge couldn't transfer the ability on paper to performances on grass. A defeat at Bradford on New Year's Day was bad, but their neighbours Leeds fell at Roker to a Nicky Pick hat-trick to give us a glimmer of hope – one which dimmed the following week when Millwall went away with the points. A hat-trick from a midfielder was obviously not in McMenemy's rulebook, so Nick was sold to Coventry. A few months later, I bumped into him while in Coventry with work, and asked him how he was enjoying life at Highfield Road. "Brilliant compared to back there," was his reply, and his FA Cup Winner's medal a year later was some compensation for being thought unsuitable to wear the red and white.

Two 2-2 draws, the second of which, against Carlisle, provided a couple of moments of sublime quality as Alan Kennedy fired in a brace of long-range efforts which would have graced any footballing stage, were simply not enough at this juncture. The following 0-2 defeat by Huddersfield saw the appearance of Andy "Officer" Dibble, on loan from Luton, in goal, with Bob "three fingers" Bolder having gone the other way on loan, never to return thanks to a summer move to Charlton. The fact that he managed five thoroughly reasonable years at the Valley is perhaps… no, definitely… proof of our manager's inability to get even the average out of better than average players.

Agboola had taken over from Corner as Benno's deputy, but his lack of height precipitated the arrival of a big centre half. While most of our recent signings had been old professionals with high level experience, Steve Hetzke had seen all of his action in the lower two divisions of football until Sunderland came along. Perhaps he was just what we needed as an antidote to the players who the manager allowed to believe that, just because they'd been successful in the past, they would be successful in the future. Maybe the manager had been listening to Billy Ocean, and decided that when the going gets tough, the tough needed to get going. Steve certainly stopped opponents, but that was as far as his game went, and he wasn't the one who was going to provide the Benno-like surges upfield, and certainly not the killer pass out of defence. His debut marked Bolder's revenge, as we lost at Charlton, but then he showed his defensive qualities by restricting our next three opponents, Hull, Bradford, and Grimsby, to a single goal apiece, and we also managed a goal a game. At Bradford, Cameron Duncan produced a penalty save in his only league game between the sticks to establish an unequalled 100% Sunderland record against spot-kicks. I suppose three draws is stemming the tide a bit, but it was turning that it needed. In an effort to do this, the manager brought on old pal, Tony Ford, on loan from Grimsby to add something extra to midfield. Steady, hard-working, and deservedly popular, Tony couldn't provide the spark we needed, but managed to run up more league appearances by the end of his playing career, if indeed it has ended yet, than just about any outfield player in the British game.

Instead of the football being the subject of the newspaper stories, it was the Batey/Cowie in-fighting that they wanted to write about – trust the journalists to take the easy option, as there was precious little to excite the reader in stories of our on-field activities. In points returns, we got nothing from Tony's debut at Sheffield United, where yet another big local lad, this time Dale White, was tried at centreforward, but with two from Proctor, beat Fulham 4-2 at Roker, then brought a point back from Norwich. Here we go? Why not likely, man. Losing by three clear goals at Wimbledon is bad enough, but when the points were needed as badly as they were, it was bad news indeed. An OG inspired win over Barnsley was followed by another capitulation in front of a small crowd, in a season when only four of the twenty-one away games attracted over 10,000, this time at Brighton. While George Michael was singing in a different corner, we were trying to get one onto someone's head, but failing. That left us two games in which to save ourselves from the jaws of Division Three, both of them at home, and maximum points needed. The Shrews were about as bad as us, and had been getting crowds small enough to fit in their famous ball-retrieving coracle – just the sort of side we could be relied upon to be beaten by. Never ones to follow convention, we won, then had to face Stoke, several places better than us in mid-table, and therefore another likely loss.

Thankfully, Gray and Proctor, with his third goal in as many games, did the business and we celebrated as if we'd won something very big and shiny. The truth was that we'd been closer to the Third Division than at any other time in the club's history, and we didn't like it one little bit. The wild scenes that followed the final whistle represented the release of so much nervous tension that you could just about taste it in the air. Officer Dibble was completely caught up in the emotion, and threw his gloves, shirt, socks, shinpads, and boots into the heaving crowd. It's not surprising that he expressed more than a little embarrassment when interviewed by the press afterwards. It just shows how much emotion a game of football, or a season of underachievement ending in a face and status-saving victory, can mean to a set of fans, and how easily that emotion can be transferred to a player – even one who is merely there on loan. On paper, fifteen goals against in only twelve appearance is hardly the stuff of legends, but we know that paper isn't always what we perform on, and the Roker crowd still remember Dibble for a brave resistance that was ultimately successful. On the other hand, I can still remember being part of a crowd that shouted the manager's name, and insisted that he join the team in a lap of honour – just showing how the joy of the moment can blind you to the blindingly obvious. The manager simply hadn't managed the bevy of talented big names and talented local lads that he had at his disposal.

My old man
Said follow Sunderland
And don't dilly-dally on the way
Off went the bus with the boot boys on it
We took Boro in half a minute
We dillied, we dallied, effed them in the alleys
La la la la la la la la la
If you haven't got a bonnet
With Sunderland written on it
You can't find your way home

1986-1987

While the board spat at each other, some little swine broke into the house and nicked some jewellery, £1.50 in loose change, and left everything else of value, portable or otherwise, just proving that your average opportunist thief is as thick as a docker's sandwich. We decided that enough was enough, and that we'd move back to town, so the house went up for sale. My summer holiday moved to Berwick, which is as close to Scotland as you can get without getting a thistle up your shorts. Davey the family Mag had bought a caravan there, so we took advantage of cheap rent and took our buckets and spades north for a fortnight, dreaming of big summer signings, the thinning out of dead wood, and a team being built around the nucleus of undoubted talent that we had. It didn't quite work out that way. Shaun Elliott had over three hundred appearances behind him in over nine years, he was the same age as me, I'd watched his career blossom alongside Arnott and Rowell, and he was an obvious choice as team captain, around whom the side could be built. At twenty-nine, he was at his prime, so we flogged him off to Norwich. Andy Dibble, unsurprisingly, headed off home to Luton, and Wallace, thankfully, went to Maritimo in Portugal (no, I'd never heard of them either).

Barry Venison was, despite his 200 appearances for us, still young, had the on-field presence to captain the team when necessary, and could impose himself on the game. So we sold him to Liverpool, albeit for a lot of money. Perhaps it was the fact that he'd got married on an island in the Indian Ocean wearing a pink leather suit, an idea Cec Irwin had toyed with but rejected on the advice of his couturier, Len Ashurst. Joint winner of footballer's haircut of the year with Venison, Dave Hodgson also had the misfortune to be relatively fit, skilful, and local, so he had to go as well – also to Norwich. They must have been laughing – not only had we given them the League Cup, but we were giving them the good bits of our team as well. Fair enough, Hodgy hadn't had the best of seasons, but any fool could see what his strengths were, but that wasn't the fool we had in charge. Howard Gayle followed the Yankee dollar to the US league, then we decided to bring in some players. Iain Hesford's dad had been a keeper, so he was as well, and he came on loan from Sheff Wed. Dave Buchanan had scored for Leicester on Gary Linker's debut, but arrived from Blyth Spartans, and it was hoped he'd repeat Alan Shoulder's success at moving from the Northern League and turning pro – but with a nice club.

So, hardly the stuff that hope is built on, and, on paper at least (there we go again…) we had a weaker squad than last season – and that squad hadn't set the world alight – but we'd better get on with it, I suppose. Tom Cowie had made way for Bob Murray to take over as chairman, and the scene was set for some changes, or so we thought. With the personal resolution to attend more away games than the previous season, when, because of two ankle-biters gnawing away at my wallet, a quick walk to Kingsway with one on my shoulders and one in the pushchair was a more feasible financial option than Wimbledon away – and Bishop were actually a good side at the time – I braced myself for the coming campaign. At least the start wasn't that tough, and we took the chance in style with a win at Huddersfield. A 1-1 draw with Brighton at home was a bit of a wake-up call, but not as loud as the one that followed. York City had beaten us 4-2 at Roker, with Cammy Duncan in goal, and he kept his place (or rather, Hesford was given a lie-down) in the second leg. We won that one 3-1, but it doesn't take Stephen Hawking to work out the away goal advantage there. Gone by September 3rd.

Continuing in alarm-clock mode, Swindlehurst might have scored one, but we let in six at Blackburn in a horror show that would have had Stephen King diving behind the couch. Alan Kennedy returned the next week, allowing Frank Gray to move upfield and score the winner against Hull, but despite this and the decent draw, thanks to Corner's goal, at Ipswich, there was still a sense of numbness that remained from the Blackburn game. Along came the pesky Full Members' Cup, and a thriller of sorts (that is, if you could be bothered to get interested in the competition) at home to Barnsley. Almost 7,000 did, and saw a draw followed by an 8-7 penalty shoot-out win that included Nigel Saddington's solitary strike for his home-town club. We'd signed big Nige from Roker FC seven months before, after his less than happy spell at Doncaster, but he only managed a handful of games before joining Carlisle a couple of years later. Being a Sunderland fan, a handful probably meant an awful lot more to him than fifty to some of the big names we were saddled with.

Steve Doyle arrived from Huddersfield, courtesy of a generous Terriers boss Mick Buxton (now where have I heard that name?) as a holding midfielder, who could never be faulted for effort or for commitment, but whose statistic of winning promotion from Division Three with three different clubs (hope I'm not giving anything away there) sums him up. Sunderland at that time was the right stage to make the most of his ability, but the results got no better. Bue-Bue-Buchanan got his first goal in the loss at Derby, then hit another four as we began to believe that he could be the answer up front. A series of iffy results culminated in a 0-3 defeat by West Brom at home, a couple of days after the Full Members' Cup (remember that one? Thought not.) campaign ended for us at Valley Parade with a 2-3 defeat. Christmas arrived with only a couple of draws and a solitary win (3-0 revenge over Blackburn) after this, and included the arrival of yet another loan keeper, Bobby Mimms. Why men in the number one shirt chose to subject themselves to the torture that must surely be a loan spell at Sunderland I'll never know, but is perhaps further proof that all goalies are radged.

What I, and all Sunderland supporters wanted for Christmas was a decent run of wins, with the odd draw thrown in, just to keep it fair, like. Not what we got. Despite scoring at Wimbledon, they managed two, and the usual phrase at this stage of a chapter rolls out again – just the league, then. The next six games were split evenly between wins and defeats, which would have been fair enough, but the players then decided that losing four off the belt was a better idea if they wanted to keep the fans on their toes. Terry Curran had been brought in during November to add some experience to the side, but no-one knew which part of the side he was supposed to bring the experience to, least of all the manager. Ostensibly a winger (probably because he had good ball skills, long hair, and a bit of an attitude), he wandered about to little effect until he managed a goal in our joint best result of the season – 3-0 against Brighton.

After only nine games, he was dumped into the reserves, took offence at some criticism from the crowd, and flashed the Vs in the general direction of the voice in question. Taxi and P45 for Curran, please. With Swindelhurst barely bothering to trouble the scorekeeper, Keith Bertschin came in from Stoke with over a hundred goals in his personal kit-bag. He only managed to produce two, despite looking the part in terms of effort and willingness, and things were looking bleak. Murray did his best day's work and handed McMenemy his P45 amid rumours of a six-figure payoff, and Big Lawrie buggered off back to Hampshire. Well in the mire, the club looked for a magician, and settled on Bob Stokoe – did he have another metaphorical white rabbit in his hat? If anyone could raise the level of contribution from the players, surely it was Bob with his spirit of 73?

While things were bad for us, the Herald of Free Enterprise showed us that things should be taken in perspective. Two hundred people drowned when the ferry rolled over and sank on its way back from Zeebrugge. Someone had left the doors open, apparently. The Prime Minister responded by visiting Moscow, buying some bread and pilchards, and getting shirty when asked by a British journalist if this was electioneering. Well, what do you expect from someone who employed a minister whose response to the AIDS threat was "Good Christians won't get AIDS." Neither would they later admit to sleeping with the party leader to sell their tawdry little book several years later.

It wasn't exactly mission impossible for a team to get the number of points we required to guarantee safety for the games we had left, but we are Sunderland, yes we are Sunderland. Bearing in mind the quality of football we had been turning out that season, Bob managed to conjure up a draw at home to Leeds, then a victory at Shrewsbury, and we danced around Gay Meadow, like you do, positive that he'd pull a white rabbit from his trilby, a bouquet of roses from his shirt pocket, and keep us safe. We celebrated around Shrewsbury that night as if we'd won the cup. Mark Proctor scored twice against Bradford for the second time in a matter of weeks – but, for the second time in a matter of weeks, they beat us 3-2. We were scoring a reasonable number of goals, but the clean sheet at Shrewsbury was the first in eleven games, and that was why we stayed a whisker away from safety. The next clean sheet came at home to Palace, and Gordon Armstrong's goal got the points. He repeated the trick at Millwall the next week, and that draw meant that all we had to do to stay out of the clarts was to beat Barnsley at home on the last day of the normal season.

Normal for us, unfortunately, meant scoring two and letting in three against a team from Yorkshire beginning with the letter B. Oh, and a missed penalty from Proctor. So that was it then – play-offs for us, as was the rule in those enlightened times, against the team just below the automatic promotion places in Division Three. As the Number One of the time said, "Nothing's gonna stop us now", so we took Bob's box of magic trips down south. Off we went to Gillingham for the first time in our history – it's such a crap place that even when we played them in a replay in 1906, we were allowed to have it at Roker – certain that Bob's magic wand was about to make an appearance. Proctor looked like being our saviour with another brace, but a certain Mr Cascarino joined the ranks of Sunderland anti-heroes, as many big centre-forwards did, with a hat-trick, and Mr Hesford had a nightmare of McDonaghian proportions. Maybe it was because it was on a Thursday, when football was never played, and we could not be expected to adjust to that. Still, we had away goals, which counted double, so we only needed to score once and that was it.

Roker was packed. It was nervous. There was more riding on this game than any other in our history – winning cups and leagues is one thing, but dropping down further than we'd ever been before just didn't bear thinking about. The nervousness was not that born of excitement, as at Wembley 73 and subsequent promotion parties, but that born of genuine fear of failure – catastrophic failure. It was one of those games that resembled a grandfather clock permanently stuck at midnight – it just kept going ding-doing, and we were either scared of the next day arriving, or we were desperate for it to do just that. They scored early to spoil things, then Gatesy put us ahead on aggregate. Then Proctor did it again – not the two goals, but the penalty miss – followed by Hesford's trip, penalty save, and some defending straight from Carry on Sunday Morning Football that allowed the ball to stay in our area long enough (it seemed like five minutes) for the save to count for nothing as the ball ended up in the Roker End net. Cascarino again. Just as it looked to be all over in their favour, Benno added further to his already legendary status by nodding over the keeper. The Fulwell exploded with relief – two minutes on the clock, and it was 5-5, away goal level, and extra time.

We'd done enough with this to raise our on-field spirits, surely, high enough to take the game. Yeah, but Gillingham's were just as high, and Cascarino scored again. Bertschin gave us brief hope, but the whistle came too soon, and it was the end of the blackest day in the club's history. I'd known relegation from an early age, I'd witnessed it first hand with deep sadness and resignation, and I'd shed tears of joy at our FA Cup triumph – but this was the first time I'd shed tears of sadness at a football match. I wasn't the only grown man with watering eyes either, not by a long chalk. I was older than more than half of our team, and the club had been part of my life for longer than it had for any of them. I was absolutely devastated, and, as we wandered away from the ground, I, like many others, just didn't know which way to look, or what to do. A big hole opening up in the street would have been a nice touch, if the council could have managed it. I didn't even want to go out and drink away my sorrows while contemplating the whys and wherefores of the season. What if Proctor had remembered how to take penalties? What if the defence had remembered how to clear a ball? What if we'd got rid of McMenemy earlier? What if Hesford had kept his occasional fluff in his belly-button where such things belong? What if Nick Pickering had been still a red and white, instead of collecting an FA Cup Winner's medal the day before?

Still, above all of this misery came the song that used to signal misery – defiance in the face of adversity – and I hated it for that.

We love you Sunderland, we do
We love you Sunderland, we do
We love you Sunderland, we do
Oh, Sunderland we love you

1987-1988

Another summer in Davey's caravan at Berwick, the house still unsold, another election win for Thatcher's Tories, and the country responded in a rather surprising way, with Oxford University refusing to give her an honorary degree – for the second time. Nice one, I thought – Oxford blue doesn't necessarily mean Tory blue. Relatively quiet on the home front, but not, as you might have expected, at dear old Roker Park. Senior professionals (old players to you and me) Hetzke (to Chester), Swindlehurst (to Cyprus), and Kennedy (to Husquvana in Sweden, Hartlepool, and all points possible before retiring aged 42) left as new manager Denis Smith brought his right hand man Viv Busby from York and proclaimed that he'd give his pay back if we didn't get promoted. Sounded like my kind of bloke, but did he really know what he was taking on? Could he really rescue something from the wreckage of the team that was left, almost as broken in spirit as the fans? Many of us had seen him play for Stoke, and could remember what a tough nut he was, and he'd done a decent enough job managing York, but would he stand up to scrutiny on Wearside? He brought John McPhail from Bristol City, and a former employee at York to partner Benno, John Kay, from Chester-le-Street via Arsenal, Wimbledon, and Boro, to show fullbacks the world over the meaning of the word hard, and Mickey Heathcote from Spennymoor, to show that the local leagues could provide talent.

A new innovation that year was the second substitute, obviously a result of frantic negotiations between the Football League and Frankie Gray, so that the latter could be somewhere near the pitch all season and keep in the manager's field of consideration for the odd game. Cammy Duncan had moved to Motherwell, and was never seen again until he turned up at our hotel in Blackpool the night before a game at Everton – in 2001 –still with fond memories of Sunderland.

The season got off to the expected start, as Keith Bertschin had the dubious honour of scoring our first ever goal in Division Three as we won at Brentford, but then we only managed a draw at home to Bristol Rovers, as they obviously saw us as the team to beat - like a few others that season. A new face to the first team was eighteen- year-old local lad Gary Owers, who had obviously impressed the new boss – he hardly missed a game all season, and could run forever. Kay and McPhail were straight into the side, with Benno and Agboola making up the defence. Owers got his first goal at Doncaster, then McPhail got two against Mansfield. Two goals? From a defender? He hadn't read his contract carefully enough. After three wins and three draws, keeper Steve Hardwick, on loan (do they never learn) and a bit of a surprise starter that season, allegedly ran out of Roker following the Bury game, jumped into a taxi, and was never seen again. And we'd offered him a permanent contract. This proves yet again that goalies are mad – especially ones who've played for the Mags.

As the removal of ourselves from that wretched division was our number one priority, we let Boro think that we were going to knock them out of the League Cup by winning at home, then letting me suffer the horrors of the Ayresome paddock (it was cheaper, OK?) and Boro scoring twice. Bye-bye to that competition.

Hesford was back for the defeat at Brighton (why do we bother going there?), and Smith brought in another old (young) boy from York. Most of us recognising his name – Gabbiadini had been fairly noticeable in the results pages the previous season, but he did no more than look very keen on his debut as we lost at home to Chester. Doncaster – Brentford – Gillingham – Chester – no disrespect to these clubs, but they were a new and unpleasant experience for most fans under the age of eighty. Then Marco scored twice as we won at Fulham, and I very nearly put the car in the ditch when the second went in, and celebrated my survival with a half and a big smile in the Thinford Inn. He decided that scoring goals for us was nice, and stuck in a couple more in each of the next two games. In the first of these he played alongside Gatesy for the first time, and the bond was immediate and effective, as his little marra scored two as well against Wigan. We saw this, and we decided that it was good.

A convenient works trip to Blackpool (it helps when you run the Sports and Social Club) coincided with our game there, and our Gary's first competitive away game. I told him he couldn't wear his plastic police helmet, as four-year-olds would get noticed in that sort of get-up. When we eventually squeezed into the shambles that had once been Bloomfield Road, he let me know what he thought of my parental discretion by pulling my ears for ninety minutes as he sat on my shoulders – he'd seen the usual collection of Flintstones, Pink Panthers, and Gorillas that accompany all trips from the North East to Blackpool at that time of year. He also got the best view of John McPhail scoring twice as Owers ran the right wing ragged and we thought "Smithy's money's safe."

Two more wins and then we had the unnecessary delight of a trip to Scarborough (Scarborough?) in the Preliminary (why preliminary? Did first not sound glamorous enough for the sponsors?) Full Members Cup, which had become Freight Rover Trophy – presumably because the Full Members wouldn't cough up the sponsorship. We cheekily played a few fringe players, and John Moore duly helped us to a 3-0 win. The league defeat at Notts County proved to be a temporary blip of the type that all championship-bound teams suffered in the days before Arsenal and Chelsea stopped that kind of nonsense. Southend, poor Southend, came up, Gatesy scored four of our seven, and we had begun to look as if we really meant business. Dickie Ord made his debut at only seventeen, and, with so little centre-half type work to do, decided to try and be Pele. John McPhail was tearing his hair out at times as Dickie surged upfield, or dribbled out of the box, but, if you're going to do that on your debut, it might as well be against Southend, 1987 vintage.

The weather that autumn was in direct contrast to our league form – miserable, wet, and windy. My out-of-town living experience got decidedly worse one evening, when the Gaunless broke its banks, and our house was the only one on our side of the street that didn't have water flowing through it. The sandbags from the council yard burst, the council tenants and the private owners good-naturedly (for the most part) argued over who had the stronger claim to those that might actually stop the floods, and the water began to lap at my doorstep. I managed to get the new three-piece upstairs, and the kids (who though it was a great laugh), before Judith got back from work and had to plodge through two feet of water to get to the front door. That was it – we'd take the first offer that came along. The best thing was, someone, obviously bereft of weather-sense, bought it before the streets were even dry. Thirteen years later, and the whole thing flooded again – twice. To get the sale completed, we'd moved in with Ma and Pa, which was fun, but the rooms were much appreciated. The media was referring to our regular front two as the G-men or the G-force, and, as is often the case with partnerships like this, the younger, less cultured partner added a couple of years to the career of his older, wiser mate.

A couple of draws preceded the Freight Rover visit of Rotherham, and we turned on the style again. Unlikely scorers Burley and Corner, as well as Moore, helped us rack up our second seven-goal haul in November, and Wembley beckoned (sorry, but you have to try and glamorise the poxy competition somehow. I can't even remember if the final was actually played at Wembley). A couple more wins, then Rotherham came back to Roker. Only a few weeks after we'd put in seven, we knocked in another four, with three from Gatesy, as their manager Norman Hunter wondered whether they'd been cursed. By the end of the season, their keeper had let in fifteen goals against us. You could only laugh, just like anyone would if it happened to us. John McPhail, a centre-half, already had eleven league goals by the end of the year (he didn't bother in any of our eight cup games that season for some reason. Must have had a bet on), ahead of Gabbiadini with nine and level with Gates, so goalscoring was not a problem.

FA Cup fun began with our first-ever competitive match with Darlington, and we fairly cruised past them with two goals from Paul Atkinson, but the problem was that this was just the first round, courtesy of us being so bad last season. And it was still only December when we nipped down to Scunthorpe for the second round. And they beat us. So next time you're in a pub quiz and somebody asks what every club but Sunderland did in 1988, you can tell them from me that it was play in the FA Cup, as our next match wasn't until January 1989, then tell them to shut up. We were concentrating on the league, OK?

On the day Barry Siddall came back to Roker with Port Vale, I was moving house. With the furniture scattered around Auckland, in a stable in Escomb, a loft in the town, and Sportsman landlord Tommy Nevin's spare house, I'd fully expected to be chasing around in Cammy's works lorry until midnight. As it turned out, the pair of us were buying Tommy Nevin a thank-you pint at half-two, but I didn't have the energy to zip through for our 2-1 win. Shame, but at least I was moved back into the town – fifty yards from where I'd started off my home-owning adventure.

As a Christmas present, Smithy bought us Tim Carter, but the lad had to wait four months to get a game thanks to Hesford's consistency. As a New Year's present, Lemon gave us two goals as we did the double over Donny (caster, not Osmond), which, let's face it, and without any disrespect to Doncaster, we bloody well ought to have. Steve Doyle's New Year's resolution, to score more goals, came true at Bury, and he duly ended the campaign level with OG on one. Obviously tired of his defensive partner hogging the limelight, and winning the traditional defenders' bet on which would score the most goals, Benno scored two in two games – his only two of the season. I guess he lost his bet. Gordon Armstrong had become Denis Smith's "First name on the team sheet" and was having a mint season. He also introduced a soon-to-be-famous kick-off ploy. Gates to Gabbiadini, or vice-versa, then hoof the ball out to Stretch on the left, where he'd invariably win the header and set us on our way.

Plenty of wins, then the odd draw, but we were coasting, really. Perhaps coasting too much when Bristol Rovers hosted us. Perhaps Tim Carter had inadvertently passed on a little too much information on his new team-mates. Perhaps it was our old Achilles' heel of a long trip and a winter's night, or perhaps it was just messing around with the formation, which rarely does Sunderland any good. Whatever the reason, we lost 4-0, then followed that with another defeat – at Northampton. Cobblers – is it all going to end in tears? We'd been following the Lads long enough to know not to take a comfy league position for granted, but surely even we could not bugger this season up. Not now. A win over Fulham looked to have done the trick, but then a home draw against Blackpool had us clutching the proverbial worry-beads again. Another draw at Wigan, the occasion of the famous mud-slides, and also of letting the opposition score twice. Yet another home draw, this time against Notts County, was not what we needed, so Smithy went out and brought in a couple of players.

Wingers/midfielders Colin Pascoe, on loan from Swansea, and Dougie Maguire, on loan from Celtic, came into the squad for the manager's return to York. Despite our recent stutters, we were still the division's top dogs, and the red and white army hit Eboracum with a vengeance. I'd even managed to arrive in town the night before, thanks to Judith's Mam having the bairns for the weekend, and prepared in style, which was probably a bad idea as I was due to run the York half-marathon on the Sunday. York obviously hadn't read the script. Armstrong had a goal disallowed, York scored twice, Maguire was awful, and Pascoe took his place from the bench and scored. Thankfully, we shook ourselves out of our malaise, and won the next two, including another pasting of Southend during which their player-manager substituted himself and was subsequently relieved of his managerial duties.

Tim Carter's first appearance was against his old rivals Bristol City, and, echoes of '75 –'76, they did their best to spoil the party by winning 1-0. Four games left to get promotion sorted, so we went to Mansfield and scored four, leaving us needing to win at Port Vale to go up. John and I dragged Pop out of Bishop for his annual taste of red and white life (he's often said that he wished that he'd chosen us over West Ham, but he's stuck to his guns for longer than most people have been following any team, so fair do's to him). No prematch pint in Burslem, or wherever Port Vale is, thanks to the home fans only policy in many pubs, but the away end was buzzing as the home side Valiantly (pun intended) kept us at bay. Would the winner ever come? Oh yes it would. Right wing corner, right in front of us, Gatesy right on the spot to force it in at the near post. Great joy and happiness. Sod off division three (lower-case intended) as the crowd cascaded down terraces and bottles of champagne mysteriously appeared amongst us. The team and manager celebrated with us, we celebrated with them, we honked our car horn all the way out of the miserable little league and up to Whaley Bridge, near Manchester, for our planned evening of celebration.

Mission accomplished – thank the Lord – and still a couple of games to go. The championship was duly clinched, as McPhail missed a penalty but still managed to score. Most of his spot-kicks were the result of Gates hitting the deck, and I asked Eric years later if he'd ever deliberately gone to ground (even I'm too polite to say dived to a Sunderland player). "Never," he replied, "but if I put myself in a place where the defender is daft enough to kick me, then that's his problem." Fair enough – I wish I'd thought of it. The last game of the season was at Rotherham (ha –poor buggers, I bet they were really looking forward to that one) and we duly stuck four past them (I think it was compulsory by then) to end the campaign in style. Fittingly, Per-er-er-er-er-erfect, was Fairground Attraction's number one, and we couldn't have agreed more. Despite a few sticky moments, once we'd found our feet, we'd never really looked back.

Here's hoping we never have to again.

Willie McFaul went into town, in a white Marina
He bought a clown for half a crown
And called him Mirandinha

Denis Smith went into town, in his Lamborghini
He bought a kid for a couple of quid
And called him Gabbiadini

1988-1989

On the recommendation of Big Kev of the Bittermen, we headed for the Mull of Galloway for our holidays, planning a fortnight of sun and fun on the beach with the kids. It hossed it down, it blew a gale, and the locals swore more than any other group of people I'd ever come into contact with. The only advantage was that you could see the black clouds coming towards you and knew when the rain was going to start. After a week, we gave up and sat on the sand in our raincoats and let the bairns get on with it – "it" being the digging of holes and throwing handfuls at each other. After another two days, we gave up altogether and headed for Davey's caravan and the positively tropical environs of Berwick, with a promise never to head north for the purposes of holidays again.

Back in Division Two, and we had to decide whether it was to be a season of consolidation, or one in which we went for promotion and endured the very real risk of stretching ourselves too far. "The only way is up," went the song, so we went for it. Tommy Lynch arrived from Limerick, and that was it until September when Tony Cullen was pinched from Newcastle reserves. No, I wouldn't call it exactly going for it either, as what was in essence last year's squad started the season, and it was hardly surprising that we didn't win a game until October. After a couple of weeks, Smith decided that we needed more beef up front, and brought in Billy Whitehurst from Hull. Subtlety was never part of Billy's game, as he played with the enthusiasm of Gabbiadini and the strength of an ox, and he soon found himself as Marco's new partner.

The League Cup had taken us to York (ticket for my birthday, thank you pet), and we managed a 0-0 draw despite McPhail forgetting the rules and pushing half of his team-mates out of the way to head his own penalty rebound into the net. Still, the pubs were now open until eleven six nights a week, and I easily made the Newton Cap for a sort-of celebratory pint. Pascoe and Marco shared the four goals in the second leg, then we let our true class show with a 0-3 defeat at home to West Ham. Marco got a goal at the Boleyn and Gary Ogilvie, brought from Dundee reserves in March, made the first of his three leaps from the bench as they made it 7-1 on aggregate. We were still a long way from the First Division on this showing.

Benno had taken a knock in the first West Ham game, and this gave Ord a run in the side, alongside Frankie Gray, who was in for John Kay. Tommy Lynch got a start (if you could call it that) and quickly earned himself the nickname "Tiddly-aye Tommy," in honour of his laid-back Irish attitude. If the man had been any more relaxed, he'd have been asleep. Benno managed a string of games at right-back, and, defeat at Walsall apart, we had a decent enough run into the winter, with one of the highlights being my unexpected attendance of the match at Oxford – they wanted me to go to London on a training course, Oxford was on the way, and we won 4-2. The downside of the day was passing the wreckage of the car in which several Sunderland fans died on their way down the A1(M). This decent run came to a bit of a halt after three consecutive 1-1 draws, the last of which included Steve Doyle's finest moment – a 30 yard strike that went in off the Roker End crossbar – with a 3-0 defeat at Brighton (yes, another failing after a long journey), then a loss at Leicester after a home draw with Watford.

As the last shipyard on the Wear closed, we shipped out Big Bad Billy to Hull, along with Hesford, who'd acquired his own anti-fan club (being, as he was, the scapegoat of the day, despite being a goalkeeper and therefore a dead easy target), bringing highly-rated keeper Tony Norman up to Wearside. Tim Carter played in the 4-1 win at Plymouth (a Sunderland win after the longest journey in English football? Never), then the home win over Barnsley. He'd also been part of the side in our Simod Cup campaign (could have been that year's version of the Full Members Cup/Freight Rover Trophy, but I'm not sure), but that only went as far as a win at Charlton in front of 1,666 people and a defeat at Blackburn in front of 4,457. I don't think the competition had quite caught the imagination of the paying public, and I can't say I was sorry to be out of it.

Tony Norman came in against Portsmouth at Roker, and kept it nice and clean as we scored four. Perhaps this was as much to do with the abandonment of the sweeper system as anything else, but the change had made the difference. Three days later, it was off to Bradford, where we were bullied, bundled, and generally battered to such an extent that we could have been forgiven for thinking that we'd turned up at the rugby ground by mistake. Still, Bradford got the win they were fighting (literally) for, and we had to watch Mick Kennedy, sent off for kicking seven bells out of Gatesy in the draw at Roker, repeat his performance but remain card-less thanks to a timely substitution. He did get fined £5,000 for writing in the Sun that he collected scalps, but the paper probably paid that for him… and their goal never crossed the line either.

Respite from the league came with an FA Cup draw, 1-1 at home to Oxford, followed by an FA Cup defeat, 2-0 at Oxford, so it was back to the league.

Against Oxford, for the third time in a week, and we managed a 1- 0 win, then repeated the job at Bournemouth, so perhaps we were back on an even keel. Down at Leeds, in the posh seats with our ties on courtesy of Cammy's company season tickets, and my first experience of just how nasty people can be even when they're in the supposed refined area of the ground. As they poked and prodded (thanks to Joe's mate – the one with the Leeds accent but the red and white heart – being unable to prevent himself from screaming "Come on Pascoe") we succumbed 2-0,and it all started to go breast-skyward for a while. Losing by three at home to Walsall was awful, as Lynch ambled around the midfield smiling nicely at the opposition and the defence crumbled, but it got worse. In our now familiar annual acquisition of a bit of experience, in came ex-England man, the much travelled and undoubtedly fantastically skilful Peter Barnes. He'll do for me, I thought – he's been around, he's got the medals – but the man made Rip Van Winkle look dynamic in his sorry, solitary appearance in the 4-1 defeat at Swindon. I don't think he even bothered to get on the team coach back north.

Back in our little cocooned world of football, Hesford came back with Hull, let in two, but, in front of the Fulwell, deliberately (in my mind at least) followed through in a challenge on Marco, and did the lad's knee. Gabbiadini didn't miss any games, but I reckon it was this injury that never quite cleared up, plagued his time at Palace, and eventually caused his retirement. That's my theory, and I'm sticking to it. Anyway, we won that one 2-0, and the game will probably be better remembered for the appearance of the German sub (ho-ho, fancy calling him the U-boat) Thomas Hauser, the next pretender to Gatesy's place up front, who soon developed a knack for coming off the bench like a man possessed, and winding up the crowd.

March 1989 also saw the appearance of A Love Supreme, a funny little photo-copied fanzine – as all fanzines were in those days, but at least you could read it. A couple of years after Sunderland's first fanzine, Wise Men Say, had first ap-peared, along came a new kid on the block, joining the ever-expanding ranks of publications produced by the fans for the fans. After years of either match day programmes, which were and always will be, of necessity, biased towards the clubs, or schoolboy favourites like Shoot! (their exclamation mark, not mine), fans had an unbiased platform from which to express their opinion, and these fanzines were growing in stature, influence, and quality as time went on. I won-der how long this one will last?

A draw at Blackburn, then four defeats in a row meant that mid-table obscurity was our best target for the season. Smithy tried the bring in the experienced professional trick to help us out, and his old mate Dave Hay came back from partial retirement, did his knee and only managed half of the game against Ip-swich. Not to worry, Marco scored a hat-trick, but spoiled it a bit by thumping a defender after scoring the third, the impetuous youth. A loss at Barnsley, a draw at home to Brum, then only 8,000 turned up for Brian Atkinson's debut against Plymouth to see the poor lad have a goal disallowed. This was a real disappoint-ment to Skinner, who, as a distant relative, had installed himself as Brian's (or Musky, as we were informed he was known back in Aycliffe) Mr ten per cent agent and promptly lost loads of bets on the lad scoring on his debut. Paul Wil-liams also got his debut that day, coming on for Atky, and we managed a win to keep us firmly in the middle of the pack. Two more debutants took their bows at Portsmouth, but this was Sean Wharton's only game for us, and the start of War-ren Hawke's Sunderland career. I won't mention his nickname, suffice it to say that it was nothing to do with his playing abilities, but rhymed with white.

Hauser eventually worked out what he was on the field to do, and scored in con-secutive games as we drew three and won three to end the season slap-bang in the middle – which we'd all have accepted the preceding August. What wasn't acceptable, on the day that Hauser got his first goal, was what happened at Hill-sborough. Stubber had taken the freebie FA Cup semi-final ticket in preference to the game at Oldham, and watched as the events of the day unfolded. Most Sunderland fans of my generation had been in the Leppings Lane End at Sheff Wed, with its nasty, dark, pokey tunnel, and the place had been made gradually less user-friendly over the years with the installation of copious amounts of fenc-ing and wire.

When somebody gave the instruction to open one of the gates, football changed forever. Ninety-four people died, in circumstances that we've all been frighteningly involved in. A big crush behind you, a big wire fence in front of you – nowhere to go. The difference that day was only one of scale – it could have happened to me a dozen times over the preceding years (York the previous season, for instance) had circumstances altered just one tiny bit. Ironically, two weeks later, fourteen Liverpool fans were locked away for their part in the Heysel tragedy four years earlier. Four years? No wonder change for the better safety of football fans was so slow in arriving.

The last few weeks of the various campaigns across the country were played out with an undercurrent of helplessness amongst the fans – the Liverpool supporters had been merely doing what they did of a Saturday, watching their team play, when so many of them died just because the authorities couldn't give a toss about them as long as they were inside the ground of their choice and off the streets. For they and their, read we and our, as we've all been there, done that, and been lucky enough to come out alive – which we'd never considered, and which is ridiculous. Football is a spectator sport, for enjoying – not one during the watching of which we should be fearful for our very survival. We've all come back from the odd game thankful that we've escaped a thumping, but we should never have to think "Ooh, I'm glad I'm still alive" when we get back on the bus after the match. Crossing the road is risky, but standing on the terraces at the match should not be.

Not the way sport should be.

Ole Ole Ole Ole
Marco
Marco

1989-1990

Following our experiences with the wind and the rain and the swearing north of the border, we'd decided to head south for the holidays – Weymouth had been just the business on our honeymoon, so that was the name on the map. Our break started earlier than usual, for a reason that I can't remember, so it was the Friday night of Arsenal's last minute championship win at Anfield that we set off – but not until the game had finished. 2-0 Arsenal, into the car, 350 miles down the road. All of this is very nice for the three passengers, who slept all of the way, but a bit of a chew on for the driver. Arriving at 7:30 in the morning, and the flat being unavailable until noon, I wanted to go to sleep. The other three woke up and wanted to go onto the beach. So we went onto the beach, they dug holes in the sand, and I fell asleep.

Britain had celebrated ten years of Thatcher, Poland saw 99 of the one hundred parliamentary seats go to Solidarity (which begs the question who the hell won the other one?) and the Chinese government dealt with student unrest in their own particularly nasty way – when the students protesting over their government's restrictions on personal freedom marched into Tiananmen Square, the army first shot at them then drove tanks over them. Perhaps they should have told them that they were on a final warning when they'd marched into the square two years earlier. There's socialism for you – it doesn't take much to tip it into fascism when certain people have been used to power for too long. In

London, as the season started, the Marchioness party boat sank into the Thames after colliding with a dredger, and took fifty one party-goers with it.

Back with the jollities of football, and Paul Bracewell had recovered from two years of ankle problems (coincidentally begun with a tackle by Billy Whitehurst when the big fella was a Mag) to resign for us, and Paul Hardyman came up from Portsmouth as cover for the left side of defence and midfield. Steve Doyle, after over a hundred games, left for Hull and Hesford. Not a lot of new faces, but then there hadn't been that much wrong with last season's faces and the initial results bore out this maintenance of most of the status quo. A win at Swindon, with the Gates and Gabbiadini partnership reinstated and Agboola filling in for Kaysie at the back. Tony Norman only managed four games before getting injured, so Carter got his best run in the side as we lost only once before defeat at Leeds in October. Marco managed a penalty-free hat-trick of the highest quality against Watford, then we passed up the chance to beat the Mags in a stalemate at Roker.

Wearing a suit and tie to Elland Road was becoming the norm, as Cammy once again came up with the freebies, but the inhabitants of the posh stand were as unpleasant as ever. Armstrong tried in vain to match Vinnie Jones by getting the early clatter in, then nearly pulling Gordon's Strachan's head off, but we couldn't get a grip of the game. Marco went off, Ricardo came on – the younger Gabbiadini's only game for us. If that was unpleasant, the five we let in at West Ham the week after were downright obscene. Thankfully, the horrors were dispelled with three wins off the belt, and included a goal at his first club Stoke from Bracewell – another of those away moments when you happen to be taking the kids out for the day and put the car in the grass when the shot hits the back of the net. (Newbiggin in Teesdale, and our Gaz fell in the river shortly afterwards.) The following week's defeat at Oldham was our last of the year, and things were panning out quite nicely – if not automatic promotion form, then the play-offs looked a certainty.

Over in Funny-Cup land, we'd done something unexpected and set off on another League Cup run. After the compulsory two legs against Fulham which saw a 3-0 win away, we obviously presumed that all rounds of the competition were to be over two games, and drew at home to Bournemouth, then won the away leg, and drew at Exeter. This game will probably be better remembered for certain players, namely Armstrong, Kay, and Williams, ending up in trouble with the law after some cars were damaged during a sprint down the street following an altercation. Details have always remained a bit sketchy, and I've never felt brave enough to ask Kaysie what really happened. Actually, it was pretty tame stuff by today's standards, as nobody ended up in hospital or went to the press with a lurid tale of debauchery. Anyway, we won the replay 5-1, which was nice, and went into the New Year with memories of 1985 stirring in the back of our minds. Along came Coventry, something of a sizeable club in those days, in an established mid-table sort of way. Benno's big brother Dave had scored the first goal in their 1987 FA Cup Final win, and he was no doubt up for the game despite a niggling kneeinjury that had seen him in and out of the side. It was one of those special Roker nights in terms of atmosphere (red hot), temperature (icy cold, and damp), and competitiveness (blood red).

David Speedie was well known as a bit of a workie-ticket, as we say in these parts and had obviously done his homework on Benno's dodgy joint. He'd already gone for it a couple of times when he finally connected, just in front of the Clock Stand, near the halfway line, and our man's reaction is part of Roker folklore. The proximity of the incident to the usual camera in the paddock made for some interesting viewing as Benno grabbed his assailant by the throat and the two of them teetered over the terracing. For Speedie's sake, it was a good job that Cyrille Regis managed to pull our man off, as they were amongst the fans, and there were a number of, shall I say, irrationally emotional characters waiting for a chance to stick one on the Coventry man. It's fair to say they'd have made a good fist of tearing him limb from limb, and big Cyrille probably saved the club a hefty fine. Rumours of Benno waiting in the tunnel for his little pal while he ran them their early bath, then confronting him, have never been confirmed – or, more interestingly, denied. It turned out to be the high (or low) point of the night, as the nastiness continued, we couldn't turn our superiority on the night into goals, and a draw took us to Highfield Road, albeit in confident mood. We shouldn't have bothered, as we concentrated too much on kicking lumps out of Speedie (or in the case of Gary Owers, giving him the elbow right in front of the ref – another early outing for the club loofah), and Steve Livingstone, whose dad once played for the Boro, scored three of Coventry's five, and that was the end of that.

Over in even Funnier Cup land, the Simod Cup had become the Zenith Data Systems Trophy, and the 7,000-odd who turned up to watch us take on Port Vale had obviously been really taken with this new, snappier moniker. I know I had. Well, the team must have been properly dazzled by it, and promptly lost 2-1.

Back in Real Business League-Land, Tony Norman had made his comeback in December (although Carter kept his place for the League Cup games), and we managed eight games unbeaten up to the turn of the year. Out in the real world, big changes were afoot. Communism was taking a bit of a battering, and the Romanians executed the man they'd ousted from office – on Christmas Day they shot Ceausescu and showed his body to the world's TV cameras. How civilised. The Czechs welcomed back Dubcek as the Politburo resigned. The Bulgarians agreed to abolish the monopoly of the Communist Party, and the Germans opened the Brandenburg Gate. It wasn't quite the end of the road, but things were moving forward in terms of democracy.

Understandably upset by our upturn in form, the powers that be decided that they'd ruin our New Year's Eve celebrations by bringing forward the kick off at Hull to something silly like 11:30. Waking up on your mate's doorstep clutching the remains of a bottle of Bell's, because you were so nervous of sleeping in that you went straight there from the party, hardly made for the best start to the day. The A19 was a convoy of sleepy drivers (bless them for their abstinence the night before) and bleary-eyed passengers, and there were many who sat on the crumbling terraces of Boothferry Park out of necessity rather than choice. The game was lost 3-2, but Hull's keeper, the familiar Iain Hesford, later admitted what the travelling fans had seen from their vantage point at the side of the pitch – that Benno's shot had been a good yard over the line when said keeper clawed it out. Injustice to the fore again, and that was the topic of conversation on the way home – at least it was until Pete suggested a stop-off in Goole "To see what it's like". If you've been you'll know, if you haven't been, don't bother.

Imagine the Anfield part of Liverpool with less bus stops, more rain, and more broken windows. The piano player stopped when we entered the Smelters Arms, or whatever grim industrial past was commemorated in the name of the pub of our choice, and we were instantly the focal point of the afternoon, due to our insistence on talking to each other. In comparison, the locals stared individu-ally into their pints, smoked Woodbines, and generally looked like an advert for the Samaritans. Which is probably what we looked like after the defeat at Elm Park the following Saturday as our FA Cup dreams died an early death yet again. January was a pretty tough month, actually, as we capitulated at Coventry in the other cup, lost 3-0 at Ayresome Park and managed a draw at West Brom with Tim Carter back in goal. Norman returned for the final game of the month, and helped us to a draw at Gallowgate, which is always nice. I genuinely fancied us to stop the rot at Blackburn, so I drove to Bradford to pick up Stubber, only to find that he'd accepted another freebie and gone to some Division One game. There's nothing quite as sad as driving to and from an away game alone, and this was no exception, apart from the Volvo constantly overheating, resulting in my calling into a pub in Gooseye (yes, it does exist – near Keighley) and asking for a half of beer for me and a pint of water for the car. We lost to the only goal, it was the last game at which I saw proper sized Wagon Wheels, and Lenny Johnrose stood on John McPhail's throat. Oh, and the exhaust fell off on the way home – does twice in ten years constitute a recurring theme? Probably not.

Over in the real world, the Russians showed that they weren't quite ready to behave themselves as their army took over in Azerbaijan, and their president, Gorbachev, tried to convince the Baltic States that breaking with mother Russia would be a bad idea. Despite this, the mood had spread, and South Africa ended restrictions on antiapartheid organisations, and released Nelson Mandela after twentyseven years of imprisonment – for being a black man with an opinion. Life's interesting, but isn't football more fun?

With the Kay/Hardyman partnership re-established, we started to play with a bit more confidence in the back four, and Hauser helped us to a draw at Watford. He then went a bit mad, and scored both goals in the win over Brighton as we encouraged Atky to watch Bracewell and learn – there'd always be a need for that sort of player, and Brace wouldn't last forever. Tommy Lynch went to Shrewsbury on loan for a snooze, turned out to be a decent turn there, and played well over two hundred games for them. It just shows how one team's laid-back Irishman can become a real star at another club. Whether this is down to something in the water, coaching methods, or the team around a man, I don't know, but it just demonstrated that a relatively poor time at one club doesn't mean that a man can't have a good time at another.

Our long-distance malaise struck again as we collapsed at Plymouth, before we steadied the ship (again) with a draw against Leicester. Win one, lose one, then along came West Ham, and the tale of the two Bradys. Liam had been everywhere, won everything, and had more T-shirts than a Bishop Auckland market stall. Kieron had made his debut in the preceding November, and had nothing to his name other than a fifty-yard goal straight from the kick-off of a youth game at Bradford. It was only his third start, but you could see that he had something special as he warmed up with all manner of jugglery-pokery, including hoofing the ball a mile into the air and catching it cleanly on his ankle. It was a game that should really be shown to anyone cynical about football, as it shows just how entertaining the game can be. As Old Brady looked on, the young pretender teased and tormented the West Ham defence. He set up goals; he won a penalty, and then scored an overhead kick as we won 4-3. West Ham made a real game of it by refusing to capitulate and repeatedly coming back into things, but it was Kieron's finest hour. The big shame was that there weren't that many hours in his career, but this one started a four-match winning streak which also included Mick Heathcote's best run in the side.

Brady did the business at Bradford the next week, after Smithy had commented that "The lad needs to remember he can't walk around the whole defence and score every week." Kieron duly waltzed past the whole Bradford midfield and defence (well, it looked like he did, and I'll always remember it that way) and slotted the ball home for the only goal, right in front of the Sunderland fans – one of those goals that generates a slightly higher level of celebration, mainly because, from the moment he picked up the ball on the half way line, we knew that he was both capable and likely to do what he did, and we had time to warm up.

After the Stoke victory, I went home for tea, got the last bus to Darlington, then the midnight coach to London, ran the marathon, had a few pints, and got the coach back to Bishop. It was cheaper if you went down and back in the same day, see. The winning streak ended after we'd discovered the Old Post Office near Barnsley and noted that it was the place where Barnsley's womenfolk were taken by Barnsley's womanising folk while their husbands were at the match. A bald guy called Agnew ran the show and scored the winner for them. "Buy him!" we cried (actually, we'd be saying that for the next few years as he dodged around Blackburn and Leicester), but we stuck with the squad we had and lost at home to Hull. Marco got the only goal at Oxford, then Armstrong got both in the draw with Portsmouth before Hardyman did a bit of a Hinnigan and scored in successive wins, at Wolves and Port Vale in what was probably Thomas Hauser's best game for us. He came off the bench and absolutely terrorised the opposing defence – why couldn't he have done that more often? Just as well that these points had put us safely in the play-offs, albeit in sixth place, as Oldham came and completed the double over us. Season over, job just about done.

The campaign had turned out OK in end, although there were arguments at home about the best way to moan about the way the poll tax had been introduced. I was all for non-payment, while Judith favoured the calmer approach of writing to MPs. Strange then, that a few years later a genuine mistake on her part lead to a big argument with my company's payroll department over a mysterious court order removing money from my pay-packet. At least I can now claim to have been a genuine poll tax protestor.

Guess who finished third in Division Two? Correct – the Mags. They came to Roker for the semi-final first leg intent on avoiding defeat, as you do, and I could only get a ticket for the Roker End, which put me painfully close to the Great Unwashed. They look on their faces when Owers tackled one of their lads with his head had to be seen to be believed, but they achieved exactly what they came for. It was almost so different, as in the last minute we won a penalty at the Fulwell – a long way from the Roker End, but I still had a decent view of Hardyman's penalty, Burridge's save, and Hardyman's follow-up. Unfortunately, the follow-up almost put Burridge's head into the back of the net, and off went Hardyman.

Consequently, Agboola moved to left back from his "sort of sweeper/ extra defender" role, and Warren Hawke came into the midfield for the second leg. The Mags clearly thought they simply had to turn up to get to the final, but we had other ideas, as we out-fought them right from the off. As is the case with all derby games, the most important thing is not to be beaten – so all we had to do was score once, and we would have been able to concede one and still triumph. Fingernails were chewed down to the wick long before kickoff, but the moment that relieved the pressure wasn't that long in coming. Owers helped on a cross from the right, and Gatesy nipped in ahead of Burridge to poke the ball in. Eruption. Joy. Tumbling down the terraces. Ugly blokes kissing ugly blokes. Laughter. Tears of happiness. Still ahead at the break, chiefly thanks to a great save from Norman, we took to chewing what was left of our fingernails, mainly because we couldn't bring ourselves to eat anything that came from the pie shop in a black and white bag, but we needn't have been nervous.

The game shifted from one end to the other, which suited us fine, as it left gaps for us to charge into, and then the inevitable happened. Hawke was involved as the usual one-two between Gatesy and Marco was executed, and the Italian one produced a typical finish, low across the keeper and inside the far post. Eruption. Joy. Tumbling down the terraces. Ugly blokes kissing ugly blokes. Laughter. Tears of happiness! All along the Wear, men ran out into the streets and jumped into the air. Job done – well not quite. In time-honoured fashion, the sensible folk of Tyneside decided that the game would be awarded to their team if they invaded the pitch. The teams went off, the police stopped the brainy army, and George Courtney told Gary Bennett that the game would be finished "If we have to stay here 'til midnight." Eventually, play resumed, play ended, I assume the Bigg Market phone box took a pasting, and we were off to play Swindon at Wembley. Swindon – we'd won at their place on day one of the season, their manager was an ex Mag, we were sorted for glory.

Picked up from the Newton Cap and onto the Willington bus (I'll travel with anyone, me), we were in that London at sunrise, which is a bit unnecessary but fun. I gave the Lamb a bit of a session, then watched in disbelief as we miserably failed to perform. Swindon looked like Brazil by comparison, and it was on the heroics of Benno and Tony Norman's finest hour that kept us in it for so long. Typically, as on our last visit, it was a cruel deflection that did for us, as Benno's attempted block ballooned up and over Norman. Thankfully, we'd only had a few days to wallow in self-pity when it was announced that Swindon were a bunch of cheats who'd been found guilty of the heinous footballing crime of failing to hide their illegal payments well enough. As the Mags claimed that they should get Swindon's place because of their third-place finish, it seemed obvious to me that, as we'd been the team defeated in the final, we should get Swindon's place. For once, the powers that be agreed with me (and, to be fair, 99.99% of Sunderland fans the world over) and we were up. Ha. If you're going to go up in such hilarious fashion, it's made quadruply - it's a new word, you won't find it in the dictionary, so don't bother looking – hilarious when you do so at the expense of your nearest and dearest rivals. Take that, Mr Magpie, stick it in your pipe and smoke it. Perhaps leaving an empty champagne bottle on Finny the Mag's doorstep over the road was a bit childish, but it had to be done.

When you're sad and feeling blue
The Fulwell End will sing for you
We'll sing a song that's oh, so grand
A song of our team, Sunderland
Sunderland will never die
We'll keep the red flag flying high

1990-1991

Still gloating from our promotion, we took our holiday in Dorset again, in the same flat, and one crazy evening spent in the company of two Sunderland boys from Ferryhill (SAFC tattooed across the knuckles gave it away as I was signing in to the Working Men's Club) recounting tales of equally crazy trips to away games and mutual red and white friends. Pos and I had our first count the football shirts on holiday competition as the trend for wearing said items as a fashion accessory really took off. England went to Italia '90 World Cup finals with a genuine chance of winning, but, as with four years earlier and the hand of God nonsense, we weren't quite there. Argentine players dived all over the place, Gascoigne was the victim of some professionalism from the Germans, and the ref in the final eventually got sick to the back teeth of the Argentinean nonsense, sent two of them off, and handed the Germans the trophy with a penalty that never was. For once, the football world agreed with the ref – the South Americans had got exactly what they deserved. Grown men crying became socially acceptable, especially if they were sportsmen, and Nessun Dorma in particular and Opera in general became inextricably linked with the beautiful game. Gorbachev took over in Russia when Yeltsin resigned, and the red flag took on a pinker hue. As we were about to kick off the new campaign, Iraq invaded Kuwait, which really upset the Americans, as their control over the world oil market would be affected.

Eric Gates left for Carlisle, job well done at Sunderland, thank you very much. In came Kevin Ball, who we'd never heard of, from Portsmouth, and Peter Davenport, who we had heard of, from Boro. With Ball suspended in the first game, Smithy chose to reward his mate John McPhail with his only game in the top flight. Game over, down the road to Hartlepool, and up the defensive pecking order for Dickie Ord. Davenport was straight in for Gatesy, and our new attacking partnership worked instantly, scoring one apiece at Norwich. It was a shame about the three that the defence let in. With Hardyman suspended for his assault on Burridge, Agboola played the first five games at left back, and his opponent for the spot moved into midfield on his return. Spurs were our first opponents at home, and, with the World Cup still fresh in everyone's mind, Roker was over-run with Gazzettes, as John called the hordes of kids in Gazza T-shirts who turned up. 0-0 was decent enough against one of the teams of the day, then along came Man Utd, and another great Benno moment.

At 1-1 and the clock running down, he flicked the ball over Gary Pallister and curled a shot into the Roker End net to secure a famous win against the Gingham tablecloth-clad Mancs. Another 2-3 defeat away from home, this time against Chelsea, proved that we could score at the highest level, but had problems preventing the opposition from doing so. A couple of 2-2 draws kept up the goals for, and the appearance of Ord and Anthony Smith in the left back berth showed the manager's uncertainty about his best defence. When Liverpool came to town, so did a 31,000 crowd, and that was a problem for me. Back in 87, we'd decided that it would be a good idea for Mike to start bringing his son, Little Michael – crowds would be smaller, it would be a nice way for him to get started. So we moved from our usual spot in the Fulwell (a few rows down and just to the left of where we'd started out) over to the Clock Stand side, under the floodlight, so that the bairn could see. We were considerate like that, and it saved having him sitting on our shoulders for ninety minutes. As there were separate turnstiles for adults and juniors, I put nephew Mat into his queue and went in. By the time kick-off arrived, he was nowhere to be seen and it was apparent that the turnstiles were closed. No mobile phones in those days (other than ones that were too big to carry, anyway), so I had no way of finding out where he was. I was getting a bit panicky – how could I explain to my sister that I'd lost her eldest child? Then all of a sudden there he was, attached to a policeman. Said policeman had noticed the lad looking forlornly at the locked turnstile, taken him in through what passed for the police station in the Roker End of the Clock Stand, under the Clock Stand itself, and through little red door into the Fulwell, where Mat had pointed to the spot where we always stood. A big thank you to the officer involved, but it was a shame that the rest of the day didn't turn out as well. After that single-goal defeat by Liverpool, we tried Hauser, Davenport, and Marco up front at Villa – and lost 3-0 as we failed to score away from home for the first time that season. A win over Luton, defeat at Arsenal and then a couple of home draws followed as the goals began to dry up. With Hardyman back in defence, Pascoe came back into the side against Coventry, along with a rare appearance for Carter.

In the League/Littlewoods/Worthington/Rumbelows/Whatever Cup, we lost at home to Bristol City in the first leg, then went a bit silly in the second, scoring six, including Bally's first. Hauser also scored, but then did his ankle. His replacement, Tony Cullen, scored his only Sunderland goal as we progressed to a third round tie at Derby, where it all went pear-shaped as we let in six without reply.

By the end of the year, Thatcher had at last taken someone else's opinion into consideration when she resigned before her own party members assassinated her. If that wasn't reason enough for a party, I don't know what was. Who cares if the Grey Man, John Major, took over – any change was a change for the better. At Sunderland, our inability to keep clean sheets when scoring goals meant that the league position was not too healthy (nineteenth out of twenty is actually very unhealthy, but I try to be positive – it's a failing of mine), with the 3-3 draw at Spurs and the 2-3 defeat at QPR highlighting the problem. Over a year after his debut in the League Cup, David Rush made his first league start in the latter of these, filling in for Marco. He kept his place for the visit of Southampton on New Year's Day (who thinks up these fixtures?), when the Saints didn't travel well, and Bally's second successful penalty in as many games gave us the points. Next was a nice easy tie to start off our FA Cup campaign – away to Arsenal. We put up a decent fight, but lost out to the only goal, and Kaysie, against the team where it all began for him, was injured.

With Paul Williams, Brian Atkinson, Dickie Ord (at right back? Haway man Smithy, that'll never work), then Gary Owers (that's more like it, Denis – an attacking right back) filling in for Kaysie, we got properly stuffed at Old Trafford, where Williams had a torrid (as they say in the newspapers) time. Atky fared better as we beat Chelsea thanks to Pascoe's goal, but Ord wasn't so lucky as we lost at Everton. By coincidence, that was our second consecutive game against Everton, as, back in December, we'd scraped past Notts County thanks to goals from OG and John Cornforth earning a draw, and successful penalty shoot-out. One win and we were into the quarter-finals – as we started in round two, simple mathematics tells me that either there were only thirty two teams who bothered to enter the competition, or there was some sort of regional system going on. Anyway, only two games from the final, and it was off to Goodison, and a stinking 4-1 defeat. Operation Desert Storm kicked off in Iraq, who responded by firing missiles at Israel and Saudi Arabia. By the time the conflict was over, the Americans had shown their gung-ho capabilities once again, by killing more British soldiers that the opposition had. Nice one, President Bush.

Just the league, then, and we spent a fairly hefty (by our standards) fee on Brian Mooney from Preston and actually won on his debut against Forest. Was he the man to save us? Well, he played reasonably in the draws at Coventry (goal-less) and Derby (3-3 – keep them out, for Christ's sake, lads), then a defeat at home to Sheff Utd with Bally getting just a bit too competitive and ending up in the bath all by himself. Should I Stay or Should I Go sang the Clash, and there were a few of us thinking just that as this game died a death. Wise Men Say, the first Sunderland Fanzine, disappointingly stopped publishing after only seventeen issues (and yes, I did have a letter in WMS 17, moaning about injustice of some sort) and it was left to A Love Supreme to champion the cause of the common man in the world of football on Wearside.

Kaysie made his comeback at Anfield with Bally suspended, but couldn't prevent a narrow defeat and the sound of alarm bells ringing. Injuries to Marco and Pascoe made the defeat even worse. We were running out of games from which to gain the points we needed, and it was only Derby's absolute ineptitude that kept us off the bottom. Having said that, we only took one point from them, so that says a lot. It got worse when Villa came to town and took all of the points, but then a 20 watt light-bulb was turned on as young guns Rush and Brady scored the goals that beat Palace. Blind optimism kicked in, and Cammy's Elland Road freebies came out of the bag again, along with our shirts and ties. Heck, we should have known better. Only the top two, Arsenal and Liverpool, had scored more home goals than the 39 Leeds had, and only Chelsea and our fellow- strugglers Luton had let in more than we had. So 5-0 to dorty Leeds shouldn't have been a surprise, but it still stung a bit, and we were stuck one off the bottom. Defeats by QPR and Southampton, despite Bally coming back into the fray, left us wondering when we'd get a win. Armstrong's sending off at the Dell wasn't going to help things either.

Thankfully, Luton away was about as easy a game as we could have wished for, and Gorgeous Gordon came up with the only goal on the dreaded plastic pitch, and the double over the Hatters was complete. Wimbledon at Roker saw Hauser back in action after recovering from his Zenith Data Systems Cup injury, and he was right in the thick of it as the ref chose to ignore a blatant rugby-tackle on Armstrong in the box. Hauser was proving a nuisance (to the opposition for a change) in the air, but on the stroke of half-time, Wimbledon took exception to his challenge for a corner (if you can't take it boys, don't dish it out) and four of them jumped on him. Bally tried to separate them, and was sent off. None of the Wimbledon players were even booked, and Hauser was leapt on in similar fashion from the resultant corner – which he looked to have put over the line. Presumably because he was scared, the ref chose to blow for half-time rather than make a decision on whether it was a goal or not. All of this nonsense meant that we stayed one off the bottom and needed other teams to slip up in order for salvation to come our way, whatever we did ourselves. We couldn't have expected much from the visit of Arsenal, who were three points clear at the top. With Warren Hawke in as Armstrong's suspension kicked in, we put up a proper fight, not the sort that Wimbledon specialised in, and kept the Gunners at bay. Shame we couldn't manage a goal ourselves. So it was off to Maine Road for the big showdown.

We set off a day early, just so that we could build up for the game in style, and Pop the Etherley Hammer made his annual end-of-season pilgrimage to follow the team he should have supported all along. We stayed at John's new place in Middlewich, having drunk the town almost dry, and met up with Reg and Stu in a pub near a canal somewhere in Cheshire. I apologise for the lack of detail, but it was becoming apparent from the amount of red and white about that we weren't the only ones who'd made a weekend of it. By the time we got to Maine Road, it was equally apparent that this was going to be something exceptional. End of season games are always a bit special, as it's your last chance to follow the Lads for a few months, so you tend to make a bit of an effort, but this was something else. It's widely reckoned that around 15,000 made the journey to shout the Lads on, and the sight of so many Stanley Pirates, cartoon cowboys, Elvi – or whatever the plural of Elvis is – and assorted furry creatures made for a brilliant sight, and an atmosphere to die for. We went for it from the word go, but Owers miscued, Quinn pounced (he played for Man City then) and we were on the back foot.

The game was a microcosm of the season – every time we did something right, we did something wrong. We couldn't be faulted for effort, as every man on the field sweated blood that day for the cause. The game went ding, the game went dong – it was an advert for end-to-end football. Marco scored, then Kaysie, switched to left back, slung a cross in front of the visiting fans, and City old boy Benno headed in. Too little, too late. The whistle went, we were down. Again. The fans stayed behind in one of those memorable displays of loyalty that makes our fans so special – one of the reasons why our club has enjoyed such an exceptional bond between players and supporters. Really, we shouldn't have done it – eight wins in a season is simply not good enough, and there was many a damp cheek amongst the red and white army.

The journey home was predictably silent, even though I should have been used to relegation by then. We go up, we go back down – that's the way it works. Back in Bish, I chucked my bag in the house, got the bike out of the shed, and rode to the Toronto Lodge for beer. It's not a pub I've ever been a regular in, it was just that I didn't want to be with anybody I knew, but God knows I didn't want to be alone. You know the feeling – sometimes you're better off in the company of strangers when you've had a day like that, at the end of a season like that. Other times you want to get it out of your system by sitting with your mates and picking over the corpse of the campaign. Whatever you do has to suit your mood, and I was in no mood for analysis. Too many mistakes were made. Thirty-six goals weren't enough, especially when we let in fifty seven. It was probably at home where we passed up the most opportunities, as we only managed fifteen goals and let in sixteen. Hell, even Steve Bruce scored four more than Marco, so that tells a story in itself. We simply weren't good enough, and probably the only positive thing to come out of it was Player of the Year Kevin Ball – despite being sent off twice.

Ooh Bally Bally
Ooh Bally Bally

1991-1992

With the kids now big enough to manage it, we went on our first camping holiday for the Whit week, just me and them – Judith had gone off tents for some reason. Basically, it was a good excuse for us to plodge in streams, climb trees, and clamber about in caves all over the Yorkshire Dales. We still had our big holiday in Weymouth, just to top up our tans and collect sympathy from people who found out we were Sunderland fans. Eastern Europe was going mad, with the Russians trying to topple Gorbachev in a coup, countries we'd never heard of (but mostly ending in stan) began to claim independence from Moscow and the various parts of Yugoslavia were blowing bits off each other. Not a very pleasant time. Closer to home, the mining industry expelled another breath of life as Dawdon pit closed. Not much of a summer holiday there.

Back in the sensible world of sensible soccer, we had no money to spend because of the cost of reducing the capacity of Roker yet again. The Taylor Report was so necessary, in the wake of Hillsborough, but all it seemed to outline was to make crowds smaller until everybody could fit seats for all, or build a new ground with seats for all. That and keeping our lovely gold cards from last season. Easy, then. It was as obvious as the belly on a Mag that Roker Park was dying a slow death, and it couldn't really be developed into anything meaningful. Talk of a new ground was inevitable, and a few choices were bandied about.

There was even some use of the ground-share word, which was quite simply a non-starter. The location that seemed to be getting the most favour amongst the powers that be was the A19 option – nice space, handy for the main road, sure, but it wasn't (and still isn't) in Sunderland. To most fans, it was also a non-starter. Nissan didn't like the idea either, claiming that Saturday crowds would upset their transport system. With all of the cash being spent on new barriers and fire exits, we tweaked our squad by promoting Ian Sampson, bought from Goole (I knew there was something decent about the place) and having made one appearance last season, to the bench, and started off with virtually the same personnel. Surely they'd be good enough to get us straight back up.

While we might have stopped drinking in the Wolsey, we still parked there, just opposite, next to the garage. The clock in the Saltgrass was always five minutes fast (still is, actually), and used to have a sticker across the front with the pub's name on it. When both hands vanished, it was time to leave, over the Alexandra Bridge, down to St Peter's, and along to our parking spot which had some dead convenient bushes that provided decent cover for a pre-match bladder relief. That was our usual itinerary until some little sod hidden in the next set of bushes, down towards the river, took pot-shots at us with an air rifle. So we started parking as close to the Fulwell as we could get, as there was always a space in one of the streets round about. It also meant that, on a good day, you could watch your car over the wall and turn the alarm off when it was activated by an over-close police horse.

As with Little Michael in 87, my two started coming more regularly on the same basis – we've just got relegated, there'll be smaller crowds, it'll be safer, they'll be able to see. We started off with Derby at home, and the game brought me another personal landmark. With Gatesy away, I was now older than any of the players. When does growing up become growing old, or do the two things remain entirely separate? With Williams at right back, Pascoe partnering Marco, and Benno and Ord in the centre of defence, 1-1 wasn't really the start we were looking for, but Derby had come down with us and were therefore familiar with our tactics. That was our excuse and I'm sticking to it, but we had to get up and running at Barnsley the following Tuesday. I took John from work and had a nice cup of tea in the sunshine in Stubber's garden in Bradford, called into the Old Post Office for a pint, and took our places in the brilliant summer evening sunshine. For once, the football matched the weather, and Armstrong, Pascoe, and Owers scored in the first half to destroy the home side.

Nice one, we thought, this isn't going to be that bad after all. Yeah, right. Milwall knocked us for four on the Saturday, and it was back to square one. With Kay back, we beat Oxford, but then lost and drew before a crazy game at Swindon in which we scored three but let in five. Shades of last season, we thought – a bit like an incontinent tramp, we couldn't keep a clean sheet to save our lives. The next week Marco scored three in little over five minutes as we won at Charlton, but couldn't find the net as we lost at home to Grimsby, and that was the last we saw of him. £1.8 million took him to Palace, and he was replaced by – nobody, actually.

A lot of people were upset that we'd let him go, but it was the only way to generate money at the time, and he'd been clearly less than 100% fit for most of the previous season. Hauser, then Rush, took his place, but simply weren't the same type of player. At least we had money to spend now, so out we went and bought Anton Rogan and John Byrne. The latter should really have been a straight replacement for Gatesy in the summer to give Marco the sort of mentor that he obviously benefited from. Davenport was a good player, but didn't quite click with Marco in the same way. Peter Beagrie also came in, on loan from Everton, and the three of them were straight into the side, but couldn't prevent defeat at the Boro. They fared better at Roker against Brighton, when we scored four and Beagrie treated us to possibly the best goal celebration ever seen by a Sunderland player, in the form of a series of somersaults. Almost worth the entrance money on its own.

In an effort to pay for the football and feed the kids, I took an extra job when it was offered – Fridays and Sundays behind the bar at the Sportsman. Never mind that the landlord had played for the Boro, it was getting paid for having a drink with your mates as far as I was concerned. If only every workplace could combine enjoyment and productivity like the Sportsman did, there would be a lot more happy people in the world. There was even some money left over at the end of the weekend to pay for the football – some weeks.

We had our usual stab at the League Cup, and contrived to lose the first leg at home to Huddersfield. Still, we thought, remember Bristol City last time around, we'll whip their collective ass in their own backyard, the cheeky Yorkshire upstarts. Ian Sampson got his second successive start in Benno's place, but it was otherwise a team you would have picked from the players we had available. Sadly, it was yet another one of those nights in that competition. Owers was dismissed as we crashed out 0-4, then carried on in the same vein at Cambridge back in the league, letting in three without reply. Not good. We stopped, or at least slowed, the rot with a flashback to the previous season – a 3-3 away draw, this time at Port Vale, but could only follow that with a home draw against Bristol Rovers. The Jarra Arra, Craig Russell, came on for his first game in the win over

Watford, with John Byrne getting his first goals, and then Armstrong won us the game at Ipswich.

Mid table was as good as it got, as we lost at Bristol City, then drew the big one at home to the Mags. Successive defeats by Plymouth (travel sick again) Southend (in an awful game), and Wolves dropped us to 19th, with Armstrong and Byrne sent off, and despite the arrival of The Don (Goodman) as our record signing at just under a million pounds, after negotiations that seemed to have lasted for months. He scored the winner in the next game, but only one more victory followed before we lost two in a row, and another nail was hammered into the coffin of our mining heritage (as that's what it was fast becoming) when Murton pit closed. That left only four pits in the county, apart from small independent affairs, and the number of lads coming off shift and going straight to Roker got smaller by the week.

After a shocker at Oxford in the second of these, Denis Smith was sacked. He'd already tried to steady things by sacking his mate and assistant, Viv Busby, but things had got worse instead of better. Malcolm Crosby, the first team coach, took charge of things and pretty soon began to regret the length of time it had taken to sign The Don, as, while waiting for his move, he'd played in the FA Cup for West Brom and was therefore ineligible to play for us in the third round against Port Vale. No matter, we stuck three past them for the second time that season, but kept them out this time. That seemed to turn things around a bit, and Crosby was beginning to look like a tactical genius a week later when The Don scored three of our six against Millwall then followed it up with another in the win at Derby.

A draw at home to Port Vale was not what we wanted, then I got the call that I was expecting from Stubber: "Fancy a freebie to Oxford? Get your tie on." Half day off work, pick the lad up at Bradford, call in at some mysterious printer's in Bicester (luckily, I'd been doing some work at another printers for a while, and actually knew which words to chuck into the conversation during the tenminute visit, along with a lot of nodding and humming), then to the match. Somehow, Stubber had got hold of tickets belonging to one of Robert Maxwell's companies – seeing as how the tycoon had drowned in mysterious circumstances two months previously, he'd not be needing them. Like the true gambling man that I am, I made Stubber keep his money in his pocket when he got all excited over the bookie offering 9-1 against John Byrne scoring the first goal. That worked. Only a few minutes in, and the blond bombshell duly scored. So did Pascoe and Hardyman, and the two that Oxford got were scarcely deserved, but we were on a Cup run – if two wins in a competition constitutes a run.

Back down to earth with a defeat and a draw, and we'd begun to believe that the play-offs were beyond our reach – certainly with the way we were playing in the League. The FA Cup, however, was a different matter, and West Ham managed to scrape a draw at our place after Byrne's cool-as-you-like goal as he guided and guarded the ball home at the Fulwell, and were probably quite justified in thinking that they'd done the hard part. What they hadn't reckoned with was the Crosby factor, or whatever it was that was coursing through our veins when the cup came along that year. We were awful in a 0-2 defeat at Southend on Saturday, magnificent in a 3-2 win at the Boleyn on Wednesday, with Rush and Byrne getting the goals. Definitely a cup run. Byrne warmed up for the quarter-final (yes, quarter-final) with a penalty winner against Wolves, and then it was off to that nice Stamford Bridge.

Colours well out of sight as we motored along the Fulham Road, then into the crumbling shell that was the ground. The away section was a real mess, and could well have been used in the picture that speaks a thousand words of the Taylor Report. Not to worry, we were the FA Cup team of the moment, memories of 73 and all that, and the visiting support were in tremendous voice. Benno got his place back from Sampson, and we played our cup forwards (Davenport and Byrne) as opposed to our League forwards (Byrne and Goodman). A win was well deserved, but we didn't get it thanks to the referee. Norman watched a shot go past the post, and his reward was to defend a corner. As usually happens with decisions like that, an opponent, in this case Clive Allen, was on hand to score an undeserved goal. Byrne was in the sort of form that brought a goal in every game, and this game was no different, so we got to bring Chelsea back to Wearside. Matches were coming thick and fast, and the league defeat at Watford was quickly put to the back of our mind as the Blues arrived.

One of those nights that will live forever in the memory of those that attended ensued, and one of those games that had cup tie, Roker Park, night game, full house written all over it – and we know what they can turn out to be. Shades of Man City in 73, albeit with a smaller crowd thanks to the safety work that had gone on since. Shot, save, and Davenport reacted with an instant left-footer into the Fulwell net. Here we go, and there we went, past half-time and still in the lead. We did our best not to think of how we were going to get tickets for the semi-final or even, dare we think the thought, the final, and, to be honest, the game was so tense, the crowd so noisy, that it was difficult to think of anything other than the action on the pitch – the real matter in hand. Just when we believed that we could hold onto the lead and start worrying about Norwich at Hillsborough, Dennis Wise popped up with a well-worked, five-a-side type goal. Well-worked, but hardly deserved, For an instant, the crowd went flat, then the individuals present merged into the entity that was the Roker Roar, and pumped back life into the shattered players. We were absolutely drained watching the match, but the players had to compete physically as well as mentally, and we could do no more than encourage them the best we could. Steam rose from the massed supporters as the minutes ticked away. "I couldn't stand extra-time," said Mick, and I knew what he meant.

Cometh the hour (or the last minute in this case) cometh the man. As we checked our watches, Brian Atkinson slung in a corner from the right, and time slowed down as we watched it curl deep, deep to the edge of the box, where Gordon Armstrong was already moving through the air at the end of a run, and the ball cannoned off his brow, over his left shoulder, and into the Roker End net. The ground simply exploded with pent-up emotion and Roker Park rocked like only Roker Park could. In the celebrations on the pitch I'm sure Gordon had sex with Atky, but we couldn't really see because a) we were going mental ourselves and b) the entire team jumped on top of the duo and it became an orgy. I don't remember what happened in the game after that, but it wasn't much. Had it gone to extra time, I doubt if we could have survived. As it was, we were through, and we remembered why it was such a special thing to be a Sunderland supporter. OK, fans of other clubs think that the relationship they have with their club is special, but it's nothing compared to what we've got, to the affinity we have with our club – we're part of it, and it's part of us.

Shame about the league, though. 3-1 defeats at home to Bristol City are hardly the performances you'd expect of FA Cup semi-finalists, but that's what we got. Then we had to go to Gallowgate, into the beginnings of the new look St James Park – which basically means that our end was a building site. The game should never have been played that day, as there was water standing inches deep in several places, but nowhere deeper than the corner just in front of the visiting fans. It was the same for both sides, but the match will be remembered for Tim Carter's super-bendy kicking, with the Armstrong on the left with a header tactic being worked to death, deliberately or otherwise. Tim could do nothing about the only goal, but Paul Hardyman probably should have, as he watched David Kelly's effort trickle (literally in this case) just inside the post. Damn. Spit. Curses. Another week of avoiding Finny the Mag and an FA Cup semi-final up next.

There's so much more to football than just the ninety minutes in the middle of it all, and the semi-final was no different. We had to get tickets for a start, which was easier said than done. "Easy," said Pos. "We'll go through after work on Friday night, take a few cans, have a bit of a laugh, get the tickets, and be home by eleven."

A fine theory, and there should have been no reason to expect failure, so I swapped shifts at the pub, put some cans in my pocket, and climbed aboard the Posmobile after tea. What greeted us at Roker changed our ideas on the simplicity of the task ahead. Thousands upon thousands of people had come up with the same plan, and the deck chairs were already out, the cans were already cracked, and the beach parties had begun. By two in the morning, some of the local residents were getting justifiably concerned about several thousand disorganised folks sitting on their doorsteps, and, in hindsight, the club should have done something to try and co-ordinate some sort of order, some queues that were actually going towards a turnstile, and some sort of litter collection service.

Fair enough, Crozza did turn up with some coffee, but he was only one man, and we were thousands. Just as I was getting comfy on my deckchair outside the Roker Bingo Office, somebody somewhere decided that it was time to move, and any vague semblance of order disintegrated in to chaos. By the time the turnstiles did open, it was a mad crush to get to any, and I finished up at the Clock Stand, behind Dunny, who'd innocently turned up at 9am, joined a queue, and bought his ticket ahead of many others who'd spent the night waiting – like me. Naughty Sunderland, bad Sunderland; must do better next time. There were even rumours that the club had deliberately left us to our own devices in order to get the fans a bad name, though I can't imagine why. The daft thing was that I already had my ticket at home, and was queuing for mates who lived down the country. Boy, the bonus points I got for that one – they were buying me beer for years afterwards.

There was supposed to be a one and a half mile alcohol-free zone around Hillsborough the day of the match, based on what I don't know. There was hardly an undercurrent of vicious hatred between the two clubs – there had even been a Friendship Cup or something similar, the winners being the side with the aggregate league win, since our dead pally match in 1985 in the League Cup Final. We thought their fans were alright, they thought our fans were alright. So that's all right then. No, it isn't, so no drinks, no socialising, no enjoyment if we can help it.

Of course, we found a pub only too happy to sell us beer, stand outside in the sun, and crack on with the Norwich lads who'd found it as well. It was a bit rough (the first question in the pub quiz was "Who are you looking at?") but it was ready, they made us welcome, and we were ready for the game. While not as intense as the Chelsea experience (especially the replay), it was some game. We were perched right at the back of what had been the Kop, and, it being made ready for the installation of seats, the steps were high and the view spectacular. It had been a bit touch and go, but it produced another one of those moments that stays in your memory bank, filed under football, and ready to replay itself at the drop of a red and white bowler hat. Rushy's through ball, Atky's lovely pass-on-aplate type cross, and Johnny Byrne writing himself into Sunderland folklore by trotting onto the cross and nodding it home. It was down the far end, but we all saw it building up and we all saw it go in – including the usual smattering of Wearsiders in the Norwich end. At the final whistle, Reg asked Mike where I was. Sitting down, crying, was the answer.

And I was, the big soft lump. There I was closer to the age of the manager than any of the players, overcome by the result of a football match. I was going to Wembley again – for the FA Cup Final. We're sorted – Sunderland had won every FA Cup Final that I'd been to. At least that was the talk on the way back, and it was more than just me saying it. Thanks to the traffic co-ordination, or rather lack of it, (the traffic police weren't going to let Reg head south, even though he lived in Ipswich) we were still in Sheffield over an hour after the end of the fun, and it was nearly ten by the time my sister picked Mat and me up from Spenny, and I'd only had time for a swift celebratory half with the bairn in the pub doorway. Thankfully, I was in the Sportsman ten minutes later. The landlord might have been a Boro boy, but, having played the game, he knew fine well what it meant to achieve something like we just had. Nice man, he bought my beer for the rest of the night – if you can't celebrate getting to the FA Cup Final, what could you celebrate?

If the league was all but forgotten about before this, it was completely forgotten about afterwards by many people, but not Stubber. "Fancy a freebie to Leicester?" was the gist of the call and the suit and tie were out again three days after Sheffield. The lad has always been one for time compression, and that night was no exception. Arriving at Belvoir (pronounce Bee-vah) suite in Filbert Street at 7:30 for a 7:45 kick-off, all we had to do was consume a three-course meal and two pints before kick-off. Thankfully, we made it, and it was just as well, as most of the action took place in the opening fifteen minutes. Benno scored, they scored – it all went a bit mental, as they say in the Times Sporting Section. The end result was a bit of a jammy win for the home side, as we say in the Auckland Chronicle. We were slipping dangerously close to the relegation places, but at least we were above the Mags, and that was at least something to shout about - well, it is when you're going to Wembley, and they're not. We lost at home to Charlton and then beat Plymouth as we began to reel in the games in with eight matches in April. Having the kids in attendance at home games meant that language had to be of the family variety, and when I lost my temper with a referee and called him a silly sausage (it was the first word that came into my head, right?) the lads from Shields who stood next to us couldn't stop laughing for the rest of the game, and I became known, for a short, sweet while, as Sausages. Childish but fun.

Davenport scored against his old employers to give us the points against the Boro, then Anton Rogan scored his only red and white goal in the draw at Brighton. That was the first of the four draws that brought the league season to an end, but the fun wasn't over. We had a trip to Wembley to sort out. By hook or by crook, we managed to get hold of or organise seventeen tickets, one for everybody in the immediate football family. I phoned far-flung clubs and asked if they were using all of their allocation. I spoke to a lovely lady at Norwich, who said "Hang on, I don't think Mr X is going, I'll just ask… yes, I'll put them in an envelope for you, with your friend's name on it." See? Norwich are nice people. Some tickets came from Brian Horton, and yet others from Robert Maxwell's estate. I tried Exeter, on the basis of them being a long way away and therefore less likely to travel. I'd forgotten that their manager was Wes Saunders, a Sunderland fan. Still, we got it sorted, and I was even presented with another two on the Thursday before the game. Judith asked me "Could I shift a couple of Final tickets?" How long had she known me? Course I could and it was a very happy Big Harrier who put the phone down ten minutes later. "Howdy Bri, fancy going to the Cup Final?" "Cheers Sobs – and where am I supposed to get a ticket?" "It's in my hand." "Whoooo –hooo! See you in the Lamb."

Of course, it's only then that your Mam chooses to ring up and ask if I know where to get a couple of tickets for her cousins. Typical – we'd managed to get in where a draught couldn't, and still there was room for improvement in the ticket-blagging front. On the basis of this, every year at work since then I've been approached with the question, "You can get FA Cup final tickets, can't you?" The answer has generally been "Not for you, you black and white so and so."

The only problem with getting tickets in this random fashion is that we had people all around the ground. We had two in the Olympic Gallery watching through their legs, some at pitch level, and young Mat in the care of Stubber in a different part of the ground to his match day guardian, yours truly. We'd got one of those family railcards for the dozen or so of us who'd travelled together, on the basis that Mat was my nephew, Mike and his two sons were amongst us, and the rest of us had played football together. A football family, if you will. Most of Bishop congregated in the Lamb, as did a number of ex pats, and we put in a better performance than the team did. As I took my seat with John from work, the chant "Sausages, Sausages, Sausages" went up. Only from half a dozen voices, but voices all the same and they were singing my name. It might be a name that only a handful of people ever knew me by, but they were singing my name – at an FA Cup Final. Unfortunately, that was as good as it got.

Byrne fluffed a decent chance in the first half, their Rush scored a tap in, our Rush didn't, Brian Atkinson became the first member of Aycliffe Big Club to play in an FA Cup Final, and the team froze. We gave them a game for half an hour, but that was about it. At onenil, there's always a chance, but when the second went in, it was over. At least we were presented with the winners' medals, but there were a lot of men staring sadly at the Liverpool celebrations from our end. When the cup was being paraded past the fans, Michael Thomas actually came up to my section of the ground and held the trophy against the fence so that people could touch it, and he wasn't being nasty. He could see the look in our eyes, knew how much football meant to us. We left the ground chanting "We came, we lost, we couldn't give a toss" which wasn't strictly true, but showed that we understood that life went on, and there was always next season. I sat on the tube listening to this noise, joining in with this noise, next to a Scouse about my age, with his young son, the pair of them looking, if not as miserable as sin, then pretty damn close. "Smile, you've just won the FA Cup," I said. "Just another day at the office," was the reply. I expect his son grew up to really appreciate the good times.

Back to the Lamb, collect various members of the footballing family together, and off to Kings Cross, then the Sportsman (Canney Hill, not my place of work – there are some times when you want to be away from those you normally drink with) for a few consolation beers with TallPaul, and a taxi to the Market Place, which was a mistake. By midnight, I was in no condition to engage in rational argument, and had to stand there in my Sunderland woolly hat and Red and White Tractor John Kay shirt being screamed at by Mr Angry, the biggest Boro fan in Bishop, and my nemesis since we were eleven. In the end, his wife dragged him off and I went home to my bed. Judith then had the bright idea of taking us to see the team come back "So the kids can have a look". For some reason, ITV interviewed me. For some reason, they didn't use it – perhaps because it was destined for the 6pm broadcast they thought there might be too many youngsters about, and I might frighten them with my miserable demeanour. Perhaps it will show up on a Tyne Tees version of "It'll be all right on the night" one day. Or perhaps not.

We went to Wembley Stadium, 'twas on the fifth of May
Nineteen hundred and seventy three, up the Wembley Way
We showed them how to drink Brown Ale
We showed them how to sup
We even showed the Magpies how to win the FA Cup

1992-1993

While the government withstood the temptation to finish off mining for good by closing our last few pits, perhaps as some sort of perverse thank-you to the nation for electing them in again, the Danes showed that democracy wasn't a thing of the past by voting against the Maastricht treaty, thus preserving a semblance of national identity. Further east, the full horrors of what had been going on in the Balkans was revealed when pictures were broadcast from the prison camps there. On a lighter note, I did the camping thing with the kids again, then the proper family holiday in Dorset for the fourth year in a row, which makes remembering where we went a bit of a doddle.

Instated as proper manager as opposed to simply the caretaker (presumably they took his brush away), Crozza went crazy and spent money. £650,000 went to Grimsby for their highly-rated midfielder Shaun Cunnington, and £220,000 to Millwall for John Colquhoun. For nothing, we got Terry Butcher from Sheff Wed, where he'd been managing the reserves. It seemed like a strange move, as the lad had obviously been unfit for some time, but his commitment to a cause could not be doubted, and perhaps his experience would help us through defensively. Paul Hardyman, rather strangely, left for Bristol Rovers, and Paul Bracewell fell out over the length of contract he was offered, and nicked off up the road, where they recognised his worth and offered him the lengthier deal he'd been seeking.

That was our squad sorted for the coming campaign. The new stadium was still being sketched onto pieces of paper with various map references at the top, but no one could decide which was best.

In an attempt to keep us happy by moving back into Division One, along came the Premier League. Whether the name-change itself would have brought about the massive changes that we've seen in the game since then is a debate that can never be answered either way, the money that came with it certainly did. As our beloved Sunderland changed status from a town to a city, Spurs came up to play in a celebration friendly. The game was memorable for two things – Darren Anderton, four months after missing a semi-final sitter against Liverpool that would have given us an all-second division FA Cup final (and certain victory over Portsmouth) scoring a hattrick, and Benno making Tony Norman's life hell by totally ignoring the new law against goalkeepers picking up back-passes.

So, back in Division One it was for us, with three new boys and one old face gone. In the defeat at Swindon on day one, Norman was injured behind a weird-looking defence of Ball, Bennett, Butcher, and Smith. All change of the next game, with Carter, Ball, Smith, Butcher, and Smith at the back, and Skinny Shaun came up with the only goal against Tranmere. Almost before the League was warmed up, some joker thought it would be funny to pair us with the side that had put us out of the previous year's League Cup (Coca Cola, as it was then called). So, despite Butcher getting his first and only Sunderland goal, we lost 2-3 at home, then substitute Davenport won us the game at Leeds Road, but the competition ended in aggregate defeat. Rogan was back for the League draw at Bristol Rovers, then an unchanged team spoiled my birthday with a defeat at home by Charlton. We messed about with the Anglo Italian Cup, but managed the strange feat of going out of the competition without playing any Italian teams, thanks to defeats by Cambridge and Birmingham.

Back in the league, Martin Gray came in at right back, and David Rush scored in three consecutive games as we won, lost and drew. Crozza gave up on Thomas Hauser, and sold him to some unheard of continental team – but it wasn't the last we heard of him, Oh no, he tried to blame a persistent ankle injury on the quality of treatment that he'd received from the SAFC backroom people. Needless to say, he tried to sue us and got exactly nowhere. Meanwhile, Byrne wasn't having the best of times in front of goal, took a bit of stick from the Fulwell after one particular miss, and reacted by having a go back – which was brave but never going to be clever. He was sold to Millwall shortly afterwards, leaving us two forwards short.

Anyhow, the Don then got off the mark as we lost at Watford, then got both as we beat Millwall. Was this the turning point? Not quite, as West Ham went daft and scored six without reply – on the telly, so that the whole world could see. I managed to borrow a Hammers shirt from Pop, and wear it to work in a display of double-bluff to keep the Mags quiet. That lasted all of a week, as they came to Roker and Liam Bloody O'Brien scored that free-kick. They'll remember that one forever, but I'll remember Benno's perfectly good goal been ruled illegal for just as long – so there. The club gave up on Kieron Brady, and let him join Doncaster Rovers, where he'd been on loan. The move lasted only a few weeks before Donny gave up on the talented youngster as well, and that was the end of Brady the professional footballer – yet another example of a richly talented and exciting player going to waste. Tales of off-the-field habits circulated, and problems with circulation in his legs were cited as being at least partly responsible for his demise. Rumours of the club being sued for incorrect medical care came to the fore again, but they were found innocent - almost six years after he left. An out-of-court settlement with the Sunderland Royal Hospital was the sad end to a sad affair.

Outside football, and for once, the government appeared to be listening to what the people had to say. When the Coal Not Dole protest marched around the capital, Michael Heseltine pooped his pants and said that they'd re-think the Coal Board's plans (or rather the Government's plans) to close thirty-one pits and lay off 30,000 miners. Instead, they'd close just ten – well thank you very much, that ain't good enough, said the rest of the House. OK, said Hezza, desperately looking for the toilet–roll, maybe we can negotiate to save some of those ten if we have a government inquiry. We'll see what happens with that, but don't hold your breath.

Lose, draw, win, was hardly going to make the season smell any better, then came a crazy game at Peterborough – yes, I said Peterborough – where we lost 5-2, and all hope seemed to be lost, especially as Anton Rogan suffered a broken leg. A bit of a rally then took place, after the defeat at home to Leicester, when we won three off the belt. Goodman got the goal at Derby, Ian Sampson his only Sunderland score against Southend when deputising for Bally, then came the local boy's magic moment. Mickey Gray had made his debut from the bench at Derby, and got his first start at home to Barnsley. Over came a corner at the Fulwell, it was partially cleared, and Mickey volleyed it back into the net from outside the box. After only half a minute. Thousands of lads over the years, myself included, have probably dreamed of doing exactly that, and can only imagine what a feeling it must be, perhaps only being bettered if it had been against the Mags. Local boy comes good, or what? While it was undoubtedly a magic moment, I doubt if it brought much seasonal cheer to Murton, where the pit had failed to escape the government's October back-down on closures.

Christmas arrived with only one more point in the bag, but at least we were given some festive cheer with a holiday win over Grimsby. The New Year's first game saw Brian Mooney's only Sunderland goal in a funny old 3-3 draw with Cambridge – he played in the next two League games then vanished in a puff of smoke, his exact location being no more than rumour. He was a fabulously skilful player, but was, unfortunately, equally inconsistent and apparently disinterested, which is all too often the case with such folks. He also featured in the FA Cup win at Notts County, and, as beaten finalists last time around, the eyes of the football world were on us as we travelled to Hillsborough for the fourth round. Being of a persuasive nature, Dunny had talked a couple of season tickets out of the Wednesday-supporting landlord of The Welcome, so it was freebies for us. No, I don't know how it worked either – Sunderland have never had the presumption to include FA Cup ties in your season ticket, but Wednesday obviously did. We turned in a fine performance, and, just as the visiting end, and the two chancers in the main stand, were about to be satisfied with taking Wednesday back to Roker, it was an easy one for Norman. Oh no it wasn't, and the man who'd performed heroics on so many occasions presented Mark Bright with the easiest of goals. Bugger, we thought. My exhaust pipe stayed on, but my windscreen wipers packed in halfway home. Simply lovely.

Just the League, then.

The board had taken about as much of that nice Mr Crosby as they were prepared to, and gave him the boot. Ironically, the man he'd brought in to bolster our defence was given the manager's job. You couldn't fault Butcher for effort, as he managed during the week and flung himself into challenges on a weekend with gusto. Maybe I was a bit cheeky when I wrote to him and suggested that providing financial support to his local Tory candidate, as he had in Glasgow, would not be such a good idea in Sunderland now that he was the manager. Sorry, I couldn't help myself. Perhaps he was entitled to write back and tell me his politics were his own business, but he did say that he might become "a bit more red." Just to make it even worse, I was, for the first time, older than the manager, but at least he was still playing, despite his knees creaking more loudly than mine did on a Sunday morning.

Performances in general didn't improve though, and it was a rare thing to get a win. When one did come along, Butcher displayed disarming enthusiasm in his post-match celebrations, going to every side of the ground and drawing greats whoops of delight from the fans with spectacular arm gestures. It was difficult not to feel uplifted, despite that fact that he didn't get to do this often enough. With the manager and first Smith, then Ordy alongside Kay and Bally, the defence tightened up a bit, and we saw a glimmer of hope with five clean sheets in a row. One of these was against West Ham, and was especially poignant because it was the first game played after the death of Bobby Moore, one of football's true gentlemen, and the only Englishman (so far) to lift the World Cup. I was disappointed to miss that one, as I would have liked to have paid my respects, but I had a previous engagement. Big Harrier had decided to join the adult world at last, and was getting married – in Dublin, so that's where I was. The groom, myself, and Tommer managed to keep an ear on proceedings at the reception, and relay the information to the rest of the Durham folks present.

What we needed was to take advantage of our new-found defensive meanness, and score some at the other end, so Butcher went out and signed his England colleague Mick Harford, who was perhaps Butcher's attacking counterpart. Experienced, hard as nails, and from Sunderland, he arrived at his boyhood heroes via all manner of clubs, including two spells up the road, the second of which had ended when the Mags couldn't afford to pay the balance of his transfer and were forced to sell him on. Right at the other end of the scale, we brought Big Chief Lee Howey, about whose brother nothing will be said, another Sunderland-born centre-forward who'd been around a bit – Ipswich, Hemptinne, Seaham Red Star, Blyth Spartans, and Bishop. Big Lee was straight into the reserves for a bit of toughening up (as if he needed it – ask Geoff Thomas or that Dutch bloke called Wolf who played for Wolves and thought he was hard), and Big Mick went straight in to the first team. While he only scored two goals himself, he did bring good things out of The Don, who scored six. Having said that, we'd started to leak goals again, never more evident than in the 2-4 home defeat by Southend, and we were hovering perilously close to the drop-zone. Lee came off the bench in the home game against Portsmouth, when we played probably our best football of the season, saw The Don get two, Armstrong one, and Martin Gray his only one. Having seen Paul Walsh miss several chances at the other end, Gray arrived on the end of a sweet passing move to tap in a goal of real quality, naturally enough said to Walsh "that's the way to do it", and received a gobful of forehead for his troubles.

Defeat at Tranmere meant that there was a very real possibility that we could go down if we lost the last game at Notts County, so there was everything to play for. Not wishing to miss any of the action, I set off with my thumb out straight from work on the Friday evening – just to see if I could still do it. And I could, arriving at my staging point of Stubber's Bradford pad in time for a night on the town. It was a subject of much debate that I'd only brought an ALS T-Shirt that bore the legend "totally obsessed with Sunderland AFC", but Stubber's way too big to borrow clothes from, so we took a chance - and had no hassle. Nottingham the next morning was the location of an "inter-branch" SAFC fans 5-a-side tournament.

I couldn't make a guest appearance for the West Yorkshire boys due to a torn hamstring (courtesy of playing football for the Bittermen in the morning and rugby 7s for the Sportsman in the afternoon – and having four pints in between), but the team in kilts looked far too fierce anyway, especially with their tartan tams and red wigs. As far as football went, it was downhill from there, with the 5-a-side being way better than anything the professionals in red and white could produce. In a thoroughly turgid affair, we went 3-0 down before Bally bobbled one in to give us something to shout about (for about two seconds, until we realised that it was only one goal, and we needed four), but when the results came in, we started celebrating properly. The other teams in the mire had contrived to lose, and we were safe. Not really a cause for celebration, you might think, but, in this game, and with a red and white shirt on your back, you take any crumb of comfort and make it a source of great joy and happiness. Things could only get better.

Sunderland's our pride and joy
And Toddo is our golden boy
We'll follow them through thick and thin
We'll cheer them on 'til Sund'land win
Sunderland will never die
We'll keep the red flag flying high

1993-1994

No FA Cup Final to plan in after the League season was over this year, so my summer routine was the same as last year, and the two before that – camping with the bairns, Dorset with the whole family. If it ain't broke, don't fix it, that's what I say. In the big bad world, the UN plans to maintain peace in Bosnia fell to pieces as the Serbs and Croats went ahead with their own plans to divide the country up between them. John Major sacked his chancellor, Norman Lamont, after the Tories miserably lost numerous local elections and the Newbury by-election. Was the country finally waking up and understanding what had been perpetrated upon their fair land? It looked like it was, especially the million or so in the NHS queues, and the men laid off when collieries at Westoe in South Shields and Vane Tempest in Seaham closed.

In jolly old Sunderland-land, Terry Butcher did something that a Sunderland manager had never done before, and spent over £2 million in virtually one go. In came Derek Ferguson from Hearts, Andy Melville from Oxford, Ian Rodgerson (whose dad had played alongside Cloughie at the Boro) from Birmingham, and Phil Gray from Luton. Pos returned from a pre-season friendly with the announcement that I'd like Gray, because "He's a bit of a thug." We didn't really get the chance to see him at his best when the season started, as the four new boys ended up in hospital with injuries ranging from a broken shoulder to glass in the eye, when Ferguson misunderstood the roundabout near St Peter's, and went the wrong way round it – much to the consternation of the oncoming traffic.

Alec Chamberlain came on a freebie from Luton as Tim Carter, after numerous loans around the country, went to Hartlepool on a permanent transfer. Warren Hawke left, playing for Raith and Scarborough before settling at Berwick before Christmas. Also, sounding like a character from Roy of the Rovers, in came Lee Power on loan from Norwich. Paul Williams left for Doncaster and first team football, but only managed eight games before having his contract cancelled. Perhaps he'd never recovered from that day at Old Trafford over two years earlier. John Colquhoun cut his losses and headed back to Hearts as part of the deal that brought Derek Ferguson south, after only 23 games and one disallowed goal. Anton Rogan joined Denis Smith at Oxford… and still no sign of where the new ground would be… and the powers that be had decided to liven things up a bit by allowing three substitutes, thus reducing the size of the typeface on match day programmes for evermore, and giving the realistic option of two proper goalkeepers in the squad.

So, the fourteen at Derby on day one looked somewhat different to that we'd watched crumble at Meadow Lane in May. Chamberlain in goal, Kay, Mickey Gray, Melville and Sampson at the back. Ferguson, Owers, Cunnington and Armstrong in the middle. Goodman and Howey up front. Five –nil to Derby, including one from Marco. Not the way things were supposed to start out. Anthony Smith joined Benno in the defence for the next game, replacing Mickey Gray, who moved up-field to replace Ferguson, and (relatively) little Lee Power replaced (genuinely) big Lee Howey. 4-0 against Charlton seemed to indicate that this was a working formation, but there were four changes made for the trip to Notts County, with local short house Craig Russell getting his first start, local short houser Stephen Brodie making his first appearance off the bench, and the team losing 1-0. We then ensured our place in the Guinness Book of Records by exiting the Anglo-Italian Cup without playing any Italians for the second consecutive season, beating Tranmere and losing to Bolton – goal difference or something going against us.

We'd made a better start in the League Cup, when Lee Power scored his only goal for us with an absolutely cracking left-footed curlywifter at the Fulwell that had us screaming for his permanent signature. Sadly, Butcher had blown the kitty during the summer, and Lee was away on a string of further loan deals before ending up at Halifax. Chester were defeated 3-1, and then held 0-0 at their place to bring us up against Leeds. Goodman and Gray (Phil) got the goals in a 2-1 home win that made the public sit up and take notice – Leeds were a pretty big scalp in those days, and we weren't expected to survive the second leg. Out came Cammy's freebies again, but this time we were located in the Captain's Bar, away from the more unpleasant inhabitants of Elland Road.

True to form, I persuaded Pos not to waste his money on a decent-odds bet on Goodman to score first, and he promised not to be too obvious in his celebrations of anything nice in red and white. You've guessed it – Owers free-kick, right in front of us, near post header from the Don (who, as a Bradford lad, must have been quite chuffed), and Pos leapt skyward, blowing all promises of decorum out of the water. After he forgave me for preventing him from collecting a tidy few quid, we noticed that about half of the people in our little stand were sweating away with Sunderland colours beneath their shirts and ties. Just before half-time, Phil Gray charged down their keeper's clearance and it was 2-0, and a bar full of smiling Mackems during the interval. They did pull one back through Noel Whelan, but we hung on to win despite Benno going off on a stretcher.

We hung back to let the crowds disperse, then collected a few autographs ("Not for the kids Gary, for me") from the Sunderland players, and called over David O'Leary, holding out a programme and a pen. "Thanks, Dave – will you nip over there and get Gary Bennett's autograph?" These things have to be done. Unfortunately, that was Butcher's finest hour as our manager, as Villa beat us 4-1 in the next round, but the result doesn't tell the whole story. Indeed, the Villa manager, Big Ron "Suntan" Atkinson, said afterwards that there was only one team in it – and they lost. Mark Bosnich played a blinder of proportions reserved by keepers for Roker Park as we laid siege to their goal.

Early October brought the sad news that Jim Holton had died, aged only forty-two. He might have only played in a handful of games for us, and a fairly inauspicious period in the club's history, but will be remembered for giving his all while with us.

In the League, two wins and two draws had steadied things a little before the game at Boro. In the last of these, against Birmingham, Kaysie went into a tackle and then tried to stand up. From the Fulwell we saw his shin buckle, and it was obvious to over 19,000 people that it was broken. Somebody should have told Kaysie, as he sat up on the stretcher and made like he was paddling a canoe. Sadly, he never played again for us, and it was an unfitting end to the Sunderland career of a man who'd redefined the meaning of the term tough full-back, earning him the nickname of the "red and white tractor" after the Leeds manager had complained about a perfectly executed tackle that had put ex-Mag Peter Haddock into the back of the net. Maybe it would have been a different

Cup Final if he'd been fit enough to play at Wembley in 92, but he was honest enough to say that he wasn't, unlike many players since. It was a shame it had to end that way, but at least he went on to have a decent few years down the divisions, where wonky legs seemingly don't matter as much.

Thanks to my weekend job at the Sportsman, I obtained two free Boro tickets from the landlord's son, who was trying to make the step up from their reserves to first team. Free tickets are all very well, but they can be in the wrong part of the ground, and that's not much fun when your team turns out in a silly "one-off limited edition" yellow and black outfit, and play like a bunch of vegetables. There might have only been about 10,000 Boro fans in the ground out of 12,772, but the one with the biggest mouths and the most sarcastic attitudes were sitting right behind us. Unfortunately, neither myself nor John from work were in the mood to keep our thoughts on our performance to ourselves, giving away our allegiance in rather vocal fashion when the Don blazed a penalty way over. When their fourth went in, the voice in my ear asking "What's the score now, Sunderland?" was the final straw, and I told its owner where to stick his head. They say that sometimes, like when speaking to a dog, the tone of your voice is more important than what you actually say, and this must have been one of those occasions. While we sat expecting an instant physical backlash, the row behind us ceased their teasing and concentrated on the game in silence. Thankfully.

Physical backlash was, unfortunately, exactly what was going on in Eastern Europe, as Moscow degenerated into virtual civil war when Yeltsin used the full force of the army to crush his opposition, and the remnants of Yugoslavia continued to knock seven bells out of each other. In world football, England contrived to let San Marino score after twelve seconds, and their seven-goal comeback was in vain as Holland avoided defeat in Poland, and the World Cup was no longer any concern of ours. Unless you liked the Irish.

A couple of new faces appeared in our team, as Butcher attempted to construct a winning run. Straight from prison (armed robbery, of course – if we're going to sign an ex-con, it might as well be a good one) came Jamie Lawrence, complete with weird pineapple haircut, and straight from the Fulwell came Martin Smith. Those amongst the crowd for the Luton game were still asking each other who the kid in the number nine shirt was when he planted a cracking freekick into the Fulwell net – shades of Mickey Gray – as we won 2-0. Perhaps a bit less chopping and changing at the back would have helped us settle – it was just as well that Butcher had retired from playing; otherwise it would have got even more complicated.

Dickie Ord scored a rare goal to beat West Bromwich the following week, and we looked to have steadied the ship. Perhaps it was the confusion over who was who – Anthony Smith, Martin Smith, Martin Gray, Mickey Gray, Phil Gray – but we couldn't have become less steady, as we lost six in a row including a 4-1 reverse at Tranmere. En route to a works cross-country race near Swansea, Tranmere was an obvious stopping point, especially when one of my travelling companions had spent time on Merseyside and had a soft spot for them. This was the day that I discovered my former flat-mate from University had turned into a Mag, which was horrible, especially when he had young children to think of. He still came to the game, watched as The Don put us ahead, then laughed into his sleeve as we allowed John Morrisey and Pat Nevin to pull a four goal second half out of the bag as we got soaked to the skin in a metal cage on the crumbling terraces.

A trip to Swansea was just what we needed, and took the whole journey to dry out. Miserable doesn't come into it. After the fifth of those defeats, the fairly predictable sacking of Butcher took place, and Bob Murray also decided to step down from the chairman's position, but stayed on the board with John Feather-stone (no, I don't remember much about him either) becoming chairman. At least the new manager was older than me – coach Mick Buxton took over, and rather than join in press conferences and the like, he put on his flat cap and walked his dog along Roker beach – far away in time, far away in style. Still, he was from Corbridge, the same place as Jimmy Adamson (as if that was a recommendation of any sort), so he should be OK. After the customary first game defeat, we won three out of four in December, including Craig Russell's first goal - off the bench to beat Millwall – and Ian Rodgerson's first appearance (of only five).

New Year's Day is never a good time to play away from home, and we duly lost out at Leicester, but Phil Gray put things right a couple of days later by scoring the goal that beat Barnsley.

Then along came the FA Cup and a visit by Carlisle, when Ferguson scored our only goal of the day, and his only one for us, knocking the ball through the wet and watching it trickle in. Unfortunately, Carlisle scored as well so it was off to an extremely clarty, wet and miserable Cumbria, where Lee Howey needed all his physical strength to score the winner, and then it was off to Wimbledon. Despite Smith's goal (sorry, Martin Smith), we went down 2-1 and could concentrate on survival.

Which wasn't looking too difficult a task, as Gray (P), Goodman, and Smith (M) got the goals that helped us win us three in a row. The last win was against the Boro, where Lee Howey came off the bench to score one of the best headers seen in my time at Roker – a thumping effort from a corner at the Fulwell End. That must have felt even better than Mickey Gray did – local rivals, local boy comes off the bench to win the game – and still rates in my top ten Roker goals. Magic. Imagine my delight when I spotted Bishop's Mr Angry, the Boro boy who'd tried to make my FA Cup Final day even worse than it already was eighteen months previously, and with whom I'd been at footballing loggerheads for best part of thirty years, standing just behind me, trying to look pleased. As he was (and still is) bigger than me, lives just down the road, and I'm not that daft, I wasn't about to point at him and shout "Boro!" instead choosing the softly, softly approach by waiting until the final whistle before saying "Hello, mate – did you enjoy the game?"

Things Can Only Get Better was at number one – was this music reflecting life? Not quite, as we slowed up with a draw and defeat in the West Midlands, then only scraped a 0-0 at home to Bristol City, before another draw and loss at Charlton and Luton respectively. Buxton decided that Owers would be better employed in a midfield role, and brought in loan star Darius Kubicki from Villa. If ever a man epitomised the term solid full-back, it was Daz. Strong at the back, he was also keen to break forward, and could put in a wicked curling, hanging cross. Completely different in style to Kaysie, but he'd do just nicely - Mick Buxton certainly knew his full-backs. Tactics were another matter, though, and after the win over Boro, we managed three goal-less draws and two 2-1 defeats in five games.

Then came three consecutive home games, with Dickie Ord back in the defence, and Ain't no fuss with the Russ got his shooting boots out as he and Phil Gray did the business in four straight wins. Even eventual champions Palace couldn't stop us, although getting back from a job in Dublin made the kick-off a bridge almost too far, and my borrowed seat in the Main Stand was only occupied with seconds to spare – but the rush proved well worth the effort. The midfield of Bally to win it, Atky to carry it, Ferguson to supply the passes and Martin Smith to provide the unexpected seemed to be working a treat, but then the same eleven crashed 4-0 at Barnsley. Never mind, Russ came back with both to defeat Bolton and then Andy Melville scored in the next two games – which we lost. At Millwall, The Don became our first substitute to be sent off, when Kasey Keller made out that he'd been punched by our number twelve. Television footage clearly showed no contact had been made, so that explains why, even to this day, the American receives such a hostile welcome from Sunderland fans – and rightly so.

Then the season sort of flattened out, as we went win, lose, win, lose, win. In the last of this sequence, Tony Norman, after what must have been a record forty-three unused substitute sits on the bench, got a game, and kept his place for the last two draws, at Wolves and Forest. At the last of these I made the perfectly reasonable request for a reduction in swearing of a bloke in front of me, seeing as our Ian was only eight and shouldn't have to hear that sort of thing. The reply, from a bloke in his fifties, probably seemed logical to him, but "I've been coming here longer than he has" just got my back up. "So have I," I said, "but I'm not effing in his ear all day." We chose to agree on a difference of opinion, but he moved far enough away for his mid-level cursing to become part of the general noise. Point made, I think, and 1-0 to Sensible Dad. Mind, you should hear the language off the bairn these days. Season over, with Buxton now in permanent rather than caretaker mode, we'd finished twelfth – shamefully, our highest position for four years – but was it a solid enough base to build on? Why aye it was – as we always say at this time of year.

Our fame is spread from shore to shore
So come and hear the Roker Roar
It will echo round the land the name of our team Sunderland
Sunderland will never die
We'll keep the red flag flying high

1994-1995

The day after the season ended, Nelson Mandela completed his journey from political prisoner to president, just showing what can be achieved by maintaining your faith and beliefs. Then Tony Blair became Labour leader, which was good, before claiming to have spent boyhood Saturdays "Sitting in the Leazes End", which was bad on two fronts – the obvious one, and the fact that the Leazes End had never contained seats until very recently. Not a good piece of PR, son. Nine months after the political parties had agreed a ceasefire in Northern Ireland, the IRA finally announced that they'd be joining it, which should have spelt more peaceful times in the province. Showing my usual concern for world affairs, I'd taken the lads on a particularly wet tour of the Dales, down a few caves and scaring the teacher in charge of one school party at Yordas Cave in Kingsdale by sending the two of them over to stand amongst the merging pupils as they were counted out. I doubt if they'd have been more scored had they been two kids down, but two extra certainly threw them. The nice old fella who owned our regular Weymouth flat having died and son taken over, the rent doubled. So we took ourselves to north Devon, stayed in a converted stable on a fish farm (presumably for sea-horses), and leaned how to surf at Bude.

Back up north, the end had come for Durham's mines, as the lads clocked off at Wearmouth for the last time, and there was simply no more coal coming out of the ground, save a very few small, private drift-mines in the south west of the county. The end of an era, but, as they say, when one door shuts, another slams in your face. Sorry, another one opens – a large piece of derelict land, half a mile from Roker, closer to the town centre and the transport links, suddenly jumped to the top of the list of likely sites for our new ground, and, as time passed, fairly quickly became the only option. Roker Park was our spiritual home, but things can't live forever.

The new season came around with little in the way of squad changes – basically, Mr Butcher had spent all of the money the previous close season, leaving Uncle Mick nothing to play with besides his flat cap and his dog. So our first line-up was virtually the same as that we'd seen finish the last – and it did pretty well with a draw at Bristol City. Mickey Gray's run on the left of midfield continued as we drew with Millwall, then won at Stoke. Roker Parklife was turning out to be pretty good. Goodman and Phil Gray were getting the goals that we had hoped for, then in came the Russ, and he got both in his second game against Boro.

Living, as I do, in south-west Durham, I come into contact with a few Boro boys. In truth, there have always been one or two, but the speed at which they came out of the woodwork upon the arrival of Bryan Robson (no, not that one, the one who actually played for England) was astonishing. One of the old guard, Paul the Gas (he worked for the Gas board, as you'd expect), was taking his annual trip to Belgium for cigarettes and alcohol, and offered me the use of his season ticket for the day. The consternation caused when it fell out of my pocket after my Sunday morning game can only be imagined, but the fact that I had it at all just goes to show that a spark of humanity does exist in the hearts of the fans of local rivals. That Paul the Gas was a decent sort was further proved when he was in charge of the traffic lights at some excavations in Crook, and, every morning for a week, kept Andy Cole waiting for up to ten minutes without another car in sight.

Anyhow, the Bittermen having been victorious at Durham, I zipped down to Teesside for the proper fun and games. It didn't take long to decide that I'd rather have paid the money and stood with the lads than sit in the main stand at Ayresome (that's where Middlesbro', as you like to call them, used to play, in case there are any of their fans reading), as the man next to me watched the whole thing on a miniature telly, and Roy Chubby Brown was five seats away. Things picked up when Phil Gray rattled the crossbar, the Russ sped away from the leaden Pearson and put us one up. My cry of joy was quickly changed to a cry of "bugger, he's fast," just in time to fend off any questions as to what Paul the Gas's mate was on about.

The second half got even better when the Jarra Arrer repeated the trick for the second, and I was, mentally at least, floating six feet above my seat. Two goals up, looking like winning after twentyfour seasons of travelling to that God forsaken neck of the woods, and it got even funnier. As the players watched a high ball drop onto the edge of their penalty box, Shaun Cunnington went up in the estimation of all Sunderland fans present by executing a perfectlytimed volley. It would have been the goal of the season had their player-manager not decided to get in the way, and Skinny Shaun almost cut him in half instead of connecting with the ball. As all eyes were on the ball, it was an obvious accident, but the home crowd instantly branded Shaun a butcher. They hadn't the benefit of having watched him for the last year or so, like I had. Presumably those around me thought that I was having a seizure of some sort as I shook and turned slowly purple, but that's what happens when you keep howls of laughter in instead of letting it out. Unfortunately, what should have been a comfortable victory turned into a hard won point as they hit us with a series of cavalry charges in the latter stages and drew level.

We followed this up with a draw at Bramall Lane and a home win over Barnsley to go eight games unbeaten, which was a canny start by our recent standards. Over in the Baltic, the ferry Estonia sank and took nearly a thousand souls down with it, and the Queen visited Russia – presumably to catch up on a few distant relatives and ask how they could have allowed the proletariat run the country for so long. In Ulster, the Loyalists followed the IRA's earlier ceasefire and laid down their arms. Or at least promised not to use them.

If there's one thing I've picked from watching Sunderland, it is that you should never get too confident, and this was a perfect example of why. We lost at Tranmere, then at Millwall in the League Cup, then Southend came to Roker, and won for the fourth consecutive time. No disrespect, but Southend were the sort of team that we'd all said we were glad we didn't have to play again when we came out of Division Three. Millwall claimed the draw that knocked us out of the League Cup, injuring Tony Norman in the process. Thus it was Alec Chamberlain who helped us beat West Brom – as did Martin Smith, back in the side after a brief try-out for Rodgerson, with a goal. Injuries above and beyond that sustained by Norman and suspensions kicked in following the dismissal of Owers at Tranmere – the fourth red card of his Sunderland career – so Uncle Mick brought in Ian Snodin on loan from Everton.

He managed six games, looking very much what he was – a reasonably classy defensive midfielder trying to get match-fit after a series of injuries. Up front, we appeared to have decent options, with Goodman and Phil Gray getting the regular starts, Russ coming up with the goods when given a chance, and the Big Scary option of Lee Howey usually on the bench. With this in mind, David Rush was allowed to go to Hartlepool, and we settled into a run of un-inspirational games, which saw our best performance in a 4-1 defeat of Portsmouth, and the goals from The Don dry up. Despite this, it didn't seem a good idea to sell him to Wolves, and it left us light on experience up front. Benno and Armstrong, both seemingly out of favour since the summer, forced themselves back into the team, but not on a regular basis. In an effort to provide money for Uncle Mick to spend, the National Lottery was launched, with fans regularly buying the manager a ticket in the hope that he'd win the millions needed to brighten things up.

After the traditional defeat at Millwall, Lee Howey made the most of a rare start with both goals against Bristol City, then Uncle Mick showed once again that he knew a good full-back, as Gary Owers opted for a change and was used as bait to bring in Martin Scott - from Bristol City. A nice Christmas present for all of us red and whites, but a bit of a surprise that Owers was allowed to leave, as he never gave less than his all, and rarely missed a match through injury, as well over 300 games in seven seasons testifies. Still, times change, things move on, but not in Russia, where they still think that they own their former neighbours. Chechenia had decided to break away from the union, but Moscow decided they couldn't, and sent the tanks in, sparking memories of Hungary and Czechoslovakia, but with much obvious unrest amongst the Soviet troops. On the bright side, peanut farmer and former US president Jimmy Carter managed to prise a ceasefire from the warring factions in Bosnia – some things never cease to amaze.

On Boxing Day, we only managed a draw with Bolton, and Benno's red card sent our disciplinary point total on the up again. If you had to point the finger at anything as a reason for our inconsistency, it would have to be at our midfield. It was completely unsettled, with Owers, Rodgerson, Atky, Martin Smith, Martin Gray, Snodin, Bally, Ferguson, Armstrong, Skinny Shaun all getting a go in the last two months of the year. Consistency in team selection is likely to produce consistency in performance, but we didn't get either.

As a bit of a joke, the FA fixed the little velvet bag, and drew us against Carlisle for the second year in a row, and, as last time around, we managed to scrape a 1-1 draw at Roker – this time thanks to a goal from the Russ. Over the A69, and another awful night weatherwise, but Gorgeous Gordon bagged two and Phil Gray the other as Big Chief Lee Howey came off the bench to rough them up a bit, which they didn't like one little bit. That took us through to a fourth round tie at home to Spurs, but they were all up to the ears in superstars at the time, and 4-1 really took the Michael – as did Benno's second red card in as many months.

Just the League, then.

At long last, and after many injuries, Steve Agnew arrived to add some shape to the centre of the park, for an outlay of £250,000. Then, in an effort to fill the void left by Goodman's departure, Paul Williams (no, not the full-back of a few years ago) came in from Palace on loan, but the fans have yet to work out why. In his three games, he played like a sulky schoolboy who'd turned up without his gym kit, had to borrow some from a much bigger boy, and wouldn't speak to anyone else as a consequence. We'd already scraped a draw at Oldham, surely the coldest ground in the professional game (I've been to Tow Law, it's a different world – hence the saying "cold as a Tow Law rabbit"), before Williams made his debut as we lost at home to Notts County. Bally won us a point at home to the mighty Port Vale before we travelled to Charlton, where Williams had made his name as a footballer. He might as well have had relegation printed on the back of his shirt, along with the rest of the team, as he cut a forlorn figure on the pitch.

Having travelled down en-masse via cheap train tickets, enjoyed a lunchtime's quaffing in the Lamb, and then being hopelessly undercharged in the Antigallican while winning 75% of the Charlton scratchcards we bought, we were in one of those moods regularly experienced when watching Sunderland play away. Hopelessly optimistic, pathetically upbeat, blindly expectant – call it what you will, it happens now and then, and you can't do anything to stop it. Unless, of course, you get all sensible and realistic – but where's the fun in that, unless you support Arsenal or Brazil? As ever, our bright mood was misplaced as we flopped rather than crashed to the only goal of a lifeless encounter. When will it end? Will the snows never cease? Are we destined to tread the path of mediocrity forever? Nah – remember, as you do at times like these, Wembley 73. Jimmy Monty, Jimmy Montgomery, Jimmy Montgomery seventy-three – and anything seems possible, if unlikely. Our alcoholic ramblings on the return from King's Cross obviously sent the right vibes to the team, as the Son of Pele, Martin Smith, popped in both goals to draw with Portsmouth, then the Russ struck to beat Watford, and Steve Agnew's first goal for us won the game at Southend.

Stupid, stupid hopeless optimism, pathetically up-beat mood, blind expectancy – home defeat by Tranmere, defeat at Wolves. Serves us right for getting a bit chirpy, I suppose, but Mary Melville got his third of the season to beat Stoke, and provide brief respite before four consecutive defeats, including one at home to the Boro on their way to the Premiership. In the middle of all this nonsense, Uncle Mick decided our defence needed shoring up (well spotted, Sherlock) and brought in our third loan ranger of the season in Dominic Matteo of Liverpool. Hardly experienced, but he did have that Liverpool thing about him, and was undoubtedly reasonably classy.

He was also undoubtedly completely unsigned, as we didn't get the papers faxed through, or some such nonsense, before putting him on the pitch. We were fined for this administrative misdemeanour, and were grateful that it wasn't points that we lost, although, had the deduction been three, we'd still have survived. Hope I haven't given too much away there. We didn't cheat our way to any points that miserable Friday in South Yorkshire, instead letting Agnew's old chums beat us 2-0. This prompted Buxton to do something many managers in his position do at that time of year, known in football circles as the panic buy. Brett Angell, surely another name straight from the pages of Roy of the Rovers, came from Everton on deadline day to save our season. On paper (wait for usual joke), he looked the part – ninety-seven goals to date, big strong lad – but on grass, it was a different matter (there it goes, couldn't resist).

Within a few days of Angell arriving, Buxton was given the chop, and the big front man's confidence was in tatters. With seven games to go, it looked likely that the only way we'd avoid Southend next year was well within our reach – relegation. Names were bandied about as they are at such times, but when the new manager was announced, it wasn't one that had been on the fans' shortlist. Peter Reid, last seen by us as gaffer of the Man City side that had sent us down five years earlier, was the surprise choice. His playing pedigree couldn't be questioned, and he'd taken City as high as they'd been for many years before being sacked. OK, he'll do for the time being, let's see how he does.

Russ got the goal as Sheffield United became April fools at Roker. Things were getting a bit silly at the old ground, partly because it was falling apart (why spend any more than the safety people tell you to when you're moving house before long?), and partly because we still treated the kids in our group as kids. You know how you start out when they're little, by standing them on the barrier, then sitting them on your shoulders (while standing right at the back, of course, so as not to obstruct anyone's view), then using one of those clever swings that hang from the barriers, then you stand behind them so that you're not in the way? Well, it was about this time that, while standing behind my two, Little Michael, and our Mat, that we noticed something glaringly obvious.

Two of the kids were actually taller than all of the adults in our little group, but we'd never even contemplated standing in front of them. Amazing what you notice when the football's not that entertaining, and, after years of my answering my mam's pre-match question of "have you got a hat?" with "yes, you know I always wear a flat cap, and anyway we're under the roof", she was right to ask. Standing, as we did, just under the edge of the Fulwell roof, we could dodge under cover if the rain got too much, and then nip back out into the sunshine if and when it decided to beam down on Roker. On the downside, the edge of the roof was where the pigeons lived, and one took the chance to do what pigeons do during that Sheffield game, and left a large message down the front of my jacket. One of the Shields lads offered me the bag his pie had come in, presumably to wipe it off. I couldn't help myself. "Thanks mate, but it'll be miles away by now." Corny I know, but far more entertaining that most of what was happening on that green bit in the middle.

Out in the big bad world, Russia was still blowing lumps out of Chechenia, the Taliban looked to have taken over in Afghanistan, and Nick Leeson managed to lose his employers, Barings Bank, tens of millions of pounds. Rumours that this cash was actually diverted to Sunderland's bank account have never been disproved, but the fact that it never arrived might be a bit of a clue as to their validity.

Then Bally got the goal that won at Derby, Phil Gray the goal that got a point at home to Luton, and we were certain that the new man had got the players moving in the right direction. Apart from one. I took our Ian to Bolton, where we feasted on cheap Easter Eggs from the supermarket, avoided taunts from local twelve year olds who were so hard that they smoked cigarettes (the bairn's first negative experience of football fans – apart from his sweary friend in the Fulwell, of course), then entered the ground. I had to explain that the funny building at the end of the stadium was the supermarket we'd just vacated, and he, with amazing insight for one of such tender years, said it was a pretty stupid place to put a shop. I could only agree.

Being in the paddock, we could stand right at the front, and be very close to the action both on and of the pitch. Off the pitch, it was the antics of Johnny, still known to my lads as the Legend. On the pitch, it was the antics of the man we'd paid a small fortune for. Brett Angell was frequently only a couple of yards from us, and, to a lad just breaking into Etherley Lane's first eleven, he showed shocking touch. "This is like watching Bishop," said Ian after another attempted trap flew down the wing, and, for the second time that day, I could only agree. Bolton won with the only goal, and we wondered if we were back to the square we frequented so often – one.

Not this time, as the Son of Pele got his shooting boots out and won the points that ensured we'd be playing Southend the following season. The win over Swindon was nice, the following to Burnley for a point was enormous, and then we had to finish it all off against West Brom. Brett Angell, six feet two and well over thirteen stone, found himself replaced by Steven Brodie, five feet seven and ten and a half stone. As well as Smith, Phil Gray, a man with a point to prove, scored to get the point that lifted us to fifth from bottom and safety. Some might say we'd had a poor season, but some might say we'd survived. Pessimist and optimists – some might say that the glass is half full, some might say that some bugger had pinched their pint.

Another season of mediocrity that almost turned really bad, but with enough signs of life in the last few games to keep us on the right side of suicidal over the summer. Peter Reid had ridden into town on his white charger, saved the day, and won himself a permanent contract. And he was older than me, if only just.

Ag-new
Ag-new
Stevie Ag-new
He's got no hair but we don't care
Stevie Ag-new

1995-1996

If you've been wondering about the lack of detail in the musical references between the mid eighties and mid nineties can I just say one word – children. The time and emotional effort you put into bringing them up means that some other things have to take a back seat, and in my case it was music. Not that I didn't listen any more, just that I stayed with what I'd already got. Thankfully, my two, perhaps through being brought up on a diet of Costello, Jam, Zep, New Order, Magazine, and the Clash (in no particular order, I must stress) amongst choice others, didn't go down the Bros/Jive Bunny kiddies' nonsense route. OK, so my nephew did, no reflection on my sister, and that was only a temporary thing.

Consequently, by the time they started to take a proper interest, it was in music in which I could also show an interest without being embarrassed. Whatever their choice was, I could roll with it, and have an excuse to start going to concerts (or gigs as the kiddies call them today) over the next few years as their tastes grew and diversified. This was, after all, the summer of Britpop, when British bands started to play songs using guitars, and singing words along to the tunes – radical stuff indeed.

With my Sunday morning team the Bittermen having taken the art of après-ski to a new level over the past fourteen years, it was nice to discover two of my team-mates were holidaying near me in Devon – Stu in the same village, and Micky Pen just a few miles away. So, as you do on such occasions, we arranged a barbecue, which Sunderland shirts to wear, and what kind of beer to bring along. On the morning of the day arranged, Judith bumped into Big Kev's wife on a crowded beach as we watched Wimbledon's youth team showing off to the besotted teenage female holidaymakers. The ladies went for a drink, Big Kev and I went for a drink, and further Barbie invitations were issued. Perhaps for the best, he had other arrangements, as Kev is of the Tyneside persuasion, and his dress sense would have spoiled the occasion, and certainly the photographs, somewhat.

Where it wasn't so sunny, the Bosnians were using the UN peacekeepers as human shields by chaining them to posts (I thought Jimmy Carter had sorted this out last year?), and Harold Wilson died. Early in the summer, Tim Gilbert died – only thirty-six, local lad, played (mostly when Joe Bolton was suspended) and scored for Sunderland. A player I'd watched, a player younger than me. It's not right when that sort of thing happens.

The new broom, Peter Reid, had decided to sweep in some changes at Roker, meaning that we'd seen the last of Benno, who eventually left for Carlisle in November after nigh on 450 games for the Lads, Ferguson went to Falkirk, Anthony Smith went to Northampton, and Tony Norman to Huddersfield, and Brodie went on loan to Doncaster, then Scarborough. West Brom swooped, if that's the word, for Shaun Cunnington. Back came le Brace from the dark side, as player/assistant manager, and in came John Mullin from Burnley, and Paul Stewart on loan from Liverpool. The first game did not go to plan, as Leicester came and won, and we failed to score at Norwich, and Reid had seen enough of Angell, and after eleven games with just one goal, Brett was off on a series of loan deals that would keep him away from our first team until his move back home to Stockport a year later.

Craig Russell stepped up from the bench to take his place, and Melville and Phil Gray got the goals to beat Wolves. Much of the summer debate amongst Sunderland fans had been Gray's discomfort, and when it became known just how much Angell's contract was worth, we understood what he was twisting about. Perhaps he'd be happier now that Brett was obviously not in Reidy's plans, but, from a fans' perspective, who would buy the lad after the time he'd had at our place?

Two wins in the opening seven games did not bode too well, but, the 3-0 at Ipswich apart (when Stewart had been injured on his debut and consequently went back to Liverpool. The taunts of who ate all the pies were probably still ringing in his ears from his appearance at Roker the previous season when on loan to Palace), we'd looked fairly solid at the back with Ord and Melville benefiting from the terminator-like presence of Bally in midfield. Bally overdid the competitive bit against Southend when a neck-high tackle (the bloke was on the ground already) got him sent off. Brace and Mickey Gray became regular parts of the midfield, but Agnew had been injured in the first game, and his place was filled by Smith or Atkinson, depending on the weather.

The League Cup was worth entering simply because we got to see Angell score at Preston as we drew in the first leg. Our thoughts of the away goal being enough were shot to pieces as North End romped to a 2-0 half time lead at Roker, and the fans were preparing for an early exit. Lee Howey then showed the worth of a fan in a red and white shirt, as he led the second half comeback with two goals, and the whole thing was made much happier with the appearance of OG. This brought up a nice tie with Liverpool and we acquitted ourselves reasonably at Anfield despite a 2-0 defeat and Mickey Gray providing the now customary penalty miss. In the second leg, in front of a house as packed as it could get on Roker's last legs, we suffered a narrow defeat, but the main talking point was Martin Smith's sending off after he'd dived in on Rob Jones, fists had been raised by the Liverpool man, and two red cards were shown.

Back in the League, Reidy had brought in ex-Mag David Kelly, a man with a decent goalscoring record, but tended to play him on the right with Phil Gray and Russell in the centre. We started to get a decent run of results together, with consecutive away wins in the south (a memorable feat in itself) at Luton, thanks to two cracking goals – a sweet strike from Mullin and a lob from Phil Gray - and Millwall. After five missed penalties, Scotty got the job at the Den, and showed how it should be done. Kelly's first goal came in the home draw with Reading, then he followed it up with the winner at Palace – but it was anything but a straightforward win.

I found my 1995 diary at work recently, and there is a note from a colleague stuck to the 5th October. It read "Lesley Coates rang from SAFC – the game is definitely on." Doesn't sound much in itself, but that note was the culmination of two weeks haranguing of the football hierarchy. As we were playing in London, I wanted to get the cheap train tickets sorted out – the sooner, the cheaper – but there were international matches coming up and there was talk of Division One games being postponed, including ours. So I rang the club and explained. They didn't know. So I rang the Irish FA and demanded to speak to someone who knew what was going on. The poor fella there knew about arranging the international games, but not about individual leagues and their decision on whether to play matches or not. So I rang the Football League, and couldn't find anybody in that marvellous organisation who either knew anything or was prepared to put me through to somebody who did. Just as I was about to get the United Nations involved, along came the call from Sunderland, to let an ordinary fan know that the weekend's game was definitely going to be played. Which was nice, and Ms Coates went to the top of my Christmas card list.

Trains booked just in time, Pos and I made rendezvous in the Lamb with Reg, now in Ross-on-Wye, that famous hotbed of Sunderland support, and made our way to the leafy suburbs of Croydon. After the novelty of having to buy a ticket at one window to present to the turnstile next door (for about £1.35 less than the advertised price. The lad probably works in the City now, worth millions – or in Burger King), the pitch just hove into view as Martyn the home keeper let the ball bounce off his chest, and we won a penalty. Scotty hit both posts and the ball went safe. Damn, we thought – this was a chance for three wins in a row in the South – we won't get a better chance than that. So we took it, when Bally knocked another Martyn rebound back into the middle and Kelly scuffed the ball in to give us the three points, and we began to believe.

There was still time for Brace to put a second penalty awfully wide, so I'm not quite sure what we believed in, but it was something along the lines of we've won a few games around London, and it's still October – what's going on? When you've had to work so hard to get one goal, it makes the pleasure amongst the fans that much greater, and there was much throwing about of folks – including Kevin Scott, ex-Mag, but Sunderland fan, standing just next to me. It might be one of the English football world's least favourite journeys, with not only 280 miles of motorway, but then at least ten miles of suburbia, to negotiate, and a three or four-part train journey, but coming back from that one wearing a smile all the way exercised facial muscles that I'd forgotten I possessed.

The home draw with Watford might have been a disappointing result, but the point, thanks to Scotty's goal, moved us up to third place, which was nice – if a little early in the season for my liking. We followed that with a trip to Huddersfield, meeting up with the family of local lad Marc Howland, with whom our Ian had struck up a friendship on our camping holiday at Whit. The choice of the Bradley Mills Social Club as our rendezvous gave me the chance to use probably the world's smallest such institution, being no more than a two-bed roomed terrace house with a bar both upstairs and down. The lad's family turned out to be as friendly as you like, and also as mad as you like, which makes for an interesting time. The barman puzzled everybody by keeping his fleece zipped up when the room was packed with steaming (hot, not drunk) bodies, and it was only when the barmaid unzipped it that we understood why.

The feckless youth was wearing a black and white shirt, complete with the badge of Satan. Either they teach them nowt in the schools of Huddersfield, or it was a bet well worth winning. I favour the former. Anyhow, Phil Gray earned us a point as both goals arrived late on then we followed up with three from the home game against Barnsley, and a Mickey-Gray inspired draw at Charlton. Phil Gray showed that he was worth more in wages than the almost-departed Brett Angell by scoring both in the win over the under-performing Sheffield United, and we were still in fourth place and starting to think the unthinkable. No, not that the Mags were actually a decent club, but that we could get better, and actually challenge for an automatic promotion spot.

A midweek trip to Stoke meant a swift finish from work and leaving TallPaul's place of employment in Darlo at five – a tight trip to the Potteries. As it was, we parked up six feet from the ground and missed the first ten seconds. The trip wasn't as tight as the match, or as tight as football's smokiest half-time concourse – which was like being in a sauna, but with tabs instead of hot coals providing the fug. Roy Wallace of Stoke took a rare chance and scored the only goal when a win would have sent us into one of the top spots, and Brace was stretchered off. Was the season slipping back into the usual groove? No, because Aggers was fit again, and Big Chief Lee Howey came up with the winner at West Brom, then Scotty was successful with the third penalty that Palace had handed us that season.

Second place – that'll do nicely, and a nice way to celebrate the fact that we'd been granted planning permission for the new ground at Wearmouth Colliery, but things got even better the next weekend when top-of-the-table Millwall came to Roker for the division's Match of the Day. For once, the game lived up to expectations, but not in the way anybody thought. It started well, as old boy Anton Rogan extended unnecessary generosity by conceding a penalty and up stepped Scotty to do the right thing (what was wrong with the people who fixed the odds at the bookmaker's in the ground? Usually 16 to one – down from his original 33 to 1 – against scoring the first goal, he was never shorter than 9 to 1, no matter how often he scored. The pound a fortnight that Pos and I invested in Scotty's trusty left boot paid for most of our pre-match beer that season) and Phil Gray, while Russ had the game of his life, scoring four and carving himself a little niche in the hearts of Sunderland supporters everywhere. We are top of the league, said we are top of the league. Our defence had become a wonderwall, and was so tight that you could get way with only scoring the odd one up the other end.

Shut up, you speak to soon. While we did manage to score the next week, Gareth Hall came off the bench and we lost 3-1 at Derby as Marco showed what we'd let go by scoring and generally tormenting. Phil Gray asked for a transfer, presumably because we wouldn't pay him as much as we were still paying Brett Angell. That was our last goal of the year, and we saw Christmas come and go with us in second place thanks to a home defeat by Norwich, and a draw at Leicester which saw Hall mark his first start with a sending off.

We were given a good chance to see what we'd be up against when the velvet bag produced a tie at Old Trafford, and we showed the world what we could do in a cracking 2-2 draw. The trip is memorable as the last time Sunderland fans could get a drink anywhere near the ground, but pulling the glass-collector's trousers down when he had his hands full (of glasses, naturally enough) probably ensured no entry for future games in one particular pub. We treated the bairns to seats in the Cantona-Free Zone behind the goal, and the visiting crowd put the home fans to shame with their enthusiasm. An opening goal from Butt had us on the back foot for a while, but then came the second half, and first Agnew with a 25 yarder, then Russ with a typical left-foot shot across the keeper, to put us ahead, tempting one Sunderland fan in the home end to give his secret away by jumping up and down for five full minutes.

Late on, a bit of a soft free-kick from their right saw Chamberlain hesitate and Cantona equalised. Still, we could treat them to a spot of the old Roker Roar in the replay, and we cranked up the atmosphere to do just that. 21,000 was all that we could get in to the dear old ground, but it would have been a few dozen more had they not erected a large shed next to where we stood, to house the TV pundits – who numbered Bryan Robson (their old boy, not ours), and it was only the sharp eyes of a steward which prevented me from snapping the padlock shut on the outside of the door. It was an act of foolish optimism to leave such a tempting opportunity begging and no-one to try and take it. Another good showing, but not enough, as, despite Phil Gray's poke into the Fulwell net putting us ahead, ex Mag Andy Cole headed the winner – also into the Fulwell net.

Well, we only wanted the League anyway.

Not that we played like we wanted it that badly for the first few weeks, despite having four games in hand over most other teams. While we hadn't been letting that many goals in, even fewer would be better, so Reidy brought in Shay Given (who?), Blackburn's nineteen-year-old reserve keeper and stuck him straight into the side. A home defeat by Norwich saw us slip to eighth, then a home draw with Leicester moved us up a place before Dickie Ord arrived at inside right to beat Grimsby. This was a good day for Dickie, but a bad day for David Kelly, whose ankle gave out and he vanished for the rest of the season, and Paul Stewart, hardly seen in his loan spell, signed permanently to fill in for the poor lad. Another home game, this time against Tranmere, saw another loan player, Man Utd's Terry Cooke, come into the team with his arrival probably having something to do with our coach, Pop Robson, having been the lad's youth team boss at Old Trafford. This game gave us the chance to move up further, but we couldn't score.

Things came to a head with a bad 3-0 defeat at Wolves, including the compulsory contribution from ex-Rokerman Don Goodman, and we needed to stop the rot quickly if we were to stay in contention. A home draw wasn't exactly what we had in mind, but we then went on the sort of run that normally only happens in the Rover. Aggers and Big Lee, playing centre half but in the right place in the last minute, got us a draw at Portsmouth, then Russ won the first of nine on the trot when partnered with Howey. Nine. OK, the second was a bit jammy, thanks to an own goal, but we were racking up league doubles, and away wins. At Southend, where a seventeen-year old called Michael Bridges made his fourth substitute appearance and got his first goal only half a minute after coming on, but thanks to the fog, there's only sketchy video footage of this big moment. The ref decided that the game was playable because he could see both ends from the middle, but neither goalie could see the other.

At Grimsby, the party started as Phil Gray's effort from about forty yards capped a stinker from the home goalie, and Bridges came off the bench to get his second in as many games. Then there was a 3-0 revenge over Derby, with a brace from Russ, and a cold, dark night at Oldham. The slightly dodgy spell was all but forgotten as we refused to look back in anger. After five consecutive clean sheets, Given actually let a goal in on the stroke of half time, but not before a lovely chip from Mickey Gray had put us ahead. Bally was in no mood to let this one slip, and he drove the team on to victory. Cramped into the little visitor's enclosure behind the goal, we were so close to the action you could have just about made a tackle if you'd wanted to.

The eruption of bodies from their seats and into the night air when Bally rose to nut in the winner in the dying minutes was another of those special moments that you get in situations like that. So was being kissed by Pete H's daughter, but that's another matter, and just made the night even better. The really big step came at St Andrews the next Sunday – another televised spectacular. We looked as if we were taking the mickey out of the Brummies with goals from Aggers and Mel, a thoroughly professional performance from our Lads.

Poor old Oldham –only eleven days after we beat them at their place, Scotty won the Lads another three points and me and Pos another few pints with the only goal – by arriving on the right hand post to knock the ball in… and he'd already hit the bar twice. He must have appreciated our thirst. This just gets better, we thought, but Huddersfield almost spoiled things. Ian's mate brought his crazy family to The Saltgrass, including his Uncle, who'd just come back from an alcohol-free six-month stint working in Saudi, and who was therefore very successfully making up for lost time. With Tony Norman returning to his old stopping-ground, they entered the last few minutes with a 2-1 lead, and we'd all but conceded defeat – on the terraces. Not on the field, though, and not in Pos's head, although he may just have been trying to impress eight-year-old son Kris upon the appearance of Michael Bridges as the seconds ticked away. "It's alright son, this Lad'll get a couple of goals."

The Lad in question duly did get a couple of goals, doing that nichecarving thing, and winning a dramatic game. Letting in those two goals must have affected us, or maybe we were just emotionally drained after winning nine games in a row, as we let in three at Watford the following game, but still managed three ourselves and stayed unbeaten. A win at Barnsley thanks to Russ, but despite Stewart's red card, and we were just about home and dry with six games till to play. Given went back to Blackburn, we passed upon the chance to sign him permanently, and the rest is his story. Chamberlain straightened himself up after sitting on the bench for three months, and carried on where the bruised young Irishman had left off. Sunderland fans hit the charts with Cheer up Peter Reid (often copied since, but never bettered) and Simply Red and White took a tongue-in-cheek swipe at our gaffer's now legendary touchline expression. Oh what can it mean, to a Sunderland supporter, to be top of the league?

Two more goal-less draws, then a three-nil thumping of Birmingham which included Stewart's first goal, left us needing a point for certain promotion, but results elsewhere meant that was achieved without kicking a ball. The draw with Stoke was more of a party than a game, and another goal-less draw at home to West Brom, made us champions. From our seats in the family area (the lower tier in the Main Stand, right next to the Roker End) we got a great view of the celebrations, and the Baggies stayed behind to join in the fun. When their largest fan was ejected for taking his shirt off and exposing a stomach of Tyneside proportions, a large section of the crowd took up the chant "We want fatty back, I said we want fatty back," and you know what? They let him back in. We were up. Not only up, but already champions. By the time we went to the Wirral in our fancy dress (1901 footballers, if you must know), we didn't really care what happened. We were going to have a party to end all parties (well, the best one for a canny while, at least). Having the new Kop end, and the whole of one side of the ground, meant that we matched the home side for support, but not the home side for football. On the field it went sadly wrong, and Aldridge was among the scorers with a penalty that we considered unfair. To be honest, it didn't matter, the stewards manfully kept the gates onto the field shut for a minute or so after the whistle, then said "Oh, get on with it" and assorted cartoon characters, pop stars (both dead and alive) and, of course, four 1901 footballers complete with stick-on giant 'taches, invaded the pitch and chaired the team and manager on high.

The Tranmere fans shook our hands, swapped mementoes (I had a Tranmere club sweater, in tasteful blue acrylic, for several years after this, but, for reasons that will become obvious in another few chapters, it's gone the charity shop route now – I think), and we then wandered back to the Shrewsbury Arms to watch the Mags spectacularly not win the Premier League. The locals looked on in disbelief as we sang the song of the moment "Silverware, silverware, the Mags have got no silverware. From Leazes Park to Eldon Square, the Mags have got no silverware."

Then we went home for a celebratory pint or two. To be honest, we'd been having them for the last three weeks after matches, but now that it was all officially over, we could officially celebrate. With eighteen games unbeaten, we had a good right to celebrate. With the championship in the bag, we had good right to celebrate. With the appearance of Breathe-rite nasal strips, we had reason to celebrate. Let the good times roll. It was going to be a good summer – promotion, sunshine, and a small matter of Euro 96 on our home turf to look forward to. Reidy might have come across as a charmless man, but he was fine by us.

He's from Murton, one thing's certain
He's not scared of these
Who needs Cantona
When we've got Dickie Ord

1996-1997

The briefest of camping trips this year, as I'd booked the Big Florida Holiday, like all good families did when the kids got to a certain age. Having bought Gaz a guitar for his birthday last year, and arranged lessons, that had been the end of peace in our house as he took to the instrument like a youth possessed. You only had to look at him sideways and he'd slope off and write a song about it, but at least he wasn't stealing cars or their radios like many of his contemporaries. Homing Pigeon Boy virtually lived in my Cavalier, and it spent as much time crashed into the kerb at the end of his street as it did outside my house. I should have given the little sod a set of keys to save him breaking into it.

Anyhow, no sooner had I booked the Disney family-thing (I had the money, it was either a big holiday or a new kitchen – no contest as far as I was concerned, although Judith did the sensible thing and thought about it for a civilised period of time before making the choice on the side of jollity) than I had to go away with work for a month – to Florida. It was a dirty job, but somebody had to do it, and I left with strict instructions not to spend my spare time doing anything that we'd do as a family. The day before my departure, I went to Sid James Park to watch the Romanians and Bulgarians draw their Euro 96 game, wearing a Sunderland tie into the Platinum club, to ward off the evil spirits.

No family-type activities in Florida was fine by me, and there wasn't that much spare time anyway, but I managed a trip in the world's slowest airboat to see the world's most docile alligators, and a weird weekend in Key West (it's a weird place, where they gather to clap the sunset. What would they do if it was cloudy?), and a lot of time in a small factory where they kept snakes in their cars, sold guns to the police, and lived for beer o'clock on a Friday.

This involved standing around in the blazing sun drinking various fizzy American beers from several iceboxes in the boots (sorry, trunks) of people's cars, wondering why the Americans insisted on wearing vests and woolly shirts at the height of their summer. We'd managed to catch the England games on the TV by getting the staff to check Fox Sports channel 77 or something equally obscure, laughed our way through the win against Spain (in a Spanish bar), cheered our way through the Holland game, and then taken an hour off work to watch the standard failure against Germany. All the while singing Three Lions, as you do. A busy trip, with work thrown in to make it even busier. As it was, I'd only been back a fortnight when it was time to head off to Orlando and more sun. Which was a nice way to spend the summer.

Big changes afoot at Roker. We knew it was going to be demolished after the season, and that we'd have a new home to go to just up the road, but the team it was a changing as well. Alec Chamberlain went to Watford (where he was still registered as a player up until last season and citing Bally as the best captain he's played with), Phil Gray left for Nancy (stop it), and we brought people in like never before. Well, not for a few years at least, as Niall Quinn became our first million-pound-plus signing, Alex Rae arrived, and so did two goalkeepers – Tony Coton we all remembered, as he'd saved a penalty against us on his debut, for Birmingham, and been all over since then, and Lionel Perez, who nobody knew. What puzzled some of the fans was why we didn't make more of an effort to sign Given for what was widely reported to be the asking price of a couple of million quid, when he'd kept more clean sheets than an empty hotel in his loan spell and was fifteen years younger.

Big changes afoot on the terraces as well, as Pos and I abandoned the Fulwell. Not a decision we took lightly, but with no season tickets for juniors in that part of the ground, it was off to the family enclosure, previously known as the Fulwell wing of the Main Stand. It wasn't that we particularly wanted season tickets, although the adults in our party had been using them for a few seasons, but the shenanigans that possession of one saved when it came to tickets for big matches made them worthwhile. To be honest, if it wasn't for the change to the all-ticket culture, I still wouldn't have one out of choice, if only because of the one big financial outlay involved.

There's nothing that gets on my nerves more than a caller to a radio phone-in opening the conversation with "I'm a season ticket holder" as if this somehow makes them a better person. It's another memento of the season to pathetically hang on to as well – I'm one of those sad folks who has the tickets for every game I've ever been to that required a ticket (apart from the Rotherham FA Cup game in 1998, when the old gadgie on the turnstile had obviously never seen a ticket before, and kept the big bit for himself, leaving me with just the stub. Oh, and the Arsenal League Cup game a few years later, but that's another story…) and they're framed up by the season, or waiting to be, while I wait for a suitable space on the wall. The season ticket books sit on the shelf at the top of the cellar steps in a neat pile that grows by the thickness of however many season tickets the household has purchased for the preceding campaign.

This campaign began against Leicester, who'd come up with us, but Quinny only made the bench and couldn't score when he did come on. At least the most important thing was achieved, in that we didn't lose, but against the play-off winners, who'd finished four places below us, it was a bit disappointing. Probably the high-point of the game was the first appearance of groundsman Tommy Porter's artistic interpretation of lawn-mowing, as the grass pattern at Roker became a subject of regular pre-match debate. At Forest, Quinny did make his first start, but was upstaged by Mickey Gray's 25-yarder opening the action, only for Bally to kill the keeper and watch the ball bounce off the Irishman's shin and in for 2-0. By half-time it was 4-1, thanks to a more conventional Niall goal and one from Dickie Ord, and the evening travellers were bouncing around the City Ground as if we'd just won the League. The same final score and we were all of the belief that we'd arrived in the big time properly, and were there to stay.

I knew what I wanted for my birthday, wanted it delivered a day early, and thought my wish had come true when Scotty's penalty went into the Fulwell net. A shot back off the post, and we were looking decidedly canny for the win. There were supposedly no Mags at the match as the clubs entered into a slightly pathetic game of tit-for-tat and banned visiting supporters. To my eternal shame, I'd got a ticket for a Mag from work, in the vain hope of reciprocal ticketing favours in the return fixture. Second-half headers from the Hunchface of Notre Dame and Ferdinand spoiled my day and that of the rest of Wearside. I made myself feel a little better when I spotted the Mag in question in his car on the way home. His wife's face was a picture as I pulled out a water pistol and squirted him though his open window. I don't know when real guns were ever made of yellow plastic, or if she was simply frightened because of her pet Mag's natural aversion to water.

Another 0-0, against West Ham, brought another point, then, just as it was looking like another one at Derby despite having Ord sent off, Gareth Hall gave away the crucial late penalty that cost us the game. The fact that Hall was playing instead of Kubicki, who had played 123 consecutive games since his arrival at the club, might go some way to explain why the fans were a bit hard on young Gareth. If you wanted consistency, it was probably the Pole's' middle name, and Hall had hardly set the Roker Park pitch ablaze with his defensive displays when given the chance. Goals were hard to come by, Forest apart, and we had to work hard to hang onto the lead against Coventry given to us by Agnew. Quinny had scored twice in the league, although he knew little about the first, and when he trod on the ball at the Fulwell End, we wondered if he was going to be of any real use. When his knee collapsed near the Clock Stand, we could see that it was serious, and that was him off the radar for a long time, probably the rest of the season.

The League Cup brought us up against Watford, but no Alec Chamberlain and Mad Alex got his first red and white goal in an aggregate 3-0 win that included an absolute screamer from Scotty that was still rising as it hit the net. Bally's goal in the game at Spurs had us in the lead until the dying stages, but we collapsed in spectacular fashion to lose 2-1, and we'd done with the trophy for another season.

A trip to Arsenal is always an excuse for a day out in the Lamb as Highbury is only three tube stops from the pub, so we stocked up on Youngs Bitter, wrote our list of daft bets (I chose Bally, Pos chose Scotty, and Steve chose Ord – despite him missing the game through suspension). If we'd put the same amount on Frankie Dettori to win every race on the card that day, we'd have been sharing over £200,000. We didn't, and had to endure the usual battering that comes with a visit to that part of the football world. We didn't help ourselves when Scotty collected a second yellow for an over enthusiastic challenge on Lee Dixon, then lone striker Stewart hit the ball with his hand after a rather hefty nudge by Bould. The look on the Arsenal man's face when the red card came out was a picture, and I'm afraid that I'd have been sent further than the stands had I been in Reidy's place in the dugout.

So there we were, down to nine men, the manager in the stands, and against one of the country's more attacking teams, at their place. And it wasn't even half time, so there was no escape to the Lamb for the faint-hearted amongst us. Tin hats and entrenching tools were passed to our defence, which pretty soon included all eight outfield players in behind sandbags with fixed bayonets. Our attacking options were reduced to hoofing the ball from the edge of our penalty box towards their corner flags, and hoping they'd get tired running back for it and slicing one into their own net. As it was, it was a remarkable defensive display and a miracle that we held on for as long as we did until Hartson got on the end of a left-wing cross to breach our tiring defence. A second late goal made it curtains for us as our brave lads were virtually dead on their feet, as if we needed an excuse for a post-match pint. At least public sympathy, for once, came our way in buckets the next day.

Dickie Ord was back for the Boro game at Roker, but he could do nothing about a thunderbolt from the bloke who looked more like a soul singer than a footballer, Emerson. Mad Alex levelled it with a penalty in Scotty's enforced absence, then Ord lost his head and trod on Barmby and Ravanelli scored for them. Russ, from the bench, saved the day and the point, but three would have been much more use. Would we get them after a long trip to Southampton? Not a chance. Getting beat was bad enough, but Coton broke his keg in about a dozen places, and that was the end of his playing days. Enter Lionel Perez, the keeper who looked more like a fairground attendant, for a real baptism of fire as we lost 3-0 and dropped further down the table.

We needed a win, and inspiration from somewhere. It was becoming apparent that Brace was not the force he had been during his previous stays on Wearside, and that the heartbeat of the team was being generated by Bally. He drove the team on against Villa, and when Bosnich gave away a penalty, Kelly fired against the post and Stewart put away the rebound. Not pretty, but effective, and I missed it, victim of a spiked drink the previous evening leaving me dozing unhappily until way past the final whistle. After my usual Friday evening shift at the Sportsman, I was exercising the bar staff's indisputable right to a bit of a stoppy-back in a little bar up the road when it all went wrong. I might have been tired, but four pints and a large Paddy's does not put you into a coma for eighteen hours. I think I know who did it but I've never been able to prove it, or understood why he did it, but I've kept a safe distance ever since.

In a season where wins were turning out to be a bit of a rarity, the last thing you need is for some nutter to make you miss one of them. Still, a win's a win, and it was a family trip to Elland Road the next week – no freebies this time, I'd discovered that you could get nice cheap seats by going as a family. So Nige became my brother-inlaw for the day and we collected our tickets for the family end, which turned out to be a few seats at the end of the Main Stand. The nightclub style bouncers, noticeably different in appearance to the "normal" matchday stewards told us to keep our mouths shut, cover up our colours, and generally behave, as they had no intention of keeping "that lot" away from us. Nice. You think that if you've gone to the effort of getting to Leeds and risking your neck, the team would at least make the effort to get something out of it. When our best chance fell to Bally, who put it over, we contrived to let the shortest man on the pitch score a header, and ended up the wrong side of three goals and only three places off the bottom. I decided to pay full whack next time, and see if it changed my luck.

It was no doubt with the team's performances in mind that work asked me to go back to Florida, probably reckoning that I could do with a bit of light relief. Had we been winning week after week, I'd have been less inclined to accept the request, but it was off from the Wearside cold and into the sun again - but not until I'd made sure that my season ticket was going to be used for every game that I'd miss, of course. The outward trip coincided with the match at Spurs (of course it did), so it was a lift from Big Harrier from Heathrow to the tube, and off to the match. They must have had something against me, as I was stuck right at the back in a nook that afforded a view of only three corner flags.

The Lads did not send me off in style, as Stewart got himself sent off, and only some comedy finishing by Spurs, including a penalty miss, kept it at just 1-0 until late on. I took the long walk to Seven Sisters tube in silence and relief that the locals no longer seemed intent on killing anyone who didn't have a Cockney accent, as they were in the seventies, and met up with Harrier in Richmond Rugby Club. The poor lad's wife had just come home from hospital with their second child, and his wonderful Irish mother-in-law was visiting. "I see you still have de earring, Paul," she said, as if such things had never been seen on a man in Dublin since I'd been at the wedding a few years earlier. Lovely woman, Mrs Bennett, but that was my last night in England for a few weeks, and it was off to the sun and the funny little factory the next morning.

The average American's interest in any sport played outside the borders of their own country – or indeed anything that happens outside their own country – is such that I had to ring The Saltgrass to find out the Sunderland scores. 1-1 with Sheff Wed was not what I wanted, and I felt guilty for not being there to urge the Lads on to the victory that they needed. I didn't hold out much hope for a victory on Reidy's return to his former home, Goodison, despite Everton hardly setting the season alight. Then again, that's exactly why football's so bloody marvellous.

I could never tell what time it was back home, and had spent five full minutes telling a blue Scouser what my team would do to his team before he told me that they already had. Just his luck to be the first English football shirt that I saw. A penalty save by Lionel, two goals from Russ, and a 3-1 win had me longing for the mists of Roker in November. Was Goodison the corner that we needed to turn to get us back up the table? The eventual newspaper reports and phone calls home seemed to confirm a good performance, and yet another Bridges-just-off-the-bench goal. Maybe he'd be the boy to do the trick, maybe the young guns of himself and Russ could be more effective than the old head (and legs) of Stewart and the outof- position Kelly.

SAFC became SAFC PLC, joining the growing trend for football clubs to throw themselves at the mercy of the stock market, and offered up shares for a minimum investment of £585. Thankfully, as it has turned out, I didn't have the money to invest and am not, as a consequence, out of pocket. Unlike hundreds of other fans. Investments can go up or down, you know, and ours went down.

And down – a bit like the team. Just when we'd shown that we could actually play football by beating Everton, we let Wimbledon trample us into our own turf, despite the return of Dickie Ord in a 3-1 defeat. That was bad news that reached the USA by phone, but the good news was that the Chelsea game was on TV. Well, I thought it was good news, but, try as I might, the magic of satellite broadcasting still could not persuade the Americans to watch anything other than baseball, ice-hockey, basketball, and that anathema to the word sport, American football. So I missed Russ firing one off someone's backside (probably Frank Sinclair, he's good at that sort of thing), Bally's most dramatic of diving headers into the Fulwell, and a cracking 3-0 win. Just what the doctor ordered and I'd be back in time for the next game.

Oh bugger. I should have stayed in the States. Man Utd had this bloke called Eric Cantona who fancied himself a bit, and, when he wasn't delivering karate kicks to fans who said naughty things about his mother, had good right to. 3-0 over Chelsea put most if us in the frame of mind that considered a trip to Old Trafford a decent opportunity to repeat the performance. Cantona thought otherwise, and capped a virtuoso display with a chip over former team-mate Lionel in a 5-0 rout that had us making nooses from our red and white scarves. Their chants of "You're in the wrong division" were typically arrogant, but didn't seem far off the mark. A much needed win came the next week when the local Lads came good on Boxing Day, in the shape of Russ and Ordy, as we beat Derby 2-0, but the win came at a cost. Bally played a good part of the first half with a broken face after a clash with Powell – the start of a long running feud between that player and Sunderland, culminating in his Dad threatening to shoot Alex Rae – only giving up the fight when he tried to head the ball and felt something wasn't right.

We were up to mid-table, and had a trip to West Ham a couple of days later to climb even further. After sharing Christmas drinks with the Hammers fans in their Supporters' Club, we watched as Radicoiou took a day off from shopping to seal the game with their second. Why can't we have players who can run fifty yards with the ball and then tuck it away? Well, the truth is that we have had them but when someone does it to you, they seem few and far between. They seemed light years away as we travelled back from that one. Coventry on New Year's Day saw a few changes in the team. Bridges and Mullin started up front on a frozen pitch, and it was probably the fact that the Coventry police didn't fancy looking after a couple of thousand matchless Sunderland fans that made the ref start the game. The hard surface meant that the football was of the tappy-lappy tiptoey variety, but our young players coped much better than their opponents. Bridges stuck one away, then Aggers put away a penalty, and the game was there to be won. When Dion Dublin lost his cool and trod on Bridges, it looked even better, but we allowed them to sneak a draw.

Then came Arsenal week. The FA Cup gave us the chance to avenge the battering they and the ref had handed out in September, and we nearly did. Mullin's persistence allowed Mickey Gray to equalise– with his wooden leg – during the coldest match I can remember in the capital, although it didn't help that TallPaul had got us tickets right at the end of the row, next to a cold metal wall right where the wind blew in. Scarves tied over numb ears were the order of the day, but the performance warmed our hearts. The next week we played them in the League, arguably a more important game as we strove to maintain the mid-table position we then occupied, and we got the better of the Gunners as Darren Williams got his first game, at centre-half, and his opposite number Tony Adams chose that day to pop the only goal into the Roker End net, while Dennis Bergkamp made a mess of Brace and was sent off. Mid-table obscurity it was, then, but the replay was still offering us a chance for a bit of a run in the cup. Unfortunately, Roker's last FA Cup tie saw the other side to Bergkamp's character, as he produced a variety of tricks and scored a goal that even the Fulwell applauded.

The League was as much as we needed to cope with, thank you very much.

Our lack of cover at the back prompted the signing of Jan Eriksson – an International footballer who'd scored the opening goal of the European Championships a few years earlier – which seemed like a good piece of business, but all we saw of him was his lumbering warm-ups down the touchline, which was a pretty close view from our little spot in the Paddock. Draws with Blackburn, when the Sun, for some obscure reason, decided to hand out thousands of inflatable red and white sticks (that'll keep us in the Premier League), and Leicester included Dazzle's first Sunderland goal and kept us firmly in the middle, but then it all went wrong. Eriksson's only start saw a shot deflect off him for the only goal at

Villa, and we failed to score in the next three games. We might have been a bit unlucky as we watched a single goal defeat at Blackburn, but the next game was a real low point.

When Pos arrived a few minutes late and we told him that we were already two goals down, he didn't believe us. Five minutes of watching a totally clueless performance convinced him of our honesty. With a natural forward (Kelly) playing on the right wing, and a natural midfielder (Rae) ploughing a lone furrow up front, Spurs could have had ten and we couldn't have complained. Well, we could and we would, but you know what I mean. Scotty had made a one game comeback against Leeds, the same day Bally returned, but the chants of "You don't know what you're doing" came from both sets of fans, and they weren't aimed at the referee. Morale after that one was as low as the morals of a Mags' director, and we could se the team going only one way.

The club then did something positive – it sold Roker Park to a builder for £1.3 million, the same amount that we'd paid for Niall Quinn – but no new players were forthcoming, despite us being linked with every unheard-of foreigner with a funny name that could wear a pair of football boots. Now the ground was officially signed away, the activities at Wearmouth Colliery became even more important. After several years, our post-match routine changed. Instead of bouncing along to the Sports Report theme tune as we crossed the Wearmouth Bridge, we nipped over to the building site and took photographs.

We'd already decided where we were going to sit, and had our little gang of thirteen already assembled and ready to move in. We located our seats, and even managed to sneak through the fence on a couple of occasions, just for a look – after all, they did keep saying it was our ground, our design for life. We visited the Portakabin for the interactive experience, and our album of photographs grew thicker with every home game. The signs said five games to go when Man Utd came to town, but we had a problem. If Man Utd won, they'd get further away from the Mags, who were chasing the Mans in second place. Ah, we thought, we'll have the points – there are plenty of games left for the Mags to win nothing – and we set about the game with a rarely seen fluency. Mickey Gary and John Mullin put us two up before Melville's annual own goal gave us a scare, but we deserved the win. If we could do it against Man Utd, surely we could do it often enough before the end of the season to stay out of trouble.

How can essentially the same bunch of players perform so abjectly one day, then so well only four days later? How indeed. So it was a smiley happy bunch of fans who nipped down the A1 to Hillsborough the next Wednesday, to Wednesday – a form team at the time, but not as good as Man Utd. At least that was the theory. Bally gave us hope, but Wednesday gave us a lesson in finishing, and it was back to square one.

Next up was Chelsea, on the telly again, and we'd already done them in front of the cameras. I wimped out, having been persuaded to do the Coast to Coast bike ride, on condition that they'd get me back to Chez Pos and the televised match after I'd dipped my wheel in the sea at Seaburn. True to their word, I was sat, Maxim in hand with two minutes to spare. I suppose the neutrals enjoyed it, and I can't argue with the fact that it was highly entertaining stuff from a distance. However, when you're emotionally involved, games like that one sting a bit if you're on the receiving end. At 0-3 down in the first half, I was wishing that I was still on my bike, but then Reidy bit the bullet, brought on Stewart and Mad Alex, and they each scored inside a couple of minutes. Game on, we thought. Correct, thought Chelsea, and banged in another three after the break.

Something spectacular was needed to keep us out of the drop zone. There might have been five teams below us, but there weren't that many points between them. Something spectacular arrived in the form of Chris Waddle, but twenty years after it should have done. At thirty-six, his game had never been about speed of foot but speed of thought, and a wise old head was just what we needed – especially if that wise old head came with a magical left foot attached to it (obviously, with a torso and legs as well – even we weren't that desperate). His arrival had the humorous side-effect of two people asking for my autograph in the wildly mistaken belief that I was Chris Waddle. I'll admit that there is a vague facial similarity, and at the time the hair wasn't that different, but did I dress like a footballer? Would any self respecting Premier League player turn up at the ground five minutes from kick-off wearing his shirt, a flat cap, and scarf, and smelling ever so slightly of Samson? (the beer, not the cat). No, he certainly wouldn't, but it was fun while it lasted.

True to form, his corner against Forest was met with a Ball volley for a spectacular goal, but we allowed Des Little to steal two points from us. Then to an all black and white Gallowgate as the no visiting fans nonsense continued, despite supporters of both clubs organising a civilised protest in the centre of Toon. Alan Johnston came from Rennes (that's in France, by the way) and immediately showed what he could do. My reciprocal ticket hadn't materialised, proving yet again to always remember – never trust a Mag. When the Waddler set up Mickey Gray to score, those that got in where a draught couldn't pulled faces from the safety of their executive boxes at the unwashed who were trying to get at them.

In front of the big screen at Roker, we saluted those brave men and women almost as much as we saluted the goal. Still only a draw, though, and we weren't making a gap between us and the dead men. At Anfield, Waddler set up Stewart for a goal, but we let them score twice and we dropped into a relegation place. One of the other places was occupied by the Boro, who had hilariously failed to fulfil a fixture at Blackburn, citing illness and injury, but managing to put out a side in a friendly the same day. They were docked three points thanks to Bryan Robson's belief that because he'd played for England and Man Utd he could break the rules and get away with it. In came Waddler's free-kick, up went Teeside's own Darren Williams, and my personal twenty-seven year wait for a win on Teeside was over. If any of their fans ever tell you that they were relegated that season because of the three points they had deducted, tell them they're wrong. Tell them they went down because of Darren Williams and Sunderland.

Out of the relegation places, and a chance for revenge over Southampton (well, most games in the second half of the season were chances for revenge, to be honest), but Quinny was hovering on the bench, itching to make up for lost time. He kept on itching, as it was way too soon to be coming back after an injury like he'd suffered, but these were desperate times. Another inept performance and we were hovering one place from disaster with only two games to go. Only one competitive match at Roker Park before the demolition men moved in and the place would be gone. What would it be remembered for?

If you're only remembered for the last great thing you did, it wouldn't be much – probably, in fact, the amount of bleeps during BBC's ultimately sad documentary Premier Passions, which we watched with a mixture of emotions somewhere between amused and bemused as Reid and Saxton effed and blinded their way through the half-time team-talks, in the process doing a great disservice to the strength of Wearside tea by comparing it to our tackling that season. It might be remembered for the win over Chelsea, or over Man Utd, but most likely the memories would be further in the past. Much further in the past.

So, along came Everton, already beaten by us, and leaving us with a rare chance to do the League double over somebody. Things in the country had taken a decidedly upward turn in the general election the previous day, when Labour had given the Tories the equivalent of a 6-0 hammering and taken the country back for the people after eighteen years. Eighteen years of that lot – virtually the whole of my adult life. It doesn't bear thinking about.

As if catching the mood, the Roker crowd lifted their spirits and willed success for their Bonny Lads. With the house as full as it could be, we actually outplayed the opposition, Stewart put away a penalty, then Waddle did the same with an exquisite free-kick, Johnston's first red and white goal put his name in the history books as the man to score the last competitive goal at Roker Park. 3-1 put us one place above the relegation places, and only a game at Wimbledon to play. At Selhurst Park. Oh great. Being a sensible sort, I left it way too late to buy a ticket, and travelled down on the Saturday morning, having a night out in Peterborough, and spending the night on the floor of a boxing hall above a pub belonging to someone's brother-in-law.

Some folks stayed at the bar all night and even had the cheek to ask for our departure to be delayed so that they could have another pint. Fair enough, but some of us still had tickets to sort out. As I queued at the ticket office, I overheard people being told that there were no more to be had, and was about to start tunnelling when the lady in front tried to return a ticket. Quick as a flash, I was in. "I'll have it," I said, £7 changed hands, and I was in – into the Wimbledon family end. I explained my predicament to a steward as soon as I got to my seat, and asked if I could be transferred to the part of the ground where all of my friends were (any of the parts of the ground where all of my friends were), but all he said was "No, and if you don't cover that shirt up, I'll throw you out."

I know when I'm not wanted, so I watched as the other three sides of the ground filled up with red and white, and by kick-off the visitors outnumbered the home fans by three to one. The highpoint of the afternoon came in the shape of a Daily Sport streaker – they'd arranged one at every Premiership game that day, apparently – then got down to the action. Listening to the home fans and watching their team's display, it was quite clear that the last thing they wanted was to send us out of the division. Quinny was back in the starting line-up, but clearly playing despite the pain instead of after it. If only Stewart's headed chance had fallen to Niall, things might have been different. If only Alex Rae hadn't remained an unused substitute, things might have been different. If only Substitute Bridges had fired to Sullivan's left instead of his right. If only we hadn't presented them with a chance that no sane man could pass up. If only the Coventry fans hadn't experienced some road-works on the M1, causing their kick-off at Tottenham to be delayed….hang on, wasn't that the same M1 that that the majority of our fans had travelled down that morning, but with the added hassle of getting across or around London to find Selhurst Park?

Forgive me if I sound a little paranoid here, but the fact that it was Coventry, yet again, who were involved… surely it's impossible it could be a coincidence. It doesn't matter that the eventual result at White Hart Lane was immaterial – why don't Sunderland fans, or the club, seem to get treated the same way as people like Coventry and Bristol City? When all of the teams apart from the Mags want us to stay up because we're fun people who spend loads of money and take all of our ticket allocations, why doesn't the "management" see it that way? Why make all of the fuss over synchronising every game on the season's final day so that no-one has the benefit of knowing exactly what result they require, then allowing some teams to start late? Why not make all of the games start late? We wouldn't have cared. When the final whistle went, I took my coat off and the steward couldn't have got me into the Sunderland end fast enough. Post-match entertainment included the now famous Mackem on a stolen police motorcycle episode, then it was yet another silent, tedious journey back home.

Walking home from Spennymoor after my drop-off, a minibus pulled up just down the road, and, as I was about to scrounge a lift, a naked man was thrown out of the rear doors. Three o'clock in the morning, this is just the sort of thing you expect at Binchester road ends. His request for the loan of some items of clothing was turned down in the time-honoured two-word Anglo Saxon fashion. I might have had eight hours on a bus to mull over the day's events, but it would take a lot longer than that to get over them.

Where had it all gone wrong? Undoubtedly, we hadn't seen the best of Quinny. Indeed, we'd hardly seen anything of him, and he'd be the first to admit that what we had seen hadn't been that impressive. In hindsight, a fit Niall Quinn would have been the difference between survival and where we ended up. That wasn't the only problem, though. Why pay all of that money (by our standards) for an attacking midfielder of Mad Alex's undoubted quality and then hardly use him, while persisting with Irish centre-forward Kelly on the wing and an ageing Brace in the middle. Paul Stewart's return of four goals, whilst more than three better than Kelly's total blank, just wasn't good enough, although it did make him joint top scorer with Russ.

Too little is probably a bit unfair on Waddle, as he blatantly wasn't too little, creating every goal we scored after his arrival, but too late is definitely correct, and not his fault. Boro might have finished beneath us, but they managed sixteen more goals. Long-term injuries at crucial times to Ball and Scott were also a big factor, and just as Mr Murray's master-plan should have seen us sailing triumphantly into the sunset from Roker Park, and up the road to Wearmouth, we'd crucially got our timing all wrong. What should have been Reid saves, Reid consolidates, Reid storms into Premiership, had become Reid saves, Reid overachieves, Reid arrives in Premiership without necessary preparation. Instead of facing a new tomorrow in a sparkly new ground, we faced an all-too-familiar tomorrow in a potential white elephant. Where were we going to find crowds twice as big as Roker could accommodate? What would the fans think of the club?

Two days after relegation, we would see exactly what the fans thought of their club when the old ground hosted its last ever match. Against Liverpool, the first ever visitors, a full house showed the team, the club, and the football world what we though of our Sunderland. Sunderland don't go away, they become part of your life. Various players from the past did a lap of honour, and when men like Charlie Hurley and Jimmy Monty passed, you could see the tears in the eyes of a thousand grown men (and women). It was all the more poignant for being a night game, as there were no distractions such as being able to see the sky – just the occasional ghostly seagull or pigeon that became illuminated in the floodlights – and memories of those big games of my supporting lifetime came flooding back.

Man City. Stoke in the League Cup. Vasas Budapest. Derby in the League Cup. Chelsea, FA Cup and League Cup. It wasn't just that we were moving to a new home, always a traumatic event in itself, but we were moving from our home of almost a century, where we had grown up – club, fans, and players alike. Even the poor adolescent who had the dubious honour of carrying the Mag's flag around the ground managed a smile. In the game itself, things could have turned naughty for us when a Fulwell Ender lobbed a can of beer towards Robbie Fowler – whether in malice or fun I can't say, but all Fowler did was to lob it gently beyond the touchline when he could have done untold damage by handing it to the referee, bless his little nylon Liverpool socks.

During the game, I went for a chat with my niece, who sat in the lower tier seats behind the family section, and a piece of red wood came off the wall in my hand. "That's not meant to happen just yet – stick it in your coat and say nowt," said the steward, I became the proud owner of a piece of the Posh Stand, and it sits next to the drawers in my bedroom to this day.

For the record, John Mullin scored the only goal, we won, and on came King Charlie with a spade, and dug up the centre-spot. A bit of a speech, and that was it. All done, all gone. Pos, Stubber, Tubby and I took the kids into the Fulwell, showed them the barrier behind which it had all begun for us as spotty youths a lifetime ago, and hawayed one last big hawayawayawayawayaway into the night air like demented werewolves. I drew the line at leaving my scarf knotted to the barrier as so many other had done. After all, life goes on, and I'd be needing it at the new ground next season.

Wise men say, only fools rush in
But I can't help falling in love with you
Sunderland

1997-1998

Another Whit week, another dad'n'lads camping trip, then the announcement of the name of the ground came up for discussion. Or rather it didn't. We'd rather naively imagined something to do with the town, or the area of town, or the proximity of the river, or even New Roker Park. Corny, I know, but acceptable – Millwall did it, even though, because no one likes them, presumably no one cares.

Sunderland, on the other hand, people do care about. Names bandied about included the logical, if rather unromantic Sheepfolds Stadium, but I suppose that was rejected because of the trouble we'd have with the Cardiff fans refusing to leave after a match. The Riverside was an obvious no-no, as it would confuse Boro fans and the Wearside Stadium might just have been a bit too obvious. The Colliery Stadium would have been fitting, but my personal favourite was, and still is, the Wearmouth Stadium. It's near the mouth of the Wear, it's a football ground – simple logic. The reaction of "You must be joking" at a few minutes after midnight when they announced the choice of what could only be two or three people wasn't restricted to my house.

Fair enough, the name Stadium of Light has grown on me a bit over the years, but only because it's been forced on me. For the first couple of years it was the new ground, then simply the stadium, then eventually the ground. The gubbins that the club put out about it representing the light of a miner's Davy Lamp is fair enough, but all of that nonsense about it having nothing to do with the Portuguese ground with which the name is shared/copied (as it is named after a district rather than a vision). It still comes across as pretentious, and that pretentiousness has only diminished because of the increase in pretentious nonsense associated with the increasing Americanisation of the beautiful game – our beautiful game. Call it something else, have a Colliery Stand, a Davy Lamp Stand, and Roker and a Fulwell End - these things would make more sense to the paying public than SoL. Enough, already - it's only a name, and, as Mr Murray had sorted the ground out for us, I suppose the least we could do would be to let him choose the name.

And so it came to pass that we arranged a game against the mighty Ajax of Amsterdam to celebrate the opening. The local Health and Safety people kept us on our toes by refusing to grant a safety certificate until most of us were on our way to the match and the whole thing was like a big party. We'd been watching and photographing the thing rising from the ashes of the Colliery for the past year, and we'd peeped inside and done the virtual tour, but nothing could prepare us for our first view of the interior in all its glory.

I entered the North West corner for the first time, and climbed those few steps to the interior for the first time – and was completely blown away. It was huge, it was beautiful, it was full, and it was ours.

The hairs on the back of my neck stood on end and I was temporarily transfixed. It was tremendous. OK, they'd messed up the seats by missing out a set of numbers with the results that some rows apparently didn't exist, and there was a row 37 at the back when in reality it only went up to 36, but that was just done to test our patience. That the game ended without goals was irrelevant – the ground had opened, it had worked, the crowd approved, and it was good. All we had to do was to get the thing in use in the Premier League as soon as possible.

The fixture list was out during our fragmented family holidays, which involved staying with my cousin in Surrey while visiting Judith's cousin when she was in the country from the States, discovering to my horror that, despite Uncle John's Sunderland-ness, and living in Surrey for most of their lives, her two brothers had turned out black and white. Thankfully his daughter hadn't, and her two lads happily accepted our gifts of Sunderland shirts to take back stateside. The admission by Uncle John that he'd only recently thrown out his 1937 Cup Final memorabilia came as another shock – I'd have walked to Epsom to collect that lot.

By the time we'd seen them off in their new colours back to New York, it was time for me to do another tour of duty in Florida. Only a month, but it was long enough, coming as close to the start of the season as it did. Phone calls home revealed that we'd tried to sign David Connolly from Watford, but come back with some unknown called Kevin Phillips. We also spent £225,000 on a Dutch goalkeeper with an entry in the Guinness Book of Records of the longest name for a professional footballer – Eduard Andreas Dominicas Hedrikus Joseph Zoetebier. So we called him Zoots. Kelly, Waddle, Howey, Kubicki, and Stewart went their various ways, and Chris Makin, Chris Byrne, Jody Craddock, of whom we knew nothing, arrived, as did Lee Clark, of whom we knew quite a bit. He wasn't getting a game up the road, he was as black and white as a Byker humbug, and he'd cost us a club record of £2.5 million – twice as much as we'd ever spent on a single player before. Clark for Bracewell seemed a logical move, but would the Mag let us down? Only time would tell.

With Coton now part of the coaching staff (prior to leaving the club and them deciding to sue us for incorrect medical care during his time when injured), Lionel, with even longer hair, took his place behind Makin, Scott, Melville and Ord, while Ball, Clark, Agnew and Gray filled the middle. Quinn and Rae were the front two, and the opposition was Sheffield United. Let's go, I thought, Floridian telephone at the ready, but a 2-0 defeat was not what I was expecting. Flying home the following Friday was a bit nerve-wracking, not because of a fear of flying, but because of the Man City kick-off time – Friday night.

After a couple of hours kip, Pos called to see if I was coming out to play, and we were off to the first real game at the new ground, along with 38,000 others. That's what the fans would think of second level football at the new ground. Our little band assembled for the first time, and watched as Phillips replaced Rae up front, and Quinny turned into the real Quinny as he accepted a stinky back-pass to score our first competitive goal at the SoL. Kinkladze seduced a penalty out of Bally for an equaliser that should have been no more than a consolation at that stage, but then this little chap reacted like lightning to a loose ball in the box, we were ahead, and Kevin Phillips had arrived. Lee Clark capped a committed display with a third, and the wheels were back on our promotion bandwagon. Someone, however, had forgotten to tighten the nuts, and they were back off a week later as Port Vale scored two early goals from which we never recovered – for another seven days, as Norwich came to Wearside, were puzzled into the deck, and hit us on the break to win.

Oxford helped us by scoring one of the three goals we got at the SoL, then it was another Friday night game, it was my birthday, and it was Bradford. Packed into the tiny away end at the Pulse FM Stadium at Valley Parade (Pretentious? Moi?), the most difficult part of the evening was using the toilets, the entrance to which was totally disorganised and potentially dangerous. Like the steward said into his radio "An entrance and an exit sign wouldn't go f****ng amiss" as we trod on his toes and spilt hot Bovril down his leg. Mickey Gray hit a belter, then Clark scored, then that nice Mr Phillips did the business, and we wound up with Johnston scoring the fourth. All before half-time. Happy birthday, Sobs.

As is often the case with 4-0 half-time leads, it became a 4-0 full-time lead despite a hatful of chances but an understandable lack of urgency. Game over, Pos took the kids back home, and Stubber and I celebrated our birthday as two Sunderland fans would after a 4-0 away win – a few pints, then, being Bradford, a weapons-grade curry and a few more beers. The train journey home was a bit subdued, what with it being Princess Diana's funeral, and the arrival at York of a dozen drunken rugby fans (at half-nine in the morning) didn't quite suit the mood of the majority. At least I had something to smile about.

Mickey Gray did the trick again the next week with the only goal at Birmingham, and in front of the cameras. Martin Smith, in the middle of a decent run in the side, got our goal in a home draw with Wolves, but the moment of the match was Melville putting Kubicki's cross into the wrong net. Oh dear. Against Boro, that soul singer bloke hit another rocket for them, and Mustoe forced another to leave us out of the game. Well into injury time, Bally forced what could be no more than a consolation into the net in front of the North Stand, but the man in the DJ booth still hit the button and James Brown belted out "AWWW. I feel good." No we bloody didn't. Kill the DJ, kill the DJ kill the DJ. Please. Remember how irritating the ice-hockey-style music was at Selhurst Park when Wimbledon won a corner and how you wished you had a rifle when you heard it?

You've probably heard of the Nighmare at Elm Park, and so you should, because that game was where it all went wrong and caused it all to go so nearly right. Darren Williams got himself sent off, and Reading hammered us 4-0. Reidy took the hint, decided that changes had to be made, and made them. Out went Melville, and in came Craddock. Before the next League game, we'd checked out of the League Cup. Having beaten Bury twice by two goals to one, I thought I'd drive to the Riverside for the next round against Boro, as I had to nip in to work to see the night shift. Never again.

Despite it being the biggest, newest building for miles, and sitting in abject loneliness in the middle of several square miles of bare, post-industrial wasteland, I couldn't find the sodding place to save my life. As driving slowly around that part of the Boro at night is inviting either arrest or the unwanted attention of a fourteen-yearold working girl, I parked up near some other cars and followed the crowd. I needn't have bothered, as the only thing of note that we did was to play Edwin Zoetebier in his second and final game for us. Presumably his name was too long, but he's gone on to win European trophies since leaving, so he can't have been that good. 0-2 flattered us a bit to be honest, but then I had to find the car, go to work when I wanted to get back to Bishop and snarl into a couple of pints, and put up with the night shift supervisor, who, conveniently, was (still is) a Boro fan.

Just as we were thinking that the drugs, or whatever it was they gave to footballers in those days, didn't work, Clark scored again, as did Smithy with a forty-yard lob that had Pele checking his family tree for connections, and Bridges did his claims for a start no good at all by scoring as a substitute as we thumped Huddersfield. The following draw at home to Swindon had seen Bishop boy Darren Holloway get his first game, but the draw wasn't the desired result. The old guard was changing into the new – we had two Darrens and a Jody in the team. What sort of names were they for proper footballers? Lee Clark then went and did a very un-Sunderland thing for a midfielder, and scored his fifth and sixth goals of the season as we won at Stoke – and it was still only October.

Bally cut his leg, and contracted blood-poisoning from something nasty that had been sprayed on the grass, or was bitten by a rabid defender, and ended up on a drip with serious worries about his survival. Thankfully, it would have taken more than the loss of a limb or two to prevent Bally from turning out for the Lads, but he was away a long time. Obviously impressed by the win, and the lengths players will go to for the Sunderland cause, the kids talked themselves into a trip to Stockport the following week, just to have another look at this all-conquering midfield maestro, so I saddled up the Sobsmobile (which had become a decidedly upmarket Rover with walnut trim, a snip from Cammycars on the proprietor's acquisition of a company car and said Rover becoming surplus to requirements, which was convenient as the Cavalier had failed its MOT on emissions, bodywork, and having been the subject of an unacceptable amount of car crime), and Pos and their Kris joined our little family outing to South Manchester.

As we parked up, one of the locals said "Please be gentle with us," which I thought a bit excessive, as we'd hardly set the football world alight just yet. The kids got what they'd gone for, as Clark scored again. Seven goals – that's almost twice as many as our top scoring forward got in the whole of the previous season. This was looking good, despite only one point won, and then first Charlton, then

Forest, similarly slowed things up with draws at the SoL. This was mid-table, and it wasn't good enough. We might have stopped getting beat, but we weren't winning enough games.

Our match-day routine had now settled into its established format for the new ground. Pick Gaz up from his Saturday morning job as a barista (no, not the kind that charges you a fortune for a thank-you letter, but the sort that can make you any kind of coffee you like, he's got the certificate and everthing) then collect Nige from his pre-pre-match pint at The Sportsman, then beer and rendezvous at The Saltgrass, park just up the road from the King's, walk over the Gill bridge, past the back of the brewery, and over the big bridge.

From there it was round the east side and the north stand to our very own McDonald's family section. Quite often, any thoughts the kids might have had of asking for burgers or whatever processed horrors Ronald McDonald was offering that day had been suppressed when walking past the brewery, as we had to pass within a few feet of the stables, and more particularly the skip full of horse-dung. Telling them that the smell was from the beer lasted only a few weeks, as they could work out that even their dads couldn't possibly drink anything that smelt that bad.

This longish walk after the match meant that we missed Sports Report, but also that the majority of the traffic had gone by the time we got to the car. Our choice of seats had proved a hit, as we'd tried to pick a place as similar as possible to our last stand in the Fulwell, and thus we looked across the pitch from just behind the North end goal line. When we'd gone to make our choice, we'd been served by the lad who spent his Saturday afternoons dressed as a cat. After this we took special interest in Samson's pre-match antics, especially the time he tackled Rory the Lion at the Riverside and broke the foot of his Boro counterpart's furry suit. A serious mascot, truly a mascot for the new age of football, and a link to the past that could be maintained into the new ground, the old ground having gone the way of all flesh.

June 21st had been a big day for me, the day that the Roker auction took place, and I couldn't bring myself to go and watch the old place be sold off in bits. I still sent a few quid along with Pos to buy my bits of turf, and our Ian pinched a couple of pieces of concrete and tarmac that still live in my back yard. Various pieces, slightly more upmarket than mine, ended up behind various bars around the county, ensuring that Roker Park will never die. Not long into the season, we paid a visit to that crazy Mr Forster who lived near the Barnes Hotel to buy some of the thousands of Clock Stand seats that he had crammed into his garage and spread over his lawn. He let us choose our own seats numbers (19 and 56 for the year of my arrival in the red and white world, if you must know), and we packed the parts into the boot and headed, heavy laden, to the match.

After dropping to the bench following the game at Stockport, and with only a handful of appearances under his belt, Chris Byrne was signed by Stockport. He'd looked lively enough, but there had been stories of him being unable to settle on Wearside virtually since the day he arrived, and a life of not-so-petty crime in the Manchester area was obviously more appealing to him, and we made a nice profit of £200,000. I don't know how that one worked, but it has to go down as a good piece of business. On a slightly more important, Craig Russell went to Man City, where he'd almost ended up in the summer, and we got part of Nicky Summerbee in return. So we paid a few quid extra and got the rest of him. The Russ had obvious strengths, including a great turn of speed and a trademark left foot shot across the keeper, but there was equally as obviously something about him that the manager didn't like.

The chance to work in Florida again came, and as we weren't playing like Real Madrid, I obliged. Coincidentally, the journey out there went via Portsmouth (honest, I had no choice in the matter), so there I was, suitcase in hand, outside the Thinford Inn for a midnight start. After the biggest of big breakfasts in the little caff in the railway arches near the docks, I met up with nephew Mat, who'd decided that if he was going to study away from home, he'd get about as far away as it was possible to get. A few pints while we watched the back-seat boys' card school in a pub that wouldn't let them play for money. A lot of matchsticks changed hands that day, and, once back on the bus for the trip to Fratton Park, they were exchanged for the appropriate amount of cash.

A small amount of that cash could have gone towards renovating Fratton Park – the visitors' end was an absolute dump, having that most inappropriate of things in an English football ground – uncovered seats. Of course, it chucked it down, the police wouldn't let us shelter under the steps because we were a fire hazard, even though we were that wet we wouldn't have burned in a blast furnace. The stewards joined in and wouldn't let us stand up, even though to sit was to put your backside in a bowl of water. "Stand up if your arse is wet" was the song of the day, and the mood should have dampened even further when Pompey went ahead. Strangely enough, there was already a feeling among the travelling fans that it didn't matter, because we already looked like we had more than one goal in us, and that's the way it turned out. By half time, Quinny – now well on his way to his Sunderland sainthood – Clark and Johnston had put us ahead, and new-boy Summerbee got a run out in the second half.

Despite very dodgy orange-trimmed boots, he scored the fourth, and the look on his face said it all. "This is going to be good!" it said, and he was right. The dream team had arrived. With Brace admitting his sell-by date was past, he left for Fulham and Al Fayed's riches, and Steve Agnew's season having ended with injury, we'd arrived by default at the Rae-Clark-Johnston-Summerbee midfield that was to be the making of the middle of the season. Oh, and the small matter of the front two. 4-1 away from home is some going, as was getting to the USA the next morning. For the first time in seven and a half years, we'd won away after letting one in – things must be on the up.

I watched Mat wander off into the streets with the sort of concern that is natural when a young relative sets off through bandit country after a match, then took the train, along with Gatesy and the Radio Metro people. I sat next to a lad about my age, whose son of about ten was as Sunderland daft as you could get - but they both had broad cockney accents. I asked if the lad's father had moved south for work. "Na, it was my Grandad." Fourth generation away from the Wear, and still living and breathing Sunderland. That's the spirit. I got to London in plenty of time for a couple of bevvies in the Lamb, from where I phoned in my match report to Pos. "That sounds like a pint of Youngs – are you in the Lamb?" he asked, his voice laced with very audible jealousy. "Have one for me." Oh, what a perfect day, win football at Fratton Park, drink Youngs beer after dark, and then smile.

Off to the sun the next morning, and the first report I got was that we'd slipped back to our old ways with a draw against Bury. After all the years I'd spent supporting Gordon Armstrong, he popped up to create their goal. The next report was of victory over a pathetically bad Tranmere side that included David Kelly, and Sand-Dancer Steve Simonsen in goal. Talk about a no-win situation, keeping goal at that magnificent ground against the team you supported. I'd had enough of this non-football life of working too far away to get to the match, and the American idea of sport is so sanitised and predict able that it is virtually impossible to get passionate about it. Their coverage of European football was bad, and the coverage of their own Major League was so corny that it wasn't true, including, as it did, some token Geordie who'd played once for the Mags, twice for Southend, and then joined Pele and company in the mid-seventies to make a small fortune in the States. He was probably called Butch. At the annual awards, in the biggest hotel in New York, Alexi Lalas (you know, the one who looked like Catweazle and played like, er, Catweazle) won the award for haircut of the season – and they were being serious. I wrote down my frustrations, faxed them to A Love Supreme, and that was me started with regular expressions of love, anger, anxiety, and angst via the medium of the written word.

Once again, coincidence brought about the synchronicity of my arrival at Heathrow and Sunderland playing nearby at QPR. I met up with the Inter City P**s

Pots at Kings Cross, and it was off for cocktails at the Jeremy Bentham, owned by the lad who used to have the Queen's, along with most of South West Durham and assorted London-based friends. He'd arranged us post-match passes to the players' lounge, so we took it canny beforehand. Like Hell we did, and we were as warm as toast by kick-off. Quinny had his best game to date for us, as he hit the bar, the post, the keeper, and then had one disallowed for what we like to call a dunsh.

That was only the first half, and he kept at it in the second, eventually hitting the winner and watching as the overhanging School End rocked in its foundations. It was one of those away games when we played well, the fans were right up for it, and we were packed in close to the pitch and felt very much part of the action. We ate most of the food before the players had arrived, chatted with Stan Bowles, and sang our way up the East Coast main line. Things were looking up.

In December, we only let in one goal, Phillips scored in six consecutive games, and we climbed to fifth. The only dropped points were at Oxford, and the game was to be televised live, so I arranged to be allowed to take the kids into the Green Tree to watch. It was terrible, so bad that it could easily have caused the cancellation of all future live games, but I felt awful about not going. If I'd been there to lend my support, they might have won, so I promised myself that I'd never again miss an away game simply because I could watch it on the telly.

First game of the New Year was at Rotherham in the FA Cup. Tall- Paul and I fancied a few pints in the town before the game, but we made the mistake of trying to do this in Rotherham, where every pub is the roughest pub you've ever been in. We found a cheap and cheerful place that the landlord admitted got wrecked every Friday night "But they're all related, so they come back first thing and fix it up again," was his reasoning. The ground was hardly any better, but Sunderland were, and little Kev scored four, including one with his chest, Chisholm-style, only a few feet in front of us, as we won 5-1. A fourth round tie at Tranmere seemed simple enough given their wimpish showing a few weeks earlier, but we managed to lose, leaving us with…

…Just the League then. In which we were doing pretty well. Against Sheff Utd, we let in two but scored four as Johnston's nickname Magic became entirely appropriate. It is a fantastic outlet to have a player to whom the ball can be passed when he has seemingly no space to work in, but with a drop of his shoulder and a feint this way and that, Magic would be away and free. The fact that he was very right footed and playing on the left was rarely an issue. The defenders knew very well that he'd be cutting it back onto his right for the inevitable cross or shot, but there was nothing they could do about it.

He could take the ball all around the world, and still plop it onto Quinny's head or Kev's toe. A win at Maine Road kept us in fourth, then we strengthened by signing someone from Serie A in Italy. He sounded Italian, but he was from London, and was obviously a back up for Quinny. Danny Dichio was the same height (about nine feet), the same build, and was a centre forward, but unlike Quinny, whose game was about beating the opponent with cunning and deft flicks, Danny's seemed to be all about seeing how quickly he could get booked after coming on when Big Niall got tired.

We spoiled things a bit by losing a game at Norwich that we should have won, and Clark's late goal almost sparked a successful surge at the death. If we thought that was bad, how do you think Bill Clinton was feeling? Monica Lewinsky, a Whitehouse Intern (I think that means work experience person) had done the dirty deed with the most powerful man in the world, kept her mucky dress, and was selling her story to anyone who'd listen – and pay. Sounds funny, would have been even funnier if it had actually mattered to the world.

Another 4-2, Port Vale this time, saw Bally back after a couple of games on the bench and his presence could be felt up in the seats. It was after this game that I decided to regress a little. After years of hitching, driving, and being driven to away games, I decided to make my occasional coach trips a regular thing, and took up permanently with the Durham Branch, with whom I'd been an irregular traveller for a few years. Wolves was the first game of my new self, taking me back to the days on the Red Lion bus in my formative years, and a whole bunch of new people became my regular away game gang.

My first stop-off in Lichfield, where I'm now on first-name terms with the bar staff in the Queen's Head, who check the fixture list to see when their quiet little town will be awash with red and white for the afternoon. Wolves the place still had a bit of a reputation for unfriendliness, and they lived up to that after the game. A rare appearance for Dickie Ord ended with Kev hitting the bar in the last minute, and Bally nodding in to send us wild with delight – it's all the better when it comes that late – and it put the locals into a Neanderthal rage that manifested itself in a couple of punch and run attacks at the burger van outside our part of the ground. Back to the seventies with the boys in old gold, back to Wearside with the points.

The ground was buzzing for the revenge mission on Reading. One of the lads at work was from Reading, and he took some mates along, on a cold, damp night in February, and was blown away by the presence of over 40,000 others, by the Prokofiev/Ready to Go music, by the noise and the passion. His team were blown away likewise, and we stayed third. It's just a shame that we had to go to Boro next, in our industrial respirators and gasmasks, because we were back to our old Teesside ways and lost 3-1.

Merson and his huge wallet supplied the bullets, and they were duly put away. The Boro boys showed a nice touch of back to the seventies as well, bravely attacking women and youngsters before running away as we had to do the chicken run past the scrap yards on the way to the conveniently parked buses. For some reason, perhaps to do with the mentality of the fans there, or the fact that the place looks like a war zone, the policing was years behind that at almost every other ground in the land in terms of planning. In the real war zone of the Balkans (aye, they were still at it) their Serbian counterparts used tanks and helicopter gun ships to quieten the Kosovans. Even the American police don't have firepower like that, which is probably just as well.

Magic had the game of his life at Huddersfield a few days later, when he scored three in the first half, but it was almost spoiled when they brought on Wayne Allison, who has plagued us in the colours of Tranmere, Sheff Utd and Huddersfield for years. They scored twice, and we were left hanging on for a win that should have been a formality. Ipswich came and forced a draw, then it was down to top-of-the-table Forest.

As it was midweek, and for some reason I had no money, I'd decided to sit this one out, but Steve and Pos were having none of it. So it was an early finish and a quick sprint to the North Brit car park, and we were off. There are some occasions when you're glad you changed your mind, and this was one of them. Bally drove his boys to the display of the season, and Mad Alex gave us a half time lead. Magic then knocked one high towards goal, and a defender's head deflected it ever so slightly, but importantly, just over Beasant's huge reach. We were going mental in the away end, and not because of the Brazilian-style antics being acted out in front of us. Down at Loftus Road, QPR were going mad and scoring goal after goal against Boro.

When Quinny looked up from the right wing, he saw his little mate racing through and delivered the pass of his life onto Kev's boot, and the half volley that followed was the high-point of the night. The pub we stopped in on the way back gradually filled with slightly bemused Sunderland fans who couldn't quite believe what they'd just seen, and as a consequence couldn't smile wide enough.

Poor little Stockport next, and the goals kept flying in. Niall got the first hat-trick at the new ground, but it was Magic who befuddled the opposition to open the doors for the big man to move us into second. Johnston's late leveller against Birmingham saved the day, then Phillips did likewise at the Valley despite Rae being dismissed. Two more home wins, then a Friday night in Tranmere. No available free time to take off work, so it was a radio for me. Which drew some strange glances, as I was at a concert (sorry, a gig) at Middlesbrough Town Hall. Come to think of it, my Sunderland badge drew some strange glances as well, but we won 2-0 and were back on track for the big time.

Unfortunately, there is always Easter to either make or break your season. QPR came up, played in a sort of blizzard, and grabbed a 2-2 draw. Then it was convoy time to West Brom, where we took three cars, dropped the womenfolk off in Birmingham for a spot of retail therapy, then headed for the Hawthorns. Don't mention the M42 to Steve, he went the wrong way, ended up coming north up the M5, and missed his pre-match pint in the Post House. He could have missed the first couple of minutes as well, as the Baggies scored, then a certain Mr Kilbane got a second and we had visions of our season turning to cabbage.

Bally then took the game by the scruff of its neck, and Quinny lobbed one back before the break. Little Kev levelled things before Mickey Gray had a slapping contest with his opposite number, and he was off. Big Niall then made our day by putting us ahead, but right at the death Lee Hughes equalised. Easter? It should be done away with. Football? It's like that; it's just the way it is.

It wasn't that bad really. We were still second, but we wanted to be clear in second, and there were four games left in which to stay in second. Crewe and Stoke were no problem, but then Ipswich showed why they were up there in the running as they beat us 2-0. That meant that we had to win at Swindon, and Boro had to lose their last game for us to get second.

Swindon meant a camping holiday, just for the one night, for me, Pos, and the boys. We got the tent up, then found a little boozer with a mad West Brom fan running it, and ate more bowls of chips than the pub had ever sold in a single evening. What is it about kids and tents that makes them eat everything in sight? We'd already had Linda's more than you can possibly eat packed lunch (that's posh for bait box), but still they wanted more.

The Cambridge Arms near the ground was packed with our boys as Swindon became Wearside for the day. As our tickets had sold out in no time, I used a work colleague from head office who lived in Swindon to get me another twenty (on Stewy's credit card – he shouldn't have left it next to the phone) and spent the previous week's dinner breaks distributing them around the factory. Consequently, the stewards quickly relaxed the rule that prevented away colours in home sections of the ground, and the County Ground was ours.

As a match, it was simply an easy win, livened up by two sub lime strikes from Phillips, as we worried about the Boro result. Of course, they won – it would have gone against logic for us to get a lucky result, 1990 and the day's opponents excepted. Play offs it was. Whatever, we'd still had a hell of a time, and we wanted to show our appreciation, so we flooded onto the pitch and mobbed the players. Someone stole Magic's boots, Reidy got a microphone and made a speech to the masses, and we sang but stopped short of dancing, as it would not have been appropriate. We had been the best team in the division since December, and had swashbuckled our way to hatful of goals in a brilliant new ground. Ninety points and still not promoted. Play offs? If that was the way it had to be, that was the way it had to be.

Sheffield United would be no pushover, but we knew we could do a job on them. There we were, high up behind the goal, and Ian's teacher Mr Johnson sat just behind us, so we gave him a song "mister Johnson, mis-ter Johnson" to the Magic Johnston tune. I don't think it helped with his exam results, but I'd like to think it did. Bally banged in following a corner to give us a quarter-time lead, but they hit us with two in the second quarter to set up the new ground's biggest match to date. Could it match Roker for the big occasion? Hell, yes. The Roker Roar had moved up the road, and came out with a vengeance that night. The darkness, the floodlights, the damp, the big away following, the roar, an own goal, a Phillips strike, and a brilliant double save from Lionel all added up to a top night, and the Blades just couldn't come up with an answer.

Wembley. Scruffy old hole in the ground that it was by then (had been for years, actually), it was where we had to do the business. The match day traffic on the A1/M1 was 90% red and white, waving at each other, waiting for the big moment. Pos having combined the match with a weekend in London (boy, he knew how to keep a lady happy). I'd packed the car with my two, along with Pete and Ade from work. We all met up in Harrow, turning the pavement bar into a little bit of Wearside down south, and then met up with nephew Mat, for some reason sporting a huge Afro wig. It was his birthday, after all- guess what his present from Uncle Paul was. Correct – one match ticket.

If you don't know what happened that afternoon on the field, then you're probably reading the wrong book. It's been variously described as the old stadium's most dramatic game, Sunderland's most dramatic game, and Charlton's most dramatic game – amongst other things. In their sweaty gold shirts, the Lads took to the field. We had a great view, sort of low down, but not too low, at the right end – and by the right end, I mean the one we were attacking in the first half. The atmosphere was atomic; if there can be such a thing. Their first goal reduced our Ian to tears, so I told him that it was only a game. It was (still is) an in-joke with our match day gang, but its utterance that day brought about 4,000 killer stares.

The fact that Sunderland's own Clive Mendonca chose to score his goal at the far end mattered not, because we had a perfect view of Quinny pointing to the spot on his forehead where he wanted Buzza to put the corner, even if we didn't believe that he'd actually put it in. We had a perfect view of our other two goals of normal time, with Bally winning a header that became the perfect through ball for little Kev's 35th goal of the season, and Quinny's far-post larrup, as they call them in Dublin. We were heading for the top when Lionel came for a cross that no goalkeeper could have reached, and found himself ten yards off his line as they bonked a header in for 3-3.

When Buzza put away our fourth, I honestly believe that both sets of fans thought that was it – we certainly did. The game had embraced more incident than ten FA Cup finals, and both teams were knackered, and both sets of fans emotionally drained. It's not just about watching, it's about being part of the game, and it was exhausting in the extreme. Mendonca then broke the hearts of a hundred schoolmates by swivelling to make it 4-4, and the nonsense began.

The penalties were at our end, and, including Quinny's first ever spot-kick, we arrived at 6-6, with the Charlton fans' vocal reaction being delayed by a split second as they watched from the other end. Then up stepped Mickey Gray, and Ilic saved his shot. Bugger.

The inevitable delay from the Charlton end, and the equally inevitable delay from our end as we struggled to come to terms with the fact that it was all over. Is that it? It can't stop now, surely? But it did. Charlton did their inevitable lap of honour, past the prostrate bodies of the Sunderland boys, and Reidy hugged Mickey Gray. I felt bad, but how did that Lad feel? He'd supported us all of his life, he'd scored on his first start, into the Fulwell End, and now he'd failed with the penalty that could have taken us up.

As we gradually drifted away from our seats and towards home, I'd never seen so many pairs of eyes looking down. What if Phillips had been able to last the whole game? What if Lionel had stayed on his line? What if Deech had connected with that glorious chance that came his way? If you could have bottled the emotions of that moment, you could have made a fortune selling glumness and resignation. Outside the tube station, the police held us up so that we could be shepherded across the road in groups, and as the mounted officer was explaining this, a voice piped up "I'm Spartacus". A split second later, a second voice did the same, then another, and within a few seconds, a host of Wearsiders were shouting it.

The policeman looked suitably befuddled, and those of us in the crowd didn't know whether to laugh or cry. It could have been the worst day of our lives, but we were Sunderland fans, and we weren't going to let a small matter like losing out on the most dramatic day that Wembley had ever experienced knock the humour out of us. They had, however, knocked the life out of us, and the 250 miles home was the quietest journey I've ever undertaken. Five people, one car, one football team, not a word.

About midnight I deposited the kids, picked up my SAFC plastic glass (if that makes sense) and a few cans, and walked across the viaduct for some solitude. As I sat at the picnic table especially erected by Wear Valley District Council as a place of solitude for Sunderland fans after long, miserable away trips, a car pulled up in the lay-by below and the young occupants began to indulge in a bout of extremely vigorous sex, involving both front seats, the back seat, and the bonnet. I didn't know whether to sneak away or applaud. I've since heard it is called dogging.

And that was the end of the football season.

Sunderland Sunderland
That's the team for me
Sunderland Sunderland
On to victory
We're the greatest team in all the land
And I hope you'll all agree
We won't give up 'til we win the Cup
And the English Football League

1998-1999

Me and the boys took to the Yorkshire Dales the next morning in our tent, complete with Gary's guitar (remember what I said about him writing songs when he got miserable – now he had May 25th to write about. God help the cheerful world, and look out Morrissey). We tried our best to forget, but couldn't help remembering. Frank Sinatra died out of sympathy, although my personal theory is that he'd already been dead for years, like the Pope, and his advisors were just waiting for the right time to announce his demise.

Even England's involvement in the World Cup failed to erase the memories, especially when Beckham rose to the bait and got himself sent off. Reidy tried to eliminate our defensive slips by buying Paul Butler, a sort of Steve Hetzke nononsense centre half, but with a bit more football thrown in, from Bury, defensive midfielder Gerry Harrison from Burnley, and Danish keeper Tommy Sorensen from somewhere in Denmark. Also bought was Neil Wainwright from Wrexham. Aggers, after virtually a full season injured, slipped down the A19 to York, and also on the way out was Lionel, allegedly following some harsh words from the manager after his Wembley display. Gary and I stopped off in Brough after a spot of hill-walking that summer, and caught Lionel saving two penalties on the TV in some Mickey Mouse three-way competition against Boro. For the Mags.

By some quirk of fate (actually Judith's only available time off work) our holidays coincided with the football for the first time. What would we do? Head south after the first home game, if it's at home, and pray for a game in the South-West the next weekend. The fixture compilers for once got it right. About the time that the Americans decided that it would be a good idea to drop some bombs on the Sudan (a chemical weapons factory cleverly disguised as a hospital, apparently) and Afghanistan, the season was underway. Not the best of games, but Kev's penalty won it despite Lee Clark's broken ankle. Nice start, straight in the car and away down to Devon, bumping into the day's linesman at the motorway services – complete with his Mag-shirt-wearing son. Was this a conflict of interests? I think so.

A week in Devon and Cornwall, where the sympathy that could be extracted from anyone who recognised the club badge was astonishing. The groundswell of public mood was definitely with us, and if we could have won promotion on good wishes, we'd have been up by the second game of the season – which, by happy coincidence, was at Swindon. Having successfully negotiated the magic roundabout (if you've been to Swindon, you'll know it, if you haven't, I'm sorry, it's a traffic system beyond description), we found the Cambridge Arms desolate in comparison to our last visit. I picked up our match tickets which had been sent directly to Swindon, had a word with Barry Dunn (wearing a woolly jumper in August, I ask you), and we sunbathed our way through the match.

Little Kev got a goal, we drew, and the high point of the match was sub Dichio getting his hand to the ball before he'd come on to the pitch and before the ball had left it. Oh, and the Ref having to change his shirt because his original was too similar to our new navy blue away kit. Only a few days before that game, I'd spent the night sitting in the car listening to our League Cup match at York, as Danny D bagged his first two goals for us. A week later, and I was still in sunny Devon, and on the radio again as Gerry Harrison played his only game for us, and we took the second leg 2-1. Then it was back home on the Friday night in readiness for the Tranmere game, a few hours kip, and into the fray again.

By half-time, we were looking at each other and wondering what was going on. If the second half of last season had been good, this was getting silly. With Summerbee and Johnston bombing down the wing, and Quinn and Phillips looking the business up front, we got two more goals from sub Danny Deech, Clark's stand-in Mullin, Phillips, and Butler. Watford were next up, and were similarly dealt with. This was good stuff, but it got even better against Ipswich, who'd done so much to frustrate our efforts last time around.

While the Northern Ireland peace process was going up in the smoke of the Omagh bomb, which claimed 29 lives, life went on in the rest of the world and

Sunderland in particular. At Portman Road Mullin scored again, and Phillips got the second as we looked every bit the top dogs and held on to top spot. A draw at home to Bristol City slowed things up a bit, then we went to Wolves, and a Mickey Gray mis-kick allowed Robbie Keane to score. Late in the game, he made a five minute exit, shaking hands with all ten of his team-mates when substituted, and in the consequential added time, little Kev scored to emphasise once again the restorative power of the late equaliser, especially away from home. Lesson learned, Mr Keane? Probably, but we couldn't be doing with League draws, because if we tolerated that, then our children would be next.

A bit of a stroll against Chester City in the League Cup, complete with Reidy's brother Shaun, should have been of no consequence, but Phillips got his toe trodden on to produce a Lineker-style injury, and that was him gone for the foreseeable future. Oh dear, what would we do now? What would Deech, or Bridges, or Smith, be able to do in the wee man's absence? More than enough, as it turned out.

Oxford were no great shakes, but could not have expected the puzzling we gave them. Bridges and Deech got two each, Mickey Gray, now established as the most attack-minded left back the club had ever possessed, got another before Mad Alex came off the bench to get another two. 7-0 could easily have been a lot more, but we weren't complaining. Back down to earth a couple of days later, and Magic got the only goal of the second leg League Cup tie against Chester.

Away down to Portsmouth, and I found myself sitting asleep on a box of bedding outside the Thinford Inn, as the information about the two hour delay in departure hadn't reached me, and it was at 2 am that we departed. With said bedding safely deposited at nephew Mat's, it was time for a few beers and a sort of satisfactory draw. Not the best result in the world, but a point after a 300-mile journey will do for me, thank you very much. It's more than we've come to expect over the years, we were top of the league, said we were top of the league.

The midweek trip to Norwich saw a very pleased landlord of the garden-centre-cum-café-with-a-bar near King's Lynn laughing all the way to the bank, along with the landlord of the Chalk Hill Brewery Tap. I must have been looking especially sensible, as one of the lads sharing my outside table confided that he was a Mag, but was working down there and liked watching us play. Takes all sorts, I suppose. A 2-2 draw almost made up for the fact that I was an unused substitute in the half-time penalty prize contest, the result of which evades me. That means we probably lost, but we did get to sing rude things about Delia Smith's cooking.

A draw wasn't what we expected against Bradford. Perhaps it was the team's way of objecting to the way we were behaving at the match. For some reason, it had become the fashion to take inflatables again. Sorry, but I had two teenage boys, Pos had one, so two silver blowy-up aliens was probably below the norm for a match day. They'd happily share our table outside The Saltgrass, sit on our knees at the match, and remain unfazed when thrown up in the air during goal celebrations or battered against each other in moments of frustration.

With my prior knowledge of the West Midlands Constabulary's sense of humour - on par with Margaret Thatcher's – the men from Mars stayed in the boot when we visited West Brom, and after a few minutes were probably glad of their imprisonment, as we went two down. The second half was a repeat of the previous season, as we stormed from behind and Bally grabbed a late winner. Ha, revenge was indeed sweet, and allowed us to accept a draw at a lively Huddersfield a few days later as we stayed second, but still wished for the presence of a sniper who could be persuaded to take out that bloody drummer at the McAlpine. If you must have a drummer, at least have the decency to a have some singers for him to drum along to. The old can't be replaced by the new, merely augmented by it, but best left alone altogether.

Deech got us the three points against Bury in recognition of Scotty's comeback, then we had the next leg of the League Cup to sort out. After over a year of pestering, Judith finally succumbed and came to the game against Grimsby. She thought it was cold, she though Quinny was nice, and then she got all medieval when it went to extra time. Big Niall's lovely winner cheered her up a bit, but she got a bit huffy when the ref didn't end it there and then.

Down at Bolton, we refused to pay a fiver for the club car park, and nipped over the motorway to a smashing pub that let the kids in. The match itself was an absolute hoot, as Johnston scored early, and we allowed them to come at us and soaked up everything they could throw at us. Quinny and Bridges, with his usual off-the-bench antics, got another two, and we laughed all the way back across the A66. At Crewe a couple of days later, the Cheshire air turned red and white as the Lads ripped into the home side. Dichio's strike, Gray's rocket, and Quinn put us three up at the break, and the locals were hiding behind their seats. Off the bench came Bridges, and got his usual goal before Makin and Sorensen got in a bit of a tangle and they pulled one back. It was a sign of the team's character that they were furious about only winning 4-1 when it should have been 4-0, and that was nice.

Smith got his first start of the league season against Grimsby, and duly scored twice. This warmed us up nicely for the League Cup tie at Everton. Actually, the whole season had warmed us up for this one. In case you hadn't noticed, this was match twenty-three, and we hadn't lost one yet – and it was mid-November. Bridges got a start, and took a clearance from Tommy in his stride, turned, and popped it away. Michael Proctor got his first game, and ran the legs off the Everton defence, helping restrict them to just an equaliser. No goals in extra time so here was a chance to lay the ghost of the Wembley penalty nightmare. Tommy did that for us with some of that penalty saving lark, and the football world began to believe that we were slightly more than a big fish in a little pond.

We carried on the good work with a win at Port Vale when Lee Clark came back, and Mo Mowlem carried on her good work by visiting loyalist prisoners in Northern Ireland to discuss their participation in peace negotiations, in an effort to end the tit-for-tat violence that had gone on through the year. Our super run came to an end in a crazy game against Barnsley at the SoL, as we scored twice but they managed three.

Still, we were top, so we went to Sheff Utd and got the frustration of Barnsley out of our system. Bridges celebrated a place in the starting eleven by having Steve Bruce's life and persuading him to pack in as a player. Two for him, two for Quinn, then the chance for his hat-trick, but he chose to put the ball into the upper tier, and we had to make four suffice. The League Cup came around again, in the form of Luton Town in the quarter final, and we quietly put them to sleep 3-0, then followed that with another couple of home wins. At this stage, we decided to have a bit of a rest and didn't score for two games, even daring to lose on Boxing Day at Tranmere, probably because it was the Christmas season and we were feeling generous. There was still enough time to get back on track with a win over Crewe, then the year turned, and it was off to Lincoln in the FA Cup.

If you've never been to Sincil Bank, let me tell you that the place is surrounded by a series of narrow canals that run between the rows of houses. So what, you may ask. OK, imagine you're the lad who dropped his ticket and had to watch it float away. I don't know if he ever got it back, but it gave us a laugh on our way to the town for a pint. There were a few notable moments during that game – Lincoln's defender Grant Brown played against his hometown team, for whom his granddad Matt Middleton had kept goal fifty-eight times before the Second World War. Darren Williams got sent off, and it was also the occasion of Gavin McCann's first goal following his move from Everton reserves a few weeks earlier – a bit of a spawny ricochet off his shin, but a goal nonetheless.

Most significant, though, was Scotty's awkward landing on a bumpy pitch that finished both his ankle and his playing career. We were through, and fighting on three fronts, surely the signs of a decent side. It wasn't long before it was just the two, and we lost at Blackburn in the next round, where Alex Rae's return to the team after treatment for what is politely described as personal problems (drink and drugs, I think) ended with a busted knee, and it was back to the League for us with his season over.

We'd been without our main goal machine since September, but had managed better than alright without him. He was straight back into the team for the game at QPR, where he behaved as if he'd never been away with a superb volley on the run into the net beneath our feet, causing the usual Loftus Road stand trembling. Bally went off to a later-rescinded red card, but we were happy enough with the result.

On the homeward journey, Shildon Pete managed to hijack first Benno, then Monty, for impromptu interviews. Top men both, they'd have talked to us all night if they'd had time. I also managed to get a chat with Nick Pickering and Gary Rowell, but the most interesting conversation went on between some Sunderland fans and the then Fulham Manager. Kevin Keegan either had very high ideas of his status in football, or had simply forgotten that he'd be sharing a train to Durham with us lot. I favour the former, as he was sat with Brace, so as I passed, I said hello to our former player and shook his hand, pointedly ignoring Keegan. A few beers later, I went back, asked for his autograph, ruffled his hair as he signed, and told him he wasn't all bad – with my fingers crossed, of course.

On to the League Cup, then, and it was the first leg of the semi at home to Leicester. McCann scored again, but we let tiny terror Tony Cottee grab the winner to leave us behind on aggregate. The second leg showed how close we were to going through, as we did everything but score more than Quinny's deft header, and a draw saw us out of the competition, but at the front of the footballing world's minds. We were on our way, and now there was only the League to concentrate on, there'd be no stopping us.

We duly beat Ipswich, then I decided to give our Ian a treat and use up the air miles gained from my flights to the USA over the last couple of years to fly the pair of us to the Watford game. We shared the plane with Bedlington Terriers, on their way to play Ford in the FA Trophy, and had a good laugh with them. It was at this point that the bairn told me he didn't like flying. He also had a broken toe, so I had to piggy-back him around London, apart from the blessed relief of the Natural History Museum, where they gave him a wheelchair. The mile from the station to the ground in Watford nearly crippled me, so he had to hop the last few hundred yards, and then the Lads went and spoiled it all by losing.

Three wins, a draw, then Rupert Murdoch tried to buy Man Utd, and, for once, the powers that be stepped in and told him that, in the interest of free trade, he couldn't. We kept seven clean sheets in a row as we stayed top and no-one looked like getting near us. Down at Bradford, it rained like it hadn't rained before, wind blew the wet in from both the front and the back of our little stand, but we didn't care.

In the claggy carts, we worked our socks off, and Quinny's halo moved into view as he scored the only goal, then kept a clean sheet between the posts after Tommy took a bang on the head. Niall Quinn's Disco Pants were clearly the best and ALS even released it as a single which charted. Off the bus at Aycliffe in the wee small hours, I biked back to Bishop, singing all the way, and surprised a copulating couple on the floor behind McDonalds. One in the morning, it was cold and raining, and they were on the floor. Only in Bishop, I thought, and went home to indulge myself with a selection from my Bushmills gift box in celebration.

At Grimsby, Pos lost his ticket, and had it instantly replaced by their ticket office upon him remembering his seat number. Top marks to them, and top marks to Phillips and Clark for getting the goals that put Grimsby to sleep in a mysterious hail of soft toys from the Sunderland end. Yet more top marks to debutant keeper Andy swing low sweet Marriott for keeping the customary clean sheet. By this stage, we looked unstoppable, and teams arrived at the stadium mentally defeated. Bolton's keeper made such a pathetically ineffective attempt to keep out Magic's swerver that we still refer to him as Flappyhands Jaaskaleinen. Palace tried to slow us up with a draw, but by this stage we could afford to drop two points and not worry, because we were nearly there.

Victory over Huddersfield on the Saturday meant that we could go up if we won at Bury on the Tuesday, and the town turned red and white as the army moved in, ready to let the world know we were back. I met up with Steve and Pos in the Rose and Crown, Stubber and Will in the ground, and then watched as we went to work. Two and a half sides of the ground didn't have long to wait, and their goalie was put to the sword four times by Phillips, and once by Quinn. The two we let in just made it a bit easier for the Bury folks to take, then the conga started, the whistle went, the shirts were off and twirling in the air, and we were on the pitch in a wild orgy of celebration. Well, like an orgy, but without the sex. Another smiley homeward journey was made even smilier because of the knowledge that victory at Barnsley on Friday would give us the championship with three games to spare.

After the sunshine of Gigg Lane, Barnsley was by contrast wet and snowy, cold and dark. The football wasn't though, and the shirts were off when Summerbee put us one up. If you've never seen Sunderland fans when we're winning away from home, winning the league, this was the night to see them, bare-chested in the snow with the steam rising from them.

Clark got the second, then Phillips did what Phillips does, won the ball out on the wing, cut inside, and curled a beaut into the net in front of us. The words icing and cake sprang to mind as we took it all in. Champion-ees champion-ees, ole, ole ole. A Perfect Moment was at number one, and it couldn't have been more appropriate.

Another 40,000 crowd saw the Lads deservedly take their collective foot off the gas against Sheff Utd, then it was off to Stockport via Stubber's in Bradford. He wasn't going to bother going until I rang and told him I was taking him (and had the necessary ticket, more to the point), but fully appreciated the effort as we won yet again. The last game didn't really matter as anything but a celebration, and we came from behind to beat Birmingham, thanks to Johnston's late goal to spark the celebrations proper.

To be honest, you would have thought we would have been all celebrated out, but we'd arranged for the ladies to come through for a swift celebratory half, then we stayed back in Sunderland to discuss what we'd witnessed since August. The most successful league season by a professional English team in the history of the game. 105 points, 91 goals, but what if Phillips hadn't got injured? How many more than his twenty-three league goals - in twenty-six games - would he have scored? What if… "Oh Sobs man, shut up and have a pint." OK, if you insist. We supped beer in The Salty, played doms in the King's, and smiled our way around the town centre until it was time to go home, still smiling.

At some stage, we were in The Londonderry, packed with jolly people. I launched into the season's anthem, and the place lifted for ten minutes solid. Sunderland were back.

On our way
We're on our way
To the Premier
We're on our way
How do we get there
I don't know
How do we stay there
I don't care
All I know is Sunderland's on their way

1999-2000

While we were eagerly awaiting the arrival of football's New Gold Dream on Wearside, the rest of the world carried on being humans. A nail bomb went off in Brixton, just to remind us that, even when there was nothing in particular to protest about, there was always someone prepared to do something unspeakable in the name of something unheard of. With our Gaz now being of an age where family holidays were about to cease being compulsory, we did the package holiday thing for the first and last time. Loret is a nice enough place, but it's too much like Blackpool with sun for my tastes. Still, we went for it, did the parascending, the banana boat rides, and the trip to Barcelona on a bus full of Huddersfield and Sunderland fans – and one with a Real Madrid shirt, as if to prove that wherever you go in the world, there'll be a football fan with no brains. Nelson Mandela decided enough was enough, and was replaced after – shock, horror – an election, and the Scottish Parliament opened, just to keep them quiet, like.

Sunday mornings were now officially free, The Bittermen having been told, individually and collectively, that the various dodgy knees, hips, and backs would take no more hung-over hammering at the hands of fitter, younger, and stronger players on the doggy toilets of Sunday morning football. To be honest, it was a bit of a relief to myself and Pop, as opposition had been increasingly hard to find, but not as hard as finding eleven Bittermen with both legs pointing in the same direction. Eighteen seasons, and we still had forty-two quid in the money-box, so that went behind the bar at The Tut, and everybody who'd ever played for us (that we could both remember and find) had a pint, a sing-song, and a bloody good laugh. I'd like to see Man Utd go that way, but it ain't gonna happen.

Back at the jolly old SoL, big changes were afoot. We'd hoped for some, as we were moving up a league and needed to cut our cloth accordingly. What we got was a catalogue of what can best be described as unforced errors. Lee Clark proved that you should never trust a Mag by having a few beers at the Cup Final and wearing a naughty T-shirt. They lost the game, by the way, and Lee was on his way to Fulham and Al-Fayed's millions.

Martin Smith, whose irregular first-team career bore testament to the manager's opinion of him, left for Sheff Utd with the quote "At least they play in red and white," and with tales of a bust-up between his missus and Paul Butler's missus at a team party. Andy Melville was allowed to leave, way too soon in my opinion, and Johnston and the manager fell out in pathetically spectacular fashion, proving to be the start of a downward spiral for a fantastically talented player. It's fair to say he's never approached the heights of his partnership with Mickey Gray since then. Michael Bridges, also after a falling-out with the manager, went to Leeds for £4.5 million. In the middle of all this nonsense, Sampdoria arrived for Bally's testimonial, despite it only being the beginning of his tenth season. I won't argue with him about that, for if ever a man deserved a testimonial, it was Bally. Typically, it ended 0-0 and the main man missed a penalty.

Off the field, things in Sunderland town had taken a turn for the worse, as Swallow Hotels went ahead with their shameful closure of Vaux Brewery. This had been threatened for months, and during the previous season they'd tried to get us to agree to wearing a Swallow logo on our shirts as part of their continued sponsorship. I made a load of alternative logos (you can stuff your swallow) that we pinned on the front of our shirts. A profitable company, a good portfolio of products, six hundred and odd jobs, and over a hundred years of history. Oh, we'll close it and make an extra £2.50 by selling the bits off.

Nothing short of disgraceful, and I think the club could have done a little more in terms of getting involved and expressing their displeasure at the way Swallow Group PLC were treating a Sunderland institution, not to mention several hundred of its fans who worked there. At least they recognised that to carry on the sponsorship deal would have been tasteless in the extreme, and would probably have resulted in replica kit sales in single figures. So local boy made good Reg Vardy stepped in, and it was his name that appeared on the famous stripes as the season kicked off.

In through the revolving door came wise old bald head Steve Bould, Kirk Douglas look-alike Carsten Fredgaard – the fastest thing in Danish football, apparently – twinkle-toed Welshman John the schoolboy Oster, Stefan Schwarz, Swedish superstar, Thomas Helmer, German superstar, and Frenchman Eric Roy pronounced rwa. These were the type of players we wanted to see – internationals with funny names and, more importantly, experience at the top level. Well, three of them were. The other three we'd have to see about.

Judith and I managed to slip in a weekend by ourselves in Weymouth, just to see if the old place was the same, and it was, just before the fun and games began at Chelsea. Oh dear, we weren't up for that one at all. After only three defeats in 46 games last term, we were off to a horrible loss at the Bridge – and after travelling overnight so that we could take in the sights as well. Chris Lumsdon played his only league game of the season, a bit of a baptism of fire, to be honest. Play-off winners Watford, one of those three teams to beat us last season, were next up, and duly seen off 2-0, with goals from Phillips, of course.

Steve Bould showed his old mates what they'd lost as he commanded our defence to a 0-0 draw. Helmer had come on for Bould, and kept his place for the trip to Leeds. Going back on my decision of a couple of years ago, I accepted another freebie, in a padded seat with the company name on it and drinks waiting for us at half time. Kev's penalty put us ahead, and we dreamed of a win, but then Alex Rae brushed past Lee Bowyer, the little bugger dived like a salmon, and our man was off. Needless to say, Leeds came back to win despite Tommy's penalty save, but in the lounge afterwards, every award presented came from the hands of a Sunderland fan. It got to the stage where the man with the microphone asked "You're not a Sunderland fan as well, are you?" as each stepped up to hand over yet another trophy to Lucas Radebe.

That was the last we saw of Helmer, who'd looked like he could play the game at two mile per hour and still outfox opponents, but he fell out with the management over some tactical thing (after all, he'd only played a thousand times helping Germany win World Cups, what did he know?), and he was packed off to Hertha Berlin on a lengthy loan.

Then came the big one, the one we'd all been waiting for – up the road to Tyneside to have a go at Gullit's underachieving Magpies. In Sunderland, fifteen thousand screamed at the big screen at the Stadium, desperately wanting to be twelve miles up the road. Twelve miles up the road, the rain hoyed down, Gullit replaced Shearer with a teenage Sunderland fan, and ballet commenced. Just to make a game of it, we let them win the first half, then we got to work.

Summerbee's free-kick was glanced in by big Niall, then Shearer came on, lost the ball in a thunderous challenge from Makin, and Summerbee set Phillips away. After his initial shot was saved, little Kev dug the ball out of the water to curl a winner into the top corner and enter Wearside folklore.

Bally was on to shore things up, and big, hard Duncan Ferguson wimped out of a challenge, causing our man to hit his own crossbar. Who cares, it was 2-1, so let it rain, let it rain. Back to The Tut, two pint glasses and a bottle of champagne, please, a bit of baiting of the Mag who didn't know the result and insisted that, as we watched the TV highlights, they could still win. They lost the highlights as well, and the empty champagne bottle ended up on Finny the Mag's doorstep over the road. As for the rest of the season, as long as we didn't go down, it could go and whistle. Why does it always rain on me? Is it because my name is Ruudi? A message to you Ruudi. Ruudi can fail. Happy days.

Draw and a win at home, and then it was down to Pride Park, allegedly named after the part of town (sorry, industrial estate) in which it stands, and nothing to do with trying to sound Americanised and corny at all. A bit like the Stadium of Light in that respect, then. We parked up at the railway station as it was cheaper, and, more importantly, next to The Brunswick, where the beer is brown, frothy, and brewed out the back. By half-time, our Ian was asking if all away games could be like this as we flattened Derby into the turf, then Phillips completed another hat-trick as we went home five goals, three points to the good, and sitting pretty in third place. Third place. Halcyon days.

A couple of days before Derby, we beat Walsall 3-2 in the League Cup, then the hardcore made the trip to Walsall's flattest of flat-pack stadia, the Bescot, to have a look at trialist Brazilian Guiseppe in the second leg. No entry to the big club near the ground, so I snuck into their supporters club under the home end. Guiseppe started on the bench, Tommy Butler played his first game, and Lumsden his last, but it was our ice-cool Frenchman who was the star of the show. "Ooh aah, he's Eric Rwa y'knaa" put his foot on the ball, sprayed passes all over the pitch, and scored a Quinn-esque header.

Deech scored a fantastic long distance scoop, added another, and Carsten Fredgaard got his only two Sunderland goals. The Brazilian fella made a cameo appearance, did several very Brazilian things, and was next heard of when Walsall signed him. He only lasted four minutes on the pitch before vanishing forever. The next round saw Bally and Deech take Wimbledon to extra time, but a late goal knocked us out. Damn.

Back in the dreamy world of the Premier League, people were beginning to take notice of us, and recognise that we were a force to be reckoned with, both as a team and a club. And a set of supporters. They loved us wherever we went (well, almost everywhere), and the jolly red and white army became one of the Premier League's big selling points. It was fun following Sunderland, it was good to belong. Schwarz hoofed in a volley of spectacular proportions to beat Sheff Wed, then we popped down to Bradford, took our places in the ground after suffering the delights of Hoagy's Bar on Lumb Lane, and watched as the Lads do what the Lads do when they play at Bradford, namely knock the stuffing out of the Bantams. 4-0 moved up to second – second – and the world was our oyster.

The standard of our ground attracted England, Kev got a cap, but the powers that be forgot that the Great North Run was on the same day, so there were a thousand runners and forty thousand football fans all trying to use the same transport system. I did my bit by doing the run, then getting the train from Shields to Sunderland, and running from the station to The Salty to collect my football clothes. I bet I smelled a treat. Shortly after this, the reserves attracted twenty thousand for the game against the Mags Overpaid Shysters Eleven (Marcelino "Ooh me fingernail" and company) at the Stadium, which carried on the following from the Liverpool reserve game last season. When times are good, we come out in droves.

Two from Kev beat Villa, and we were still there or thereabouts in third, and ready to move on up as we hit the Boleyn and West Ham. Phillips put us ahead, Bould was off, and we were hanging on into the dying minutes when sub Deech missed a chance, the ball went down the other end, and Trevor Sinclair put away the equaliser. We could have gone top, but we held our nerve and Quinny took the proverbial out of Sol Campbell against Spurs to get both goals and another win. About this time, someone decided to put too many trains on the same line, one went through a red light at Ladbroke Grove, and 31 people died. Just the sort of thing to keep your feet on the ground.

Down on Teesside, after our compulsory early start and wait on the A19, Michael Reddy showed his much-vaunted pace by racing onto Kev's saved penalty to put away the rebound and earn us another point, despite Makin's sending off. Liverpool then got a bit clever by beating us at our place, before we won a ding-dong 3-2 at Watford, where TallPaul refused to enter the toilets on the grounds that they were too far underground to be safe. With only one entrance/exit, I had to agree. The game also marked the end of an era, as Bally left for a nice pay check at Fulham, and good luck to him.

Then came Chelsea, and things didn't look too promising. Ball, Butler, McCann, and Bould were missing, so the central midfield was Roy and Thirlwell. Not what you would choose, but the result was probably the best performance the Stadium had seen so far. Roy pulled more strings than a manic violinist, while his partner in crime Thirlwell nicked more balls than a drunken vasectomist. Eric the Frenchman's roll into the box for the first was sublime, then Phillips hit a beaut from distance as he and Quinn racked up two apiece by half time.

The second half was by necessity an anticlimax, but 4-1 against Chelsea in that sort of style is something to remember, cherish, and bring out of the memory bank every now and then on the way to an away game. Another win, over Southampton, when we sported our new boy Kevin Kilbane, to a backdrop of Baggies complaining that we'd got him cheap, then it was the Boxing Day trip to Everton. For the last thirty years, I'd offered my Mam a trip to the match on Boxing Day, as a birthday treat, and every year she'd refused. Ian and I wished we'd gone to her house for tea instead, as we collapsed like a Mag on a Saturday night, five goals the wrong side of a defeat.

Strangely enough, it was at this time that Jeffrey Archer was proved in court to be a pathological liar. Which explains his years at the top of Conservative politics. Sorry, dear, I just happened to see a prostitute at Kings Cross, so I gave her a bag of money. Sounds obvious.

2-2 at home to Man Utd ended the year, then we popped down to the delightful Selhurst Park for our annual disappointment against Wimbledon. We looked about right for at least a draw until a little thug called Thatcher stuck the most obvious of elbows into Buzza's face, took the ball up-field and created the only goal. That sort of challenge on a Sunday morning would probably see the perpetrator in prison, but he got away with it. Truly the masses against the classless, and the masses were the losers that day, which was probably the start of Wimbledon's long slide out of popularity and down to Milton Keynes. Thank goodness.

So welcome to the new millennium. And welcome to George W Bush, amazingly elected into power in the USA despite his father's performance in office and his failure to reach double figures in an IQ test. Over in the Balkans, things got no better, as the self-styled warlord known as Arkan ended up in the gutter, full of bullets. Those who live by the sword…

For some reason known only to TV, the FA Cup third round had seen us beat Portsmouth in December, and therefore face Tranmere (again) in January in the fourth round. I shared a couple of beers in the Gloucester Tavern with former flatmate Rob, then watched in disbelief as we played one up front. They moved heaven, earth, and the advertising hoarding to allow their enormous long throws to be accommodated, and then had Clint Hill sent off.

They managed to bring a sub on at the same time, and still ended up with eleven men on the field for ninety minutes. Once the mistake was realised, the ref didn't do the obvious and sensible thing of allowing us the added time that they'd been illegally a man up, but simply allowed the whole thing to stand. And don't even suggest that John Aldridge was an innocent party in this, because he knew fine well what he was doing, but got away with it. I'm not biased, though I would admit to being paranoid, but I won't because if I did they'd spot me because they're watching. The fiends, they're everywhere.

Back in the jolly old Premier League, it was down to the Arsenal, and we'd barely time to settle our pre-match Lamb pints before we were 3-0 down at half time. You have to keep the faith, but times like these stretch your loyalty a bit. The two Shildon Petes managed to persuade the jobsworth on the gate that they'd be better off on the outside, and by the time we got back to The Lamb the wrong side of a 4-1 thumping, they were the wrong side of the best part of a barrel of Winter Warmer and happily oblivious to the slaughter a couple of miles away. Until we described it in detail, that is. While we were drowning our sorrows on the East Coast main line, most of our defence was trying to prove just how Premier League we really were by doing what we mere fans only dream about – providing the tabloids with several days' worth of news by cavorting with Melanie Sykes (model, TV presenter, generally nice looking lady) and her pal. The jammy sods.

A home defeat to Dorty Leeds, then the return of the Big One, and Phillips got both goals in a 2-2 draw with them from up the road. Their fans were hilarious, with their wobbly stomachs, pastry-encrusted faces, and huge cartoon tattoos. They'd pathetically ridiculed the coaches that had taken us to Tyneside in August, but at least ours had glass in the windows. Four points to us, just the one on its way back to the Dark Side. Top dogs, I think.

A defeat at Coventry held us up a bit, but then we had Derby at home. We'd popped in five at their place, so a slaughter was definitely on the cards. The day before, I was cycling to work, as I had for years, when there was a big bang and I woke up on the roadside being stared at by the young lass whose Metro had made such an impression on my mountain bike, and crowd of concerned onlookers. Broken bike helmet, broken back, the Derby game was strictly off limits as they took their time to find a hospital that actually treated folks with broken bones, and I could get no radio reception in the Memorial. I did manage to get a red and white shirt shipped in for the occasion, but Pos and Stubber called in to tell me that I'd been better off where I was rather than at the match. I knew what they meant, but I couldn't agree, as I was within a titchy bit of agreeing to swap my back for a black and white shirt at that stage.

Only the generous intervention of morphine prevented me from selling my soul to the devil, and it's a shame they wouldn't give me a gallon of the stuff to share out with fellow red and whites in future seasons. Luckily, I held out, but the planned trips to Leicester and Liverpool were off limits. They propped me up in the corner of The Tut for the former, and it went stupid with a Heskey hat-trick and a 5-2 defeat. Heskey promptly joined Liverpool, the team he'd supported as a boy despite having a Leicester season ticket since before he could remember, and plagued our life the following week. At least at Anfield we could rightly say that his tit-for-tat shirt pull on Williams was scarcely deserving of a penalty, but we came away with a draw, and I just survived the pub, having entered into a vigorous discussion of Heskey's merits as a footballer, or rather a big fat girl's blouse in my opinion, with a rather gobby scouser. Down to ninth, then only a draw with the Boro at home, and a win over Everton took us back to seventh. Lads on the bus opened a bank account and began to save up for the inevitable European away games next season.

Our constant search for new talent brought us to a new low – literally, as four foot two Milton Nunez arrived with a fake CV and a receipt for a couple of million quid, one of the biggest cons that our great club has ever been the victim of. He made his debut against Wimbledon, looked smaller than the ball, and jumped about like Jimmy Krankie as we won. Another win, then down to Old Trafford and a four-goal knackering, but seventh place was still ours. Down to Sheff Wed on the train, a really friendly pub next to the Crucible Theatre for two dads and two lads, and the tram out to Hillsborough, on which we met Michael from school. Some things never change, Michael certainly doesn't. "They do my head in, this team, but I still love them." Sounds about right. Two goals from SuperKev took the points, then we did the unthinkable and let Bradford win at our place. Quinny's bobbly goal at Villa earned a point, then we snuck past West Ham at home thanks to another Phillips goal.

So the end of the season, away to Spurs and I scrounged a lift with the two Petes, nicely sprawled across the back seat. Things looked encouraging early on, when, after almost three years of us screaming shoooooot, Chris Makin did just that and scored. Not the thunderbolt we'd been expecting, but a clever one two and dink past the keeper. Bloody hell, what was all that about? That was as good as it got, as Mad Alex lived up to his name by applying his elbow rather forcibly to ex-

Mag Ginola's chin, presumably because ee was worth eet, and off he went. The European place was one position away thanks to our 3-1 defeat, but we were a million miles above where we'd expected to be.

We weren't there, but we were in the elite. We were some of the Premier League's chosen people. Our manager was a media darling, appearing on Question of Sport, and adding his expert opinion to match commentaries. Quinn and Phillips were the mystery guests on Question of Sport. We were fun, we were trendy, and we were still my Sunderland. Above all, we were nice people, and that went a long way. If them up the road could actually survive as a football club for over two years after the unbelievably disgusting behaviour of their two main directors, we were laughing. How any football club can allow two individuals like those to remain in any way connected with the club is beyond me, but apparently on Tyneside it's perfectly acceptable for board members to call their female fans dogs, laugh at the prices they charge for replica shirts, and question the character of their team's captain – while being filmed in a brothel. Hey, you're welcome to them, their money's tainted, and I wouldn't touch them with a bargepole.

Niall Quinn's disco pants are the best
They go up from his arse to his chest
They are better than Adam and the Ants
Niall Quinn's disco pants

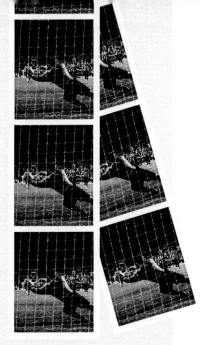

2000-2001

No more camping holidays with the boys, as our Gaz had reached an age at which he wanted to go camping with his mates, and was too big to tell otherwise, so it was a couple of nights up Weardale with Ian, resisting the requests to join in the Bridge team at the Cowshill Hotel. Had it been Snap, we'd have been in like a shot, but Bridge was a game too far.

Ian then won two tickets for the Euro 2000 semi-final France against Portugal. It was only third prize, which meant no transport or accommodation, so it was a swift ride down the East Coast Main Line, pint in The Lamb (of course), then the Eurostar to Brussels. We arrived at the King Boudewijn Stadium, formerly Heysel but now unrecognisable as the place where all that nonsense had occurred fifteen years previously, resplendent in our Sunderland shirts. Eusebio sitting just in front of us, Zidane and Figo were in their pomp, and Xavier was a big clumsy oaf. Controversial penalty (not really, it looked obvious to me), compulsory protests, sending off, and a 2-1 win to France. A nice little break, if a bit exhausting. With one night in Belgium, we'd only been out of the house for thirty hours.

Jude and I had found Weymouth so unchanged last summer that we booked a week there, after a week in the Peak District, but after the delights of our previous stays, the reality of the accommodation was a bit of a shock. Location-wise, it was great, but the fact that the carpets only touched the walls in the corners of the room (held there with drawing pins) was a bit of a stinker. Apart from that, it was fine. We caught fish, we plodged in the sea, we sent Gaz to the USA to stay with his cousin, and I went to see Dorchester Town play Southampton, because it was there.

Meanwhile the big world had seen Rover be bought by the Phoenix Consortium for £1 (oh, how I wish I'd saved up) and watched as the Kursk submarine had sunk and the Russians had waited for ten days before accepting offers of technical help. A bit too late, as it turned out, and all 118 men on board drowned, suffocated, or did whatever you do in such circumstances.

"It is 13:15. All personnel from sections six, seven and eight have moved to section nine. There are 23 of us here. We have made this decision because none of us can escape… I'm writing this blind…"

It's only a game.

So off we went in pursuit of that elusive European place and Reidy's search through the list of players with dodgy names gathered pace. In came Macho, Varga, Thome, Arca, Peeters (damn, nearly) and Hutchison (get in, a normal one), and, again amid rumours of a difference of opinion with the management, Summerbee was off on a tour of the football world. Quinny did the business at home to Arsenal, despite Vieira breaking Dazzle's nose, and we were up and running from day one.

Stan Varga, he of the scandalous haircut, had played an absolute stormer in that one, being both strong in the tackle and scarily accurate with the forty-yard passes. Down at Maine Road, we fell to pieces as he fell to pieces. He ended up with something like a hundred stitches in his leg; we produced a storming second half but still ended up 4-2 down. While the fuel price protestors slowed the nation's traffic, we crawled down to Ipswich, the landlord of The Bridge put his beer up by twenty pence especially for us, and we fell foul of Titus Bramble's surge upfield and goal. Thome made his debut against West Ham the next week, and had us doubting his Brazilian credentials with a display of defensive excellence and passing hilarity.

Also starting for the first time that day was Hoooolio (insert as many "O"s as you like depending on his last performance) and he came up with our goal in a draw. A horrible hammering at Old Trafford, now with no away-friendly bars anywhere near the ground, and the highest concentration of unsociable bouncers this side of Vladivostok, preceded a win over Derby, then it was off to Anfield. I took our Ian, as part of his teenage visit to as many grounds as you can growing up thing, and was showing him the Hillsborough memorial when someone rode past on a bike and spat on it. Who he was or where he'd come from I couldn't tell, but I thought everyone in Liverpool loved each other and their cheeky Scouse sense of humour. That one I didn't understand. SKP (as he was now known) what with his England caps and everything hit the ball wonderfully early in to the Kop end net, and we held on for a draw.

In October the railway track at Hatfield fell to pieces, the train came off the rails, and people died because of bad maintenance. By the time our jaunt to Spurs came along, there were still no trains, so we hired a seven-seater and big Pete donned the bairn's red and white Viking hat for the day in honour of the national team's new manager, and was referred to for the duration as Sven.

We parked up at Enfield, met up with Paula from Uni in the pub in the market place (no, I can't remember the name of it, but it's near the world's first cash point machine, if that helps), where we had great banter with the locals and discovered that pork scratchings dipped in tabasco sauce are something else. We lost, we drank exotic beers and vodkas (with fresh fruit, of course) and we sang our way back, the part where Bohemian Rhapsody kicked us into a Wayne's World head banging mayhem almost causing several passing drivers to leave the road. That's life on the road with SAFC. Steve Bould's toe forced his retirement, and Mickey Gray, the quiet man on the field, became team captain.

November also brought the end of a legend, as Shack died. "I'm not biased against Newcastle, I don't care who beats them," is probably his most famous quote, and I make no excuses for using it again. The end of the great entertainer.

Draw, win, draw, win, loss, draw, and we were decently mid-table and awaiting the trip to Tyneside and a repeat of last season's fun in the rain. Kilbane had seen red for a bout of harmless flappy-handing with renowned hard-man Le Saux (actually, despite his Guardianreading persona, he was a bit of a niggly bugger) to earn a suspension, but was back for the trip north. Off the convoy went, and as with last year, we let them sneak one in just to make a game of it, and cause Willa to pull his shirt over his head for the rest of the first half. Then Hutch ignored the obvious foul on Quinny to equalise, took a moment to realise what he'd just done, then decided it was OK to celebrate.

Several light years later, the images reached us up at the back, and we were off, out of our seats, lifting the roof, waving to our loved ones back home in the distance. Off went Makin, on came Arca, and Rae set up Mickey Gray, who produced the run and cross of his life, right on Quinny's head, and there it was, over Given and into the top corner. Praise be to Saint Niall. We were even further down the road to nowhere mentally, and all over the stand physically as we laughed, cried, and took fits of joy. Quinny then made the classic forward's mistake of thinking that he could defend, and gave away a penalty near the end. Up stepped Mary Poppins (Hall's quote, not mine) and down went Tommy to write his name in massive letters in the book of Great Big Red and White Heroes.

As we kissed and cuddled each other in our little compound afterwards, there was a commotion, the fence burst, and two Mags appeared, fists at the ready. A quick glance that said "forty-odd busloads, only two of you" and they were back into the Byker Wall faster than you could say "Greggs of Gosforth", while we simply continued our great big Mackem love-in. Yes, we were officially Mackems now, as every bunch of fans in the Premier League is required by law to have a nickname, as is every club. They won't be happy until we're called the Wearside Ferocious Felines, or something equally as banal and stupid, but money talks and sense walks. They even had the cheek to tell us we couldn't have our traditional black cat badge (sorry, logo) on our shirt-sleeves because they hadn't endorsed it. Well stuff you, Mr Premier League, do I try and tell you what pattern you can or can't have on your tie? Get a life, for goodness sake, and leave ours alone.

Into the Valley, and we toasted Quinny, SKP, and all things red and white with several bottles of Jameson's in the Antigallican (holidays courtesy of SAFC fans), then watched Mad Alex hit a screamer to win the game, despite being the subject of crowd abuse (if you can get abuse at Charlton) because of his former affiliation with Millwall. We were climbing up the league, and Everton were brushed aside back at the good old SoL. After a few years, it was starting to bed in, and we were feeling comfortable in our seats. They were extending the North Stand, we were glad that they were, and we collected our free rain capes that would keep us dry while the roof was off. We'd grown accustomed to the faces around us – the lad who looks a bit like Ian Rush, the lad who looks a bit like Alan Rickman's Sheriff of Nottingham, the lad with the glasses a few rows down who never stops shouting, and the miserable bloke next to our Ian who called the Lads worse than cack from half two until five every Saturday, win, lose, or draw. Thankfully, he's moved on; otherwise the bairn would have been sitting somewhere else by now.

We eventually beat the Boro thanks to Mickey Gray, then lost at Leeds (I was wrong, paying for my ticket made absolutely no difference) before the fixtures went a bit mental. Way back in September, we'd beaten Luton 3-0 at home, then gone to Kenilworth Road, scarily once at the cutting edge of stadium development in this fair land, but now boasting views into people's bathrooms, and watched Reddy score and Nunez run through defenders' legs.

Then Hutch scored both as we braved the flooded South West to defeat Bristol Rovers before Man Utd reserves were put away thanks to an extra-time penalty from SKP. It was still very wet when we passed through central London on our way to Palace, and a radgie Rastafarian drove into the side of the bus and tried to blame us for the big rusty dent on his car. Forty pairs of eyes told him it was a bad idea, then the weatherman spoiled the day by announcing that the game was off. At least we got home early, but I'd run out of holidays, it being December, and the re-arranged match was thus beyond my reach. It was beyond the reach of the Lads as well, and we slipped quietly away 1-0.

Back in the Big League, we squeezed past City, then took our regular trip to Hoagy's, and the Pulse FM KFC McDonald's Stadium at Valley Parade, or whatever they were calling it at the time. You know what happens down there, and it happened again, as SKP knocked in a hat-trick and still had time to miss a penalty as Quinny added the fourth. I love Bradford, me, apart from the wobbly concrete floors in the only-opened-yesterday corner that we were housed in, but especially because they had so far refused to toe the Premiership line, and were charging under £2 a pint.

So it was high spirits down to Arsenal, as always. What we'd do if there wasn't The Lamb only three tube stops away, I don't know. Some wide boy tried to pick a fight with me at Highbury station, so I smiled sweetly, shook his hand, and went for some Youngs to numb the pain of the inevitable early collapse. The second half was a different story, as SKP put away a penalty, then Alex drove into Vieira with more gusto than the Frenchman had ever seen, the ball broke to McCann, and he scooped away one of those efforts that had been my speciality on a Sunday morning. Well, I'd done it twice in eighteen years, but it did help me feel extra specially jolly when the ball nestled in the back of the net just in front of me. Quinny almost nicked it late on, but 2-2 and fourth place was what you might call canny away, like.

New Year's Day, and poor old Ipswich had to make the nightmare journey to Wearside. Where's the personal intervention and common sense in the fixture list? You can't tell me that it doesn't get fiddled with, but that only happens when it's Man Utd or Arsenal trying to have a bit rest after or before a European game. Why is it never because Plymouth have to travel to the North East on a Tuesday night?

Whatever, they had an even worse journey home, with a 4-1 defeat to come to terms with. Then came the FA Cup – against Palace. You couldn't make these fixtures up. A goal-free game at home, with Stan the Man being sent off, took us to deepest suburbia, and we came from behind to take them to extra time before substitute Deech was sent off and we came away 4-2 winners after a crazy old game. Quinny's chest and volley special, two cracking finishes from Kev that took him to 104 goals, and a lovely run and calm slotaway from Killa were four top quality goals. That gave us Ipswich (I told you that these fixtures couldn't be made up), and Deech made amends by getting the only goal. That brought West Ham up North in February, and we ran out of FA Cup puff, 1-0 losers.

Back in the league, we'd done West Ham at their place, good and proper, as they say in the East End. A cracking header from Stan the Man won the first half, and a sneakily quick free-kick from Don made it two. TallPaul's brother Will had been transported from the airport to the match on his return to good old County Durham, and found himself jet-lagged and helpless with laughter as we went one up and turned the Hammers' song back on them. I can't print it exactly, but it went along the lines of "eff off DiCanio", and was hilarious. We then went three games without scoring, and the home defeat to Man Utd saw Mickey Gray off for being too gobby, and Mad Alex for refusing to be nutted by Andy (that's Andy, not Andrew) Cole. The home draw with Liverpool should have been a win but for the twenty yard dive into the box by old cheat Gary McAllister. Wasn't he at Coventry for a while? Figures.

Never mind, we were still fourth, and the passports were being checked. Nicky Summerbee, long the victim of some unspoken feud, finally got away to Bolton, and the shape of the side had changed forever. We'd managed most of this season without the wingers of the past two years (Oster's fleeting appearances apart), and were relying more on Hutchison's guile and Rae's enthusiasm alongside the calmness of Schwarz, plus what was now recognised as the best front two in the League, if not the universe. Paul Butler, now down the pecking order, went to Wolves, and Eric Roy (that's Rwa) went back to France, and we went down to Filbert Street.

If you've ever been, you'll understand why it was nothing ridiculous for Benny to end up in someone's front room, asking for a cup of tea. What you won't understand is how we lost 2-0 to a very average side, as hard man (I think not, actually) Robbie Savage picked a fight with the massive John Oster, and got our man sent off. Still in the European places, though. A draw at home to Villa didn't exactly have us phoning the travel agents, but then we went to Chelsea, and the St Patrick's Day (nearly) massacre took place. Having taken advantage of the two for one offer on the black stuff in the Lamb, we were already underway when I arrived. What followed convinced me that we were well and truly on the world map of football. Sometimes you can't make it on your own, but we did that day, and came away 4-2 winners, bursting with pride and pies all the way home.

The defeat at home to Leeds was a bit of a show-stopper, and the draw with the Boro didn't help, but then we let a two goal lead turn to a defeat at the hands of Spurs, and we were wondering just what was going on. It was almost as bad - no, it was worse, this is Sunderland, my Sunderland that we're on about here – as the Labour Party's gradual turning into the Conservative party, and Tony Blair still telling us all how he'd loved sitting in the Leazes End as a child. Isn't it a shame when something you've craved for so long (eighteen years, to be precise) eventually arrives, gets into a comfortable position, and then starts to sound very much like the thing they've replaced? And pretends to be a Mag, just for the showbiz, man of the people angle? Still, I take it as the lesser of two evils as far as I was concerned. They had a bit of bother on their plates as foot and mouth was first identified – naturally enough sourced from a farm at Heddon on the Wall, so he was probably a Mag. Near Selby, someone fell asleep at the wheel and managed to knock a train off the rails and kill ten people. It's only a game.

Chris Makin had been the subject of some pretty unsavoury rumours, and when that happened under Reidy, you were out of the picture. So in came Patrice Carteron (remember him?), a floppy-haired Frenchman who was more tact and guile compared to Shooot's blood and thunder. Along came the stinky Mags, Hutch pointed to where he wanted Pat to go, and go he did, nipping the ball under Given. Only a draw, but, again, top dogs and bragging rights to the boys in red and white.

I was praying for a televised game at Southampton, as I was at a family wedding in Surrey and had an escape route planned to see our last ever game at the Dell, but Sky said no, and it was the radio to the ear and weird tales of Killa's spectacular winner as William and Kai said yes. So Europe was still on the cards if we won our last two and other people didn't. Charlton came, made a great contest of a 3-2 win for us, then it was off to Everton. Or rather Blackpool if you were on the Durham bus, and a chance meeting in our hotel with Cammy Duncan (remember?), warm as toast and still watching our scores with interest.

Outside Liverpool, we seamlessly linked up with the day bus – quite worrying how precise it was, actually – and took our seats in the Netley. Or rather, someone else's seat – that being the seat from which narcotics were regularly dispensed in that part of the world. They had to go down-market that day and do their business in the toilets. A 2-2 draw was fair enough, despite Hutch being sent off against one of his former employers, but we were only seventh and one place away from the promised land of Europe. Never mind, we'd probably have been drawn against someone from Iceland or somewhere ending in stan anyway.

Season over, did very well, but could have done a bit better.

Oh, Tommy Tommy
Tommy Tommy Tommy Tommy Sorensen

2001-2002

Up there with the elite, but only one desperate place away from being one of the real big guns in terms of international perception. Phillips had bagged fourteen to follow his golden-boot performance of the previous year when he got thirty (yes, thirty, by a Sunderland player, in the top flight, you're not dreaming), and Quinny was still virtually unmarkable, despite his back being an obvious problem. A whole summer to find another striking option, a whole summer to fix those niggly little problems that had been appearing since the turn of the year.

We split our holidays that year. A week in Norfolk replaced the usual camping extravaganza as our Ian breathed a sigh of relief that my dodgy back prevented me hauling him along the eighty-odd miles from Ilkley to Windermere that is the Dales Way. We'd tried it a few years ago, and he and Gaz had used up all of my money on food in three days, so it was a halfway stop and a quick phone-call for a lift home. A week in a cottage near the beach was much more relaxing from his point of view. Out in the big bad world, they were still trying to make the peace process work in Ulster, and then we went back to the eighties with race riots in Bradford and Oldham.

Who was to be the new Quinn? Dichio was the same size and build, but not the same player, so off he went. The fact was that Quinn could not be replaced, as there could be only one. We had to find another way. In came another French-man, called Lilian, to try out as a centre-forward, and a Swiss called Bernt Haas, to be the new Chris Makin. Jan Koller, and any other European over six foot two was always on the verge of signing, but none of them ever did.

Until now, I'd not been one for pre-season friendlies unless it was the reserves at West Auckland or Bishop, or a swift trip up to Berwick, preferring to save my readies for the real thing. However, the fact that the Durham branch put on a coach to Celtic persuaded me that it would be worth a try. Ian and I took Austin, the Bhoy from work, along to see his team, we had a few beers in the Horseshoe Bar, where Travis had played their first gig, and then had Austin hooked on Sun-derland as his second team. Several thousand had made the journey, and we took the atmosphere with us. Try as we might, we couldn't get any sort of reac-tion from the surprisingly quiet home fans until we were leaving the ground, and we struck up the Hello, Hello, We are the Sunderland Boys song, and the Jocks went ballistic.

Austin explained that it was the lyrics of verse four, and the bit about being knee-deep in Fenian blood that upset them. Oh well, you live and learn, and I was all in favour of pre-season friendlies all of a sudden. The price of the train down to Torquay couldn't be sniffed at, so it was off to the English Riviera with Ian and the two Petes, via a long stop in the sweltering heat of Devon as the train broke. My match report to Pos stated categorically that Laslandes was the business, and he'd fill in nicely when Quinny decided to call it a day. Also on the way in was French sprinter Daveeed Bellion, soon to replace Fredgaard in the reserves as the man the fans shouted "take the ball with you" at.

The Celtic game, a comfy win at Torquay and a great weekend with the travellers changed my views on such games. Why on earth would several hundred people travel 400 miles for a meaningless game to sing red and white army for twenty-five minutes without drawing breath? I don't know, but they did, and it made me glad that I was one of them.

Then came the second part of the holidays, in the Lakes, where foot and mouth had knocked the tourist trade for six. More importantly, the holiday began about three hours after we'd beaten Ipswich at home, and included a bus, two trains, an unscheduled two-hour wait in a field north of Tamworth, a swift beer in The Lamb, the wrong tube, and a taxi from Earls Court to Craven Cottage. All that for Lee Clark to be injured, us to lose, and an overnight stay before the first train back to the holiday the next morning. A great way to warm up for the trip to Tyneside, and we could be forgiven for being slightly disappointed with only a draw after the fun and games of the previous two visits. We did get to exercise our annual privilege, afforded to Sunderland fans since 1909, of wazzing on Leazes Moor.

A win over Blackburn on September 8th, then came September 11th, when the world took terrorism to the USA's doorstep for the first time. Maybe now they'd realise that funding the IRA wasn't such a good idea. And perhaps now they'd realise that kicking ass in the Balkans wasn't just a game.

Trips to Villa were becoming about as stale as a week-old cake, and it was probably only the pre-match refreshments in Lichfield that kept us going, and they chose to put this one on the TV. As we prepared to leave Lichfield, an old chap asked me who we were playing. "Villa," I replied. "Home or away?" came his next question. I give up, and the 0-0 probably made many people give up on their Sky TV subscriptions. The stadium announcer then read out the substitutes, and the pronouncement Darius Vassel as Darr-Aye–Uss Vass- Ell had us in stitches.

Only one point from the home games against Spurs and Charlton, and we weren't looking too clever. Then we went to Bolton, and Jody Craddock did what we'd long since given up on him ever doing. If Jody had an attacking trick, it was to look one way and clip a fifty-yarder to the other side of the field. It certainly wasn't scoring goals, but that's just what he did, adding to Kev's opener. Even Kylie jumped on the bandwagon, topping the charts in memory of the event. Can't Get You Out Of My Head (Jody), she sang to Blue Monday's drum beat. This should have been the springboard for development, but far from the team strengthening, bits were falling off it.

Alex Rae left, for no apparent reason (insert falling out with gaffer), and then Hutch decided their lass didn't like shopping at the Bridges. The fact that he was straight back down to West Ham and an extra £10,000 a week (conservative estimate) obviously had nothing to do with his decision that we weren't good enough for him. Like I've said before, never trust a Mag, but we desperately needed his sort of professional badge-kisser to progress, or even stand still, in this league. He was a clever player, very much a Premiership player, and it's a shame that his type of cunning has become such an integral part of the game.

Where now for our midfield? Schwarz was slowing down, and our other options were limited. In came Jason MacAteer, head banger extraordinaire. A few years ago, I'd been drooling at the prospect of him and Mickey Gary bombing down the flanks as wing-backs, but what we needed was experience and a calm head, not an admittedly influential and enthusiastic player and all-round good bloke to have a pint with, but a complete nutter. Paul Thirlwell was there on the fringes, and Arca was occasionally weaving his magic spells down the left, but what we needed was a commander in the centre.

In the League Cup, we gave big Lil a chance, and he scored, but Michael swear-a-lot Ingham was beaten twice by a then very poor Sheff Wed side. We'd tried to make it a fun night by taking Kazoos and other wind powered instruments as an objection to the Hillsborough Band and their incessant Great Escape drum-banging, but our on-field performance knocked the edge off that.

October week saw Stubber's lad Will staying for the week, so, being the responsible type, I took him to the game at Boro, complete with industrial respirator (facemask to you). Political correctness and lack of humour had gone mad by this stage, and we were required to deposit said items in an amnesty bin, and collect a nice letter from the local constabulary explaining that the wearing of such things could cause offence to the home supporters, the poor dears. We folded the letters into facemasks and put them over our mouths, then watched the lads fold 2-0. The curse of Teesside and their plastic stadium had struck again, along with the highly irritating sing along Pig Bag music.

I then had the dubious responsibility of getting two teenagers in Sunderland shirts from the away end to the bus unharmed, which was no mean feat at the Riverside. Thankfully, I managed, despite them ignoring my requests to fasten their coats and stop moaning about the result for two minutes. Schwarz, amid rumours that he wanted to fly to the moon as soon as there was an available flight, earned us a draw against his old team Arsenal, then we went to Leicester sure of victory. The reason for this ultimately futile belief was that they had, statistically, the worst forward in the world.

One of the tabloids, probably the Sun, had done all the maths on Adi Akinbiyi and concluded that he was the least effective frontman of all time. Well, that can mean only one thing. Two actually, because his partner, Benjamin, was much worse on the day, but the inevitable result was that he scored the winner with a miss-hit shot in off Thome's shin. Our cause wasn't helped when Varga went off injured, but it was a dismal performance all round. Stan, you've got some issues, I think you need some counselling. My tea's gone cold, I'm wondering why I got out of bed at all. Anyone with a record as bad as Leicester's can guarantee that the run will end against us, it's in the rules, so watch the newspapers and get your bets on as soon as you can.

We stuttered along, beating Leeds, losing at Liverpool, and beating West Ham before drawing with Chelsea, then brought in Claudio Reyna from Rangers. Captain of the good old US of A, he was pretty much a straightforward replacement for Schwarz, being strictly of the play it simple but effective school of midfielders. He took his bow at Southampton, where we arrived after an overnight trip and the driver heading back out of town, paying the toll on the bridge both ways. It wouldn't be an away game if we didn't become geographically challenged at least once. After being accosted by Morris Dancers, we discovered the delights of Weatherspoons early opening breakfasts specials, and warmed ourselves up therein.

It's just a shame that the players hadn't done likewise, as they laid down and died quietly. We gave big Lil his final try-out before giving up and sending him to Corsica or somewhere equally obscure on extended loan. Whether he'd been given a fair run in the side is still open to question, but the fact is that he didn't do that well in the games he did get (Torquay apart) and if I hadn't mentioned him, you'd maybe have never remembered him. Our attacking options were therefore down to the bare bones of Quinn and Phillips, with Kyle beginning to knock a few centre-halves about at reserve games, and Michael Proctor running around like a madman alongside him. Besides them, there were a lot of keen youngsters flying around New Ferens Park, but nobody who looked like the Next Big Thing.

Just as Woodgate and Bowyer were being found not guilty of beating the living daylights out of Safraz Najeib (the clue's in the name), and Woody's pal was getting six years for the same incident (what's the chance of that happening, eh?), Captain America got the only goal against Everton to steady the ship. Thoughts of an upturn in form came to the fore when we went to Blackburn for our Christmas treat, and went goal crazy – by our standards.

Big Niall had one of those games where he could do no wrong, and Killa added to the Irishman's brace, and we snuck into the top half of the table. All happy again, I made the mistake of letting a young Mag buy me a pint out of his first pay-packet at The Castle, and consequently slept in and missed the bus to Ipswich. Ever heard the term "one over the eight"? Stan the ticket-man, as opposed to Stan the centre half man, managed to sell it to some poor sod. Ever heard the term "survivor's guilt"? That was me, sitting at home with a bottle of Black Sheep, playing trivial bloody pursuits as the Lads were being cut to ribbons. At least we only let in one in the second half, but it was the four in the first that did the damage.

We pulled ourselves together with a draw at home to Villa, hardly a thriller, and then looked to the FA Cup to give us some impetus. We shouldn't have been so optimistic, and the Baggies came, showed pace that we didn't have, and won 2-1.

So it was just the League then, which was just as well, but we didn't take advantage of the rationalisation of competitions, losing at Everton, drawing with Fulham, losing to the Boro (at home, the buggers), and then capitulating at Old Trafford. I'll freely admit to sitting out the back for a good part of second half with a beer (United Pilsner, or some such rubbish) in my hand rather than watch the slaughter on the grass. I know it was wrong, but I just wasn't in the mood to watch my favourite eleven people be put to the sword like that.

Jocky Bjorklund, another of the been there, done that school must have wondered what he'd let himself in for. Down to Derby, and a nice stop off in Matlock where we laughed at big Steve for losing his ticket to the previous game. Perhaps it wasn't a good idea of mine to take his ticket for the day's game out of his pocket while he was asleep, especially when he nearly knocked the driver across the car-park when he awoke at Pride Park to find it missing. I might be getting older, but I certainly wasn't going to get any more sensible.

Quinny scored the only goal, and we were more than happy to move up to eleventh, but it turned around a week later, when we lost at home to them from up the road. Only one point out of our dear neighbours wasn't good enough, and the fans were getting restless.

Yet another new Niall had arrived in the shape of Patrick Mboma, and he came off the bench in that one to at least give us a chance to use his song-friendly name. He scored at Spurs the following week, but we still lost, and he kept his place for a month as Quinny was restricted to late cameo appearances.

Late cameo appearances were becoming a feature of our games, with none of the three subs getting more than a few minutes on most occasions, and consequently having little time to influence the game. Just my opinion and I wasn't picking the team. We were hovering just above the naughty part of the league table, and stayed there with a narrow win over Bolton, then made it fourteen goals in three visits to Chelsea. The shame was that we'd scored only four of them, and they were all in last season's game.

Another only moderate home draw, then it was off to Arsenal, and the very definite possibility of yet another thumping. The bookies were offering fourteen to one for us to be unbeaten by the end of the match, so, fuelled by the usual three hours in The Lamb, we had a whip round, and once in the ground, sent Heather to place the bet. By the time she sat down, we were two down, and the rest was a damage-limitation exercise. After the heroics of our performance there last season, this was a major back to reality moment. We'd gone back-over in a big way instead of going forward.

A Reyna double against Leicester took us up to the dizzy heights of fourteenth, but three defeats in a row, including a horror show at West Ham, left us one place from disaster. A draw at Charlton, when we'd actually looked like winning, then another in our final game at home to Derby, kept us up, and still in front of full houses.

At least the faith was still strong in them. A little less conversation, a little more action was what we wanted, but what we'd had was a stuttering season with no advances in style or tactics. Phillips had managed eleven goals and Quinn six, but the rest of the Lads only managed another twelve between them. The games at Chelsea and Arsenal probably summed up our lack of progress: last season we'd come close to winning at Highbury, and won well at the Bridge.

This season we'd been thumped twice, and hadn't looked half the side of twelve months before. Rae and Hutchison had left and not been replaced. We'd had wonderkid Nic Medina (he comes from Argentina) for a year and he'd looked lost in the reserves. I know that it's only football, and I shouldn't get so upset about it when thirty-odd million people in Africa were facing starvation, but it's what's close to my heart, so it's what hurts.

Things were wrong, and things were going wrong.

Julio-o
Always believe in your soul
You've got the power to know
You're indestructible
Always believe it

2002-2003

We had to get better, we'd sort it out in the summer with some shrewd signings – or so the more optimistic of us thought. Those of the glass half empty inclination said that maybe Man City had been right to get rid of Reid after he'd taken them to their two highest league finishes for years. They reckoned that he'd run out of ideas, and that a change should have been made at the beginning of last year. At least we had plenty to argue about over the close season, and lively debate keeps you focused. Immediately after the season ended, Niall Quinn played his testimonial game against the Republic of Ireland. The fact that he'd not been at Sunderland ten years and therefore didn't really qualify didn't matter. Nobody in the game would argue against football's all-round nice guy being deserving of such an occasion, and the fact that he was going to give all the money to charity confirmed his status as Saint Niall of Durham.

I took half a day off and joined in the day's jollity as half of the green half of Glasgow hit Wearside, along with most of Dublin. Obviously forgetful of our experience at Parkhead recently, a Sunderland fan who shall remain nameless but may be referred to as Bambi, decided to sing "hello hello, we are the Sunderland bffffff" as I clapped my hand over his mouth and explained away his ignorance as the result of a terrible childhood accident when he fell out of the Main Stand and landed on his head.

Quinny moved from hero to superhero, and even had the chance to create Robbie Keane's goal that took the Republic through to the second round in the World Cup. His generosity made a lot of super- rich footballers think twice about testimonials, especially when their original purpose was remembered. These games were meant to provide a nice lump sum for long serving and near retirement players so that they could buy a pub, not for them to do a Giggs and present all of the players in the match with £20,000 watches as a thank-you.

Judith's boss loaned us his caravan for the holidays, over near the Lakes, and we'd just spent the day cruising and walking around Ullswater when her phone went. I assumed, from the look on her face, that one of the kids had set the house on fire, or got themselves locked up, but that didn't come close. "Derek's died," she said, and that was the end of the holidays. Ageing relatives, even parents, eventually run out of steam, and it's sort of expected that things work out like that, but when your contemporaries die… well, that's another matter. Especially when it's someone who had been there with me through Sunderland thick and Sunderland thin for the last thirty-odd years.

Pos had kept the faith through some rough times in red and white and remained fiercely loyal, but not blindly so. He'd reckoned Reid should have gone, but he never made it to the start of the season to shout the Lads on. His most famous quote was frequently made to anyone who came up with the old chestnut "I like to see all the North East teams do well…"
"Rubbish."

My pre-season football was restricted to a trip to Berwick for their game against Raith Rovers, half of whom were Spanish. At least they sounded exotic, but our reserves would have taken them apart. Nobody there to suggest as the new Quinny.

Changes were needed, and changes were afoot as we signed Babb, Piper, Stephen Wright, Myhre, and then, with a mysteriously secret and complicated £10 million double deal, Marcus Stewart and Tore Andre Flo. £10 million? By Sunderland? Here we go again, but with an empty seat in front of me. We kept it empty for the whole of the season by asking anyone who sat there if they'd mind moving, and explained why. Nobody ever objected. It just didn't seem right for anyone else to sit there, except Pos.

The opening day draw at Blackburn was dull but satisfactory, made tolerable thanks to our usual lunchtime refuelling in Lancaster. Wright and Babb were new faces, and were joined by Piper in the next game. Unfortunately, soon to be a by-word for the season, the blues won, and I lost my temper.

37,000 people could see what was going wrong and where, but nothing was changing, so I went to the bench and told Reid to get it sorted. A dozen others individually did the same, but he didn't get the hint. Phillips and Kilbane were up front, backed up by Reyna, McAteer, McCann, and Tommy Butler, and with a defence of Babb, Bjorklund, Wright, and Gray. At Elland Road, on a Wednesday night, McAteer scored the only goal, and my decision to slum it with the travelling army looked well justified. "Not many teams will come here and win," I said. The fact that most teams did and they only just stayed up shows how much I know. Flo raised spirits by scoring against Man Utd on his debut, and a point, but then we went to the Riverside and laid down 3-0 as Stewart played his first game.

It got worse. Fulham came to Wearside, but were so bad that they probably wouldn't have won if we'd stayed off the field. As it was, we didn't stay off the field, and they scored three. It got even worse, as the abject lack of spirit at Gallowgate allowed them to stroll in 2-0. Brief respite came when Daveed Bellion scored a great goal on his first start, showing speed that left the opposition trailing in his wake. Maybe he could save our season. Maybe George Bush could, as he was about to save the world from itself. He decided to invade Iraq, but he kept it a secret until the UN agreed to help out, so that it would look like it was their fault.

Arsenal was what we'd come to accept at Arsenal, where they put Derek's name in the special section of the programme reserved for such memorials – which was nice, as he'd arranged all of our ICPP trips down there. A broken arm for Sorensen, but at least Jody Craddock doubled his goal tally with a consolation. Well, that was some consolation, but enough was enough, Reidy was sacked and in came the dream team of Howard Wilkinson and Steve Cotterill.

Why not McCarthy, as it was obvious that despite his success with the Irish, his days there were clearly numbered after the Keane nonsense. He said something about a contract. Haway Mick, man, this is football. Since when did contracts mean anything? I'll freely admit to thinking, and saying, that Wilko could be just what we needed: someone to bring a bit of discipline back to a squad that had gone seriously off the rails – and he was considerably older than me, unlike Reidy, who was virtually the same age. Cotterill I knew nothing about, but he had all of the badges and was well thought of by those who knew, or pretended to know. Let's see what these two can do.

The Arsenal game had been preceded by the start of our League Cup campaign, away at Cambridge – Jody Craddock's first club. A chance to try a new ground for some of us and a chance to knock a few more pubs off the list for the Ship's Charity Challenge. Spotted languishing on the touchline was a rather down-at heel Lionel Perez, apparently working at a nearby sports centre. He could probably have played and scored, as we went crackers and put in seven, with two apiece for Flo and Stewart.

That took us to Arsenal, where they put out half of their reserves and took a 2-0 half-time lead. Our second half comeback was the stuff of legends, as the smallish but perfectly formed travelling army bounced around the away end. At 2-1 and piling forward, we were having a whale of a time in the crowd, but unnecessary and over the top intervention by one particular boy in blue soured the taste a little, and the words which were exchanged when the Billericay Mackem was ejected resulted in the Bishop Mackem following him out through the in door.

Consequently I missed the second and third goals, despite much swapping of jackets and pulling of hats over our eyes and trying to get back in, and had assumed the cheering, being so loud, was in celebration of scores by the home side. It was only when the crowd came out that I was told the score, and it was a fairly jolly minibus back home.

Much of the next day was spent writing letters to both Arsenal and Sunderland, explaining the events of the previous evening, and I got replies to both saying that I was still welcome at both grounds. The Arsenal one said that a steward had filed a report which stated that the policeman involved (number and station provided) had been unnecessarily harsh in his actions, and was followed a couple of weeks later by a second, which said that no police report had been filed, even though they're supposed to be. Maybe I should learn to keep my mouth shut in such situations, but I don't see why arrogant little Hitlers like that should be allowed to get way with it, and I guess I'll keep telling them that.

Sheffield Utd for the next round, but I was knackered with whatever version of flu was doing the rounds at the time, and couldn't even get out of bed. The match ticket is still on the bedside drawers, a reminder that I should have made the effort and shouted the Lads on to victory. As it was, we were well beaten, and back to reality.

A home defeat at the hands of West Ham didn't give Wilko the start we wanted him to have, and Quinny called it a day, the end of a great career. "I learned my trade at Arsenal, became a footballer at Man City, but Sunderland got under my skin. It hurt me deeply to leave. I love Sunderland." What a nice man.

Over in the USA Enron collapsed, having been unable to come up with an excuse for lying about losing £1 billion, and the consequences spread though the States like wildfire, as trust in any financial institution came under scrutiny. In Bali, terrorists blew up two hundred holidaymakers, and in Moscow a similar number died when Chechens held a theatre full of people hostage. The world can be a nasty place.

It's only a game. At Bolton, fans turned up in plastic army hats bearing the words Sergeant Wilko's Red And White Army, Mickey Gray scored a rocket, Myhre did his thigh muscle, and on came Macho to earn us a draw. Flo repeated the trick at Charlton the next week, then again the week after. Phillips got his first of the season to make it 2-0 over Spurs, but we were still just above the drop zone, and the last thing we wanted was a trip to Anfield.

They'd just defended as if their life depended on it to bring a draw back from Barcelona, but they'd seen nothing like the defending that we were about to show them. Macho played like a man possessed, the other ten defended like demons, and we occasionally got the ball into their half. By the last few minutes we'd decided that they wouldn't score past Jurgen in a month of Sundays, and were laughing as much as cheering each time he pulled off another improbable save. On the way back to the bus, a local shouted that we were a disgrace to football and that we should at least have tried to attack. "You should have let us have the ball, then," I told him, "and by the way, Barcelona."

Back to reality, and a home defeat to Birmingham, followed by the usual at Chelsea, but by only three goals this season, and they didn't arrive until late on. The same result at home to Man City, then it was Liverpool again. Gavin McCann, and Michael Proctor, local boy made good, scored the goals that made it four points out of the Reds. I'd love to be able to say that this was the start of the revival, but there's no dressing up the fact that it was all downhill from there.

We did manage our annual thriller at the Hawthorns, as Phillips got both of our goals as we came back from two down to earn our last point of the year. Two more defeats saw us in the third relegation spot, and Reyna's knee injury meant that his season was over. What's the last place you want to go in the middle of a run like that? Old Trafford, on New Year's Day, meant a relatively quiet night, strictly a two-pint job, then an early busload of red-eyed travellers. Glory be, after only a minute or so Gav's ball in bounced off Veron's expensive head and in. Here we go. We should have known better, as Man Utd had spent the last few weeks scoring last minute winners. We held out until the second half, we held out for most of that. They equalised, then they did the dirty when Macho, for once, made the wrong decision, and that was us gone.

A bit of light relief with the FA Cup, then, but what we got was two marathon games against Bolton and Blackburn. Phillips got us a draw at the Reebok, then the replay went to extra time before Arca and Proctor won the game. Then we drew 3-3 at Blackburn, and the replay went to extra time, 2-2, and a three-nil penalty shoot out victory. We must have used up all of our ideas and energy in those two, as Watford came up and nicked a 1-0 win.

Just the League, then. Oh dear. While the USA were deploying an extra 62,000 troops in the Persian Gulf, making things look a bit bleak for Iraq – especially when the weapons inspectors found some things that actually looked like weapons. Pity the Iraqis had declared them.

Blackburn at home again, and a dull, dull 0-0 was the last point we got. That's right, January 11th, and the last point of the season was already in the bag. Shaun Thornton came into the side on and off, and showed enough to convince us that he might have a future in the game, but we'd just about given up on there being any footballer in creation who could save us. Well, some of us did. Some of us believed against belief that while there was still a mathematical chance of staying up, we had hope.

Judging by the away following, there were quite a few of that disposition, and there were still around forty thousand at home games. What an optimistic lot. What a masochistic lot. In came Morrocan El Karkouri, who looked as cool as you like, and out went Varga, Schwarz, and Macho. We scored four goals in a game and lost, because only one was for us. Proctor managed two own goals and Wright one in a matter of minutes, and the football world looked on in disbelief and Charlton fans laughed all the way back down the A19.

Around the world, people were marching in protest at the seemingly inevitable invasion of Iraq and in the USA the space shuttle exploded on re-entry. It's only a game.

Amid rumours of an extra payment should he move on from fortynine appearances, Emerson Thome played his last game. Another two defeats, then a mad day out in London on the way to Fulham at Loftus Road. How Kilbane's effort stayed out is beyond me, as we pezzled the Londoners and did everything but score. Needless to say, they snuck one, and the lucky mascots we'd brought, four soft toy monkeys, ended up on top of the goal net as I risked another ejection by disregarding Premier League rules on the distribution of cuddly toys. You had to laugh, or else you'd cry.

With the good ship Sunderland well and truly adrift, McCarthy eventually arrived as Wilko and Cotterill were given their P45s. Good grief, the manager was younger than me. It had been another step into age when first one and then both of my lads were watching lads younger than them pull on the famous stripes, but being senior to the manager was worse.

Two more defeats, then a decent performance against Chelsea that should have brought a win thanks to a masterful display by Thornton and his ever-changing hair. Just like Mickey Gray a few years earlier, young Shaun couldn't decide which colour suited him best, but he appeared to have the skill to go with it. We were clutching at straws in terms of entertainment, and this was the last bright spot of the season. At least it was better than SARS, the new thing that was allegedly sweeping across Asia.

Me, I think a lot of these supposed pandemics or epidemics are just a name that someone applies to a dozen deaths in China, where there are hundreds of millions of people, or even more than that. Everything has to have a name these days, rather than be accepted as an unfortunate thing that just happens. Or natural causes, if you like.

As Baghdad fell, our last chance for survival came at Birmingham. Poom got his first game, but we were thoroughly miserable, and the only bright spot of the day was Marcus Stewart at last losing his temper and kicking his marker up the arse. As one glum face in a sea of glumness, the Daily Mirror picked mine as the one that summed up the way we felt, and the Sunderland Echo decided on a full colour version.

The Mirror entitled it "Sad: a choked fan." "You look like you've been drinking" was Judith's comment. She'd seen the results, what else did she think kept me going on away trips? Down, out and still a month and five games to go. The day of our home defeat to West Brom, the war in Iraq started. The week after, the traffic at the Trafford Centre held us up for an hour, and I was able to get a whole busload of signatures on my petition for the abolition of all such creations. The sooner these are all closed down, the better for society – at least that's my opinion.

This meant that we missed the first fifteen minutes, which at least meant that the torture was shorter that day. 3-0 to Man City, then a horrible home defeat at the hands of them from up the road. By this stage, we were shell-shocked anyway, so we could have taken anything the game could have thrown at us, as it had been all season.

A weekend in the original Crossroads Motel wrapped itself around the last away game, at Villa, and I spent the Friday in the company of Davey the Carlisle fan from University. We'd arranged to meet up in a certain pub, and I thought it hilarious that he arrived in an identical shirt and leather jacket to me. When he told me it was a wellknown gay pub, I thought it even funnier. The Saturday was spent in a little cricket club behind the hotel, where Ronnie explained the intricacies of fives and threes dominos to the bemused locals. They were puzzled enough that we were still going to the match given the way the season had gone, but they didn't understand that we were Sunderland, which means that it goes with the territory.

Being the last game, the away end was full to bursting, we sang our heads off, and Alex Rae's little daughter stared in disbelief at the seemingly endless queue of red and whites waiting to shake her dad's hand and the whole end singing his name. Needless to say, we lost, just to set up the final fling, against Arsenal. Oh, give us a break. They were there to entertain, we were there to make up the numbers, and they put on a display that had us applauding, they gently tore us apart, and some of them even broke sweat.

George Bush said that the fighting in Iraq was over, and it certainly was at the SoL. Mick had given several youngsters like Ryan, Black, and Dickman runs out, presumably to see what use they'd be next season, and because several of the senior players were wandering around the pitch with faces like thunder, picking their noses and talking on their mobile phones.

On the way home, I took Ian to see comedy act Men in Coats, and had thought front row seats would be nice. At the end of a season like we'd just had, the front row of a comedy night, wearing our Sunderland shirts, probably wasn't the best idea. The turns took pity, and said nothing. The fact that one of them was a mime act probably helped.

Four years on from having the most successful league season in professional football in this country, we'd produced the worst season the Premier League had seen. In case you hadn't been paying attention, we only won four games, scored only twenty-one goals, and lost fifteen in a row. I needed a holiday.

Oh Alex Rae
Alex Alex Alex Rae
Alex Alex Alex Rae
Alex Alex Alex Rae

2003-2004

Like I said, I needed a chance for quiet contemplation, and with Ian now following his brother down the musical route, there was always a house full of guitars and associated amplification. Although Gaz wasn't living at home any longer (but it was summer, so he might just show up) he was never far away, and his band would be playing locally anyway.

One of the reasons that I've dropped off the musical references in recent chapters is that there was so much of it around, as in rubbish music in the charts and noise coming from the upstairs rooms. The upside was that I, being the one with the car, got to go to see the likes of Radiohead, The Manics, The Stereophonics, and various others as Mr Taxi Man - which was nice. Peaceful it wasn't, but fun it was.

So, needing to prove that my back was back to something like useable again, I hopped on the train to Ilkley and did the Dales Way. Lack of planning meant that the first night was spent on a bench, but hey, I was on holiday, I could do that sort of thing. Fellow walkers regarded me as some sort of nutter. Not for doing the walk, but for wearing a Sunderland hat. Surely I would have been better off hiding my allegiance in the circumstances? Nah, it made me look mad, bad, and dangerous to know. No messing with this boy.

If there was a dead rabbit on the road, I'd be allowed first pickings. Apparent madness has its advantages and the Sheffield Wednesday lads I fell in with bought me a pint out of sympathy. Four nights, five days, and eighty-odd miles later, I was home triumphant, sore of foot and clear of mind. Last season had only been a blip and Mick McCarthy was the man to turn us straight around and have us back to the top in no time.

In no time it became big news that we were virtually bankrupt. We were no-where near as far in debt as them up the road, or Chelsea for that matter, but the fact that they were in the Premier meant that it was acceptable. The fact that we weren't meant that it wasn't, and we were in big trouble. The net result as far as the manager was concerned was that every carbon-based life-form at the club in possession of more than one leg (and that included the stadium cat) was for sale. Not even necessarily at the right price, any price would do, just so long as we got some money in the bank.

My proper holiday, shared between Cornwall, the Lakes, and Northumberland, was interspersed with spells watching the TV in disbelief at the knock-down prices we were letting the Lads go for in the biggest sale of fire-damaged goods in football history. The biggest surprise was that Man Utd agreed to give us a scandalous amount of money for Bellion, who'd spent the year to date complaining that his head wasn't right, and sloping off to France whenever the manager wasn't looking. Phillips off to Southampton, Craddock to Wolves, Reyna, dodgy knee and all, to Man City, Sorensen to Villa, McCann to Villa, and a whole host of lay-offs amongst the stadium employees. The day these redundancies were an-nounced, Michael Gray arrived for work with a brand-spanking new Ferrari. Not the kind of diplomacy to go down well at the time.

Having retained the pre-season bug, I was one of an amazing several thousand that made a big day out in Edinburgh. Pete and I dusted off our hybrid Sunder-land-Eire shirts, just to ingratiate ourselves with the Hibs fans, and it worked a treat until some buffoon decided that we were insulting the flag, or some such nonsense. By this time, we'd drawn 2-2, having allowed Heather twenty minutes shopping (as it was a friendly. Had it been a league game she'd have had to abide by the rules that allow a lady to be part of our day out: nee shopping, nee looking at the sights – unless it was a precursor to plodging in a fountain, drink pints, stand your round), and had a big get-together in the Guildford Arms.

We even took Denty the Mag, just so that he could see what it was like follow-ing a proper team, and Kyler had us hoping he'd be scoring like that regularly. Kilmarnock wasn't on my itinerary until halftime, when Russell somehow got my name down for the minibus, so it was another trip north. Less of a result, as we didn't really look that clever. Only a friendly, though, and another massive turn-out for a nothing game - especially after the season we'd just had.

From despair to where? Would I be going back? I was asked that question many times over the summer. People had seen my picture in the papers from the Birmingham game (that's me in the corner, that's me in the spot light, losing my religion – almost), and assumed that enough was enough. The fact was I'd had my season ticket ordered from the first opportunity, and I couldn't wait for whatever Lads we had left to get out there and put things right. The thing was Mick didn't know who he'd have at his disposal, as the scavenging clubs were waiting for the last minute, in order to snap up the cheapest bargains.

After a seemingly endless chase, Jeff Whitley arrived to become the manager's first signing, then came Gary Breen and Colin Healy, both of whom McCarthy had worked with for Eire. Nic Medina, after all of the hype, had managed a decent game for the reserves at West Auckland, one league start, and vanished into thin air with more international honours than Arca.

We started off at Forest in a real sweltering hot-box of an away stand, and watched as the Lads failed to gel. Not the new beginning we were looking for, but the League Cup gave us, in theory, a chance to get a few goals and restore our confidence, as we were drawn against Mansfield. Flo made his last appearance. Jeff Clark's lad Jamie played for the opposition, they scored an own goal, Kyle replaced Flo, scored an own goal and then got the winner. That gave us Huddersfield at home a month later, another chance to get a few goals. Well, Kyle managed two, but the Terriers managed four, Ben Clark was sent off, and that was the League Cup over and done with for another season.

Mickey Gray was apparently un-saleable, so he went on loan to Celtic, Champions' League football, and a place alongside Stan Varga. Millwall came north and simply bullied us out of the game. Things were looking grim as we set off for Preston with the nation's press hot on our tails. If we lost that one, we'd become officially the worst side in League history by going past Darwen's 100-and-something year-old record of consecutive defeats. Officials of that club made the short trip to Deepdale to witness the occasion.

We steeled ourselves for the possibility by relaxing in Lancaster for a couple of hours, then took our places in the seats to await whatever fate would deliver. Thornton capped a masterly display with a goal, and Stewart ended all thoughts of defeat with the second. Blessed relief, we'd won a League game for the first time since December. Colin Healy made his debut after leaving Celtic and the gaffer was starting, albeit slowly, to get his own players in the team. Piper went off injured, as he tended to do, so changes were necessary for the next game. No matter, Stewart scored, and, with a mad gallop from the back and cool finish, so did Stephen Wright, and there were another three points, thank you very much.

Two wins in a row. Where would you choose to go to extend that run? Correct. Bradford, the poor dears, had been exceedingly generous to us over the years at their place, and things didn't change. Arca scored a fantastic goal to add to the other three, and we were laughing our way back from West Yorkshire. Everton then nipped in with a million quid for Killa, and that was the end of the sale.

A win over Palace took us up into fourth, but then the best pub team in the League at the time, Stoke, in another identikit flat-pack stadium in the middle of an industrial estate, beat us 3-1. Craig James, fresh from a season's loan at Hibs, European football and all, made his debut and Thornton was sent off. At Derby, with Arca back in defence for James, we should have had the game sewn up well before they scored a last-minute goal, and our heads could well have gone down.

They didn't, and history was made as Poom (insert as many Os you like after this performance) loped up field for an injury-time corner and thumped in a legend-making header. The power of the late equaliser can never be underestimated, but when the keeper does it, away from home, against his former club, it's like winning the cup (not a cup with a capital C, obviously, just a minor trophy, but a trophy nonetheless). Mart's goal inspired a dozen games of let's do what our keeper's just done in the car park, and a thousand threehour homeward conversations. Oster made a rare start and scored as we beat Reading, then did likewise to Ipswich. In came another player, Tommy Smith from Watford, to give us another option up front.

Kyle was beginning to look every inch the big scary centre-forward that we'd hoped he'd become, and his diving header in front of the visiting fans at Bramall Lane epitomised his performances at the time. Cardiff came and shut us out, then we had a bit of a flat spell as we snuck past Walsall, drew with Rotherham, then had Oster sent off for a rather obvious hoof on his tackler as we lost at Norwich. Another goal-free extravaganza against West Brom, and we were hovering around the bottom end of the play-off places.

Around this time, music in the North East was going through a bit of a renaissance, and Sunderland in particular was experiencing something of an explosion, ignited by The Futureheads. Showing the close links between music and sport (if you like music and sport, that is), some lads from A Love Supreme promoted (coughed up the cash and took a share of the profits) some of the dates on the band's first UK tour, and able support was provided by other local boys doing good The Golden Virgins. Both bands have since done the city proud, and showed their love for their hometown by re-investing most of their new-found wealth into The Ivy House. Well, into the tills thereof, but it's a start.

Down to deepest Kent, and the world's worst football ground – official. Even the G of Gillingham was missing from the stand. Only the flimsiest wire fencing separated us from a swift descent into the Brian Moore refreshment area, but new loan star Stewart Downing lit up the game and helped us to a 3-1 win. Up to fourth, but the flat spell returned as neither side could muster a goal when Coventry visited, but Crewe should have provided us with a way back and we dominated for long periods but somehow succumbed to the deadly finishing of Dean Ashton and came away an unbelievable 3-0 down. At least we'd caught the end of England winning the World Cup during our stop off in Knutsford, even if it was only the rugby.

Kyle earned us a point at home to Burnley, then Downing, very much the man of the moment, scored in consecutive 1-1 draws. Before the second of these, at Highfield Road, no-one had told the stewards that the away fans were no longer welcome in the Sky Blue Bar to which they directed us, and my discussion with the thug - sorry, doorman - resulted in being manhandled down the stairs. Only a timely intervention by Rob prevented him from sealing the meeting with a punch to the back of my head. The game will be best remembered, if best is the correct word in these circumstances, for the horror tackle that snapped Colin Healy's leg. Replays and subsequent photographs have shown it to be both very high and very late. The players understandably lost their stomach for the game after that incident.

At West Ham, we thought we'd turned the corner. We thought we finally got back on our footballing feet. We'd taken over the upper floor of the East Ham Social Club, from where you could actually see into the ground, then took our seats and watched the Lads storm into a 2-0 half-time lead. This was the business. No it wasn't. If there's one thing any opposing manager should know about us, it is that we just can't cope with great big centre-forwards, especially if they're called Brian Deane. Two-nil up became three-two down, and I felt like finding the Queen Vic and picking a fight with the Mitchell brothers.

Thankfully, Wimbledon were next to visit, and they were falling apart faster than a Magpie European campaign. Homeless, they moved to Milton Keynes, and the sooner this sort of thing is stopped, the better. If you're Wimbledon, you play somewhere near Wimbledon, or you just pack it all in. None of this American-style franchise nonsense where you simply buy someone else's place and move the whole lot across the country. Not that anyone paid any more for the team, but allowing them to become the Milton Keynes Dons was a shocking decision.

Anyhow, we won (hurrah!) then did it again against – Bradford. I love Bradford, most seasons. Not only do they let us win handsomely at their place, they quite often collapse on Wearside as well, but even they usually put up a better fight than this 3-0 win for my favourite team. We popped down to Rotherham and Stewart got both goals, then we had the fun and games of a visit by Hartlepool in the FA Cup.

Last time we'd played them in a real game, they'd won the Freight Rover (or something like that) at Roker Park, and this time they brought twice their home gate up the A19. They played out of their skins, and we snuck past them 1-0 to earn a fourth round game at Ipswich. Darren Williams won a ball that was 70-30 against him, and Smith put away his cross, then Arca pounced on an awful defensive cock-up to make it two, and they could only manage one in reply. A Cup run? We'd have to see.

Back in the really important bit, we'd brought in another loan winger, Alan Quinn, probably the steadiest-away player we've ever had, to help out in the continued absence of Piper and the increasingly weird Thomas Butler, who swayed between injury, stress, personal problems, and invisibility. We beat Forest and then had a joyful trip down to that nice Millwall. As there is no way any sane fan will try for refreshments anywhere near the place, we called in at Charlton, where the landlord of our usual watering-hole was more than pleased to see a busload of Sunderland fans make up for the lack of a game at The Valley. Sadly, we lost, as loan winger (sound familiar?) Kevin Cooper played his only game.

Then came the news that Bob Stokoe had died, the man who'd led the club to their only big trophy since 1937. The man who'd given me Wembley 73, my biggest day as a Sunderland fan, in fact, one of Wembley's biggest days and arguably the biggest shock in FA Cup history. Bob's trilby. Bob's Mac. Bob's FA Cup. Our FA Cup.

One of football's good guys, and someone who will hold a special place in the heart of every Sunderland fan.

That same week we could only manage a draw at Watford with a goal from new faster-than-lightning Darren Byfield. Then came the long trip to Cardiff, and their back to the seventies football experience. If you like it unfriendly, badly policed, and intimidating, then Cardiff is the place for you. Its one positive point is that you can stand, which is where I met Reg and Little Michael, Bishop Boys in exile, but that's where the fun ended. Off went Bjorklund, away went the resultant free-kick, then it was Earnshaw's shiny blue boots that did the damage. If the journey down had been long due to Benny's atomic innards, the journey back seemed twice the distance.

It's funny how the same bunch of players can turn in a performance so vastly different in the space of a few days. Just before the trip to Wales, Birmingham had held us to a draw in the FA Cup, and shortly after the trip to Wales, we went to the Midlands with the spots of cup fever clearly visible. We held them until extra time, then Tommy Smith produced his finest moments in a red and white shirt. The sight of him racing goalwards to clinch it was truly awesome, and another wonderful night of cup action entered the annals of Sunderland's history.

There was much dancing and hugging of rarely-seen friends in the car-park afterwards, and everyone who'd been at the away games in the dark days of a year ago was celebrating the re-emergence of their Bonny Lads as a decent team again. That momentous win meant that we had Sheffield Utd in the Quarter Final - Quarter Final, get in. So along they came, and Smith did the job again with the winner. Was he turning into this campaign's Johnny Byrne? Let's hope so. Millwall in the Semi Final, and a chance for revenge for every nasty game in the last few years.

Back in the League, a win over Walsall, then a crazy 3-3 draw with Preston, in which Whitley was sent off, preceded the defeat of West Ham, where Whitley added to Kyle's opener by charging down a clearance and thus getting his first goal for us via a tackle. Stoke then pinched a point at our place, and at Reading we were comfortable winners despite Whitley's second dismissal in ten games. Colin Cooper, lifelong Sunderland fan, finally got his run-out in red and white in this game, and came on twice more from the bench in his three-game loan spell.

Our involvement in the FA Cup meant that the games were coming thick and fast, and successive 2-1 wins ended seven matches in April, and took us to Old Trafford and the FA Cup Semi Final. This was going to be the game in which we exorcised the ghosts of recent matches with Wise's rotters. It was going to be Jason McAteer's last big hurrah, and he was going to be the man to keep us on the straight and narrow as we refused to be intimidated by the off the ball stuff that we'd been subjected to in recent seasons.

There had been such demand for seats on our bus that Ian had to go on the Station Minibus which set off early. Traffic meant that our bus got nowhere for a pre-match snifter, while he was on the phone singing when we were still forty miles short of the ground. We were housed in the new, high bit above what used to be the Stretford End, and the pair of us met up and had two seats by ourselves behind the steps. I'd already found Alan and Heather, but refused to pay £3 for a can of Boddingtons that had cost Man Utd all of forty pence, if that.

Our fans were magnificent, those of our opponents noticeable by their inability to sell all of the tickets they'd been offered, meaning that huge swathes were empty while Sunderland fans were watching on TV because they couldn't get tickets. McCartney got in a tangle, Poom saved, and the ball eventually was put away for the game's only goal. Arca had a good chance, as did McCartney, but McAteer went against his word, lost his head, and was sent off, ending the game as a contest.

Just the League, then, and we were back with a vengeance and a 3-0 win over Sheffield Utd, but then the packed itinerary seemed to catch up with us. We didn't score for four matches, and at Palace, Poom became our first ever keeper to be sent off. The 3-0 defeat had us biting our nails and accepting that the play-off was as good as it was going to get. Thoughts that were confirmed when Whitley rescued a point with a proper goal against Crewe. Yet another loanman, Carl Robinson, scored the only goal against Norwich, who were already up, and so it was the end of season trip to Burnley. Well, it should have been, but as they're not that friendly there, we decided on two nights in Liverpool, the country's most liver-unfriendly city.

On the first evening, I met up with Susanne from Uni before hitting the town with the lads, and on the second night with Rob from Uni, who just happened to be her ex as well as the same Rob who'd turned into a Mag while living in Tranmere. I must give special thanks to Ron, John and Lee for forgiving him his black and white sins as he guided us around the city. Two nights in The Adelphi, which is exactly as it appeared on the TV, and it was Sunday in Burnley. The away end was a collection of tired fans, fancy dress, and injured players. Oh, and Samson The Cat, who decided that I looked like I needed a cuddle. A 2-1 win, a rousing reception for departing home manager Stan Ternent, lifelong Sunderland fan and the holder of one unused substitute appearance for the Lads, from both sets of supporters.

Play-offs. Don't we just love them? No, actually, I don't. I think that if you're up you're up, despite our good fortune in 1990. For the second time, we were in there from third place, and against Palace. Down we went to bloody Selhurst

Park, hit the local Wetherspoon's with a vengeance, as we were on first name terms with the staff after the frequency of visits, and despite Lee sending Pete and me off to the wrong platform at Victoria. At least he felt sorry for me, and there was a pint on the table when we eventually arrived.

at half time, the second half went crazy with penalties, us ahead, them ahead, and what seemed like every Sunderland fan, shirts off, in the front row screaming the Lads on. Then came a desperate late winner for the home side. Then their fans were on the pitch, taunting, throwing coins, and we were getting blamed for it. Another night of high drama, another long, miserable, frustrated trip home. Another short night's sleep, another thundery day at the office.

Three days later, and we had the chance to make use of the away goals we'd scored in the first leg. On a slightly sour note, there were still ten thousand empty seats, proving that a lot of people were still hurting from the events of the previous season. The absentees probably still loved Sunderland, but couldn't yet bring themselves to like them. 2-0 up at half-time, they took it to extra time, and the away goals counted for nothing. Shows what I know.

Oster hit the post with our first penalty, then Smith, Babb, Robinson and Breen scored to take it to sudden death. Sudden death – the only thing we're worse at than penalty shoot-outs themselves. Despite heroics at the other end, McAteer and Whitley (with an effort Julian Clarey would have been ashamed of) both missed, and it was 5-4 to them. Arse, if you'll pardon my French. Of course, Palace won the final, as teams finishing sixth tend to do, which moved the playoff system to a par with Alan Shearer in the Wearside popularity stakes.

Maybe we can blame the slightly duff patch in October and November, maybe we cam blame the inability to come to terms with physical sides like Millwall (boo, hiss), Cardiff, and Stoke. Maybe it was a minor miracle that McCarthy had turned the season into anything at all, considering that he'd had to oversee the demolition of his entire squad and had to build a new one. Next year we'd be ready, because the power of persuasion is no match for anticipation, and we'd be pointing in the right direction when we started.

I needed a holiday.

And I would walk five hundred miles
And I would walk five hundred more
To be a Sunderland fan who's watching
Kevin Kyle each time he scores
La la la la…

2004-2005

That was some season that was. Fifty-six games – a personal record – plus various and random non-league jobs and not counting friendlies or England games. It had seen me ditch my flat cap as well and for the first time in thirty-odd years, folks at the match could see my hair. I thought I'd better let them have that privilege before it all fell out. For the first time in living memory, I missed the FA Cup Final, as I couldn't bring myself to watch Wise and company on the turf that we should have been running about on, choosing to go to Scotland on anti-FA Cup day. Linlithgow Rose against Hill of Beath Hawthorn was a much better prospect.

Holiday. Whit week, all the way to the Outer Hebrides with a telescope, just me, the roof off the car, a tent and a whole lot of peace and quiet. It was also a chance to stay with Gaz, now living in Edinburgh, and for him to show me the sights. Foolishly, perhaps, I'd got us tickets to see Scotland play Trinidad and Tobago, and we chose to wear our Sunderland shirts. The tickets were only a tenner, but the Scots don't think much of the English until you explain that you're from the North East, and they sort of accept that you're not so bad. At least I got to see Steve Caldwell, on for his brother as a sub, and one of our summer targets, so I felt as if I was doing McCarthy a favour.

At the end of the week, I joined the musical subdivision of ALS who were on an acoustic tour of the Highlands. Providing backing vocals at their Inverness gig was interesting, as was explaining my Space Invaders Mag baiting T-shirt to the local Goths, but it was an excellent end to the week.

The real holidays got a bit special, with a week in Cornwall followed by a heli-copter flight to the Isles of Scilly. I'll not say how good the place was, because I want to keep it too myself, and they support Plymouth, despite it being about a hundred miles away.

Back on planet Sunderland, out went Babb, McAteer, Bjorklund, Thirlwell, and Smith. In came Caldwell, Whitehead, Lawrence, Robinson on a permanent con-tract, Elliott, Mark Lynch (amid rumours that Man Utd let us have him in lieu of paying the rest of the Bellion fee), and Neill Collins. That's right, I'd only heard of Lynch as well, apart from Robbo, who we already knew. I resisted all preseason games apart from the trip to Barnsley, just because I wanted to see what a re-developed Oakwell looked like. It looked just the same as the old one, but with one new stand in place of the old away end, and very nice it was. Liam Lawrence was refused entry to the club car park, presumably because he had an Audi TT and that was far too flash for Barnsley. The home side was robust to say the least, Julio was brilliant, and we won. Yippee.

When the real thing came along, it was first to Coventry, managed by Peter Reid – so it was a mixed reception for him. He'd overseen the biggest changes in the club's modern history, given us three and a half years of swashbuckling, gung-ho football which was the most consistently exciting of my time as a fan, so I wouldn't boo him. Mind, he'd stayed a bit too long, allowing things to go hor-ribly wrong, so I wouldn't clap him either. The 2-0 defeat should have been ex-pected, as we never seem to do much on day one, and the best part of the day was re-acquainting ourselves with our longlost fellow supporters, not seen for… oooh, three months in some cases.

The following home games brought only four points, then the trek to Plymouth brought none. Spending four hundred plus miles each way in the company of Mr Winks and his inflatable away-game companion LiloLil is bad enough, espe-cially when he's been fed lamb and mint sauce crisps and morphs into the Green Haze, but to then watch the team fall victim to the newly-promoted syndrome was awful. This wasn't what we'd expected. A draw with Wigan, then another long trip to Reading, and another shoddy defeat.

Kyle's dodgy hip finally gave out, and that was the last we saw of him that season. If our travels hadn't been bad enough, the clever fixture-machine then took us to Gillingham, and some decidedly unfair ticket prices. £28 to sit in the open air in a building site was exceedingly excessive, especially when other clubs were charged half that amount. Still wanting something on the wing, McCarthy had brought in Simon Johnson on loan – probably the thinnest player ever to wear the stripes, and I saw Bridges when he was a lad. Thankfully, the rain that had chased us in from the beer garden in Gravesend had gone by the time we took our rickety seats, and Mr Stewart treated us to a master-class in finishing, with Elliott adding a spectacular header to make it 4-0 against an awful home side. Highly satisfactory, and we followed it up with a 2-0 win over Forest at home with Wright scoring a classic header.

In the League Cup, only 11,000 turned up to see us knock out Chester, which was a reflection of how much football costs in the 21st century. People are becoming so priced out of the game that even the FA Cup, the world's most famous knock-out trophy, isn't attracting the crowds any more. We put out a mostly reserve side down at Crewe in the next round, and saw a 3-3 draw, extra-time, and penalties. Two goals from Chris Brown came twenty-five years after his dad got two for us, including a last minute equaliser, at Gallowgate in the same round of the same competition. We won the penalty shoot-out back in 1979 (it was my birthday, the second win there in the space of seven months) but we lost it in 2004.

Brian Clough, Sunderland goalscoring machine and football management's first superstar, died in September, leaving a gap in the game that will never quite be filled.

A home win over Preston, which saw the goal-scoring arrival of Darren Carter, then it was down to Leeds, who'd finally imploded and gone from Champions' League Semi Finalists to the second tier of English football in a few short years. Funny what money can do. Suddenly, they couldn't afford their wage bill, just like us the year before, and another sale was on. It's crazy that relegation should mean almost automatic bankruptcy, but not as crazy as docking clubs points for going into administration. That's a bit like breaking someone's fingers because they can't write neatly. Robbo scored the only goal, then we got mugged just down the road where Frankie Gray's lad Andy and Gary Breen looked at each other in a funny way, and both were sent off. That defeat was followed by a home draw with Derby, and we were lying seventh. Must do better.

The game against Millwall was nothing to get excited about, but it was won thanks to an own goal by Kevin Muscat, some sort of justice for a man who's spent the greater part of the last decade kicking people up in the air. I'll take any form of victory over that lot. A draw at Watford, then down to Rotherham, where we took over the Phoenix Club adjacent to the ground, and everyone brought the kids for an October half term treat. Everybody except George, who missed his first game in about five years thanks to TV's decision to switch the game to an evening kick-off, so it was phone reports to Spain to keep him up to date. The story was that Elliott could have had six goals, but Whitehead got the only one. A win over Brighton, then three goals of top quality from Lawrence and Elliott saw off Wolves and took us up to third.

Millwall again, and some genius thought it a good idea to put this on the telly, on a Friday night. Lynch gave away a penalty, Wise scored, they added a second, and it was a damp squib of a bonfire night for us.

In Iraq, more people had died since George Bush's declaration that the fighting was over than during the official war. In Sunderland, we tried to keep our minds off such things by watching our local music scene go national. When supporting The Futureheads on Tyneside, another local outfit burst onto the scene, with the gig, or concert, if you will, being interrupted by chants of "Sunderland, Sunderland, Sunderland." Which was nice and preceded Maximo Park reaching the top twenty, or hit parade, if you will.

At Leicester, we found ourselves in another identikit stadium, were berated in the press for interrupting a tribute to Keith Weller that we'd not been told about thanks to the £2.50 tannoy system, and witnessed a moving march-past by ex-servicemen in the Remembrance Day parade. We applauded them, and the old lads smiled and applauded back. It's only a game. Browny did everything but score, then Steve Caldwell scrubbed a bit of the black and white from his system with the only goal past an extremely fat goalkeeper who couldn't get off the ground. Don't care, we won.

Browny's first League goal came the next week and we beat Ipswich, then came a blast from the past. Michael Bridges, once as cool as fridges, had come back on loan, and Bolton were paying his wages because we're such nice people. They must be OK as well. At Stoke, after years of waiting, right in front of the travelling fans, and from about a foot, Michael struck the only goal of the game to keep us third. Not a classic game by any means, but one of those occasions where team spirit and a special moment for someone did the trick. We don't usually need much reason to celebrate, and this was an excuse. You'd think we'd won the league. They say that laughter is the best medicine, although I'd recommend antibiotics a lot of the time, but there's a lot to be said for the restorative powers of a Sunderland goal away from home. They do you the world of good.

Sticking to the theory that you should buy when you're doing well, McCarthy spent 47 pence on winger Andy Welsh from Stockport reserves, and gave up altogether on John Oster, who joined the list of extremely talented but ultimately frustrating players. Curran, Brady, Mooney all had undoubted talent, but something missing in the attitude department, and Oster sits comfortably with them.

With Ben Clark having gone to join Hartlepool, in came Danny Collins from Chester, just to keep the fans on their toes and add to our growing collection of centre-halves. Darren Carter had been a real find – how was he not getting a game at Birmingham? His loan spell ended in the home game with West Ham, when things went a bit wrong and we lost 2-0. Some old bloke called Sheringham added a second goal late on to finish us off, but we stayed third. Third wasn't good enough. We'd had the play-offs last time around, and we didn't want them again, thank you very much, although Wigan and Ipswich were doing their level best to keep us there.

No nonsense at Cardiff this year, as Lawrence and Whitehead struck goals from a distance, and the police treated us nicely, choosing not to keep us in after the game and lock the toilets, thus avoiding shouts about their role in the miners' strike. To be honest, the strike had ended when most of the officers present were still in nappies, so they probably wouldn't have known what we were on about if we had repeated last year's protests. Darren Williams had recently gone to South Wales on loan, and was the last man off the pitch as he did what he always did – give the Sunderland fans a great big clap. It would have been nice if more of the fans had been as nice to him while he was with us, as he never gave less than his best. We all knew he suffered from his own versatility, as he wasn't the best centre-half, full-back, or midfielder at the club, but neither was he the worst. Darren Williams, I salute you as the only recent Sunderland player to get a mention in Stanley Matthews' autobiography. Sir Stan liked Darren's attitude, and you can't say fairer than that.

Burnley were next at home, and another goal from a couple of inches out by Bridges sealed the win after Arca had scored. This gave us a chance to celebrate the closest we'd get to a derby on Boxing Day, at home to Leeds, but we slipped up and guess what? A great big centre-forward called Brian Deane did for us as they won 3-2, in front of 43,000. It's open to debate whether many of the extras in that holiday crowd would have come back the next week, but we'll never know, and it was a good chance missed to find out.

When we got home from the match, the news was decidedly unseasonal. One of those natural disasters that come along every few hundred years had taken place in the Indian Ocean. An underground earthquake had caused a massive wave, a Tsunami, and there's nothing you can do about them. I knew straight away that you'd be talking in hundreds of thousands of lives. Some folks have tried to apportion blame, but what could anyone have done? Welded the sea floor together? It would be like trying to put a cork in a volcano.

It's only a game.

Back to the City Ground after a Christmas drink in Retford with the landlord who looks like Alan Whicker's twin brother and a display of comical finishing by the home side, and Stewart's first goal in ages to get us the three points to put us back on course. Some joker had decided on another game on New Year's Day, so it was another quiet night, and an early start to Preston. Our usual haunt in Lancaster did us proud (I'm not telling you the name, you'll all want to go), then it was a tour of the National Football Museum, and a game of table football before the real thing. The kick off was in doubt as the rain came down, games were called off nearby, and Sunderland must have had one hell of a New Year's party the night before. We looked absolutely out of touch as they raced three goals ahead by the break, then Thornton came on and took the game by the scruff of its neck. He got us back to 3-2, and could have sneaked us a point.

That was followed by a home draw with Gillingham, which did little to disperse the gloom of Deepdale, but along came the FA Cup to provide a welcome distraction. Palace and a chance for revenge. For once, we took it, and gave the supposed Premiership side a lesson in hard work. That took us to Everton, and chance to do the same to another top flight team. Straight off the bus after our eventual arrival at Goodison following the impromptu visit to Anfield (all football grounds look the same these days), we hopped into a taxi for the town centre. We'd found more good pubs than you could shake a stick at during our weekend there last season, so we took in an unplanned dinner-time session with half of South West Durham in the Caernarvon Castle. Taxi back to the ground, and a huge red and white following ready for action, but not the sort that we got. Kilbane gave Wright a rough ride, and they ended up as comfortable 3-0 winners as you're likely to see. Rotten result.

Time to concentrate on the League, and off to Derby, on a Sunday, meaning no stop-off in Matlock, and a twelve o'clock start, so no nipping into town for a swifter snifter. It was only when Ron and I had circled the ground twice, and he'd got the teas in, that somebody broke the news that there was a bar open inside. Tea hoyed, straight in, double round of Pedigree, and away we went. Myhre in goal meant no chance of last season's goalscoring goalkeepery nonsense, but it was the two Collinses in central defence that were the big surprise of the day. They did their bit, and Elliott and Whitehead did the business up the other end against a fairly decent looking Derby side – a good sign, but we were still third.

A home win over Sheffield Utd, then it was off to Molineux for another nail-biter. Stephen Elliott produced one of the season's best goals to add to the three corkers we'd scored against them at our place. A draw was the best we could manage, and we seemed destined for another play-off position. A bit of an unnecessarily entertaining 4-2 win against Watford saw Stewart produce his second hat-trick, and it was now two months since we'd failed to score in a league game.

Brighton was always going to be an awkward trip, the council didn't like them using the Withdean, it was a long way away, and we only got seven hundred tickets. The Withdean is probably one of the most scenic grounds in the league, as it's mostly surrounded by trees and gardens, but it certainly put us off playing football. Somehow against ten men we went behind and Thornton's second half performance just wasn't quite enough. A lot of harsh words were directed at the players as they left the field from a lot of tired and upset fans, and there was nowhere to hide. They heard every word, they saw every angry and frustrated face. They took it to heart.

Thornton produced two Brazilian free-kicks in our four goal win over poor Rotherham. No wonder they did in the First Division what we'd done in the Premier two seasons before and finished fifteen points adrift. Then wins over Cardiff, at Burnley where their substitute Ade Akinbiyi lasted two minutes before trying to remove McCartney's head, and at Crewe, and we were hovering between first and second place. Could we stay there? Well, if we couldn't, we'd die trying. Five goals against Plymouth had us drooling, and feeling more than a little sympathy for their fans. Walloped away from home, midweek and a million miles before bed. Been there, done that, got the programme.

We managed a narrow win over Coventry, then the ICPP went to town. I'd booked train tickets for everybody who'd asked, then two denied ever having asked, so it was a mad scramble to get seats sold. Being Sunderland, it was always a question of when rather than if, and our new member turned out to have been taught by one of our long standing members, who promptly whacked him with a newspaper and told him to sit down and shut up. It's great to organise the seating arrangements.

The Lamb was once again full of red and whites sneakily eating their own pies from under the tables, and chatting away to the old lad who always seemed to find himself in our midst. London-based nephew Mat and his better half were coming to the game, and it was to be Amy's first-ever football match v QPR. Oh dear, maybe we should have warned her. A quick rendezvous in Shepherd's Bush Green, then on to the business of the day. The first half was awful, and we managed to concede a goal to someone called Shittu. I know I shouldn't make fun, but come on, how could you resist? The second half was barely a few seconds old when Andy Welsh whacked in the leveller, then Brown and Arca completed the job. Amy said that watching Sunderland hurt, but that was me throwing her in the air each time we scored. Mat should have warned her.

3-1 in London is always good, so we celebrated some more, and did the ten minute walk to King's Cross in five minutes, stopping only to break up a domestic dispute in the street. Leave them to it, that's my recommendation. It might seem like a good idea to step in when some drunken bloke is threatening to knock his wife's head off, but not when you're two minutes from your train leaving. We are top of the League, said we are top of the League, and we had a chance to cement that position a couple of days later at Wigan. Half of Wearside turned up for this one, and Stewart's early goal was followed by a top-class defensive display. That was the clincher, that was the day that we knew we were up. Which was just as well, because we lost at home to Reading at the weekend. In an effort to prevent him scoring against us or anyone else, we signed Brian Deane.

A weekend in Great Yarmouth, including the game between Yarmouth and Diss Town – it would have been rude not to go – was wrapped around the game at Ipswich. Myhre's back kept him out, and Ingham got a rare game. A shaky game, as it turned out, as Stewart's nerve failed him from the spot against his old club, and we went a goal down. Deane set up Elliott, and Robbo put us ahead, but it ended 2-2 and still not certain of promotion.

Going a goal down against Leicester wasn't in the script, but Alnwick kept us in it with his foot, then Stewart equalised and Caldwell won us promotion. The job was done, the time had come, we could relax, and there were still two games to go. As we were at West Ham, it was played on a Friday night, and we had our pre-match party in the motorway services with Tom's Top Buffet, champagne and all. As Alnwick played his second game, he played like a keeper of ten year's standing. Again, we went a goal down, but Arca lev elled. Then Elliott came off the bench to win us the title with a great finish, and the end of season fancy dress party erupted into a madness of joy, sweat, beery breath, and flying crisps.

Don't be eating crisps when we score away from home, you'll just lose most of them. Champions and two whole days in London to celebrate. By the time we got back to the hotel, Sky were showing the match as live, so we were able to re-live the whole experience until about three in the morning. Then it was break-fast, back to the Lamb, and a jolly good celebration. Life's sweet when you're winning, and there are plenty of times when you're not, so make the most of it.

A full house, a load of nonsense with fireworks, music, presentations, funny hats and a 1-0 win over Stoke thrown in for good measure. The boys were back, seven points clear at the top. Now all Mc- Carthy, Pope Mick the first, had to do was build another side. One to compete in the Premier League – and one that would stay there.

Mick McCarthy's red and white army
Mick McCarthy's red and white army
Mick McCarthy's red and white army
Mick McCarthy's red and white army

2 0 0 5 - 2 0 0 6

So the close season began again, another bird-watching trip to Scotland, but I'll admit to cheating this time. No tent, as my sister had booked a cottage in the Hebrides and kindly offered me a room and she cooked two meals a day, which was a little more cordon bleu than my usual efforts with the paraffin stove. I repaid this kindness by taking her to the various birding hotspots while her other half spent the day standing waist deep in some obscure loch waving a fishing rod about. Each to his own, I get my non-football kicks lying in the grass staring down a telescope, which isn't everybody's idea of fun, and our Brian gets his trying to entice trout onto a hook.

There was another trip to the Scillies, and another pre-season friendly – this time in Holland. I get worse, I really do. I used to do the odd pre-season game, but I've found that the more you go to, the more you want to go to. You just get used to going to the match, and there's the added bonus of an exotic trip and maybe a new ground, if you're a bit of a "ticker" – and there are a few of us about like that. Off to Holland this time, by car through the Chunnel – a personal first, although really quite similar to the Eurostar, and the car wasn't that much slower when we got to the Continent. The turn-out of Sunderland fans was more than impressive and their antics in the Alkmaar supporters' club and on the terraces were equally so. Ninety minutes plus of socialising with the locals (and the Rotterdam branch of the Feyenoord/SAFC supporters club) was followed by ninety minutes plus of constant singing at the match. On the pitch, the there was no more Myhre, no more Byfield, no more Deane. Mick McCarthy had shifted out those for whom he foresaw no future at SAFC and splashed what cash he had been given on a plethora of new faces.

So it was hello to Davis, with a very encouraging display, hello Bassila, Hoyte, Nosworthy, Stead, Gray (I used to watch your dad), Miller, Stubbs, and everybody else. A good performance, an encouraging win against a side that had performed well in European competition the previous season, and we could be forgiven for thinking that the good times might indeed be just around the corner that the new season offered. There were also games in the USA and Canada, but that was a bit beyond my means. Maybe one day. Off the field, there was another summer of man's inhumanity to man, what with the London Tube bombers bringing carnage to our doorstep, and the peacekeepers and Iraqis being killed by the Iraqis. And by the Americans as well, of course.

Just to spice things up on the home front, our Gaz decided that he'd had enough of Edinburgh and moved back, which was nice. Except our house wasn't built for four adults and the assorted friends who provide unexpected obstacles to my safe passage out of the house of a morning when they decide to sleep on the couch. Or the floor. Or the big chair. Still, it made for cosy times.

As ever, we planned our lives for the next nine months or so according to the fixture list, which this time pitted us against the big names of the domestic game. Off we went again on our trains and coaches, and in our cars, baffling bar staff the length and breadth of the land by calling the female variety "hinny" and the male variety "bonny lad." We greeted each other like long-lost relatives, just as we did every August, with the time-honoured words of "alreet marra" as we set off on another season of amazing the rest of the football world with our displays of loyalty and passion – in the middle of the week, hundreds of miles from home.

You only have to be with our club a while before it gets you – Peter Davenport was only here a couple of years, comes from Liverpool, and played for Forest and Man Utd (and Boro, poor bairn), but he's brought his kids up as Sunderland supporters. It's not just about following your team because they win things (although a trophy or two wouldn't go amiss) but because they're your team, and you shouldn't forget that you don't choose your team, they choose you. Full of hope and optimism despite what football had dealt us over the preceding decades, we set out again to watch the Lads doing the business.

Or at least that was the plan.

A home starter against Charlton hardly had us quaking in our boots, but despite a debut goal from Andy Gray – surely the precursor to a goal-laden season, we thought – we found ourselves on the wrong end of, amongst other things, a Murphy free-kick and a burst of pace from Darren Bent. We'd spent a fair amount of time chasing Bent, allegedly, and it was a bit of a bugger to see him show our defence a clean pair of heels for his goal. Still, it was only one game, and we're quick learners. Aren't we? What we didn't need was a trip to somewhere like Liverpool, which is what we got. Actually, we put up a decent fight, but were caught again when we conceded a free-kick just outside the box and another piece of Premiership quality undid us. Against Man City at the SOL a couple of games later, we had the lion's share of the possession, but old boy Reyna helped to sink us despite loan man Anthony Le Tallec scoring his first goal in the stripes. Surely, if he's French, he should be Antoine Le Tallec? Whatever, another defeat, then it was off to Wigan, where we'd barely taken our seats when Breen lost his head and gave away the game's decisive penalty, and it was four defeats in a row. What happened to the masterly display we'd produced last season at the JJB? Not good, but a trip to Chelsea, or Chelski as they were known by then, was next. Baptism of fire or what? Where we'd spent a few million on a dozen players, they'd been spending about that amount on the annual salary of each of their new boys, and their substitutes had cost over £60 million, allegedly. At £48 a ticket, we could have been forgiven for staying at home, or buying some shares in a brewery, but we went, and once again the Lads put up a good show until Davis hoyed the ball to a defender who wasn't expecting it, and Geremi banged it away. The second underlined how much we had to learn, despite the presence of Alan Stubbs, brought in to "do a Bould" and provide some experience and stability at the back.

Perhaps what we needed was a break, and good old England provided one. Being a lucky sort, I'd been invited on a longish weekend in Spain with the back seat of the Durham bus. Originally we were headed for Shagaluf, or so I was told, and then we had a change of destination and headed for Benidorm on Silent Bob's Tours – but not until three of us had watched the England game in the New Derby. Just for old time's sake. It was handy for George, and it was my first visit in years. The place had been done up a treat, the beer was better than I remember, the telly was a lot bigger, and England beat Wales, which was nice. Victory accomplished, it was a quick dash to Ponteland airport, then over the sea to sunny Spain, where we celebrated my birthday as only five middle-aged Sunderland fans can. Bob, George, Tom, Willa, and I hoyed some Euros in the kitty and drank Stokoe's bar close to dry, and made a decent impression on a few other hostelries, as well as almost making fools of ourselves in the water park. Rest and recuperation – you can't beat it when it's SAFC you're resting and recuperating from.

In the big, bad, world, a date was set for the trial of Saddam Hussein, which we all predicted would be a perfectly fair and unbiased affair, conducted away from the glare of publicity.

West Brom were next to the SOL, and we took an early lead through Breen and looked well worth a win, but didn't get the second, and were stunned into silence when they levelled in added time – that most deflating of things, a last-minute goal against. What we needed was a win, and we needed it soon. Thankfully, there was the League Cup, and there was a home tie against Cheltenham Town. Being Sunderland, we tore the lower-league side to shreds, scoring a hatful of goals in the process. Sorry, I was drifting off a bit there. What we actually did was struggle against a side sixty-odd places below us in the league, try Le Tallec, Stead, and Elliott up front, and finally get the only goal in extra time. Hardly the sort of performance that indicated an upturn in our Premiership fortunes, but we had a trip to Boro next, for a Sunday four o'clock start, and, as their fans think it's a derby, we had to do something spectacular. After our invasion of that nice family pub at Wolviston services – a quick check of the fixture list by the manager, or a quick phone-call from the police, and it could have been so much easier for the staff, who were treated to a couple of hundred Sunderland fans trying to take full advantage of the unexpected chance of a couple of pints. And let's not forget the poor lad in the Mag shirt, supposedly celebrating his tenth birthday. Anyway, without being too clever, the Lads on the pitch did the business thanks to Tommy Miller's shin and a peach of a curling free-kick from Arca. There we go then, lessons all learned, we're sorted now, and we're ready for lift off. We'd be alright, especially now that we'd overcome our live TV jinx, and the cameras were at the SOL the next Saturday tea-time for the visit of West Ham, who'd picked up eleven points to our four.

Things were looking decidedly canny, thanks to Tommy Miller's second of the season, but once again we failed to build on the lead, and the Hammers nicked a point. At least we got out of the bottom three on the back of a four game unbeaten run. I'm all for statistics, especially when they make Sunderland look good (or better than they are), but that was stretching things a bit, calling that a run of any kind.

As with his sister a year ago, Nephew Mat had invited us to his wedding – during the football season. In Bristol. Of course I accepted, as family comes first, but the lad must be psychic, or have studied the England fixture list, and we decamped to the South West for the weekend with no match to miss. The wedding went a treat, my kids managed to win the Keith Richards award for the state of their hotel room, and England managed to beat Austria. A good day all round.

Back to the business, and another home defeat, this time to Man Utd, but the really big one was the following week at Sid James Park. We assembled at the stadium, which is actually the same distance from our house as our ultimate destination, then the expeditionary force convoy through Washington, Gateshead, and the back end of Newcastle. We'd been often enough to the place to know that there would be stairs, but they always come as an unpleasant surprise, and they go on forever. At least the view's canny from the top – you can see the sea, and the Stadium of Light. In contrast to most of the season to date, we put up a good display, scored two great goals through Liam Lawrence and Stevie Elliott, were denied a blatant penalty, but the home side scored three. It might have gone down in the records as one of the better derbies, football-wise, in recent times, but I think that defeat went a long way to establish the losing mentality that was creeping into the players' minds. We played well, we were unlucky to lose, but lose we did, even though the Mags who could string together a sentence generally agreed that their side had been fortunate to come away with the three points. Not the one in the Derby when I got back to Bishop, who I didn't know, but who tried to lace straight into me by referring to Sunderland as a small town in Durham. I simply asked him where he lived, which was Bishop, a small town in Durham. I'd remained quite calm up to this point, but then the red mist descended, and I reminded the callow youth that he was a County Durham boy, and that Sunderland were the team for County Durham boys. If he was a typical pale-faced youth when I walked in, he was paler than a pint of milk when I supped up and left to grumble the evening away at home.

Well, if the league wasn't going to plan, there was always the League Cup, and we had Arsenal at home. That might not sound too promising a second step in a formative cup run, but that nice Monsieur Wenger had stated his intention to play his youth team, and we had one of the better Arsenal youths in Justin Hoyte. Wembley here we come, if they finish it in time. Perhaps we'd better book the bus to go to Cardiff instead. Our experienced professionals would teach the Arsenal whippersnappers a lesson or two. Yeah, right. They gave us a football seminar, and the three nil defeat probably flattered us a bit, and that losing mentality began to grow. When Portsmouth came to town, everything went wrong. We scored first through a Whitehead penalty, and went into the second half expecting to build on that lead, but, after the equaliser, Stubbs and Davis ran into each other, Pompey scored, and it all fell apart. When Taylor scored a beaut from all of forty yards, there was little Davis could have done, but it was too much for one fan, who ran onto the pitch and vented his anger very vocally at our keeper. It was wrong, it was daft, and it cost him his seat, but I understand exactly how he was feeling. Me, I moved round to the South West Corner, just so that I could sit near some people who were enjoying themselves, the Pompey fans. If I'd had any sense, I would have realised that losing a game in that manner probably meant that we were on our way out of the division, but, as ever, I held on to my belief that we'd turn things around, that Mick McCarthy would sort things out, that we'd be fine.

Just to put things in perspective, 22 people died in the Bali bombings, then 54,000 – that's a whole Roker Park full – died in the Pakistan earthquake that left 2.5 million – that's a whole North East – homeless. And 2,000 US servicemen died in Iraq. Football's only a game.

We'd be fine. That's OK then, so we nipped down to Arsenal on bonfire night, via a great afternoon in The Lamb, to start the process of putting things right. Unfortunately, if there was a corner to be turned, it wasn't anywhere near Highbury, but we did manage a goal. They, on the other hand, managed three. But we'd still be alright, because we had three home games in a row coming up, and we'd sort it. Hell, if they can have elections in Iraq for the first time in a quarter of a century, if the third world can arrive in New Orleans via Hurricane Katrina, if the IRA can destroy their arsenal of weapons, if George Weah can come second in the Liberian elections to Africa's first female head of state since Cleopatra, Ellen Johnson-Sirleaf... then there's got to be a chance of something unusual happening to Sunderland.

We lost all three. Three one to Villa, despite another penalty that had Whitehead in danger of going on a goal spree. In a bad week for football, George Best passed away, it having been a minor miracle that he'd survived as long as he did. There's not much I can say to describe the abilities of the man, just that he was up there with the best of all time. As is typical of the genius type, there was with George a self-destruct button that was pressed with alarming regularity. As with many of his ilk, it was the drink that got him. Without it, he'd probably have postponed his first retirement from playing by ten years, and, purely from a selfish point of view, the football public would have seen a lot more of him. In the end, it was his life, and it was up to him to do with it as he saw fit. After all, he's the one he hurt the most. It was a well-respected minute's silence before the Brum game, and then it was back to the business of getting beaten. Two points from home games is not the stuff of which survival is made, as Jon Stead defiantly refused to score and Le Tallec was all Gallic flicks and twazzles but no heart and no end product. Ben Alnwick had replaced the hapless Davis, but he couldn't prevent the defeat, and there was an air of inevitability about the Liverpool game. The fans were becoming numbed to the pain of it all, shell-shocked if you like. I know I was. We turned up, we watched the Lads get pummelled, we went home. It became the way Saturdays were.

As Tottenham aren't famed for good beer in friendly surroundings, we hopped off our bus and onto a train to Enfield, home of the world's first cash point machine, and a Christmas market that had a real reindeer, which was a bit unexpected, not to say scary. A few pints later, we watched the Lads put up a fight at Spurs, perhaps because there was a bit less pressure away from home, less of an atmosphere of dread, and managed to score twice. Of course, there were three at the other end, but we had something to smile about for a while. Whitehead scored with a great free-kick, but we let Spurs get ahead before Le Tallec equalised. Two moments of joy became three when young Alnwick saved a penalty, but just when we thought there was light at the end of the tunnel, that light turned out to be Michael Carrick's toothy grin when he rolled a late winner through Breen's legs and past Alnwick.

Another loss, again in London at Charlton. Another no contest, and the BBC chose that one to send roving reporter Kevin Day along. Quite what he made of Rob's tirade in answer to the perfectly innocent question of "How do you think that went," will probably never be revealed, but he looked more than a little taken aback. At least George managed to keep it just the right side of profane and our thoughts on yet another timid display were broadcast to the nation the following evening. Then it was Christmas, and the big Boxing Day game was Bolton at home. For us, it was a welcome if pretty useless point as we bumped along at the bottom of the league, ending the year on New Year's Eve with another defeat. We had had high-ish hopes of getting something from the game at Blackburn a few days earlier, but all we got was cold and wet, as the snow forced the game to be postponed, and we simply headed north from Lancaster instead of south, straight back home.

New Year, new direction for the club, we thought – up. It was the only way we could go, to be honest. Off to London again, this time Fulham via The Lamb and a shocking pub near the tube at the Fulham end, and seats in the temporary stand, beyond the "neutral" section. Packed with non-committal tourists, that part of the ground. That and passing Australian bar staff on a rare day off. Apparently, the football world thought we were bright and enthusiastic. I'll agree with that to a point. Lawrence scored one that made it to the goal of the month competition, but as soon as they equalised, the old Sunderland returned and it was defeat number sixteen for the season. Our previous record as the worst team in Premiership history looked seriously at risk of being lost – to ourselves.

Well, at least there was the FA Cup to keep us warm. As the price of oil went up in response to Russia cutting off Ukraine's supply – their response to an argument over price – we warmed our hearts by putting three past the mighty Northwich

Victoria, not that we could continue the form against Chelsea the week after despite scoring our first league goal from open play for 500 minutes. Fifty-five points between the two clubs showed in the way we simply faded from the match after our traditional, if pointless, bright start. Our game at West Brom was a tea-time game, meaning that we could have a leisurely afternoon in Lichfield, and then we did the unexpected by actually winning. For the second time in the season. In January. Le Tallec sort of claimed the goal, which took a huge deflection off former Mag Steve Watson. Oh all right then, it should really have gone down as an own goal, but who cares. Was this the corner turned?

Was it heck. Brentford were our opponents in the FA Cup fourth round and our first visit since the bad old days of the Third Division. A novelty, and a welcome one, was the opportunity to stand and watch the Lads lose rather than sit and watch the Lads lose. Thinking back, we should all have put huge bets on us to lose, as we were playing a team in red and white, we were the team out of form, and they had a forward with a silly name. DJ Campbell did the business, Arca fluked in a cross, DJ Campbell did the business again, and we were out.

Just the league, then.

At home to Boro, we wimped out in spectacular fashion, if being walloped without putting up any sort of fight can be considered spectacular, then lost to West Ham. Daryl Murphy won us a last-minute point at home to Spurs. It was just one point, it wasn't much use, but in the context of the season we were having, it felt like we'd won the cup, and we travelled home singing and celebrating. Be thankful for small mercies, that's what we thought, and that point might just be the point that would be "a platform to build on," as footballers and managers like to say. Well, that was February and in March we knocked the legs off that platform we were supposed to be building on by losing four games, laying down what arms we had faster than the Basques in Spain and Southern France. After the first of these, when we'd had to take our pre-match refreshment in the supermarket car-park due to the lack of away-friendly pubs - or pubs of any kind – anywhere near the City of Manchester Stadium, and collapsed faster than a sandcastle hit by a tidal wave, I took a couple of days off work. Everybody needs a break, to climb a mountain or jump in a lake. Some folks go to exotic places, others go to Galway Races. Me, I just packed up the car, and drove to the Lakes, it's not too far. In fact, we didn't even get that far before the news came through. It was in the little café in Brough where my mobile chirruped into life (aye, I'd become a techno, moving into the nineties at last) and the call brought the news that Mick McCarthy had been sacked. The official club line was that it was "In the best interests of both parties for him to leave immediately," which seems fair enough.

A nice enough bloke, one with whom I'd gladly sit down and talk football over a pint, but one who'd never been able to make it work in the Premiership. He'd taken over the worst team in that division, with no real hope of saving them, and taken only two years to get us back up after a play-off semi-final and an FA Cup semi-final. On the other hand, whether it was spreading his tiny transfer budget too thinly or just an inability to manage at the highest level remains a subject for debate and no doubt will do so for years to come. It can't be denied that several of his high profile players had failed miserably to do what they were brought in to do – Stead, Gray, and Davis are names that spring to mind – but the reasons for this probably lie with the whole team's performances, and that it the responsibility of the manager.

So it was up to Kevin Ball, hoyed into the hot-seat from the academy, to save the good ship Sunderland, sinking faster than it had been when his predecessor had put his hand on the tiller. Nobody would shirk their responsibilities with Bally in charge, but could he do enough to save the day? We duly lost Kevin's first three games, just to get him used to things. We were a ridiculous number of points adrift of the next team – sixteen or so, more than it was worth counting, really – but at Everton something strange happened. Everton taking an early lead wasn't strange, and neither, really was Rory Delap's first Sunderland goal since his recent arrival. No, not even Everton's inevitable second was that strange. Jon Stead scoring a goal, on the other hand, was the strangest thing we'd seen in a long while. Nine months to score your first goal is what you might expect from a defender, not a forward. We might even have won the game when Delap's drive hit the post, but it was not to be. We would have been technically relegated (a lovely phrase, one that had been hanging over our heads for several weeks) if West Bromwich had won the evening game, but they managed to lose to Liverpool. So we lived to fight another week, and the end of that week brought Fulham, proud owners of the worst away record in the division – aye, even worse than ours – to Wearside. As befitting a relegation battle, the sky as we climbed Houghton Cut was black as coal, and by the time we de-bussed - or whatever the technical term for getting off the coach for a pint is – the weather was looking decidedly dodgy. When we emerged from the warmth of the bar, we almost turned around and went straight back in. It was blowing a blizzard of horrible wet snow, and the fifteen minute walk through the town and over the bridge saw us arrive at the turnstiles literally soaked to the skin. I was fully expecting our inevitable victory to come at a price – pneumonia. We were actually behind when the ref decided that enough was enough for Sunderland, never mind the Southern Softies of Fulham. The early finish meant that we could watch the Grand National live for a change, with the terrifying addition of a horse with an on-board camera, which had most of the watchers ducking for cover at every fence. I didn't back a winner or even a place, but at least we hadn't lost the football, and I could enjoy my evening out without having to explain to various interested parties the manner of the day's defeat. A pleasant change.

We didn't lose the next game either, making it twenty-one whole days undefeated, at Old Trafford. Having taken refreshment, we decided that we'd have a whip-round and a daft bet, as they were offering 14-1 against us not losing. Eighteen quid would have brought us a canny return, but it being Good Friday, the bookmakers' were all closed. As if to rub it in, the team turned in a good display and came away with a 0-0 draw. Unfortunately, and unlike the Everton game, the other results went against us and we were down. While the season as a whole was a great big flop, we could at least hold our heads up and say that we went down with a fight in Manchester. We won relegation. Wonderful.

Having held up our heads for a week, the Mags came to town on the back of a series of fragile defensive performances, offering up a chance to give us something to remember the season for. We took a first-half lead when Justin Hoyte, Hoyte, Hoyte did a Carteron by starting and finishing a sweet move, and our simple cousins were there for the taking when we came back out for the second half. There was a real feeling that we would do the necessary and salvage a bit of pride from a stinking season, but then we did what we'd been doing with embarrassing regularity since August. In seven minutes, we went from heroes to zeroes, as Davis, who'd previously blamed lack of communication with his defensive colleagues on losing his voice due to shouting at them too much, didn't talk to Caldwell, and Chopra scored with his first touch. We should buy him, you know, they'll never appreciate him up the road. A Shearer penalty and a third from N'Zogbia had us heading for the exits before Luque, a £10 million pound striker who couldn't hit a cow's arse with a handful of gravel 364 days a year, scored the fourth. The post match feelings were awful – worse than the day we were relegated, because at least then we looked like we made an effort. Where we'd been unlucky on a few occasions through the season, that day we'd thrown away a great chance to get one over on our nearest and least dear, in a fashion that would have been comical had it not been so personal.

After that nonsense, the end of the campaign couldn't come soon enough, despite the need to win a home game. The last game on the fixture list was Arsenal, but we also had Fulham to squeeze in. Arsenal did what Arsenal do, and put on a show that was worth the ticket money. A certain Niall Quinn was at the match, a guest of Bob Murray, and he saw that Tut Henry give a display that almost made you cry, it was so good. We lost 3-0, the crowd rose to a man to applaud Henry from the field, and there was a strange feeling of... I don't know what it was, but it wasn't the feeling you'd expect when an already relegated team loses 3-0 at home. Perhaps it was the rumours that were beginning to circulate about Niall Quinn getting together a team of fantastically rich backers to save the club he'd grown to love... Perhaps, perhaps, perhaps. The win over Fulham had an air of inevitability about it, but we let them score a late goal just to make it interesting as we scored twice at home for the first time that season at the last attempt, and just avoided being the first team in the Premiership to go a whole season without a home win. We had enough unwanted records already, as we were guaranteed to beat our own lowest points total whatever happened at Villa on the last day. Needless to say we lost that one as well. Davis saved a penalty, Danny Collins scored, but we still contrived to lose, and we had to spend the rest of our weekend in Birmingham at a football wake. Sunderland were officially dead, let's have a party, and let's wait for the rebirth.

If I was glad when the 19 point season ended, then I was ecstatic when this debacle finished. There was precious little to take from it that was positive, and I'd been forced to spend my Saturday nights in sombre contemplation of defeat after defeat rather than celebration of victories. Any sort of non-football entertainment had been welcome, just to take my mind off things of a red and white nature, so I got myself out to as many comedy events as possible, just so I didn't forget how to smile. I was getting a bit old to follow the current musical trends – I still try, but it gets harder – so I took to listening to the bairns. They'd been in several bands separately over the years, a few incarnations of which had been quite decent, but now they'd decided to join forces, and I was quite often the oldest face in the audience, having driven them and a decent amount of the gear to the venue. No mean feat that, in a Daihatsu Charade, which, if you don't know them, are about the size of a Mini that's been left in a hot wash for a week or two. At least our Ian passed his test and took that task away from me, but the house was, and still is, a mass of amplifiers and guitars. At least there's always something to strum on. They've promised me that when they're rich and famous, a sort of Durham version of the Gallagher brothers but without the attitude and two eyebrows each, they'll see me and Judith right - a season ticket would do for starters, the mansion can wait.

Over and out. After the drab sterility of the last few FA Cup Finals, which had been enough to drive us to dominoes by half time, Ron, Lee and I decided to drag Denty the Mag along to the Scottish version, where former Northern League Gretna were playing Hearts. They were also funded by Brooks Mileson, a Sunderland lad made good who apparently survives on a diet of tabs and Lucozade, so there were enough connections to make a trip to Hampden a viable alternative to an afternoon in front of the TV being bored to death. Having come out of the blocks at lightening pace Hearts eventually scored after half an hour and the game, as well as Gretna's fairytale, looked to be over. However, the little village side showed the sort of spirit we'd lacked all season and fought back, grabbing an equaliser with quarter of an hour left, and putting the SPL under heavy pressure for the last ten minutes or so. They pushed all the way to penalties, losing 4-2 on spot kicks in the end. It was no disgrace and a canny day out for a good few from the North East, despite the traffic and lack of bus-ticket meaning only half an hour to take in the surroundings before kick-off. For once, the English Cup Final produced the goods, as Liverpool beat West Ham by four goals to three. Bugger. Still, we had a great day out, and the lads who stayed in The Grand had a great day in.

A bright spot at the end of a dismal season, and that bright spot not even provided by Sunderland. I needed a holiday.

And it's Sunderland
Sunderland FC
We're by far the greatest team
The world has ever seen

2006-2007

Need a holiday? After the debacle of the season just ended, in which we'd gone beyond ridicule and were looked on at away games with a rather sympathetic eye by the locals, I needed one more than ever, and couldn't get away fast enough. As had become my regular habit, I headed for the Western Isles, but this time I took no chances on the bird-watching front and went to Mull, booking myself on an RSPB accompanied trip to see Itchy and Scratchy. No, not the cartoon characters in the cartoon on the Simpsons (if you get my meaning), but the Sea Eagle chicks. After two consecutive holidays searching for them in vain on the Outer Hebrides, I took the easy, perhaps slightly cheaty option, but fair's fair, I deserved a bit of assistance after the hours I'd spent scanning the skies from various damp and windy locations in the far North West. There was plenty of other birdlife about, and plenty of rain. I impressed the locals in the pub by correctly predicting that Sol Campbell would score the first goal in the Champions' League Final, and then by winning the quiz under the name of Sunderland, all by myself, before almost drowning in the rain on the way back to the tent. After a season in which we'd won only five games out of forty-four, a sixth triumph for Sunderland, in whatever competition, was a bit of a rarity. Thirty-one defeats, six draws, and a whole load of heartache had left me, and I suspect more than a few others, wondering if there was an alternative to a season of football. I could try weekends of bird-watching, exploring the country on foot, or something else more interesting and less unpleasant.

The big question, of course, was whether or not I could tear myself away from the beautiful game in general and Sunderland in particular. Even when the first team was stinking to high heaven, there had been the reserves at Durham, and a chance to stand at a match and watch people who were either trying to get into the first team for the first time, or after injury, or who were just biding their time until a transfer came along. I always found it interesting to see which ex-pro was coaching the visitors and whether I could remember his efforts against the Lads. You were also able to see the reaction to the hilariously witty comments of those in the crowd in the past referred to as wags (no, not wives and girlfriends, just amusing people in the crowd), as it was a much more personal arena than the SOL when it came to hurling comments at officials and opposition players. Oh, and let's not forget the underachievers in our own squad, of which there were many that season. So when it became apparent that we weren't to have a reserve team in a league in the coming season, it was more than a bit of a disappointment. There was also Bishop, my home town team, for weekday evenings, but if you'd added their points total from the recently-ended season to Sunderland's, we'd still have been relegated. There was also the never-ending saga of the new ground for the Bishops. Hell, my Mam now lives in a nice flat somewhere near the edge of the Town End penalty box, and the Two Blues were dodging from Shildon to Spennymoor and back to play their home games. Hardly a situation to attract the part-time watcher.

Rumours of Quinny's imminent arrival turned into confirmation from the Big Man that he was indeed heading back to Wearside with a posse of Irish squillionaires hot on his heels – but only once he'd had his legal people go through the books with the legal equivalent of a fine tooth comb. Not only the books, but the magazines, newspapers, post-it notes, and the graffiti on the toilet walls. This slowed things up considerably, but in the light of what had happened at several other clubs with accusations of dodgy dealings and underhand financial activities, Niall wanted to be seen to be as squeaky clean as possible.

In preparation for the forthcoming World Cup, Jamaica came to Old Trafford to play England, so a few of us popped down for a day out in Manchester and a swift half in York on the way home. The Reggae Boys seemed to have been at a bit of a party the night before, and England had a football party, winning 6-0. We also answered the eternal question of how many people it takes to start a Mexican Wave, when, after fifteen minutes of effort, four of us set one away. High hopes for the finals with a score like that, eh? June also saw us at our first Stadium of Light wedding, along with most of the Durham Branch, as George and Marion tied the knot, and the Black Cats Bar was taken over for the day. For a view from a post-wedding party, there can be few better than the interior of the

SOL from one side of the room, and Southwick from the other with a sunset over the Wear as a backdrop. If, like me, your Great Granny came from Southwick, it adds a bit more interest.

While Niall was paving the way for the Irish investment, and the appointment of a world-class manager, we shot off to the South West again for the proper holidays. England, in the meantime, headed off to the World Cup in Germany with high hopes. I watched the victory over Paraguay in Evesham, the victory over Trinidad and Tobago - more of them later, as it transpired – in the Mermaid on St Mary's, and the draw with Sweden in the Scillonian Club. I was back in Bishop for the decisive Portugal game, and back in The Grand with the England second-half Domino boys. As ever seems the way, they fell to a penalty shoot-out, which kept us off the dominoes, but predictably failed and shambled our way out of the tournament.

Back at Sunderland, the club seemed to have been brought back to life after the slow death of the previous campaign. Bob Murray had long wanted to be out of Sunderland, but he rightly waited until he was sure he had the right person to hand over to. Drumaville came to town, all shillelaghs, Guinness, and, more importantly, a barrow-load of Euros. The pre-season was announced, along with Quinny's disappointment that there were to be no competitive games for the reserves – a particularly silly legacy of the previous regime. I cast aside the post-season blues and all thoughts of a football-free life, and accepted a lift down to Rotherham for the friendly, took the train to Carlisle, and the coach to one of the most pleasant football locations I've ever visited – Forest Green, where Julio Arca scored his final goal for the Lads before risking his lungs with a move to the Boro. Old Boy Bobby Saxton had been brought back from retirement to add a bit of experience behind the scenes as Niall began the task of stabilising the playing side of things. There was still no world-class manager, as Martin O'Neill (favourite for the job) dragged his heels and eventually decided Sunderland weren't for him, Alan Curbishley decided that the time wasn't right, and Sam Allardyce also decided against us. Our options were becoming fewer by the day, so we headed across the Irish Sea for the game at Shelbourne without a boss-feller, and it was scarcely a surprise when we got a text message headed "new manager on the way" but a bit of a shock when the manager in question was revealed to be none other than Peter Reid. The fact that we were in the pictures at the time (sorry, attending the cinema) and that most of the other watchers of the latest Superman epic were probably not interested in who the next Sunderland manager was explained their reaction to our reaction.

As you'll have gathered by now, the information was erroneous in the extreme. Surely that appointment would have been desperate measures indeed, but we took our minds off it with the hurling, where the participants tried to take their minds off with big sticks and a ball like a little rock. We chatted with recently-signed Kenny Cunningham's dad in the pub before the game, and he confirmed that the average Irish man-on-the-street loves his Guinness, or his beer, and that they were chuffed to bits to see us. When he returned from a trip to see his son at the ground, he bore a spare match ticket. Generous man indeed. At the main event, Niall Quinn walked long the touchline to receive acclaim the like of which is rarely seen. Fans of both sides cheered, clapped, and simply wanted to see the man himself. No manager, so Niall had a go, as he had with everything else. If it needed doing, Niall did it. I've a feeling that he flew the plane over for that match, or used the magic carpet of his now famous analogy.

We'd had the fixture list for a few weeks by now, and once again we started at Coventry. By the time we got there, for a Sunday dinner-time start, Niall was still the manager, and had been shopping. He'd brought in Frenchman William Mocquet and previously-mentioned former Irish team-mate Kenny Cunningham – another in the Bould mould, not the Stubbs mould, we hoped - but was still chasing his old partner Kevin Phillips, who was on his way out of Villa. Hardly a lot shopping, really. Kevin Kyle, after spending what seemed like years having different body parts sawn off and nailed back on, left for Coventry. Naturally, we were on the crest of a wave after the summer of change, but the appearance of an ex-player generally meant a goal for them.

It didn't arrive, and, indeed, it looked like we were off to a flyer when Murphy scored for us, but Stern John (we should sign him, he could be useful, you know) equalised with a lovely goal. Ex-players don't always score (it just seems that way) but they also set goals up, and that's exactly what Don Hutchison, hardly the most popular former player anyway, did. Well, not exactly, but when his quick free-kick was ordered to be retaken, we fell asleep and we were a goal down. Clive Clarke, a target in the past, was signed before the visit of Birmingham, and made his mark for the wrong reason. As Steve Caldwell limped off, on came Clive, and promptly gave away the crucial penalty for the only goal of the game. Arnau arrived from Barcelona (reserves), and along came Plymouth – surely a win for the Lads was on the cards. Tobias Hysen had also signed from Swedish club Djurgarden, which should have given our squad a boost, as we'd actually heard of him, being an international footballer and all that.

It started well with another goal from Murphy, but then we went to pieces and allowed Plymouth to score twice before Niall threw on Stead and Brown to join Murphy and Elliott and up front. OK, with that number of strikers on the field, a goal was the least we should have got, but there was another mistake, and another goal against, another defeat to take. Three in a row is a bad start, even by our recent low standards, but worse was to follow. At Southend, crammed into the tiny away end, we watched an even first half end in disaster as they went ahead right at the death. On came Arnau early in the second half, and proceeded to show more heart, guile, and commitment that the rest of his teammates. By the time Jon Stead scored in a manner which said "Look, I can score you know" it was past ninety minutes and they'd scored another two. Mr Quinn's magic carpet was beginning to look like a second-hand clippie mat that had been left in front of an open fire for too long, and it suffered more severe burns a few days later. As in several other seasons that had started badly, we were thrown a lifeline of sorts in the form of a League Cup tie at the worst team in the league – Bury. As in several other seasons that had started badly, we buggered it up in classic style. It was a shame, not just from a football point of view, but because it spoiled a good day out. A bit like mostly every game last season, if you like. We managed to sneak the bus into Skipton, where they don't allow things like coach-loads of football supporters apparently, but it was sunny, the pubs and the locals were friendly, the beer was good, and there are more sock shops per head of population than anywhere else in the UK and probably the world. We were still discussing hosiery related statistics, and how well the Sunderland socks suited Arnau, when we started looking for him on the pitch. A clip round Ron's ear from his cousin Clive was followed by a curt "he's been sent off, yer daft buggers." Apparently, we'd been looking the other way when he was shown the red card after about two minutes, and it was downhill from there. Two nil against the basement club, and we teetered on the precipice of a season which had the potential to become as bad as the last.

At least we weren't in the Middle East, where the Hezbollah and the Israelis were blowing each other to pieces despite the pleas of the western world to agree a ceasefire. Well, Blair and Bush sort of pussyfooted around telling them to stop killing each other, while back in Blighty the firemen threatened strike action. Having just sweated our way through the hottest July on record, they were probably just taking advantage of our aversion to heat. Strike while the iron's hot, if you like. With our football season well underway, they thankfully started upgrading the A66, just to help us get to our next defeat in the North West a bit quicker.

In an effort to give life away from the green grass of Sunderland's latest stumbling start a try, our Gaz made a bid for Hollywood by joining several hundred other local lads to mill about on Redcar beach for a few days, dressed in khaki and hoping in vain to catch a glimpse of Keira Knightley. His brother thinks much more of Ms Knightley, to be honest, but he also thinks more of his hair, and flatly refused to have a World War Two military short back and sides. So only one Dobson in what would surely be a classic film, Atonement, but one film star per household is way above the average for South West Durham anyway, so that's good enough for me.

Five defeats off the belt, none of which we'd looked like winning, and highly fancied West Brom, complete with their new boy Kevin Phillips, were the next visitors, so we could have been forgiven for expecting the worst. We could have expected the worst, but we didn't, because something strange happened to change the mood. Sitting in the stand was a famous face, and the subject of the most recent of manager rumours, a certain Roy Keane. The crowd, a very big crowd considering they'd just watched their side play like clowns for a season and a month, made him more than welcome, showed them how much they cared, and cheered on the Lads to a comfortable win. Mr Phillips came on as a substitute, managed very little, and goals from Whitehead and Neill Collins (in for Caldwell) won the day, and it was as if a cloud had lifted from over Wearside – and my part of Bishop. I know it's on the Wear as well, but it's Wear Valley and not Wearside. In fact, the metaphorical black cloud lifted from the metaphorical sky above every Sunderland supporter - it must have made the whole country seem a brighter place. Just to top off a tremendous day, Roy Keane went out the back, borrowed a pen, and signed a contract. Roy Bloody Keane – sorry, Roy Maurice Keane - Sunderland manager. It had a nice ring to it, and still does. We all know that he'd become a manager one day, but I don't think many people, myself included, considered him a likely candidate for the job at Monkwearmouth. As it turned out, he'd turned down Niall's original offer a few months before because he wanted to "Do his badges" and learn how to be a coach. A thorough man indeed.

Well, that was a win that was, and there followed a period of almost two weeks without a game, so Roy went and signed everybody he could of think of from his recent past. Varga, Wallace, Miller (no, not that one, this one's called Liam), Yorke (yes, the Dwight Yorke), David Connolly (at the third or fourth time of asking, which seemed like trying too hard to me), Graham Kavanagh, and a hatful of others all arrived before the dreaded transfer window, yet another attempt by the authorities to mess up the game, closed. And that was it for August, and the first weekend of September was that weekend off. Having signed all of those players, we needed the time for them to introduce themselves to each other. I needed the weekend off to celebrate a significant birthday by means of a night at the Theatre (comedy club, no high-brow nonsense) in Durham, and a chance encounter with Kenny Cunningham outside the Half-Moon. I mix with the stars, me.

A week later, we took over Derby, showed the world what Quinny had been talking about when he talked of Sunderland having the potential to be something spectacular, and won convincingly. A few days after that, after I'd taken another couple of days off work and spent them in deepest Yorkshire, just to get into the atmosphere, like, we did the same at Leeds, where a home fan or two apparently tried to confront our new manager. Rather them than me, I thought, along with "we're off and flying." It was a bit of a bumpy take-off, as it turned out, with a home draw thanks to a goal from Hysen and then a real bit of turbulence at Ipswich as we lost. The BBC screened a much publicised documentary in which they promised to blow the lid of underhand payments in football, following Mike Newell's naming of names earlier in the year. In fact, all the Beeb did was reel off all of the managers you'd have suspected of being implicated in slightly dodgy dealing, purely because of the number of deals they make in a year. Allardyce, Redknapp, Souness ("How much for Boumsong? Aye, gan on then") and a few others. One of the few others was Kevin Bond, who was quickly sacked by Freddie Shepherd without any actual proof being provided of his guilt.

A home win over Wednesday ended September on a high, then came the obligatory defeat at Preston. Everybody seems to have a bogey side, and Preston were about to become ours. 4-1 there, then a few days later 1-2 at Stoke, where our man Rory Delap broke his leg. While playing on loan for Stoke. At least we beat a rather toothless Barnsley at home, then had a trip to Hull. It was also our Ian's twenty-first on the Friday, and when asked what he'd like for this special birthday, he said "Have a fancy-dress at The Grand, and go to Hull with you, our Gaz, and Stainy."

Easily pleased, some folks, but if you'd seen the state of them on the bus in the morning, you'd have seen that they didn't take it that easy. With a combined total of three hours kip between the pair of them (two hours and fifty plus ten) it was a wonder we got them on at all, but we've all done it in our reckless youth. I know I did, anyhow. They perked up a bit during our stop at Beverley, what with the beer in Nellie's being so cheap, and the place being lit by gas. Ross Wallace carried on his personal mission to remove his shirt as often as possible in breach of the rules, but we forgave him as he'd scored the winner right near the end. Back on track, we thought, but were proved wrong with a home defeat to Cardiff. Brown scored once, Chopra scored twice. We should sign him, he could do a job for us despite his black and white roots.

So the football wasn't that clever, but bearing in mind what it had been like the season before, it was pretty canny, and we all realised (well, most of us did) that Roy Keane had a long term plan, and that if it didn't happen this season, then it would be because it was part of his plan to build for next season – which would be fine by me. For the first time in my time in a red and white scarf, we seemed to have a management team (chairman and team manager) that had a plan for more than the next eighteen months. Following on from last season, I maintained am "alternative entertainment" agenda, and was a regular visitor to the various comedy nights at The Gala. There was live music at least one night a week at The Grand, and the bairns (they will be forever known thus) played gigs – a modern term used by beat combos of the current generation to refer to a live performance – around the town and county, so there was always something to see and listen to. I've seen, over recent years, many of the bands the bairns like, with the excuse that I had to drive them there anyway, so I might as well get a ticket. Travis, Radiohead, The Stereophonics, the Red Hot Chili Peppers, but I also maintained an interest in stuff from my past. The Stranglers (getting on a bit, mind), The Buzzcocks (getting not quite as far on, but still 100mph), Bad Company (getting on a bit looking fitter than thirty years ago), and John Mayall (old as my mam). I took our Gaz, as part of his musical education –something he's never shirked from expanding – to the John Mayall gig at the Sage. I was one of the younger attendees, so Gaz was amongst not just the generation before him, but the one before that as well. With the lad being a bit of a guitar man, watching his jaw drop as he listened to Buddy Whittingham do things with a guitar that most mere mortals can only dream of was a sight to behold. Keep on learning, son.

Still, the football was the most important entertainment, and a free train trip, first class, to Norwich. We lost, the heel came off my shoe, and the first class service was suspended on the way back. Bad day at Carrow Road, but it signalled the end of the doldrums, all because of my enforced change of match-day footwear. Everybody has their little match-day superstitions –yes you do, you fibber – and one of mine was to wear the same gear game after game. It's obviously less important if we're losing, but if we're winning, the possibility of a lucky pair of shoes being unavailable could be a terrifying thought. Anyway, my new football shoes, a rather natty pair of brogues, proved a bit of a winner, as we sailed unbeaten through the rest of November, although David Connolly's decision to start scoring probably had a lot to do with it. Sky TV had obviously taken a fancy to Keane and Quinn's New Sunderland, and stuck us on the telly on a Friday night at Wolves. They were obviously expecting a Celebrity Death Match as Roy Keane met Mick McCarthy for the first time since the infamous Saipan bust-up. Thankfully, and predictably considering his behaviour in the season so far, it was a perfectly amicable encounter off the field, and a welcome point on it.

The winning carried on through December, and included a last minute equaliser by Mr Connolly at Burnley – Andy Gray would no doubt have scored, but he was sitting with the Hetton Boys in the bar at half time nursing a broken foot - in front of a huge away following, producing a result that felt every bit as good as a victory. Last minute goals, don't you just love them? There was also a defeat at Palace, but that's a place we've come to dislike for numerous reasons. This one was the Friday night before Christmas, traditionally the busiest travelling day of the year, the weather was so foggy that kick-off was in doubt, the tickets were ridiculously expensive, and we had to leave The Lamb after one drink because Will's daughter was under eighteen –and the family were visiting all the way from the USA. Bad day all round. We also lost to Preston at the end of the month, something else that was becoming a habit, on the same day as Saddam Hussein was executed in one of the most inevitable conclusions to the overturning of an oppressive regime there has ever been.

On a slightly more local level, there was the small matter of some alleged mates of one or two players selling the story of a "footballers with a lass" evening to the papers. Some mates, those lads, and despite the admittedly grainy image of the pair of them bearing an uncanny resemblance to my two, the story was every-where. Woods had already left the club, Chris Brown was the cameraman and Ben Alnwick the male lead, while Liam Lawrence also had a hand in proceedings. End of the road for the three of them? Eventually. Lawrence was off to Stoke quicker than you could say "get yer hair cut," Alnwick went to Spurs as part of the deal that brought Fulop (our first Hungarian) to Sunderland, and someone on the board said that Brown had played his last game for us. As if to emphasise who really was the boss, Roy played Brown once more before flogging him to Norwich.

Up the road, the American group, Polygon, pulled out of a proposed takeover (sensible sorts, I say), and Tesco in Kingston Park started selling square melons (daft sorts, I say). The rest of the world suddenly decided to start measuring its carbon footprint, which I always though was that mark on the carpet just out-side the coal hole in the cellar, and any subject of a marketing campaign had the words "green" or "eco-friendly" stuck in front of it.

We passed up on the New Year revelry, or most of it, so that we could get to Leicester to watch the Lads win more easily than the 2-0 score-line suggests, and see Peter Hartley make his debut. Of course, we were drawn at Preston in the FA Cup, and they did us for the third time in the season.

Just the league, then.

And bearing in mind the way the league was going, it was maybe a good thing. Carlos Edwards became our third Trini boy, and scored early in his career in the

4-2 win at Hillsborough. Perhaps the most important thing after the three points in front of a huge travelling support, and the creation the Hey Jude Keane song thanks to a bit of a dim half-time disc jockey, was Roy Keane's angry reaction to the two goals we let in. Perfectionist that he is, this was a sign of the standards at New Sunderland. Oh, and we spectacularly refrained from taking part in the attempt at the world's biggest air guitar riff, despite the antics of Saxon, last seen on stage by me at the Boilermakers before that 6-3 win over Sheffield United all those years ago. Sent us to the top of the league, that did, with a hat-trick from Wilf Rostron. After what seemed like months, mainly because it was months, we finally signed Anthony Stokes from Arsenal to bolster our attack even more. So we got ten points in January, followed by thirteen in February, including a cracking game at Birmingham when Carlos Edwards produced a moment of class to endear himself further in our hearts. I was beginning to behave like a kid again where football was concerned – we were going to storm the league, in my head. The thing was, we were heading upwards past many teams who were ahead of us in the promotion stakes, so maybe I wasn't behaving like a kid after all.

What would March bring? After the last February game, when high-flying Derby were beaten by the only thing better than a last-minute equaliser – a last minute winner – we felt even better about our lot in life. Talk about that cup winning feeling. We felt great, we'd won in style, but their manager chose to tell the football world that they would still finish above us. We felt so great, in fact, that we headed off to see England play Spain at Old Trafford in a friendly. It does help when TallPaul's daughter works there, and can get you tickets – all paid for, mind you, but an upgrade at half-time was most welcome. It's a shame she couldn't have upgraded the performance of the team, who played with Kieron Dyer as the lone striker and Crouch mostly on the wing. Any fool could see what was wrong except the manager, and the loss was deserved.

March brought another thirteen points, starting with a win at the home of another of the high-flyers, West Brom, and again the defeated manager chose to tell the football world that they would score more goals and finish above us. These fellers seemed to be going out of their way to make fools of themselves, and to give us the extra incentive to get above them in the league. In West Brom's case, claims that they were the better footballing side had a hollow ring to them, as they'd been pretty cynical in the way they'd kicked Carlos Edwards into a few weeks' injury-enforced absence. Stoke were the only side to break our winning sequence, and that came with that last-minute thing again, this time from Daryl Murphy, and towards the end of the win at Cardiff, the sound of "They tried to take the ball off Nyron, he said No, No, No" echoed around Ninian Park. We were getting noticed around the football world, Roy Keane was the Next Big Thing, he was giving the press good, original quotes, he wasn't head-butting linesmen as predicted, he had a genuine sense of humour, and we sensed that he wanted to be that Next Big Thing at Sunderland. While the red half of Manchester told us that he was just warming up before a return to Old Trafford as boss and a lot of neutrals agreed with them, we told them that he was happy with what he was creating on Wearside. As if to propel himself back into the limelight, as if that were necessary, Niall Quinn paid for taxis for Sunderland fans wrongly ejected from the flight home after that win in Cardiff, and in so doing, wrote himself into football folklore.

As the newspapers filled up with stories of Mr Quinn's generosity – "These are my people" – there was obviously (and predictably, given their recent history) a PR fight-back from Tyneside, where Mr Shepherd announced plans for a multi-multi million pound investment in a ground extension (Where, for crying out loud? Underground, with periscopes?) and the inevitable hotel. In the wider world of sport, England were having a go at the World Cup in the Caribbean, but vice-captain Freddie Flintoff, the ashes hero of little over a year before, and a man noted for not being frightened of a pint, made the headlines for attempting a pedalo ride in the early hours. Perhaps unsurprisingly, the team missed him and failed to impress, allowing those nice modest Australians to win the tournament.

On came April as the fixtures began to run out, but it brought another twelve points. After the home win over Wolves, which included a decent reception for Mick McCarthy, we were off to Southampton, another win, and another Quinn master-class in PR. After a couple of our ALS coaches had their windows put out by some disaffected, non-football, local youth, he sent the team coach back from the airport after dropping the players off, and took the stranded fans home. The sound of Freddie Shepherd scratching his head as he desperately tried to come up with something to throw to the fans could be heard in Pennywell. There was also a defeat, our first since January and our first in the league all year. Colchester were just too "up for it" in their tiny little ground, where my lucky shoes had a big lump knocked out of them in the packed away end. Quinny continued his gospel tour of the North East, where he turned up at packed clubs to preach the red and white cause. I'm that soft I went twice, even getting him to sign my Disco Pants CD. "Jeez, don't let anybody see that" he implored, but in vain. I still show it off now. He was all over the back pages, the front pages, the middle pages, and the Sunday supplements, in the spaces between the Keane articles and features. You could have been forgiven for thinking that we were Real Madrid, and had already won the European Cup. This was in the Irish press as well as the English, and Irish accents at Sunderland games became increasingly common.

At the end of the month, on a Friday night, Burnley came to town, and contributed to the game of the season. As you'd expect, our former flop Andy Gray scored for them, the game see-sawed in favour of either side, then along came Carlos with another moment of magic. Three penalties, one of which we missed, and it was standing at 2-2 with ten minutes to go when he got on the end of a ball forward from Murphy, came inside, and unleashed one of the SOL's finest goals, still rising as it hit the net from well outside the box. A fitting end to a great game of football, and it sent us top of the league for the first time, with promotion almost guaranteed. What a nice feeling, especially when I'd taken along a Burnley-supporting mate, just so that I could slap his nice baldy heed when we scored. Promotion would be sorted a couple of days later if Palace could beat Derby, and it was a very strange feeling sitting in the pub, cheering on one of the teams that have given us more reason than most to bear a grudge against them. Bless them, they beat Derby and sent us up. Nice old Crystal Palace, for once. That just left the trip to relegated Luton to finish things off.

Only one game to go, we were into May, and things were going to change, and not just at Sunderland. Tony Blair had announced his decision to stand down from the position of Prime Minister. He probably deserved a break, as he'd aged twenty-five years in his decade in office, and the constant worry over the decision to send the troops into Iraq was obviously eating at him. Hell, the war had been over for ages, but there were just as many people, civilian and military, being killed. Shouldn't have trusted George Dubya Bush so much, you daft Mag. At least you'll have more time to watch your beloved (allegedly) team play – do you think? I doubt it. The handover to Gordon Brown, as we all knew fine well it would be, was scheduled for the end of June, but Tone was on wind-down already. Farewell tours and all that. The report spurred into existence by the BBC football bungs documentary finally appeared, no managers were sacked, and the main finding was that agents in football are mostly very bad men, and that clubs should watch out for them. Strangely enough, Sam Allardyce found himself the new manager at Sid James Park, the very place that had booted out Kevin Bond for having the temerity to be named by Panorama nine months previously. Whiter than white, that lot.

The weekend in London leading up to our game at Kenilworth Road was the usual blast, incorporating a match at Barnet on the Saturday with a surprisingly high Sunderland content in the crowd, an evening at The Blues Bar where a friendly Welsh lad bought us all a pint simply because I'd bothered to make conversation with him, and an eight o'clock start in the pub next to the hotel on Sunday. Kenilworth Road had Sunderland fans in every part, and the team did what we'd been threatening to do for a while, winning 5-0, while Charlie

Hurley sat next to Niall Quinn and saluted the fans. It was one of those days that restores your faith in football in general and Sunderland in particular.

The sun shone, the goals flew in, we dominated, we had fans all over the ground thanks to the generosity of some supporters of the already-relegated home side, and we had others in the home end just because Sunderland fans can usually get in where a draught couldn't. It made me proud to be one of us, and put my faith back on track. Promotion was already won, but, even if we hadn't decided as fans that we wanted the Championship, we knew that it was exactly what Roy wanted. Preston, three times our betters during the season, did a Palace and beat Birmingham, and we were champions of the Championship for the second time in three years. Let's hope it's a habit we're going to get out of.

Premiership? Bring it on.

Niall Quinn's Taxi Cabs are the best
You can stick it up your arse, EasyJet
Fat Freddie wouldn't do it for the Mags
Niall Quinn's Taxi Cabs

2007-2008

Season over, faith restored, as the campaign just over had been as joyous as the previous one had been heartbreaking, and my desire to celebrate like a lunatic on the Sunday night was tempered by the knowledge that I had to be at the wheel early the next morning. Aye, that's right, bird-watching again, but this year with a difference. Judith had decide that she'd like to come, so it was no tent, but a nice hotel in Portree, then a bed and breakfast on Benbecula. Maybe she thought I spent the week sitting in the pub, but she soon found that licensed premises in that neck of the woods are as common as black and white shirts in Monkwearmouth. A great week, a football-free week, but I was back in time to join the domino boys at The Grand for the FA Cup Final. The bones stayed in their box, but only just as Chelsea beat Man Utd in the first final at the new Wembley – years behind schedule, tens of millions over budget, and horribly expensive, it will probably serve as a monument to English football's obsession with money above all else.

Gordon Brown duly took over from Tony Blair in perhaps the least surprising political event in recent years, and it looked like more of the same, but with a slightly Scottish accent. With a bit of luck, he won't spend as much time smiling at George W Bush and doing all he can to keep the good old US of A happy with us.

There was no international competition for England to capitulate in, but there was a lot of weather. Most of the Midlands seemed to disappear underwater, and Sheffield Wednesday's pitch resembled a boating lake for long periods. Unlike 2000, Durham escaped the worst – in fact, it wasn't that bad at all, and our holidays in Cornwall saw only the one really wet day. Unfortunately it was the day we chose to go to the outdoor theatre, but that's life. At least it was just us and our clothes that got soaked, not our homes. We had a holiday, but I suspect Niall and Roy didn't, judging by the amount of work they were getting through. Greg Halford arrived from Reading – memories of an impressive performance against us for Colchester, perhaps – followed by Russell Anderson, one of the stars of the Scottish Premier in recent years, then Dickson Etuhu, Paul McShane, Kieron Richardson, and Michael Chopra. Chopra's arrival polarised the fans for a while – after all, he was a Mag who'd scored against us a few times. Perhaps the biggest signing of the summer – and I mean in the whole Premiership, not just Sunderland, was Craig Gordon, at £9 million or something like that, a record for a goal keeper. The pre-season was in Ireland – probably the footballing equivalent of Brown following Blair in the surprise stakes –and, with the cheap flights being available (not from EasyJet, of course), the attendance was large, happy, and full of optimism. Ireland took us to heart; the place was full of taxi and bus drivers who appeared to know everything about Sunderland. In Cork, everyone was related to Charlie Hurley or Roy Keane. As with everything Niall Quinn touched, it was a PR masterpiece, and we came back home for a rare home friendly to celebrate ten years at the SOL.

Ten years? I can still remember sneaking a peep inside as they built it; still remember the hairs standing up on the back of my neck the first time I walked up the steps and into the arena itself. Ten years. Hell's bells. Walking from The King's to the Wearmouth Bridge, we passed the still derelict former Vaux site. Seven years on from the disgraceful selling off by the Swallow Groups asset-strippers, plans are still being knocked back for various retail and residential developments. Not living in Sunderland, I'm not as close to the issue as those who do, and I don't see the details as closely, but I still see it as a horrible waste of a prime site in the city centre. If I did live in the city, I've a feeling I'd be screaming at the council on a regular basis. In the middle of all of this Roy Keanery, Judith and I passed the twenty-five year milestone, and celebrated the fact with a night out at the Charlaw, where we'd had our reception all those years ago.

August also saw the death of Tony Wilson – an ordinary name for an extraordinary man, one who'd created Factory Records, brought us Joy Division and New Order, and thus gave me something to associate with around the end of the seventies and the beginning of the eighties, something for the slightly miserable youth of the era to identify with. Yet another musical icon from my past gone the way of all flesh. The current focus of my musical attention, the bairns, played a gig in Derby. Derby – that's some distance. Anyone remember that little rough pub up a side street opposite Derby station? That was the one they played, one hundred and forty miles or so to perform for an hour in that less than salubrious venue. There's dedication. They also played Richmond Live, on the same stage as the Buzzcocks, no less, and seem to be embracing the rock 'n' roll bohemian lifestyle a bit too much. After their gig, in a display of typical unity, the drummer went home early because he had work the next day, our Ian came home because he can drive and was trying to impress his latest flame by being in one piece the next day. The other two stayed the night, but Graham the singer, every inch the front man, came back the following afternoon, having woken next to a campfire with someone pouring lighter fuel over him and brandishing a tab-lighter. Having escaped that, he was then stabbed (only a little stab, mind) for not handing over his mobile phone to would-be muggers. He and our Gaz had been asked for autographs, apparently – signed on at least one young lady's chest. Rock and roll! Gaz eventually came back to the land of the living via a phone-call the day after that, something along the lines of "I've got no money honey, can someone rescue me from the Wetherspoons?"

Bohemians, Darlo, Scunny, Galway, Cork, and Juventus – for the second year, I got in a full pre-season. Like I said, I get worse, and I actually felt disappointment when the Berwick game (reserves) proved to be a non-starter as far as I was concerned, but Keane was signing players. The summer had been one of speculation about huge international superstars, but they never materialised. Perhaps the shopping in Sunderland isn't that good, as Roy launched a scathing attack on the WAG culture. It made entertaining reading, and rang true, especially if the comments that came out of a few players are to be taken as a sign of the truth hurting.

Right then, let's get on with this football business, the proper competitive stuff, not the jolly, let's-get-fit-introduce-the-new-players-to-the-fans stuff, but the real business. Spurs at home, not a bad start, and that's the way it turned out. Noon kick-off, quick pint in town, off to the match. Back to life, back to reality. To be honest, I'd have taken a point, but just as I was about to say that, as the ref checked his watch, up popped Chops to win it. Great start. Birmingham away a few days later matched us with our nearest rivals from last season, and once again it was a great few beers in The Queen's in Lichfield and a cracking game of football, with that man Chops scoring late on, and their old boy Stern John winning us a point. Still a great start, so Wigan had better watch out. Heskey and Bramble in the same team? We're laughing. Oh no we weren't, as Heskey scored and we gave away two daft penalties to be well beaten. At least the County of Durham had something to celebrate as the cricketers won the Friends Provident Trophy by beating Hampshire. Some sensible Sunderland fans had chosen that game above Wigan, and it proved a good choice. The Wigan result was what we didn't need with Liverpool and all of their spending next up. We put up a decent show, but their quality told, and we thanked our lucky stars that we had the chance to get our shooting boots back on with a League Cup tie at Luton.

Aah, Luton. Remember them? 5-0 only a few months back, and we'd spent a fortune in the meantime. As a deliciously aromatic cloud of curry flavoured smoke billowed across the pitch, Paul Furlong rose from the dead to put us out of the competition. Remember Luton? Remember Bury, more like. Just what we needed when our next game was at Old Trafford. As the transfer window closed, Roy brought in Andrew/Andy/Andra Cole and swapped Stern John and a bit of cash for Kenwyne Jones. Danny Higginbotham had also arrived, bringing our outlay to somewhere just short of £40 million. £40 million? That was only behind Man Utd and Liverpool and somebody else, and many times more than we'd ever spent in a season before. It also meant that Roy Keane, in just one year, had presided over no less than fifty-six transfers, which was enough to make you wonder what Sunderland was coming to. New Sunderland indeed – if that was what it takes to move the club forward, then that's what Roy and Niall would do.

September, as it tends to, brings my birthday so we headed off into deepest Yorkshire again – same hotel, as it happens, where Stubber (same birthday) and Kath joined us for a spot of walking, then us lads watched England while the ladies went shopping. If you've ever been to Kettlewell, you'll know that there's an outdoor shop and a village store, so shopping is a short-lived experience. England actually did what they were supposed to for once, winning 3-0, with a telling contribution by Heskey. You might have gathered that I'm not the man's biggest fan, but credit where credit's due. Perhaps McLaren had arrived at the line-up because his first choice players were injured (no Rooney, no Lampard, and Crouch suspended) but at least he kept an unchanged side for the Russia game a few days later, where the domino lads were kept interested in the football by another 3-0 win, courtesy of Barry, Heskey, and the rest.

In the big world of sport, England's rugby side went into their World Cup in turmoil, with mumblings of discontent from within. They proved right, with a shocking defeat, nay, humiliation, at the hands of South Africa, 0-36, after the initial defeat of that huge rugby nation, the USA. Heroes to zeroes in the space of four years.

Old Trafford after a thumping at Luton... the portents were not good. Logically, any way. In the minds of us Sunderland fans, it was a chance for a fresh start, and there were impressive debuts for Danny Higginbotham and Kenwyne Jones. OK, so we lost, but only just, and we really upset the few United fans who were bothered by singing louder than them. Craig Gordon had played another good game, and was making his transfer fee look value for money. Remember Brian Clough, and his transfer record for Peter Shilton? Build the team from the back. Well remembered, Roy. If we're still in this division next May, which we will be, any points saved by outstanding goalkeeping performances will make him well worth the money.

Along came Reading, a game we had to win to get back on track, and we did win. The game was a tribute to Ian Porterfield, who passed away on the 11th of September after a battle with cancer. Ian Porterfield, the man who scored probably the most important single goal in our club's history. Ian Porterfield, the man who won the FA Cup in 1973 in a flash of magic that gave football one of its most memorable moments. Along with Monty's save, Ian's goal provided an image that will live with me, and all other Sunderland supporters whether they were alive at the time or not, for the rest of our lives. It will remain part of FA Cup folklore. Porter deserved a good send-off, and the presence of most of his team-mates from that wet May day all those years ago helped created the atmosphere. The playing of the commentary of the goal, followed by the applause, and the scoreboard reading "Sunderland 1, Leeds 0, Porterfield 32" made it even better. A good performance and a good win, with a stunning first goal from Kenwyne Jones, was fitting, but the spontaneous "Stand up for Porterfield" moment towards the end of the game absolutely made the occasion.

At the Boro, they had the Rory the Lion's share of the game, but we did what we did many times in the previous season, and hit a last minute equaliser. Last minute goals – don't you just love them?

We're up and running, we're in the Premier League (I hate that pretentious name. What's wrong with First Division?), and we've just spent more money than the national debt of a small Central American country. We're still in our shiny new ground, and ten years on it's still miles better than the vast majority of those that are being hoyed up all over the country in terms of facilities, quality of construction, and proximity to both town centre and spiritual home. I travel the same roads to the match, but the pit heaps are no longer grey and pointed, they are smooth and green. The pitheads are gone completely, replaced by technology parks and executive housing; the pithead bath's a supermarket now. There are no more shipyards on the Wear. Northern Rock, one of the local companies to rise from the ashes of heavy industry with some sort of success, overstretched itself (see what happens when you get involved with them up the road) and had to be bailed out by the Bank of England. One small crumb of consolation is that many SAFC fans closed their accounts when NR put their name on the front of black and white shirts, but that doesn't help those that didn't.

I'm travelling up Houghton Cut, past the graveyard where some of my Houghton ancestors lie, still using a bus that picks up from a pub in Bishop. Thirty-seven years ago, when my journey began in earnest, that pub was The Sun Inn, but that's now famously rebuilt in Beamish Museum, so now it's The Station. The faces on the bus are the same, lads I've known for forty years in some cases, but those faces are a little older, a little wiser. The same people, a bit thinner on top and thicker around the middle, but still with the same passion for Sunderland, a passion grown stronger by decades of adversity mixed with years of unbridled joy. I've gone through the various stages of a supporter's life – older than some players, older than all of the players, as old as the manager, older than the manager, having children older than most of the players, just like many of us have, and we're still there, still as daft as the proverbial brush. The big difference is that we've got a manager who believes he was born to manage Sunderland.

At the Stadium, the bus having parked on the street where my Great Grandfather was born, a few hundred yards from the shipyard his father and father-in-law worked, I sit above the colliery where other ancestors has dug coal. The fans are every bit what they've always been – part of the team. That's the way it should be, and that's the way it will always be at Sunderland. It's been good, it's been bad, it's been everything you want and didn't want, and while I'm one of those who thinks that folks who say "I wouldn't change a thing" are mad, as I'd certainly change a few things, but I wouldn't change my team.

Keep the Faith

Notes From The Author's Sons

I was born June 12th 1983 and named after Gary Rowell. It was hoped that my name would ensure the foundations of a successful career in football, but apparently not… From a very young age I was intrigued as to who this Rowell fellow was and what these red and white clad warriors he represented stood for. It wasn't long after I was born before I was suited in the correct Mackem attire and was off to my inevitable first match. I have many, many wonderful memories from my experiences home and away and no doubt some will be documented in this very book. The loyalty and devotion my dad has shown over the years to SAFC has rubbed off and left me with a love for the red and white and a loathing for all things black and white. My old man has also taught me there's no point in doing anything unless you do it with strong faith and integrity. That is why twenty-two years, five relegations, six promotions and what seems like thousand of games later I can't call myself the biggest Sunderland fan, just the son of him.
Gary Dobson

It speaks volumes for a Sunderland fan when, after all the ups and downs the club has been through, this fella and thousands of others still follow them, and sings with the same passion he did at his first match, all those hundreds of years ago. I know this, because I live under the same roof as him, and when I ask, after a defeat, "What went wrong?" he simply answers "We were sh*t."

Or, if it was a close thing, I get a ten-minute explanation of what went wrong and why. When we win, he celebrates like it was thirty-two minutes past three on the fifth of May 1973, and the bloke I'm named after had just scored that goal. My brother and I occasionally ask him what he wants to be when he grows up. We don't get an answer to that one but we think that if it does ever happen, he'll be a Sunderland fan.
Ian Dobson